THE QURAN

English Meanings

Edited by
Saheeh International

Published by
AL QURAN D'AWAH CENTER USA

THE QURAN
English Meanings

Edited by
Saheeh International

Published by
Al Quran Da'wah Center Inc.
A non-profit 501(c)3 institution
1033 Glenmore Avenue, Brooklyn, NY 11208, USA
Phone: (718) 235-3300, (347) 951-6829, (917) 294-4966

Email: alqurandc@gmail.com
www.alqurandc.org

Published
Al Quran Dawah Center 3rd Print: December 2021
Al Quran Dawah Center 1st Print: February 2020

© Copyright reserved by Al-Quran Dawah Center Inc.

$5.00
ISBN 978-1-7371044-0-7

Please Contact us to Collect Your Copy

☾ Phone ☾

(718) 235-3300
(347) 951-6829
(917) 294-4966

Email alqurandc@gmail.com

to know details Please visit
www.alqurandc.org

Send your Donation to
Al Quran Da'wah Center Inc.
1033 Glenmore Avenue, Brooklyn
NY 11208, USA

Donate by Quick Pay

Zelle/PayPal alqurandc@gmail.com

or

Pay directly AlQuranForAll.com

▸ All donations are tax-deductible ◂

[This is] a Book which We have revealed to you, [O Muhammad], that you might bring mankind out of darknesses into the light

[Al Quran 14: 1]

• • •

Indeed, this Qur'an guides to that which is most suitable and gives good tidings to the believers who do righteous deeds that they will have a great reward.

[Al Quran 17: 9]

Availability

▶ MICHIGAN ▶

AL-QURAN ACADEMY OF MICHIGAN
12500 McDougall St.
Detroit, MI 48212,
Phone: (313) 368-5308

▶ NEW JERSEY ▶

MCSJ Masjid As-Salam
400 Erial Road
Pine Hill, NJ 08021
Phone: (856) 669-8796

▶ CALIFORNIA ▶

4430 Fountain Ave.
Unit # 3
Los Angeles, CA 90029
Phone: (213) 926-2959

▶ NEW YORK ▶

**BAITUL MAMUR MASJID &
COMMUNITY CENTER
&
MUNA BOOK SERVICE**
1033 Glenmore Ave
Brooklyn, NY 11208
Phone: (917) 355-4538

Please be a sponsor for free Quran distribution project, inspire others to be a sponsor and get rewards.

Table of Contents

Introduction		11
History of Quran Compilation		13
01	Surah Al-Faatihah	17
02	Surah Al-Baqarah	17
03	Surah Aali Imraan	47
04	Surah An-Nisaa	65
05	Surah Al-Maaidah	84
06	Surah Al-An'aam	98
07	Surah Al-A'raaf	114
08	Surah Al-Anfaal	132
09	Surah At-Tawbah	138
10	Surah Yunus	151
11	Surah Hud	160
12	Surah Yusuf	170
13	Surah Ar-Ra'd	179
14	Surah Ibrahim	184
15	Surah Al-Hijr	188
16	Surah An-Nahl	193
17	Surah Al-Israa	203
18	Surah Al-Kahf	211
19	Surah Maryam	220
20	Surah Taa-Haa	226
21	Surah Al-Anbiyaa	234
22	Surah Al-Hajj	241
23	Surah Al-Muminoon	247
24	Surah An-Noor	254
25	Surah Al-Furqaan	260
26	Surah Ash-Shu'araa	265

27	Surah An-Naml	274
28	Surah Al-Qasas	280
29	Surah Al-Ankaboot	288
30	Surah Ar-Room	293
31	Surah Luqman	297
32	Surah As-Sajdah	300
33	Surah Al-Ahzaab	302
34	Surah Saba	309
35	Surah Faatir	314
36	Surah Yaa Seen	317
37	Surah As-Saaffaat	322
38	Surah Saad	329
39	Surah Az-Zumar	333
40	Surah Ghaafir	339
41	Surah Fussilat	346
42	Surah Ash-Shura	350
43	Surah Az-Zukhruf	355
44	Surah Ad-Dukhaan	360
45	Surah Al-Jaathiya	362
46	Surah Al-Ahqaf	365
47	Surah Muhammad	368
48	Surah Al-Fath	372
49	Surah Al-Hujuraat	375
50	Surah Qaaf	376
51	Surah Adh-Dhaariyat	379
52	Surah At-Tur	381
53	Surah An-Najm	384
54	Surah Al-Qamar	386
55	Surah Ar-Rahmaan	389
56	Surah Al-Waaqiah	391
57	Surah Al-Hadid	395

58	Surah Al-Mujaadila	398
59	Surah Al-Hashr	400
60	Surah Al-Mumtahana	402
61	Surah As-Saff	404
62	Surah Al-Jumu'ah	405
63	Surah Al-Munaafiqoon	406
64	Surah At-Taghaabun	407
65	Surah At-Talaaq	409
66	Surah At-Tahrim	410
67	Surah Al-Mulk	412
68	Surah Al-Qalam	414
69	Surah Al-Haaqqa	416
70	Surah Al-Ma'aarij	418
71	Surah Nooh	419
72	Surah Al-Jinn	421
73	Surah Al-Muzzammil	423
74	Surah Al-Muddaththir	424
75	Surah Al-Qiyaama	426
76	Surah Al-Insaan	427
77	Surah Al-Mursalaat	429
78	Surah An-Naba	431
79	Surah An-Naazi'aat	432
80	Surah Abasa	434
81	Surah At-Takwir	435
82	Surah Al-Infitaar	436
83	Surah Al-Mutaffifin	437
84	Surah Al-Inshiqaaq	439
85	Surah Al-Burooj	440
86	Surah At-Taariq	441
87	Surah Al-A'laa	441
88	Surah Al-Ghaashiya	442

89	Surah Al-Fajr	443
90	Surah Al-Balad	444
91	Surah Ash-Shams	445
92	Surah Al-Lail	446
93	Surah Ad-Dhuhaa	446
94	Surah Ash-Sharh	447
95	Surah At-Tin	447
96	Surah Al-Alaq	448
97	Surah Al-Qadr	448
98	Surah Al-Bayyina	449
99	Surah Az-Zalzala	449
100	Surah Al-Aadiyaat	450
101	Surah Al-Qaari'a	450
102	Surah At-Takaathur	451
103	Surah Al-Asr	451
104	Surah Al-Humaza	451
105	Surah Al-Fil	452
106	Surah Quraish	452
107	Surah Al-Maa'un	452
108	Surah Al-Kawthar	452
109	Surah Al-Kaafiroon	453
110	Surah An-Nasr	453
111	Surah Al-Masad/Lahab	453
112	Surah Al-Ikhlaas	453
113	Surah Al-Falaq	454
114	Surah An-Naas	454

• • •

بِسْمِ اللهِ الرَّحْمٰنِ الرَّحِيْمِ

INTRODUCTION

All praise is due to Allah; and blessings and peace be upon His messenger and servant, Muhammad, and upon his family and companions and whoever follows his guidance until the Day of Resurrection.

There is clearly a need for a presentation of the meanings of the Holy Quran in English which is precise enough to be useful as a reference for Muslims and students of Arabic yet also suitable for dawah purposes to non-Muslims. The Arabic Quran has always spoken for itself – to those who discover it for the first time as well as to those who study it in depth. The general meanings in a translation should thus be correct, as far as human ability permits, and clear, in a readable and uncomplicated expression.

Al-Muntada al-Islami has selected this edition by Saheeh International (first published by Abul-Qasim Publishing House, Jeddah, Saudi Arabia) as the one most suitable for distribution. Widely acknowledged for improvement over previous translations, its language closely adheres to that of the original text while remaining lucid and intelligible.

Without going into excessive detail, a word is due about the methodology of this abbreviated edition. Three main objectives served as guidelines for the work:

1. To present correct meanings, as far as possible, in accordance with the aqeedah of Ahl as-Sunnah wal-Jam'ah
2. To simplify and clarify the language for the benefit of all readers
3. To let the Quran speak for itself, adding footnotes only where deemed necessary for explanation of points not readily understood or when more than one meaning is acceptable

Each verse was reviewed in Arabic with reference to several works of tafseer and grammar. Where differences arose, explanations were generally taken from an authentic hadith or, in the absence of such, those by the most knowledgable of the sahabah and tabiu'n as quoted by Ibn Katheer.

English word order was chosen to conform more closely with that of the Arabic text. This facilitates comparison for the student, and the reader is brought somewhat closer to the feel of the original expression. Transliterated Arabic terms have been avoided wherever an English definition could serve, keeping exceptions to a minimum. Necessary clarifications or additions are given in footnotes. Care has also been taken to avoid the definitions of modern Arabic dictionaries, which are often variant with the language of the Quran and reflect the degree of change which has crept into the understanding of certain concepts with the passing of time. Instead, classical definitions were applied.

In compliance with standard regulations, words not derived from the Arabic text but added for the purpose of clarification or the completion of English meaning have been enclosed in brackets. The exception is in regard to the frequently occurring expressions of "association of another with Allah" (shirk) and "fearing Allah" (taqwa), where the divine name, although not always included in the Arabic text, is understood to be an integral part of that concept. Throughout this work there is an endeavor to be consistent in the translation of oft-repeated words and phrases from the text. There are, however, specific instances where some adjustment is required for accuracy, necessitating exceptions to the rule.

• • •

HISTORY OF QURAN COMPILATION

1. In addition to its memorization in entirety by many of the sahabah (the Prophet's companions), written recording of the Quran began during the Prophet's lifetime. As it was recited by him, his scribes wrote down the revelation on pieces of leather, bone and palm leaves, and its verses were ordered and arranged as Allah revealed. Initially, the Quran was not compiled in one volume, although some of the sahabah had made personal copies for themselves after memorizing it from the Prophet (ﷺ).

2. Collecting and compiling the Quran followed soon after the Prophet's death, during the caliphate of Abu Bakr as-Siddeeq. Upon the advice of Umar bin al-Khattab, Abu Bakr charged Zayd bin Thabit to bring all of the Quran together on written sheets (suhuf). These were checked for accuracy against what had been memorized by a great number of the sahabah. After the death of Abu Bakr and then Umar, the collection remained with Umar's daughter, Hafsah, who was also the Prophet's wife.

3. The standardization of one authentic volume (mushaf) took place during the caliphate of Uthman bin Affan. The copy kept by Hafsah was obtained and, upon the order of Uthman, it was transcribed with great care by four of the most knowledgeable scribes: Zayd bin Thabit, Abdullah bin az-Zubayr, Saeed bin al-Aas and Abdur-Rahman bin al-harith bin Hisham. Copies were sent to each of the various Islamic territories to replace all other collections in circulation. Uthman kept a copy in Madinah, and the original suhuf were returned to hafsah. There is consensus by the sahabah that what is contained in this standard copy is the true revelation received by Muhammad (ﷺ) from Allah, the Exalted.

4. The mushaf of Uthman had no dots or vowel marks, as they were unnecessary for those who knew the pure Arabic tongue. With the spread of Islam among other peoples, there arose a need to guard against incorrect reading and misinterpretation of the Quran. At first, scholars were reluctant about these

additions, but it was finally agreed that they did not affect the text itself and were merely aids to proper pronunciation and understanding. They were introduced in three stages:

- Short vowel sounds were first represented by dots positioned above, below and to the left of the letter. This system was introduced during the caliphate of Muawiyah bin Abu Sufyan by Abul-Aswad ad-Du'li after he had heard serious errors in recitation of the Quran.

- Similarly written letters were differentiated by another system of dots above and below them during the caliphate of Abdul-Malik bin Marwan. At the caliph's order, his governor, al-hajjaj, appointed two scholars, Nasr bin a'sim and hayy bin Ya'mur, to implement this improvement.

- The presently used system of short vowel symbols was devised by al-Khaleel bin Ahmad al-Faraheedi during the Abbasine period.

...

THE QURAN

English Meanings

| Verses: 07 | **Surah 01 Al-Faatihah** | Makki |

01. In the name of Allah, the Entirely Merciful, the Especially Merciful.
02. [All] praise is [due] to Allah, Lord of the worlds -
03. The Entirely Merciful, the Especially Merciful,
04. Sovereign of the Day of Recompense.
05. It is You we worship and You we ask for help.
06. Guide us to the straight path -
07. The path of those upon whom You have bestowed favor, not of those who have evoked [Your] anger or of those who are astray.

| Verses: 286 | **Surah 02 Al-Baqarah** | Madani |

In the name of Allah, the Entirely Merciful, the Especially Merciful.

01. Alif, Lam, Meem.
02. This is the Book about which there is no doubt, a guidance for those conscious of Allah -
03. Who believe in the unseen, establish prayer, and spend out of what We have provided for them,
04. And who believe in what has been revealed to you, [O Muhammad], and what was revealed before you, and of the Hereafter they are certain [in faith].
05. Those are upon [right] guidance from their Lord, and it is those who are the successful.
06. Indeed, those who disbelieve - it is all the same for them whether you warn them or do not warn them - they will not believe.
07. Allah has set a seal upon their hearts and upon their hearing, and over their vision is a veil. And for them is a great punishment.
08. And of the people are some who say, "We believe in Allah and the Last Day," but they are not believers.
09. They [think to] deceive Allah and those who believe, but they deceive not except themselves and perceive [it] not.
10. In their hearts is disease, so Allah has increased their disease; and for them is a painful punishment because they [habitually] used to lie.
11. And when it is said to them, "Do not cause corruption on the earth," they say, "We are but reformers."

12. Unquestionably, it is they who are the corrupters, but they perceive [it] not.
13. And when it is said to them, "Believe as the people have believed," they say, "Should we believe as the foolish have believed?" Unquestionably, it is they who are the foolish, but they know [it] not.
14. And when they meet those who believe, they say, "We believe"; but when they are alone with their evil ones, they say, "Indeed, we are with you; we were only mockers."
15. [But] Allah mocks them and prolongs them in their transgression [while] they wander blindly.
16. Those are the ones who have purchased error [in exchange] for guidance, so their transaction has brought no profit, nor were they guided.
17. Their example is that of one who kindled a fire, but when it illuminated what was around him, Allah took away their light and left them in darkness [so] they could not see.
18. Deaf, dumb and blind - so they will not return [to the right path].
19. Or [it is] like a rainstorm from the sky within which is darkness, thunder and lightning. They put their fingers in their ears against the thunderclaps in dread of death. But Allah is encompassing of the disbelievers.
20. The lightning almost snatches away their sight. Every time it lights [the way] for them, they walk therein; but when darkness comes over them, they stand [still]. And if Allah had willed, He could have taken away their hearing and their sight. Indeed, Allah is over all things competent.
21. O mankind, worship your Lord, who created you and those before you, that you may become righteous -
22. [He] who made for you the earth a bed [spread out] and the sky a ceiling and sent down from the sky, rain and brought forth thereby fruits as provision for you. So do not attribute to Allah equals while you know [that there is nothing similar to Him].
23. And if you are in doubt about what We have sent down upon Our Servant [Muhammad], then produce a surah the like thereof and call upon your witnesses other than Allah, if you should be truthful.
24. But if you do not - and you will never be able to - then fear the Fire, whose fuel is men and stones, prepared for the disbelievers.

25. And give good tidings to those who believe and do righteous deeds that they will have gardens [in Paradise] beneath which rivers flow. Whenever they are provided with a provision of fruit therefrom, they will say, "This is what we were provided with before." And it is given to them in likeness. And they will have therein purified spouses, and they will abide therein eternally.

26. Indeed, Allah is not timid to present an example - that of a mosquito or what is smaller than it. And those who have believed know that it is the truth from their Lord. But as for those who disbelieve, they say, "What did Allah intend by this as an example?" He misleads many thereby and guides many thereby. And He misleads not except the defiantly disobedient,

27. Who break the covenant of Allah after contracting it and sever that which Allah has ordered to be joined and cause corruption on earth. It is those who are the losers.

28. How can you disbelieve in Allah when you were lifeless and He brought you to life; then He will cause you to die, then He will bring you [back] to life, and then to Him you will be returned.

29. It is He who created for you all of that which is on the earth. Then He directed Himself to the heaven, [His being above all creation], and made them seven heavens, and He is Knowing of all things.

30. And [mention, O Muhammad], when your Lord said to the angels, "Indeed, I will make upon the earth a successive authority." They said, "Will You place upon it one who causes corruption therein and sheds blood, while we declare Your praise and sanctify You?" Allah said, "Indeed, I know that which you do not know."

31. And He taught Adam the names - all of them. Then He showed them to the angels and said, "Inform Me of the names of these, if you are truthful."

32. They said, "Exalted are You; we have no knowledge except what You have taught us. Indeed, it is You who is the Knowing, the Wise."

33. He said, "O Adam, inform them of their names." And when he had informed them of their names, He said, "Did I not tell you that I know the unseen [aspects] of the heavens and the earth? And I know what you reveal and what you have concealed."

34. And [mention] when We said to the angels, "Prostrate before Adam"; so they prostrated, except for Iblees. He refused and was arrogant and became of the disbelievers.

35. And We said, "O Adam, dwell, you and your wife, in Paradise and eat therefrom in [ease and] abundance from wherever you will. But do not approach this tree, lest you be among the wrongdoers."
36. But Satan caused them to slip out of it and removed them from that [condition] in which they had been. And We said, "Go down, [all of you], as enemies to one another, and you will have upon the earth a place of settlement and provision for a time."
37. Then Adam received from his Lord [some] words, and He accepted his repentance. Indeed, it is He who is the Accepting of repentance, the Merciful.
38. We said, "Go down from it, all of you. And when guidance comes to you from Me, whoever follows My guidance - there will be no fear concerning them, nor will they grieve.
39. And those who disbelieve and deny Our signs - those will be companions of the Fire; they will abide therein eternally."
40. Children of Israel, remember My favor which I have bestowed upon you and fulfill My covenant [upon you] that I will fulfill your covenant [from Me], and be afraid of [only] Me.
41. And believe in what I have sent down confirming that which is [already] with you, and be not the first to disbelieve in it. And do not exchange My signs for a small price, and fear [only] Me.
42. And do not mix the truth with falsehood or conceal the truth while you know [it].
43. And establish prayer and give zakah and bow with those who bow [in worship and obedience].
44. Do you order righteousness of the people and forget yourselves while you recite the Scripture? Then will you not reason?
45. And seek help through patience and prayer, and indeed, it is difficult except for the humbly submissive [to Allah]
46. Who are certain that they will meet their Lord and that they will return to Him.
47. Children of Israel, remember My favor that I have bestowed upon you and that I preferred you over the worlds.
48. And fear a Day when no soul will suffice for another soul at all, nor will intercession be accepted from it, nor will compensation be taken from it, nor will they be aided.
49. And [recall] when We saved your forefathers from the people of Pharaoh, who afflicted you with the worst torment, slaughtering your [newborn] sons and keeping your females alive. And in that was a great trial from your Lord.

50. And [recall] when We parted the sea for you and saved you and drowned the people of Pharaoh while you were looking on.

51. And [recall] when We made an appointment with Moses for forty nights. Then you took [for worship] the calf after him, while you were wrongdoers.

52. Then We forgave you after that so perhaps you would be grateful.

53. And [recall] when We gave Moses the Scripture and criterion that perhaps you would be guided.

54. And [recall] when Moses said to his people, "O my people, indeed you have wronged yourselves by your taking of the calf [for worship]. So repent to your Creator and kill yourselves. That is best for [all of] you in the sight of your Creator." Then He accepted your repentance; indeed, He is the Accepting of repentance, the Merciful.

55. And [recall] when you said, "O Moses, we will never believe you until we see Allah outright"; so the thunderbolt took you while you were looking on.

56. Then We revived you after your death that perhaps you would be grateful.

57. And We shaded you with clouds and sent down to you manna and quails, [saying], "Eat from the good things with which We have provided you." And they wronged Us not - but they were [only] wronging themselves.

58. And [recall] when We said, "Enter this city and eat from it wherever you will in [ease and] abundance, and enter the gate bowing humbly and say, 'Relieve us of our burdens.' We will [then] forgive your sins for you, and We will increase the doers of good [in goodness and reward]."

59. But those who wronged changed [those words] to a statement other than that which had been said to them, so We sent down upon those who wronged a punishment from the sky because they were defiantly disobeying.

60. And [recall] when Moses prayed for water for his people, so We said, "Strike with your staff the stone." And there gushed forth from it twelve springs, and every people knew its watering place. "Eat and drink from the provision of Allah, and do not commit abuse on the earth, spreading corruption."

61. And [recall] when you said, "O Moses, we can never endure one [kind of] food. So call upon your Lord to bring forth for us from the

earth its green herbs and its cucumbers and its garlic and its lentils and its onions." [Moses] said, "Would you exchange what is better for what is less? Go into [any] settlement and indeed, you will have what you have asked." And they were covered with humiliation and poverty and returned with anger from Allah [upon them]. That was because they [repeatedly] disbelieved in the signs of Allah and killed the prophets without right. That was because they disobeyed and were [habitually] transgressing.

62. Indeed, those who believed and those who were Jews or Christians or Sabeans [before Prophet Muhammad] - those [among them] who believed in Allah and the Last Day and did righteousness - will have their reward with their Lord, and no fear will there be concerning them, nor will they grieve.

63. And [recall] when We took your covenant, [O Children of Israel, to abide by the Torah] and We raised over you the mount, [saying], "Take what We have given you with determination and remember what is in it that perhaps you may become righteous."

64. Then you turned away after that. And if not for the favor of Allah upon you and His mercy, you would have been among the losers.

65. And you had already known about those who transgressed among you concerning the sabbath, and We said to them, "Be apes, despised."

66. And We made it a deterrent punishment for those who were present and those who succeeded [them] and a lesson for those who fear Allah.

67. And [recall] when Moses said to his people, "Indeed, Allah commands you to slaughter a cow." They said, "Do you take us in ridicule?" He said, "I seek refuge in Allah from being among the ignorant."

68. They said, "Call upon your Lord to make clear to us what it is." [Moses] said, "[Allah] says, 'It is a cow which is neither old nor virgin, but median between that,' so do what you are commanded."

69. They said, "Call upon your Lord to show us what is her color." He said, "He says, 'It is a yellow cow, bright in color - pleasing to the observers.' "

70. They said, "Call upon your Lord to make clear to us what it is. Indeed, [all] cows look alike to us. And indeed we, if Allah wills, will be guided."

71. He said, "He says, 'It is a cow neither trained to plow the earth nor to irrigate the field, one free from fault with no spot upon her.'" They said, "Now you have come with the truth." So they slaughtered her, but they could hardly do it.

72. And [recall] when you slew a man and disputed over it, but Allah was to bring out that which you were concealing.

73. So, We said, "Strike the slain man with part of it." Thus does Allah bring the dead to life, and He shows you His signs that you might reason.

74. Then your hearts became hardened after that, being like stones or even harder. For indeed, there are stones from which rivers burst forth, and there are some of them that split open and water comes out, and there are some of them that fall down for fear of Allah. And Allah is not unaware of what you do.

75. Do you covet [the hope, O believers], that they would believe for you while a party of them used to hear the words of Allah and then distort the Torah after they had understood it while they were knowing?

76. And when they meet those who believe, they say, "We have believed"; but when they are alone with one another, they say, "Do you talk to them about what Allah has revealed to you so they can argue with you about it before your Lord?" Then will you not reason?

77. But do they not know that Allah knows what they conceal and what they declare?

78. And among them are unlettered ones who do not know the Scripture except in wishful thinking, but they are only assuming.

79. So woe to those who write the "scripture" with their own hands, then say, "This is from Allah," in order to exchange it for a small price. Woe to them for what their hands have written and woe to them for what they earn.

80. And they say, "Never will the Fire touch us, except for a few days." Say, "Have you taken a covenant with Allah? For Allah will never break His covenant. Or do you say about Allah that which you do not know?"

81. Yes, whoever earns evil and his sin has encompassed him - those are the companions of the Fire; they will abide therein eternally.

82. But they who believe and do righteous deeds - those are the companions of Paradise; they will abide therein eternally.

83. And [recall] when We took the covenant from the Children of Israel, [enjoining upon them], "Do not worship except Allah; and to parents do good and to relatives, orphans, and the needy. And speak to people good [words] and establish prayer and give zakah." Then you turned away, except a few of you, and you were refusing.

84. And [recall] when We took your covenant, [saying], "Do not shed each other's blood or evict one another from your homes." Then you acknowledged [this] while you were witnessing.

85. Then, you are those [same ones who are] killing one another and evicting a party of your people from their homes, cooperating against them in sin and aggression. And if they come to you as captives, you ransom them, although their eviction was forbidden to you. So do you believe in part of the Scripture and disbelieve in part? Then what is the recompense for those who do that among you except disgrace in worldly life; and on the Day of Resurrection they will be sent back to the severest of punishment. And Allah is not unaware of what you do.

86. Those are the ones who have bought the life of this world [in exchange] for the Hereafter, so the punishment will not be lightened for them, nor will they be aided.

87. And We did certainly give Moses the Torah and followed up after him with messengers. And We gave Jesus, the son of Mary, clear proofs and supported him with the Pure Spirit. But is it [not] that every time a messenger came to you, [O Children of Israel], with what your souls did not desire, you were arrogant? And a party [of messengers] you denied and another party you killed.

88. And they said, "Our hearts are wrapped." But, [in fact], Allah has cursed them for their disbelief, so little is it that they believe.

89. And when there came to them a Book from Allah confirming that which was with them - although before they used to pray for victory against those who disbelieved - but [then] when there came to them that which they recognized, they disbelieved in it; so the curse of Allah will be upon the disbelievers.

90. How wretched is that for which they sold themselves - that they would disbelieve in what Allah has revealed through [their] outrage that Allah would send down His favor upon whom He wills from among His servants. So they returned having [earned] wrath upon wrath. And for the disbelievers is a humiliating punishment.

91. And when it is said to them, "Believe in what Allah has revealed," they say, "We believe [only] in what was revealed to us." And they

disbelieve in what came after it, while it is the truth confirming that which is with them. Say, "Then why did you kill the prophets of Allah before, if you are [indeed] believers?"

92. And Moses had certainly brought you clear proofs. Then you took the calf [in worship] after that, while you were wrongdoers.

93. And [recall] when We took your covenant and raised over you the mount, [saying], "Take what We have given you with determination and listen." They said [instead], "We hear and disobey." And their hearts absorbed [the worship of] the calf because of their disbelief. Say, "How wretched is that which your faith enjoins upon you, if you should be believers."

94. Say, [O Muhammad], "If the home of the Hereafter with Allah is for you alone and not the [other] people, then wish for death, if you should be truthful.

95. But they will never wish for it, ever, because of what their hands have put forth. And Allah is Knowing of the wrongdoers.

96. And you will surely find them the most greedy of people for life - [even] more than those who associate others with Allah. One of them wishes that he could be granted life a thousand years, but it would not remove him in the least from the [coming] punishment that he should be granted life. And Allah is Seeing of what they do.

97. Say, "Whoever is an enemy to Gabriel - it is [none but] he who has brought the Qur'an down upon your heart, [O Muhammad], by permission of Allah, confirming that which was before it and as guidance and good tidings for the believers."

98. Whoever is an enemy to Allah and His angels and His messengers and Gabriel and Michael - then indeed, Allah is an enemy to the disbelievers.

99. And We have certainly revealed to you verses [which are] clear proofs, and no one would deny them except the defiantly disobedient.

100. Is it not [true] that every time they took a covenant a party of them threw it away? But, [in fact], most of them do not believe.

101. And when a messenger from Allah came to them confirming that which was with them, a party of those who had been given the Scripture threw the Scripture of Allah behind their backs as if they did not know [what it contained].

102. And they followed [instead] what the devils had recited during the reign of Solomon. It was not Solomon who disbelieved, but the

devils disbelieved, teaching people magic and that which was revealed to the two angels at Babylon, Harut and Marut. But the two angels do not teach anyone unless they say, "We are a trial, so do not disbelieve [by practicing magic]." And [yet] they learn from them that by which they cause separation between a man and his wife. But they do not harm anyone through it except by permission of Allah. And the people learn what harms them and does not benefit them. But the Children of Israel certainly knew that whoever purchased the magic would not have in the Hereafter any share. And wretched is that for which they sold themselves, if they only knew.

103. And if they had believed and feared Allah, then the reward from Allah would have been [far] better, if they only knew.

104. O you who have believed, say not [to Allah 's Messenger], "Ra'ina" but say, "Unthurna" and listen. And for the disbelievers is a painful punishment.

105. Neither those who disbelieve from the People of the Scripture nor the polytheists wish that any good should be sent down to you from your Lord. But Allah selects for His mercy whom He wills, and Allah is the possessor of great bounty.

106. We do not abrogate a verse or cause it to be forgotten except that We bring forth [one] better than it or similar to it. Do you not know that Allah is over all things competent?

107. Do you not know that to Allah belongs the dominion of the heavens and the earth and [that] you have not besides Allah any protector or any helper?

108. Or do you intend to ask your Messenger as Moses was asked before? And whoever exchanges faith for disbelief has certainly strayed from the soundness of the way.

109. Many of the People of the Scripture wish they could turn you back to disbelief after you have believed, out of envy from themselves [even] after the truth has become clear to them. So pardon and overlook until Allah delivers His command. Indeed, Allah is over all things competent.

110. And establish prayer and give zakah, and whatever good you put forward for yourselves - you will find it with Allah. Indeed, Allah of what you do, is Seeing.

111. And they say, "None will enter Paradise except one who is a Jew or a Christian." That is [merely] their wishful thinking, Say, "Produce your proof, if you should be truthful."

112. Yes [on the contrary], whoever submits his face in Islam to Allah while being a doer of good will have his reward with his Lord. And no fear will there be concerning them, nor will they grieve.

113. The Jews say "The Christians have nothing [true] to stand on," and the Christians say, "The Jews have nothing to stand on," although they [both] recite the Scripture. Thus the polytheists speak the same as their words. But Allah will judge between them on the Day of Resurrection concerning that over which they used to differ.

114. And who are more unjust than those who prevent the name of Allah from being mentioned in His mosques and strive toward their destruction. It is not for them to enter them except in fear. For them in this world is disgrace, and they will have in the Hereafter a great punishment.

115. And to Allah belongs the east and the west. So wherever you [might] turn, there is the Face of Allah. Indeed, Allah is all-Encompassing and Knowing.

116. They say, "Allah has taken a son." Exalted is He! Rather, to Him belongs whatever is in the heavens and the earth. All are devoutly obedient to Him,

117. Originator of the heavens and the earth. When He decrees a matter, He only says to it, "Be," and it is.

118. Those who do not know say, "Why does Allah not speak to us or there come to us a sign?" Thus spoke those before them like their words. Their hearts resemble each other. We have shown clearly the signs to a people who are certain [in faith].

119. Indeed, We have sent you, [O Muhammad], with the truth as a bringer of good tidings and a warner, and you will not be asked about the companions of Hellfire.

120. And never will the Jews or the Christians approve of you until you follow their religion. Say, "Indeed, the guidance of Allah is the [only] guidance." If you were to follow their desires after what has come to you of knowledge, you would have against Allah no protector or helper.

121. Those to whom We have given the Book recite it with its true recital. They [are the ones who] believe in it. And whoever disbelieves in it - it is they who are the losers.

122. Children of Israel, remember My favor which I have bestowed upon you and that I preferred you over the worlds.

123. And fear a Day when no soul will suffice for another soul at all, and no compensation will be accepted from it, nor will any intercession benefit it, nor will they be aided.

124. And [mention, O Muhammad], when Abraham was tried by his Lord with commands and he fulfilled them. [Allah] said, "Indeed, I will make you a leader for the people." [Abraham] said, "And of my descendants?" [Allah] said, "My covenant does not include the wrongdoers."

125. And [mention] when We made the House a place of return for the people and [a place of] security. And take, [O believers], from the standing place of Abraham a place of prayer. And We charged Abraham and Ishmael, [saying], "Purify My House for those who perform Tawaf and those who are staying [there] for worship and those who bow and prostrate [in prayer]."

126. And [mention] when Abraham said, "My Lord, make this a secure city and provide its people with fruits - whoever of them believes in Allah and the Last Day." [Allah] said. "And whoever disbelieves - I will grant him enjoyment for a little; then I will force him to the punishment of the Fire, and wretched is the destination."

127. And [mention] when Abraham was raising the foundations of the House and [with him] Ishmael, [saying], "Our Lord, accept [this] from us. Indeed You are the Hearing, the Knowing.

128. Our Lord, and make us Muslims [in submission] to You and from our descendants a Muslim nation [in submission] to You. And show us our rites and accept our repentance. Indeed, You are the Accepting of repentance, the Merciful.

129. Our Lord, and send among them a messenger from themselves who will recite to them Your verses and teach them the Book and wisdom and purify them. Indeed, You are the Exalted in Might, the Wise."

130. And who would be averse to the religion of Abraham except one who makes a fool of himself. And We had chosen him in this world, and indeed he, in the Hereafter, will be among the righteous.

131. When his Lord said to him, "Submit", he said "I have submitted [in Islam] to the Lord of the worlds."

132. And Abraham instructed his sons [to do the same] and [so did] Jacob, [saying], "O my sons, indeed Allah has chosen for you this religion, so do not die except while you are Muslims."

133. Or were you witnesses when death approached Jacob, when he said to his sons, "What will you worship after me?" They said, "We will worship your God and the God of your fathers, Abraham and Ishmael and Isaac - one God. And we are Muslims [in submission] to Him."

134. That was a nation which has passed on. It will have [the consequence of] what it earned, and you will have what you have earned. And you will not be asked about what they used to do.

135. They say, "Be Jews or Christians [so] you will be guided." Say, "Rather, [we follow] the religion of Abraham, inclining toward truth, and he was not of the polytheists."

136. Say, [O believers], "We have believed in Allah and what has been revealed to us and what has been revealed to Abraham and Ishmael and Isaac and Jacob and the Descendants and what was given to Moses and Jesus and what was given to the prophets from their Lord. We make no distinction between any of them, and we are Muslims [in submission] to Him."

137. So if they believe in the same as you believe in, then they have been [rightly] guided; but if they turn away, they are only in dissension, and Allah will be sufficient for you against them. And He is the Hearing, the Knowing.

138. [And say, "Ours is] the religion of Allah. And who is better than Allah in [ordaining] religion? And we are worshippers of Him."

139. Say, [O Muhammad], "Do you argue with us about Allah while He is our Lord and your Lord? For us are our deeds, and for you are your deeds. And we are sincere [in deed and intention] to Him."

140. Or do you say that Abraham and Ishmael and Isaac and Jacob and the Descendants were Jews or Christians? Say, "Are you more knowing or is Allah?" And who is more unjust than one who conceals a testimony he has from Allah? And Allah is not unaware of what you do.

141. That is a nation which has passed on. It will have [the consequence of] what it earned, and you will have what you have earned. And you will not be asked about what they used to do.

142. The foolish among the people will say, "What has turned them away from their qiblah, which they used to face?" Say, "To Allah belongs the east and the west. He guides whom He wills to a straight path."

143. And thus we have made you a just community that you will be witnesses over the people and the Messenger will be a witness over you. And We did not make the qiblah which you used to face except that We might make evident who would follow the Messenger from who would turn back on his heels. And indeed, it is difficult except for those whom Allah has guided. And never would Allah have caused you to lose your faith. Indeed Allah is, to the people, Kind and Merciful.

144. We have certainly seen the turning of your face, [O Muhammad], toward the heaven, and We will surely turn you to a qiblah with which you will be pleased. So turn your face toward al-Masjid al-Haram. And wherever you [believers] are, turn your faces toward it [in prayer]. Indeed, those who have been given the Scripture well know that it is the truth from their Lord. And Allah is not unaware of what they do.

145. And if you brought to those who were given the Scripture every sign, they would not follow your qiblah. Nor will you be a follower of their qiblah. Nor would they be followers of one another's qiblah. So if you were to follow their desires after what has come to you of knowledge, indeed, you would then be among the wrongdoers.

146. Those to whom We gave the Scripture know him as they know their own sons. But indeed, a party of them conceal the truth while they know [it].

147. The truth is from your Lord, so never be among the doubters.

148. For each [religious following] is a direction toward which it faces. So race to [all that is] good. Wherever you may be, Allah will bring you forth [for judgement] all together. Indeed, Allah is over all things competent.

149. So from wherever you go out [for prayer, O Muhammad] turn your face toward al- Masjid al-Haram, and indeed, it is the truth from your Lord. And Allah is not unaware of what you do.

150. And from wherever you go out [for prayer], turn your face toward al-Masjid al-Haram. And wherever you [believers] may be, turn your faces toward it in order that the people will not have any argument against you, except for those of them who commit wrong; so fear them not but fear Me. And [it is] so I may complete My favor upon you and that you may be guided.

151. Just as We have sent among you a messenger from yourselves reciting to you Our verses and purifying you and teaching you the

Book and wisdom and teaching you that which you did not know.

152. So remember Me; I will remember you. And be grateful to Me and do not deny Me.

153. O you who have believed, seek help through patience and prayer. Indeed, Allah is with the patient.

154. And do not say about those who are killed in the way of Allah, "They are dead." Rather, they are alive, but you perceive [it] not.

155. And We will surely test you with something of fear and hunger and a loss of wealth and lives and fruits, but give good tidings to the patient,

156. Who, when disaster strikes them, say, "Indeed we belong to Allah, and indeed to Him we will return."

157. Those are the ones upon whom are blessings from their Lord and mercy. And it is those who are the [rightly] guided.

158. Indeed, as-Safa and al-Marwah are among the symbols of Allah. So whoever makes Hajj to the House or performs 'umrah - there is no blame upon him for walking between them. And whoever volunteers good - then indeed, Allah is appreciative and Knowing.

159. Indeed, those who conceal what We sent down of clear proofs and guidance after We made it clear for the people in the Scripture - those are cursed by Allah and cursed by those who curse,

160. Except for those who repent and correct themselves and make evident [what they concealed]. Those - I will accept their repentance, and I am the Accepting of repentance, the Merciful.

161. Indeed, those who disbelieve and die while they are disbelievers - upon them will be the curse of Allah and of the angels and the people, all together,

162. Abiding eternally therein. The punishment will not be lightened for them, nor will they be reprieved.

163. And your god is one God. There is no deity [worthy of worship] except Him, the Entirely Merciful, the Especially Merciful.

164. Indeed, in the creation of the heavens and earth, and the alternation of the night and the day, and the [great] ships which sail through the sea with that which benefits people, and what Allah has sent down from the heavens of rain, giving life thereby to the earth after its lifelessness and dispersing therein every [kind of] moving creature, and [His] directing of the winds and the clouds controlled between the heaven and the earth are

signs for a people who use reason.

165. And [yet], among the people are those who take other than Allah as equals [to Him]. They love them as they [should] love Allah. But those who believe are stronger in love for Allah. And if only they who have wronged would consider [that] when they see the punishment, [they will be certain] that all power belongs to Allah and that Allah is severe in punishment.

166. [And they should consider that] when those who have been followed disassociate themselves from those who followed [them], and they [all] see the punishment, and cut off from them are the ties [of relationship],

167. Those who followed will say, "If only we had another turn [at worldly life] so we could disassociate ourselves from them as they have disassociated themselves from us." Thus will Allah show them their deeds as regrets upon them. And they are never to emerge from the Fire.

168. O mankind, eat from whatever is on earth [that is] lawful and good and do not follow the footsteps of Satan. Indeed, he is to you a clear enemy.

169. He only orders you to evil and immorality and to say about Allah what you do not know.

170. And when it is said to them, "Follow what Allah has revealed," they say, "Rather, we will follow that which we found our fathers doing." Even though their fathers understood nothing, nor were they guided?

171. The example of those who disbelieve is like that of one who shouts at what hears nothing but calls and cries cattle or sheep - deaf, dumb and blind, so they do not understand.

172. O you who have believed, eat from the good things which We have provided for you and be grateful to Allah if it is [indeed] Him that you worship.

173. He has only forbidden to you dead animals, blood, the flesh of swine, and that which has been dedicated to other than Allah. But whoever is forced [by necessity], neither desiring [it] nor transgressing [its limit], there is no sin upon him. Indeed, Allah is Forgiving and Merciful.

174. Indeed, they who conceal what Allah has sent down of the Book and exchange it for a small price - those consume not into their bellies except the Fire. And Allah will not speak to them on the

Day of Resurrection, nor will He purify them. And they will have a painful punishment.

175. Those are the ones who have exchanged guidance for error and forgiveness for punishment. How patient they are in pursuit of the Fire!

176. That is [deserved by them] because Allah has sent down the Book in truth. And indeed, those who differ over the Book are in extreme dissension.

177. Righteousness is not that you turn your faces toward the east or the west, but [true] righteousness is [in] one who believes in Allah, the Last Day, the angels, the Book, and the prophets and gives wealth, in spite of love for it, to relatives, orphans, the needy, the traveler, those who ask [for help], and for freeing slaves; [and who] establishes prayer and gives zakah; [those who] fulfill their promise when they promise; and [those who] are patient in poverty and hardship and during battle. Those are the ones who have been true, and it is those who are the righteous.

178. O you who have believed, prescribed for you is legal retribution for those murdered - the free for the free, the slave for the slave, and the female for the female. But whoever overlooks from his brother anything, then there should be a suitable follow-up and payment to him with good conduct. This is an alleviation from your Lord and a mercy. But whoever transgresses after that will have a painful punishment.

179. And there is for you in legal retribution [saving of] life, O you [people] of understanding, that you may become righteous.

180. Prescribed for you when death approaches [any] one of you if he leaves wealth [is that he should make] a bequest for the parents and near relatives according to what is acceptable - a duty upon the righteous.

181. Then whoever alters the bequest after he has heard it - the sin is only upon those who have altered it. Indeed, Allah is Hearing and Knowing.

182. But if one fears from the bequeather [some] error or sin and corrects that which is between them, there is no sin upon him. Indeed, Allah is Forgiving and Merciful.

183. O you who have believed, decreed upon you is fasting as it was decreed upon those before you that you may become righteous -

184. [Fasting for] a limited number of days. So whoever among you is ill or on a journey [during them] - then an equal number of days [are to be made up]. And upon those who are able [to fast, but with hardship] - a ransom [as substitute] of feeding a poor person [each day]. And whoever volunteers excess - it is better for him. But to fast is best for you, if you only knew.

185. The month of Ramadhan [is that] in which was revealed the Qur'an, a guidance for the people and clear proofs of guidance and criterion. So whoever sights [the new moon of] the month, let him fast it; and whoever is ill or on a journey - then an equal number of other days. Allah intends for you ease and does not intend for you hardship and [wants] for you to complete the period and to glorify Allah for that [to] which He has guided you; and perhaps you will be grateful.

186. And when My servants ask you, [O Muhammad], concerning Me - indeed I am near. I respond to the invocation of the supplicant when he calls upon Me. So let them respond to Me [by obedience] and believe in Me that they may be [rightly] guided.

187. It has been made permissible for you the night preceding fasting to go to your wives [for sexual relations]. They are clothing for you and you are clothing for them. Allah knows that you used to deceive yourselves, so He accepted your repentance and forgave you. So now, have relations with them and seek that which Allah has decreed for you. And eat and drink until the white thread of dawn becomes distinct to you from the black thread [of night]. Then complete the fast until the sunset. And do not have relations with them as long as you are staying for worship in the mosques. These are the limits [set by] Allah, so do not approach them. Thus does Allah make clear His ordinances to the people that they may become righteous.

188. And do not consume one another's wealth unjustly or send it [in bribery] to the rulers in order that [they might aid] you [to] consume a portion of the wealth of the people in sin, while you know [it is unlawful].

189. They ask you, [O Muhammad], about the new moons. Say, "They are measurements of time for the people and for Hajj." And it is not righteousness to enter houses from the back, but righteousness is [in] one who fears Allah. And enter houses from their doors. And fear Allah that you may succeed.

190. Fight in the way of Allah those who fight you but do not

transgress. Indeed. Allah does not like transgressors.

191. And kill them wherever you overtake them and expel them from wherever they have expelled you, and fitnah is worse than killing. And do not fight them at al-Masjid al- Haram until they fight you there. But if they fight you, then kill them. Such is the recompense of the disbelievers.

192. And if they cease, then indeed, Allah is Forgiving and Merciful.

193. Fight them until there is no [more] fitnah and [until] worship is [acknowledged to be] for Allah. But if they cease, then there is to be no aggression except against the oppressors.

194. [Fighting in] the sacred month is for [aggression committed in] the sacred month, and for [all] violations is legal retribution. So whoever has assaulted you, then assault him in the same way that he has assaulted you. And fear Allah and know that Allah is with those who fear Him.

195. And spend in the way of Allah and do not throw [yourselves] with your [own] hands into destruction [by refraining]. And do good; indeed, Allah loves the doers of good.

196. And complete the Hajj and 'umrah for Allah. But if you are prevented, then [offer] what can be obtained with ease of sacrificial animals. And do not shave your heads until the sacrificial animal has reached its place of slaughter. And whoever among you is ill or has an ailment of the head [making shaving necessary must offer] a ransom of fasting [three days] or charity or sacrifice. And when you are secure, then whoever performs 'umrah [during the Hajj months] followed by Hajj [offers] what can be obtained with ease of sacrificial animals. And whoever cannot find [or afford such an animal] - then a fast of three days during Hajj and of seven when you have returned [home]. Those are ten complete [days]. This is for those whose family is not in the area of al-Masjid al-Haram. And fear Allah and know that Allah is severe in penalty.

197. Hajj is [during] well-known months, so whoever has made Hajj obligatory upon himself therein [by entering the state of ihram], there is [to be for him] no sexual relations and no disobedience and no disputing during Hajj. And whatever good you do - Allah knows it. And take provisions, but indeed, the best provision is fear of Allah. And fear Me, O you of understanding.

198. There is no blame upon you for seeking bounty from your Lord [during Hajj]. But when you depart from 'Arafat, remember Allah

at al- Mash'ar al-Haram. And remember Him, as He has guided you, for indeed, you were before that among those astray.

199. Then depart from the place from where [all] the people depart and ask forgiveness of Allah. Indeed, Allah is Forgiving and Merciful.

200. And when you have completed your rites, remember Allah like your [previous] remembrance of your fathers or with [much] greater remembrance. And among the people is he who says, "Our Lord, give us in this world," and he will have in the Hereafter no share.

201. But among them is he who says, "Our Lord, give us in this world [that which is] good and in the Hereafter [that which is] good and protect us from the punishment of the Fire."

202. Those will have a share of what they have earned, and Allah is swift in account.

203. And remember Allah during [specific] numbered days. Then whoever hastens [his departure] in two days - there is no sin upon him; and whoever delays [until the third] - there is no sin upon him - for him who fears Allah. And fear Allah and know that unto Him you will be gathered.

204. And of the people is he whose speech pleases you in worldly life, and he calls Allah to witness as to what is in his heart, yet he is the fiercest of opponents.

205. And when he goes away, he strives throughout the land to cause corruption therein and destroy crops and animals. And Allah does not like corruption.

206. And when it is said to him, "Fear Allah," pride in the sin takes hold of him. Sufficient for him is Hellfire, and how wretched is the resting place.

207. And of the people is he who sells himself, seeking means to the approval of Allah. And Allah is kind to [His] servants.

208. O you who have believed, enter into Islam completely [and perfectly] and do not follow the footsteps of Satan. Indeed, he is to you a clear enemy.

209. But if you deviate after clear proofs have come to you, then know that Allah is Exalted in Might and Wise.

210. Do they await but that Allah should come to them in covers of clouds and the angels [as well] and the matter is [then] decided? And to Allah [all] matters are returned.

211. Ask the Children of Israel how many a sign of evidence We have given them. And whoever exchanges the favor of Allah [for disbelief] after it has come to him - then indeed, Allah is severe in penalty.

212. Beautified for those who disbelieve is the life of this world, and they ridicule those who believe. But those who fear Allah are above them on the Day of Resurrection. And Allah gives provision to whom He wills without account.

213. Mankind was [of] one religion [before their deviation]; then Allah sent the prophets as bringers of good tidings and warners and sent down with them the Scripture in truth to judge between the people concerning that in which they differed. And none differed over the Scripture except those who were given it - after the clear proofs came to them - out of jealous animosity among themselves. And Allah guided those who believed to the truth concerning that over which they had differed, by His permission. And Allah guides whom He wills to a straight path.

214. Or do you think that you will enter Paradise while such [trial] has not yet come to you as came to those who passed on before you? They were touched by poverty and hardship and were shaken until [even their] messenger and those who believed with him said, "When is the help of Allah?" Unquestionably, the help of Allah is near.

215. They ask you, [O Muhammad], what they should spend. Say, "Whatever you spend of good is [to be] for parents and relatives and orphans and the needy and the traveler. And whatever you do of good - indeed, Allah is Knowing of it."

216. Fighting has been enjoined upon you while it is hateful to you. But perhaps you hate a thing and it is good for you; and perhaps you love a thing and it is bad for you. And Allah Knows, while you know not.

217. They ask you about the sacred month - about fighting therein. Say, "Fighting therein is great [sin], but averting [people] from the way of Allah and disbelief in Him and [preventing access to] al-Masjid al-Haram and the expulsion of its people therefrom are greater [evil] in the sight of Allah. And fitnah is greater than killing." And they will continue to fight you until they turn you back from your religion if they are able. And whoever of you reverts from his religion [to disbelief] and dies while he is a disbeliever - for those, their deeds have become worthless in this

world and the Hereafter, and those are the companions of the Fire, they will abide therein eternally.

218. Indeed, those who have believed and those who have emigrated and fought in the cause of Allah - those expect the mercy of Allah. And Allah is Forgiving and Merciful.

219. They ask you about wine and gambling. Say, "In them is great sin and [yet, some] benefit for people. But their sin is greater than their benefit." And they ask you what they should spend. Say, "The excess [beyond needs]." Thus Allah makes clear to you the verses [of revelation] that you might give thought.

220. To this world and the Hereafter. And they ask you about orphans. Say, "Improvement for them is best. And if you mix your affairs with theirs - they are your brothers. And Allah knows the corrupter from the amender. And if Allah had willed, He could have put you in difficulty. Indeed, Allah is Exalted in Might and Wise.

221. And do not marry polytheistic women until they believe. And a believing slave woman is better than a polytheist, even though she might please you. And do not marry polytheistic men [to your women] until they believe. And a believing slave is better than a polytheist, even though he might please you. Those invite [you] to the Fire, but Allah invites to Paradise and to forgiveness, by His permission. And He makes clear His verses to the people that perhaps they may remember.

222. And they ask you about menstruation. Say, "It is harm, so keep away from wives during menstruation. And do not approach them until they are pure. And when they have purified themselves, then come to them from where Allah has ordained for you. Indeed, Allah loves those who are constantly repentant and loves those who purify themselves."

223. Your wives are a place of sowing of seed for you, so come to your place of cultivation however you wish and put forth [righteousness] for yourselves. And fear Allah and know that you will meet Him. And give good tidings to the believers.

224. And do not make [your oath by] Allah an excuse against being righteous and fearing Allah and making peace among people. And Allah is Hearing and Knowing.

225. Allah does not impose blame upon you for what is unintentional in your oaths, but He imposes blame upon you for what your hearts have earned. And Allah is Forgiving and Forbearing.

226. For those who swear not to have sexual relations with their wives is a waiting time of four months, but if they return [to normal relations] - then indeed, Allah is Forgiving and Merciful.

227. And if they decide on divorce - then indeed, Allah is Hearing and Knowing.

228. Divorced women remain in waiting for three periods, and it is not lawful for them to conceal what Allah has created in their wombs if they believe in Allah and the Last Day. And their husbands have more right to take them back in this [period] if they want reconciliation. And due to the wives is similar to what is expected of them, according to what is reasonable. But the men have a degree over them [in responsibility and authority]. And Allah is Exalted in Might and Wise.

229. Divorce is twice. Then, either keep [her] in an acceptable manner or release [her] with good treatment. And it is not lawful for you to take anything of what you have given them unless both fear that they will not be able to keep [within] the limits of Allah. But if you fear that they will not keep [within] the limits of Allah, then there is no blame upon either of them concerning that by which she ransoms herself. These are the limits of Allah, so do not transgress them. And whoever transgresses the limits of Allah - it is those who are the wrongdoers.

230. And if he has divorced her [for the third time], then she is not lawful to him afterward until [after] she marries a husband other than him. And if the latter husband divorces her [or dies], there is no blame upon the woman and her former husband for returning to each other if they think that they can keep [within] the limits of Allah. These are the limits of Allah, which He makes clear to a people who know.

231. And when you divorce women and they have [nearly] fulfilled their term, either retain them according to acceptable terms or release them according to acceptable terms, and do not keep them, intending harm, to transgress [against them]. And whoever does that has certainly wronged himself. And do not take the verses of Allah in jest. And remember the favor of Allah upon you and what has been revealed to you of the Book and wisdom by which He instructs you. And fear Allah and know that Allah is Knowing of all things.

232. And when you divorce women and they have fulfilled their term, do not prevent them from remarrying their [former]

husbands if they agree among themselves on an acceptable basis. That is instructed to whoever of you believes in Allah and the Last Day. That is better for you and purer, and Allah knows and you know not.

233. Mothers may breastfeed their children two complete years for whoever wishes to complete the nursing [period]. Upon the father is the mothers' provision and their clothing according to what is acceptable. No person is charged with more than his capacity. No mother should be harmed through her child, and no father through his child. And upon the [father's] heir is [a duty] like that [of the father]. And if they both desire weaning through mutual consent from both of them and consultation, there is no blame upon either of them. And if you wish to have your children nursed by a substitute, there is no blame upon you as long as you give payment according to what is acceptable. And fear Allah and know that Allah is Seeing of what you do.

234. And those who are taken in death among you and leave wives behind - they, [the wives, shall] wait four months and ten [days]. And when they have fulfilled their term, then there is no blame upon you for what they do with themselves in an acceptable manner. And Allah is [fully] Acquainted with what you do.

235. There is no blame upon you for that to which you [indirectly] allude concerning a proposal to women or for what you conceal within yourselves. Allah knows that you will have them in mind. But do not promise them secretly except for saying a proper saying. And do not determine to undertake a marriage contract until the decreed period reaches its end. And know that Allah knows what is within yourselves, so beware of Him. And know that Allah is Forgiving and Forbearing.

236. There is no blame upon you if you divorce women you have not touched nor specified for them an obligation. But give them [a gift of] compensation - the wealthy according to his capability and the poor according to his capability - a provision according to what is acceptable, a duty upon the doers of good.

237. And if you divorce them before you have touched them and you have already specified for them an obligation, then [give] half of what you specified - unless they forego the right or the one in whose hand is the marriage contract foregoes it. And to forego it is nearer to righteousness. And do not forget graciousness between you. Indeed Allah, of whatever you do, is Seeing.

238. Maintain with care the [obligatory] prayers and [in particular] the middle prayer and stand before Allah, devoutly obedient.

239. And if you fear [an enemy, then pray] on foot or riding. But when you are secure, then remember Allah [in prayer], as He has taught you that which you did not [previously] know.

240. And those who are taken in death among you and leave wives behind - for their wives is a bequest: maintenance for one year without turning [them] out. But if they leave [of their own accord], then there is no blame upon you for what they do with themselves in an acceptable way. And Allah is Exalted in Might and Wise.

241. And for divorced women is a provision according to what is acceptable - a duty upon the righteous.

242. Thus does Allah make clear to you His verses that you might use reason.

243. Have you not considered those who left their homes in many thousands, fearing death? Allah said to them, "Die"; then He restored them to life. And Allah is full of bounty to the people, but most of the people do not show gratitude.

244. And fight in the cause of Allah and know that Allah is Hearing and Knowing.

245. Who is it that would loan Allah a goodly loan so He may multiply it for him many times over? And it is Allah who withholds and grants abundance, and to Him you will be returned.

246. Have you not considered the assembly of the Children of Israel after [the time of] Moses when they said to a prophet of theirs, "Send to us a king, and we will fight in the way of Allah "? He said, "Would you perhaps refrain from fighting if fighting was prescribed for you?" They said, "And why should we not fight in the cause of Allah when we have been driven out from our homes and from our children?" But when fighting was prescribed for them, they turned away, except for a few of them. And Allah is Knowing of the wrongdoers.

247. And their prophet said to them, "Indeed, Allah has sent to you Saul as a king." They said, "How can he have kingship over us while we are more worthy of kingship than him and he has not been given any measure of wealth?" He said, "Indeed, Allah has chosen him over you and has increased him abundantly in knowledge and stature. And Allah gives His sovereignty to whom

He wills. And Allah is all-Encompassing [in favor] and Knowing."

248. And their prophet said to them, "Indeed, a sign of his kingship is that the chest will come to you in which is assurance from your Lord and a remnant of what the family of Moses and the family of Aaron had left, carried by the angels. Indeed in that is a sign for you, if you are believers."

249. And when Saul went forth with the soldiers, he said, "Indeed, Allah will be testing you with a river. So whoever drinks from it is not of me, and whoever does not taste it is indeed of me, excepting one who takes [from it] in the hollow of his hand." But they drank from it, except a [very] few of them. Then when he had crossed it along with those who believed with him, they said, "There is no power for us today against Goliath and his soldiers." But those who were certain that they would meet Allah said, "How many a small company has overcome a large company by permission of Allah. And Allah is with the patient."

250. And when they went forth to [face] Goliath and his soldiers, they said, "Our Lord, pour upon us patience and plant firmly our feet and give us victory over the disbelieving people."

251. So they defeated them by permission of Allah, and David killed Goliath, and Allah gave him the kingship and prophethood and taught him from that which He willed. And if it were not for Allah checking [some] people by means of others, the earth would have been corrupted, but Allah is full of bounty to the worlds.

252. These are the verses of Allah which We recite to you, [O Muhammad], in truth. And indeed, you are from among the messengers.

253. Those messengers - some of them We caused to exceed others. Among them were those to whom Allah spoke, and He raised some of them in degree. And We gave Jesus, the Son of Mary, clear proofs, and We supported him with the Pure Spirit. If Allah had willed, those [generations] succeeding them would not have fought each other after the clear proofs had come to them. But they differed, and some of them believed and some of them disbelieved. And if Allah had willed, they would not have fought each other, but Allah does what He intends.

254. O you who have believed, spend from that which We have provided for you before there comes a Day in which there is no exchange and no friendship and no intercession. And the

disbelievers - they are the wrongdoers.

255. Allah - there is no deity except Him, the Ever-Living, the Sustainer of [all] existence. Neither drowsiness overtakes Him nor sleep. To Him belongs whatever is in the heavens and whatever is on the earth. Who is it that can intercede with Him except by His permission? He knows what is [presently] before them and what will be after them, and they encompass not a thing of His knowledge except for what He wills. His Kursi extends over the heavens and the earth, and their preservation tires Him not. And He is the Most High, the Most Great.

256. There shall be no compulsion in [acceptance of] the religion. The right course has become clear from the wrong. So whoever disbelieves in Taghut and believes in Allah has grasped the most trustworthy handhold with no break in it. And Allah is Hearing and Knowing.

257. Allah is the ally of those who believe. He brings them out from darknesses into the light. And those who disbelieve - their allies are Taghut. They take them out of the light into darknesses. Those are the companions of the Fire; they will abide eternally therein.

258. Have you not considered the one who argued with Abraham about his Lord [merely] because Allah had given him kingship? When Abraham said, "My Lord is the one who gives life and causes death," he said, "I give life and cause death." Abraham said, "Indeed, Allah brings up the sun from the east, so bring it up from the west." So the disbeliever was overwhelmed [by astonishment], and Allah does not guide the wrongdoing people.

259. Or [consider such an example] as the one who passed by a township which had fallen into ruin. He said, "How will Allah bring this to life after its death?" So Allah caused him to die for a hundred years; then He revived him. He said, "How long have you remained?" The man said, "I have remained a day or part of a day." He said, "Rather, you have remained one hundred years. Look at your food and your drink; it has not changed with time. And look at your donkey; and We will make you a sign for the people. And look at the bones [of this donkey] - how We raise them and then We cover them with flesh." And when it became clear to him, he said, "I know that Allah is over all things competent."

260. And [mention] when Abraham said, "My Lord, show me how You

give life to the dead." [Allah] said, "Have you not believed?" He said, "Yes, but [I ask] only that my heart may be satisfied." [Allah] said, "Take four birds and commit them to yourself. Then [after slaughtering them] put on each hill a portion of them; then call them - they will come [flying] to you in haste. And know that Allah is Exalted in Might and Wise."

261. The example of those who spend their wealth in the way of Allah is like a seed [of grain] which grows seven spikes; in each spike is a hundred grains. And Allah multiplies [His reward] for whom He wills. And Allah is all-Encompassing and Knowing.

262. Those who spend their wealth in the way of Allah and then do not follow up what they have spent with reminders [of it] or [other] injury will have their reward with their Lord, and there will be no fear concerning them, nor will they grieve.

263. Kind speech and forgiveness are better than charity followed by injury. And Allah is Free of need and Forbearing.

264. O you who have believed, do not invalidate your charities with reminders or injury as does one who spends his wealth [only] to be seen by the people and does not believe in Allah and the Last Day. His example is like that of a [large] smooth stone upon which is dust and is hit by a downpour that leaves it bare. They are unable [to keep] anything of what they have earned. And Allah does not guide the disbelieving people.

265. And the example of those who spend their wealth seeking means to the approval of Allah and assuring [reward for] themselves is like a garden on high ground which is hit by a downpour - so it yields its fruits in double. And [even] if it is not hit by a downpour, then a drizzle [is sufficient]. And Allah, of what you do, is Seeing.

266. Would one of you like to have a garden of palm trees and grapevines underneath which rivers flow in which he has from every fruit? But he is afflicted with old age and has weak offspring, and it is hit by a whirlwind containing fire and is burned. Thus does Allah make clear to you [His] verses that you might give thought.

267. O you who have believed, spend from the good things which you have earned and from that which We have produced for you from the earth. And do not aim toward the defective therefrom, spending [from that] while you would not take it [yourself] except with closed eyes. And know that Allah is

Free of need and Praiseworthy.

268. Satan threatens you with poverty and orders you to immorality, while Allah promises you forgiveness from Him and bounty. And Allah is all-Encompassing and Knowing.

269. He gives wisdom to whom He wills, and whoever has been given wisdom has certainly been given much good. And none will remember except those of understanding.

270. And whatever you spend of expenditures or make of vows - indeed, Allah knows of it. And for the wrongdoers there are no helpers.

271. If you disclose your charitable expenditures, they are good; but if you conceal them and give them to the poor, it is better for you, and He will remove from you some of your misdeeds [thereby]. And Allah, with what you do, is [fully] Acquainted.

272. Not upon you, [O Muhammad], is [responsibility for] their guidance, but Allah guides whom He wills. And whatever good you [believers] spend is for yourselves, and you do not spend except seeking the countenance of Allah. And whatever you spend of good - it will be fully repaid to you, and you will not be wronged.

273. [Charity is] for the poor who have been restricted for the cause of Allah, unable to move about in the land. An ignorant [person] would think them self-sufficient because of their restraint, but you will know them by their [characteristic] sign. They do not ask people persistently [or at all]. And whatever you spend of good - indeed, Allah is Knowing of it.

274. Those who spend their wealth [in Allah's way] by night and by day, secretly and publicly - they will have their reward with their Lord. And no fear will there be concerning them, nor will they grieve.

275. Those who consume interest cannot stand [on the Day of Resurrection] except as one stands who is being beaten by Satan into insanity. That is because they say, "Trade is [just] like interest." But Allah has permitted trade and has forbidden interest. So whoever has received an admonition from his Lord and desists may have what is past, and his affair rests with Allah. But whoever returns to [dealing in interest or usury] - those are the companions of the Fire; they will abide eternally therein.

276. Allah destroys interest and gives increase for charities. And Allah

does not like every sinning disbeliever.

277. Indeed, those who believe and do righteous deeds and establish prayer and give zakah will have their reward with their Lord, and there will be no fear concerning them, nor will they grieve.

278. O you who have believed, fear Allah and give up what remains [due to you] of interest, if you should be believers.

279. And if you do not, then be informed of a war [against you] from Allah and His Messenger. But if you repent, you may have your principal - [thus] you do no wrong, nor are you wronged.

280. And if someone is in hardship, then [let there be] postponement until [a time of] ease. But if you give [from your right as] charity, then it is better for you, if you only knew.

281. And fear a Day when you will be returned to Allah. Then every soul will be compensated for what it earned, and they will not be treated unjustly.

282. O you who have believed, when you contract a debt for a specified term, write it down. And let a scribe write [it] between you in justice. Let no scribe refuse to write as Allah has taught him. So let him write and let the one who has the obligation dictate. And let him fear Allah, his Lord, and not leave anything out of it. But if the one who has the obligation is of limited understanding or weak or unable to dictate himself, then let his guardian dictate in justice. And bring to witness two witnesses from among your men. And if there are not two men [available], then a man and two women from those whom you accept as witnesses - so that if one of the women errs, then the other can remind her. And let not the witnesses refuse when they are called upon. And do not be [too] weary to write it, whether it is small or large, for its [specified] term. That is more just in the sight of Allah and stronger as evidence and more likely to prevent doubt between you, except when it is an immediate transaction which you conduct among yourselves. For [then] there is no blame upon you if you do not write it. And take witnesses when you conclude a contract. Let no scribe be harmed or any witness. For if you do so, indeed, it is [grave] disobedience in you. And fear Allah. And Allah teaches you. And Allah is Knowing of all things.

283. And if you are on a journey and cannot find a scribe, then a security deposit [should be] taken. And if one of you entrusts

another, then let him who is entrusted discharge his trust [faithfully] and let him fear Allah, his Lord. And do not conceal testimony, for whoever conceals it - his heart is indeed sinful, and Allah is Knowing of what you do.

284. To Allah belongs whatever is in the heavens and whatever is in the earth. Whether you show what is within yourselves or conceal it, Allah will bring you to account for it. Then He will forgive whom He wills and punish whom He wills, and Allah is over all things competent.

285. The Messenger has believed in what was revealed to him from his Lord, and [so have] the believers. All of them have believed in Allah and His angels and His books and His messengers, [saying], "We make no distinction between any of His messengers." And they say, "We hear and we obey. [We seek] Your forgiveness, our Lord, and to You is the [final] destination."

286. Allah does not charge a soul except [with that within] its capacity. It will have [the consequence of] what [good] it has gained, and it will bear [the consequence of] what [evil] it has earned. "Our Lord, do not impose blame upon us if we have forgotten or erred. Our Lord, and lay not upon us a burden like that which You laid upon those before us. Our Lord, and burden us not with that which we have no ability to bear. And pardon us; and forgive us; and have mercy upon us. You are our protector, so give us victory over the disbelieving people."

| Verses: 200 | **Surah 03 Aali Imran** | Madani |

In the name of Allah, the Entirely Merciful, the Especially Merciful.

01. Alif, Lam, Meem.
02. Allah - there is no deity except Him, the Ever-Living, the Sustainer of existence.
03. He has sent down upon you, [O Muhammad], the Book in truth, confirming what was before it. And He revealed the Torah and the Gospel.
04. Before, as guidance for the people. And He revealed the Qur'an. Indeed, those who disbelieve in the verses of Allah will have a severe punishment, and Allah is exalted in Might, the Owner of Retribution.
05. Indeed, from Allah nothing is hidden in the earth nor in the heaven.

06. It is He who forms you in the wombs however He wills. There is no deity except Him, the Exalted in Might, the Wise.

07. It is He who has sent down to you, [O Muhammad], the Book; in it are verses [that are] precise - they are the foundation of the Book - and others unspecific. As for those in whose hearts is deviation [from truth], they will follow that of it which is unspecific, seeking discord and seeking an interpretation [suitable to them]. And no one knows its [true] interpretation except Allah. But those firm in knowledge say, "We believe in it. All [of it] is from our Lord." And no one will be reminded except those of understanding.

08. [Who say], "Our Lord, let not our hearts deviate after You have guided us and grant us from Yourself mercy. Indeed, You are the Bestower.

09. Our Lord, surely You will gather the people for a Day about which there is no doubt. Indeed, Allah does not fail in His promise."

10. Indeed, those who disbelieve - never will their wealth or their children avail them against Allah at all. And it is they who are fuel for the Fire.

11. [Theirs is] like the custom of the people of Pharaoh and those before them. They denied Our signs, so Allah seized them for their sins. And Allah is severe in penalty.

12. Say to those who disbelieve, "You will be overcome and gathered together to Hell, and wretched is the resting place."

13. Already there has been for you a sign in the two armies which met - one fighting in the cause of Allah and another of disbelievers. They saw them [to be] twice their [own] number by [their] eyesight. But Allah supports with His victory whom He wills. Indeed in that is a lesson for those of vision.

14. Beautified for people is the love of that which they desire - of women and sons, heaped-up sums of gold and silver, fine branded horses, and cattle and tilled land. That is the enjoyment of worldly life, but Allah has with Him the best return.

15. Say, "Shall I inform you of [something] better than that? For those who fear Allah will be gardens in the presence of their Lord beneath which rivers flow, wherein they abide eternally, and purified spouses and approval from Allah. And Allah is Seeing of [His] servants -

16. Those who say, "Our Lord, indeed we have believed, so forgive us our sins and protect us from the punishment of the Fire,"

17. The patient, the true, the obedient, those who spend [in the way of Allah], and those who seek forgiveness before dawn.
18. Allah witnesses that there is no deity except Him, and [so do] the angels and those of knowledge - [that He is] maintaining [creation] in justice. There is no deity except Him, the Exalted in Might, the Wise.
19. Indeed, the religion in the sight of Allah is Islam. And those who were given the Scripture did not differ except after knowledge had come to them - out of jealous animosity between themselves. And whoever disbelieves in the verses of Allah, then indeed, Allah is swift in [taking] account.
20. So if they argue with you, say, "I have submitted myself to Allah [in Islam], and [so have] those who follow me." And say to those who were given the Scripture and [to] the unlearned, "Have you submitted yourselves?" And if they submit [in Islam], they are rightly guided; but if they turn away - then upon you is only the [duty of] notification. And Allah is Seeing of [His] servants.
21. Those who disbelieve in the signs of Allah and kill the prophets without right and kill those who order justice from among the people - give them tidings of a painful punishment.
22. They are the ones whose deeds have become worthless in this world and the Hereafter, and for them there will be no helpers.
23. Do you not consider, [O Muhammad], those who were given a portion of the Scripture? They are invited to the Scripture of Allah that it should arbitrate between them; then a party of them turns away, and they are refusing.
24. That is because they say, "Never will the Fire touch us except for [a few] numbered days," and [because] they were deluded in their religion by what they were inventing.
25. So how will it be when We assemble them for a Day about which there is no doubt? And each soul will be compensated [in full for] what it earned, and they will not be wronged.
26. Say, "O Allah, Owner of Sovereignty, You give sovereignty to whom You will and You take sovereignty away from whom You will. You honor whom You will and You humble whom You will. In Your hand is [all] good. Indeed, You are over all things competent.
27. You cause the night to enter the day, and You cause the day to enter the night; and You bring the living out of the dead, and You bring the dead out of the living. And You give provision to whom You will without account."

28. Let not believers take disbelievers as allies rather than believers. And whoever [of you] does that has nothing with Allah, except when taking precaution against them in prudence. And Allah warns you of Himself, and to Allah is the [final] destination.

29. Say, "Whether you conceal what is in your breasts or reveal it, Allah knows it. And He knows that which is in the heavens and that which is on the earth. And Allah is over all things competent.

30. The Day every soul will find what it has done of good present [before it] and what it has done of evil, it will wish that between itself and that [evil] was a great distance. And Allah warns you of Himself, and Allah is Kind to [His] servants."

31. Say, [O Muhammad], "If you should love Allah, then follow me, [so] Allah will love you and forgive you your sins. And Allah is Forgiving and Merciful."

32. Say, "Obey Allah and the Messenger." But if they turn away - then indeed, Allah does not like the disbelievers.

33. Indeed, Allah chose Adam and Noah and the family of Abraham and the family of 'Imran over the worlds -

34. Descendants, some of them from others. And Allah is Hearing and Knowing.

35. [Mention, O Muhammad], when the wife of 'Imran said, "My Lord, indeed I have pledged to You what is in my womb, consecrated [for Your service], so accept this from me. Indeed, You are the Hearing, the Knowing."

36. But when she delivered her, she said, "My Lord, I have delivered a female." And Allah was most knowing of what she delivered, "And the male is not like the female. And I have named her Mary, and I seek refuge for her in You and [for] her descendants from Satan, the expelled [from the mercy of Allah]."

37. So her Lord accepted her with good acceptance and caused her to grow in a good manner and put her in the care of Zechariah. Every time Zechariah entered upon her in the prayer chamber, he found with her provision. He said, "O Mary, from where is this [coming] to you?" She said, "It is from Allah. Indeed, Allah provides for whom He wills without account."

38. At that, Zechariah called upon his Lord, saying, "My Lord, grant me from Yourself a good offspring. Indeed, You are the Hearer of supplication."

39. So the angels called him while he was standing in prayer in the chamber, "Indeed, Allah gives you good tidings of John, confirming a word from Allah and [who will be] honorable, abstaining [from women], and a prophet from among the righteous."

40. He said, "My Lord, how will I have a boy when I have reached old age and my wife is barren?" The angel said, "Such is Allah; He does what He wills."

41. He said, "My Lord, make for me a sign." He Said, "Your sign is that you will not [be able to] speak to the people for three days except by gesture. And remember your Lord much and exalt [Him with praise] in the evening and the morning."

42. And [mention] when the angels said, "O Mary, indeed Allah has chosen you and purified you and chosen you above the women of the worlds.

43. Mary, be devoutly obedient to your Lord and prostrate and bow with those who bow [in prayer]."

44. That is from the news of the unseen which We reveal to you, [O Muhammad]. And you were not with them when they cast their pens as to which of them should be responsible for Mary. Nor were you with them when they disputed.

45. [And mention] when the angels said, "O Mary, indeed Allah gives you good tidings of a word from Him, whose name will be the Messiah, Jesus, the son of Mary - distinguished in this world and the Hereafter and among those brought near [to Allah].

46. He will speak to the people in the cradle and in maturity and will be of the righteous."

47. She said, "My Lord, how will I have a child when no man has touched me?" [The angel] said, "Such is Allah; He creates what He wills. When He decrees a matter, He only says to it, 'Be,' and it is.

48. And He will teach him writing and wisdom and the Torah and the Gospel

49. And [make him] a messenger to the Children of Israel, [who will say], 'Indeed I have come to you with a sign from your Lord in that I design for you from clay [that which is] like the form of a bird, then I breathe into it and it becomes a bird by permission of Allah. And I cure the blind and the leper, and I give life to the dead - by permission of Allah. And I inform you of what you eat

and what you store in your houses. Indeed in that is a sign for you, if you are believers.

50. And [I have come] confirming what was before me of the Torah and to make lawful for you some of what was forbidden to you. And I have come to you with a sign from your Lord, so fear Allah and obey me.

51. Indeed, Allah is my Lord and your Lord, so worship Him. That is the straight path."

52. But when Jesus felt [persistence in] disbelief from them, he said, "Who are my supporters for [the cause of] Allah?" The disciples said, "We are supporters for Allah. We have believed in Allah and testify that we are Muslims [submitting to Him].

53. Our Lord, we have believed in what You revealed and have followed the messenger Jesus, so register us among the witnesses [to truth]."

54. And the disbelievers planned, but Allah planned. And Allah is the best of planners.

55. [Mention] when Allah said, "O Jesus, indeed I will take you and raise you to Myself and purify you from those who disbelieve and make those who follow you [in submission to Allah alone] superior to those who disbelieve until the Day of Resurrection. Then to Me is your return, and I will judge between you concerning that in which you used to differ.

56. And as for those who disbelieved, I will punish them with a severe punishment in this world and the Hereafter, and they will have no helpers."

57. But as for those who believed and did righteous deeds, He will give them in full their rewards, and Allah does not like the wrongdoers.

58. This is what We recite to you, [O Muhammad], of [Our] verses and the precise [and wise] message.

59. Indeed, the example of Jesus to Allah is like that of Adam. He created Him from dust; then He said to him, "Be," and he was.

60. The truth is from your Lord, so do not be among the doubters.

61. Then whoever argues with you about it after [this] knowledge has come to you - say, "Come, let us call our sons and your sons, our women and your women, ourselves and yourselves, then supplicate earnestly [together] and invoke the curse of Allah upon the liars [among us]."

62. Indeed, this is the true narration. And there is no deity except Allah. And indeed, Allah is the Exalted in Might, the Wise.

63. But if they turn away, then indeed - Allah is Knowing of the corrupters.

64. Say, "O People of the Scripture, come to a word that is equitable between us and you - that we will not worship except Allah and not associate anything with Him and not take one another as lords instead of Allah." But if they turn away, then say, "Bear witness that we are Muslims [submitting to Him]."

65. People of the Scripture, why do you argue about Abraham while the Torah and the Gospel were not revealed until after him? Then will you not reason?

66. Here you are - those who have argued about that of which you have [some] knowledge, but why do you argue about that of which you have no knowledge? And Allah knows, while you know not.

67. Abraham was neither a Jew nor a Christian, but he was one inclining toward truth, a Muslim [submitting to Allah]. And he was not of the polytheists.

68. Indeed, the most worthy of Abraham among the people are those who followed him [in submission to Allah] and this prophet, and those who believe [in his message]. And Allah is the ally of the believers.

69. A faction of the people of the Scripture wish they could mislead you. But they do not mislead except themselves, and they perceive [it] not.

70. People of the Scripture, why do you disbelieve in the verses of Allah while you witness [to their truth]?

71. People of the Scripture, why do you confuse the truth with falsehood and conceal the truth while you know [it]?

72. And a faction of the People of the Scripture say [to each other], "Believe in that which was revealed to the believers at the beginning of the day and reject it at its end that perhaps they will abandon their religion,

73. And do not trust except those who follow your religion." Say, "Indeed, the [true] guidance is the guidance of Allah. [Do you fear] lest someone be given [knowledge] like you were given or that they would [thereby] argue with you before your Lord?" Say, "Indeed, [all] bounty is in the hand of Allah - He grants it to whom He wills. And Allah is all-Encompassing and Wise."

74. He selects for His mercy whom He wills. And Allah is the possessor of great bounty.

75. And among the People of the Scripture is he who, if you entrust him with a great amount [of wealth], he will return it to you. And among them is he who, if you entrust him with a [single] silver coin, he will not return it to you unless you are constantly standing over him [demanding it]. That is because they say, "There is no blame upon us concerning the unlearned." And they speak untruth about Allah while they know [it].

76. But yes, whoever fulfills his commitment and fears Allah - then indeed, Allah loves those who fear Him.

77. Indeed, those who exchange the covenant of Allah and their [own] oaths for a small price will have no share in the Hereafter, and Allah will not speak to them or look at them on the Day of Resurrection, nor will He purify them; and they will have a painful punishment.

78. And indeed, there is among them a party who alter the Scripture with their tongues so you may think it is from the Scripture, but it is not from the Scripture. And they say, "This is from Allah," but it is not from Allah. And they speak untruth about Allah while they know.

79. It is not for a human [prophet] that Allah should give him the Scripture and authority and prophethood and then he would say to the people, "Be servants to me rather than Allah," but [instead, he would say], "Be pious scholars of the Lord because of what you have taught of the Scripture and because of what you have studied."

80. Nor could he order you to take the angels and prophets as lords. Would he order you to disbelief after you had been Muslims?

81. And [recall, O People of the Scripture], when Allah took the covenant of the prophets, [saying], "Whatever I give you of the Scripture and wisdom and then there comes to you a messenger confirming what is with you, you [must] believe in him and support him." [Allah] said, "Have you acknowledged and taken upon that My commitment?" They said, "We have acknowledged it." He said, "Then bear witness, and I am with you among the witnesses."

82. And whoever turned away after that - they were the defiantly disobedient.

83. So is it other than the religion of Allah they desire, while to Him have submitted [all] those within the heavens and earth, willingly or by compulsion, and to Him they will be returned?

84. Say, "We have believed in Allah and in what was revealed to us and what was revealed to Abraham, Ishmael, Isaac, Jacob, and the Descendants, and in what was given to Moses and Jesus and to the prophets from their Lord. We make no distinction between any of them, and we are Muslims [submitting] to Him."

85. And whoever desires other than Islam as religion - never will it be accepted from him, and he, in the Hereafter, will be among the losers.

86. How shall Allah guide a people who disbelieved after their belief and had witnessed that the Messenger is true and clear signs had come to them? And Allah does not guide the wrongdoing people.

87. Those - their recompense will be that upon them is the curse of Allah and the angels and the people, all together,

88. Abiding eternally therein. The punishment will not be lightened for them, nor will they be reprieved.

89. Except for those who repent after that and correct themselves. For indeed, Allah is Forgiving and Merciful.

90. Indeed, those who reject the message after their belief and then increase in disbelief - never will their [claimed] repentance be accepted, and they are the ones astray.

91. Indeed, those who disbelieve and die while they are disbelievers - never would the [whole] capacity of the earth in gold be accepted from one of them if he would [seek to] ransom himself with it. For those there will be a painful punishment, and they will have no helpers.

92. Never will you attain the good [reward] until you spend [in the way of Allah] from that which you love. And whatever you spend - indeed, Allah is Knowing of it.

93. All food was lawful to the Children of Israel except what Israel had made unlawful to himself before the Torah was revealed. Say, [O Muhammad], "So bring the Torah and recite it, if you should be truthful."

94. And whoever invents about Allah untruth after that - then those are [truly] the wrongdoers.

95. Say, "Allah has told the truth. So follow the religion of Abraham, inclining toward truth; and he was not of the polytheists."

96. Indeed, the first House [of worship] established for mankind was that at Makkah - blessed and a guidance for the worlds.

97. In it are clear signs [such as] the standing place of Abraham. And whoever enters it shall be safe. And [due] to Allah from the people is a pilgrimage to the House - for whoever is able to find thereto a way. But whoever disbelieves - then indeed, Allah is free from need of the worlds.

98. Say, "O People of the Scripture, why do you disbelieve in the verses of Allah while Allah is Witness over what you do?"

99. Say, "O People of the Scripture, why do you avert from the way of Allah those who believe, seeking to make it [seem] deviant, while you are witnesses [to the truth]? And Allah is not unaware of what you do."

100. O you who have believed, if you obey a party of those who were given the Scripture, they would turn you back, after your belief, [to being] unbelievers.

101. And how could you disbelieve while to you are being recited the verses of Allah and among you is His Messenger? And whoever holds firmly to Allah has [indeed] been guided to a straight path.

102. O you who have believed, fear Allah as He should be feared and do not die except as Muslims [in submission to Him].

103. And hold firmly to the rope of Allah all together and do not become divided. And remember the favor of Allah upon you - when you were enemies and He brought your hearts together and you became, by His favor, brothers. And you were on the edge of a pit of the Fire, and He saved you from it. Thus does Allah make clear to you His verses that you may be guided.

104. And let there be [arising] from you a nation inviting to [all that is] good, enjoining what is right and forbidding what is wrong, and those will be the successful.

105. And do not be like the ones who became divided and differed after the clear proofs had come to them. And those will have a great punishment.

106. On the Day [some] faces will turn white and [some] faces will turn black. As for those whose faces turn black, [to them it will be said], "Did you disbelieve after your belief? Then taste the punishment for what you used to reject."

107. But as for those whose faces will turn white, [they will be] within the mercy of Allah. They will abide therein eternally.

108. These are the verses of Allah. We recite them to you, [O Muhammad], in truth; and Allah wants no injustice to the worlds.

109. To Allah belongs whatever is in the heavens and whatever is on the earth. And to Allah will [all] matters be returned.

110. You are the best nation produced [as an example] for mankind. You enjoin what is right and forbid what is wrong and believe in Allah. If only the People of the Scripture had believed, it would have been better for them. Among them are believers, but most of them are defiantly disobedient.

111. They will not harm you except for [some] annoyance. And if they fight you, they will show you their backs; then they will not be aided.

112. They have been put under humiliation [by Allah] wherever they are overtaken, except for a covenant from Allah and a rope from the Muslims. And they have drawn upon themselves anger from Allah and have been put under destitution. That is because they disbelieved in the verses of Allah and killed the prophets without right. That is because they disobeyed and [habitually] transgressed.

113. They are not [all] the same; among the People of the Scripture is a community standing [in obedience], reciting the verses of Allah during periods of the night and prostrating [in prayer].

114. They believe in Allah and the Last Day, and they enjoin what is right and forbid what is wrong and hasten to good deeds. And those are among the righteous.

115. And whatever good they do - never will it be removed from them. And Allah is Knowing of the righteous.

116. Indeed, those who disbelieve - never will their wealth or their children avail them against Allah at all, and those are the companions of the Fire; they will abide therein eternally.

117. The example of what they spend in this worldly life is like that of a wind containing frost which strikes the harvest of a people who have wronged themselves and destroys it. And Allah has not wronged them, but they wrong themselves.

118. O you who have believed, do not take as intimates those other than yourselves, for they will not spare you [any] ruin. They wish you would have hardship. Hatred has already appeared from their mouths, and what their breasts conceal is greater. We have certainly made clear to you the signs, if you will use reason.

119. Here you are loving them but they are not loving you, while you

believe in the Scripture - all of it. And when they meet you, they say, "We believe." But when they are alone, they bite their fingertips at you in rage. Say, "Die in your rage. Indeed, Allah is Knowing of that within the breasts."

120. If good touches you, it distresses them; but if harm strikes you, they rejoice at it. And if you are patient and fear Allah, their plot will not harm you at all. Indeed, Allah is encompassing of what they do.

121. And [remember] when you, [O Muhammad], left your family in the morning to post the believers at their stations for the battle [of Uhud] - and Allah is Hearing and Knowing -

122. When two parties among you were about to lose courage, but Allah was their ally; and upon Allah the believers should rely.

123. And already had Allah given you victory at [the battle of] Badr while you were few in number. Then fear Allah; perhaps you will be grateful.

124. [Remember] when you said to the believers, "Is it not sufficient for you that your Lord should reinforce you with three thousand angels sent down?

125. Yes, if you remain patient and conscious of Allah and the enemy come upon you [attacking] in rage, your Lord will reinforce you with five thousand angels having marks [of distinction]

126. And Allah made it not except as [a sign of] good tidings for you and to reassure your hearts thereby. And victory is not except from Allah, the Exalted in Might, the Wise -

127. That He might cut down a section of the disbelievers or suppress them so that they turn back disappointed.

128. Not for you, [O Muhammad, but for Allah], is the decision whether He should [cut them down] or forgive them or punish them, for indeed, they are wrongdoers.

129. And to Allah belongs whatever is in the heavens and whatever is on the earth. He forgives whom He wills and punishes whom He wills. And Allah is Forgiving and Merciful.

130. O you who have believed, do not consume usury, doubled and multiplied, but fear Allah that you may be successful.

131. And fear the Fire, which has been prepared for the disbelievers.

132. And obey Allah and the Messenger that you may obtain mercy.

133. And hasten to forgiveness from your Lord and a garden as wide as the heavens and earth, prepared for the righteous

134. Who spend [in the cause of Allah] during ease and hardship and who restrain anger and who pardon the people - and Allah loves the doers of good;

135. And those who, when they commit an immorality or wrong themselves [by transgression], remember Allah and seek forgiveness for their sins - and who can forgive sins except Allah? - and [who] do not persist in what they have done while they know.

136. Those - their reward is forgiveness from their Lord and gardens beneath which rivers flow [in Paradise], wherein they will abide eternally; and excellent is the reward of the [righteous] workers.

137. Similar situations [as yours] have passed on before you, so proceed throughout the earth and observe how was the end of those who denied.

138. This [Qur'an] is a clear statement to [all] the people and a guidance and instruction for those conscious of Allah.

139. So do not weaken and do not grieve, and you will be superior if you are [true] believers.

140. If a wound should touch you - there has already touched the [opposing] people a wound similar to it. And these days [of varying conditions] We alternate among the people so that Allah may make evident those who believe and [may] take to Himself from among you martyrs - and Allah does not like the wrongdoers-

141. And that Allah may purify the believers [through trials] and destroy the disbelievers.

142. Or do you think that you will enter Paradise while Allah has not yet made evident those of you who fight in His cause and made evident those who are steadfast?

143. And you had certainly wished for martyrdom before you encountered it, and you have [now] seen it [before you] while you were looking on.

144. Muhammad is not but a messenger. [Other] messengers have passed on before him. So if he was to die or be killed, would you turn back on your heels [to unbelief]? And he who turns back on his heels will never harm Allah at all; but Allah will reward the grateful.

145. And it is not [possible] for one to die except by permission of

Allah at a decree determined. And whoever desires the reward of this world - We will give him thereof; and whoever desires the reward of the Hereafter - We will give him thereof. And we will reward the grateful.

146. And how many a prophet [fought and] with him fought many religious scholars. But they never lost assurance due to what afflicted them in the cause of Allah, nor did they weaken or submit. And Allah loves the steadfast.

147. And their words were not but that they said, "Our Lord, forgive us our sins and the excess [committed] in our affairs and plant firmly our feet and give us victory over the disbelieving people."

148. So Allah gave them the reward of this world and the good reward of the Hereafter. And Allah loves the doers of good.

149. O you who have believed, if you obey those who disbelieve, they will turn you back on your heels, and you will [then] become losers.

150. But Allah is your protector, and He is the best of helpers.

151. We will cast terror into the hearts of those who disbelieve for what they have associated with Allah of which He had not sent down [any] authority. And their refuge will be the Fire, and wretched is the residence of the wrongdoers.

152. And Allah had certainly fulfilled His promise to you when you were killing the enemy by His permission until [the time] when you lost courage and fell to disputing about the order [given by the Prophet] and disobeyed after He had shown you that which you love. Among you are some who desire this world, and among you are some who desire the Hereafter. Then he turned you back from them [defeated] that He might test you. And He has already forgiven you, and Allah is the possessor of bounty for the believers.

153. [Remember] when you [fled and] climbed [the mountain] without looking aside at anyone while the Messenger was calling you from behind. So Allah repaid you with distress upon distress so you would not grieve for that which had escaped you [of victory and spoils of war] or [for] that which had befallen you [of injury and death]. And Allah is [fully] Acquainted with what you do.

154. Then after distress, He sent down upon you security [in the form of] drowsiness, overcoming a faction of you, while another faction worried about themselves, thinking of Allah other than

the truth - the thought of ignorance, saying, "Is there anything for us [to have done] in this matter?" Say, "Indeed, the matter belongs completely to Allah." They conceal within themselves what they will not reveal to you. They say, "If there was anything we could have done in the matter, some of us would not have been killed right here." Say, "Even if you had been inside your houses, those decreed to be killed would have come out to their death beds." [It was] so that Allah might test what is in your breasts and purify what is in your hearts. And Allah is Knowing of that within the breasts.

155. Indeed, those of you who turned back on the day the two armies met, it was Satan who caused them to slip because of some [blame] they had earned. But Allah has already forgiven them. Indeed, Allah is Forgiving and Forbearing.

156. O you who have believed, do not be like those who disbelieved and said about their brothers when they traveled through the land or went out to fight, "If they had been with us, they would not have died or have been killed," so Allah makes that [misconception] a regret within their hearts. And it is Allah who gives life and causes death, and Allah is Seeing of what you do.

157. And if you are killed in the cause of Allah or die - then forgiveness from Allah and mercy are better than whatever they accumulate [in this world].

158. And whether you die or are killed, unto Allah you will be gathered.

159. So by mercy from Allah, [O Muhammad], you were lenient with them. And if you had been rude [in speech] and harsh in heart, they would have disbanded from about you. So pardon them and ask forgiveness for them and consult them in the matter. And when you have decided, then rely upon Allah. Indeed, Allah loves those who rely [upon Him].

160. If Allah should aid you, no one can overcome you; but if He should forsake you, who is there that can aid you after Him? And upon Allah let the believers rely.

161. It is not [attributable] to any prophet that he would act unfaithfully [in regard to war booty]. And whoever betrays, [taking unlawfully], will come with what he took on the Day of Resurrection. Then will every soul be [fully] compensated for what it earned, and they will not be wronged.

162. So is one who pursues the pleasure of Allah like one who brings

upon himself the anger of Allah and whose refuge is Hell? And wretched is the destination.

163. They are [varying] degrees in the sight of Allah, and Allah is Seeing of whatever they do.

164. Certainly did Allah confer [great] favor upon the believers when He sent among them a Messenger from themselves, reciting to them His verses and purifying them and teaching them the Book and wisdom, although they had been before in manifest error.

165. Why [is it that] when a [single] disaster struck you [on the day of Uhud], although you had struck [the enemy in the battle of Badr] with one twice as great, you said, "From where is this?" Say, "It is from yourselves." Indeed, Allah is over all things competent.

166. And what struck you on the day the two armies met was by permission of Allah that He might make evident the [true] believers.

167. And that He might make evident those who are hypocrites. For it was said to them, "Come, fight in the way of Allah or [at least] defend." They said, "If we had known [there would be] fighting, we would have followed you." They were nearer to disbelief that day than to faith, saying with their mouths what was not in their hearts. And Allah is most Knowing of what they conceal -

168. Those who said about their brothers while sitting [at home], "If they had obeyed us, they would not have been killed." Say, "Then prevent death from yourselves, if you should be truthful."

169. And never think of those who have been killed in the cause of Allah as dead. Rather, they are alive with their Lord, receiving provision,

170. Rejoicing in what Allah has bestowed upon them of His bounty, and they receive good tidings about those [to be martyred] after them who have not yet joined them - that there will be no fear concerning them, nor will they grieve.

171. They receive good tidings of favor from Allah and bounty and [of the fact] that Allah does not allow the reward of believers to be lost -

172. Those [believers] who responded to Allah and the Messenger after injury had struck them. For those who did good among them and feared Allah is a great reward -

173. Those to whom hypocrites said, "Indeed, the people have gathered against you, so fear them." But it [merely] increased them in faith, and they said, "Sufficient for us is Allah, and [He is] the best Disposer of affairs."

174. So they returned with favor from Allah and bounty, no harm having touched them. And they pursued the pleasure of Allah, and Allah is the possessor of great bounty.

175. That is only Satan who frightens [you] of his supporters. So fear them not, but fear Me, if you are [indeed] believers.

176. And do not be grieved, [O Muhammad], by those who hasten into disbelief. Indeed, they will never harm Allah at all. Allah intends that He should give them no share in the Hereafter, and for them is a great punishment.

177. Indeed, those who purchase disbelief [in exchange] for faith - never will they harm Allah at all, and for them is a painful punishment.

178. And let not those who disbelieve ever think that [because] We extend their time [of enjoyment] it is better for them. We only extend it for them so that they may increase in sin, and for them is a humiliating punishment.

179. Allah would not leave the believers in that [state] you are in [presently] until He separates the evil from the good. Nor would Allah reveal to you the unseen. But [instead], Allah chooses of His messengers whom He wills, so believe in Allah and His messengers. And if you believe and fear Him, then for you is a great reward.

180. And let not those who [greedily] withhold what Allah has given them of His bounty ever think that it is better for them. Rather, it is worse for them. Their necks will be encircled by what they withheld on the Day of Resurrection. And to Allah belongs the heritage of the heavens and the earth. And Allah, with what you do, is [fully] Acquainted.

181. Allah has certainly heard the statement of those [Jews] who said, "Indeed, Allah is poor, while we are rich." We will record what they said and their killing of the prophets without right and will say, "Taste the punishment of the Burning Fire.

182. That is for what your hands have put forth and because Allah is not ever unjust to [His] servants."

183. [They are] those who said, "Indeed, Allah has taken our promise not to believe any messenger until he brings us an offering which fire [from heaven] will consume." Say, "There have already come to you messengers before me with clear proofs and [even] that of which you speak. So why did you kill them, if you should be truthful?"

184. Then if they deny you, [O Muhammad] - so were messengers denied before you, who brought clear proofs and written ordinances and the enlightening Scripture.

185. Every soul will taste death, and you will only be given your [full] compensation on the Day of Resurrection. So he who is drawn away from the Fire and admitted to Paradise has attained [his desire]. And what is the life of this world except the enjoyment of delusion.

186. You will surely be tested in your possessions and in yourselves. And you will surely hear from those who were given the Scripture before you and from those who associate others with Allah much abuse. But if you are patient and fear Allah - indeed, that is of the matters [worthy] of determination.

187. And [mention, O Muhammad], when Allah took a covenant from those who were given the Scripture, [saying], "You must make it clear to the people and not conceal it." But they threw it away behind their backs and exchanged it for a small price. And wretched is that which they purchased.

188. And never think that those who rejoice in what they have perpetrated and like to be praised for what they did not do - never think them [to be] in safety from the punishment, and for them is a painful punishment.

189. And to Allah belongs the dominion of the heavens and the earth, and Allah is over all things competent.

190. Indeed, in the creation of the heavens and the earth and the alternation of the night and the day are signs for those of understanding.

191. Who remember Allah while standing or sitting or [lying] on their sides and give thought to the creation of the heavens and the earth, [saying], "Our Lord, You did not create this aimlessly; exalted are You [above such a thing]; then protect us from the punishment of the Fire.

192. Our Lord, indeed whoever You admit to the Fire - You have disgraced him, and for the wrongdoers there are no helpers.

193. Our Lord, indeed we have heard a caller calling to faith, [saying], 'Believe in your Lord,' and we have believed. Our Lord, so forgive us our sins and remove from us our misdeeds and cause us to die with the righteous.

194. Our Lord, and grant us what You promised us through Your messengers and do not disgrace us on the Day of Resurrection. Indeed, You do not fail in [Your] promise."

195. And their Lord responded to them, "Never will I allow to be lost the work of [any] worker among you, whether male or female; you are of one another. So those who emigrated or were evicted from their homes or were harmed in My cause or fought or were killed - I will surely remove from them their misdeeds, and I will surely admit them to gardens beneath which rivers flow as reward from Allah, and Allah has with Him the best reward."

196. Be not deceived by the [uninhibited] movement of the disbelievers throughout the land.

197. [It is but] a small enjoyment; then their [final] refuge is Hell, and wretched is the resting place.

198. But those who feared their Lord will have gardens beneath which rivers flow, abiding eternally therein, as accommodation from Allah. And that which is with Allah is best for the righteous.

199. And indeed, among the People of the Scripture are those who believe in Allah and what was revealed to you and what was revealed to them, [being] humbly submissive to Allah. They do not exchange the verses of Allah for a small price. Those will have their reward with their Lord. Indeed, Allah is swift in account.

200. O you who have believed, persevere and endure and remain stationed and fear Allah that you may be successful.

| Verses: 176 | **Surah 04 An-Nisaa** | Madani |

In the name of Allah, the Entirely Merciful, the Especially Merciful.

01. O mankind, fear your Lord, who created you from one soul and created from it its mate and dispersed from both of them many men and women. And fear Allah, through whom you ask one another, and the wombs. Indeed Allah is ever, over you, an Observer.

02. And give to the orphans their properties and do not substitute the defective [of your own] for the good [of theirs]. And do not consume their properties into your own. Indeed, that is ever a great sin.

03. And if you fear that you will not deal justly with the orphan girls, then marry those that please you of [other] women, two or three

or four. But if you fear that you will not be just, then [marry only] one or those your right hand possesses. That is more suitable that you may not incline [to injustice].

04. And give the women [upon marriage] their [bridal] gifts graciously. But if they give up willingly to you anything of it, then take it in satisfaction and ease.

05. And do not give the weak-minded your property, which Allah has made a means of sustenance for you, but provide for them with it and clothe them and speak to them words of appropriate kindness.

06. And test the orphans [in their abilities] until they reach marriageable age. Then if you perceive in them sound judgement, release their property to them. And do not consume it excessively and quickly, [anticipating] that they will grow up. And whoever, [when acting as guardian], is self-sufficient should refrain [from taking a fee]; and whoever is poor - let him take according to what is acceptable. Then when you release their property to them, bring witnesses upon them. And sufficient is Allah as Accountant.

07. For men is a share of what the parents and close relatives leave, and for women is a share of what the parents and close relatives leave, be it little or much - an obligatory share.

08. And when [other] relatives and orphans and the needy are present at the [time of] division, then provide for them [something] out of the estate and speak to them words of appropriate kindness.

09. And let those [executors and guardians] fear [injustice] as if they [themselves] had left weak offspring behind and feared for them. So let them fear Allah and speak words of appropriate justice.

10. Indeed, those who devour the property of orphans unjustly are only consuming into their bellies fire. And they will be burned in a Blaze.

11. Allah instructs you concerning your children: for the male, what is equal to the share of two females. But if there are [only] daughters, two or more, for them is two thirds of one's estate. And if there is only one, for her is half. And for one's parents, to each one of them is a sixth of his estate if he left children. But if he had no children and the parents [alone] inherit from him, then for his mother is one third. And if he had brothers [or sisters], for his mother is a sixth, after any bequest he [may

have] made or debt. Your parents or your children - you know not which of them are nearest to you in benefit. [These shares are] an obligation [imposed] by Allah. Indeed, Allah is ever Knowing and Wise.

12. And for you is half of what your wives leave if they have no child. But if they have a child, for you is one fourth of what they leave, after any bequest they [may have] made or debt. And for the wives is one fourth if you leave no child. But if you leave a child, then for them is an eighth of what you leave, after any bequest you [may have] made or debt. And if a man or woman leaves neither ascendants nor descendants but has a brother or a sister, then for each one of them is a sixth. But if they are more than two, they share a third, after any bequest which was made or debt, as long as there is no detriment [caused]. [This is] an ordinance from Allah, and Allah is Knowing and Forbearing.

13. These are the limits [set by] Allah, and whoever obeys Allah and His Messenger will be admitted by Him to gardens [in Paradise] under which rivers flow, abiding eternally therein; and that is the great attainment.

14. And whoever disobeys Allah and His Messenger and transgresses His limits - He will put him into the Fire to abide eternally therein, and he will have a humiliating punishment.

15. Those who commit unlawful sexual intercourse of your women - bring against them four [witnesses] from among you. And if they testify, confine the guilty women to houses until death takes them or Allah ordains for them [another] way.

16. And the two who commit it among you, dishonor them both. But if they repent and correct themselves, leave them alone. Indeed, Allah is ever Accepting of repentance and Merciful.

17. The repentance accepted by Allah is only for those who do wrong in ignorance [or carelessness] and then repent soon after. It is those to whom Allah will turn in forgiveness, and Allah is ever Knowing and Wise.

18. But repentance is not [accepted] of those who [continue to] do evil deeds up until, when death comes to one of them, he says, "Indeed, I have repented now," or of those who die while they are disbelievers. For them We have prepared a painful punishment.

19. O you who have believed, it is not lawful for you to inherit

women by compulsion. And do not make difficulties for them in order to take [back] part of what you gave them unless they commit a clear immorality. And live with them in kindness. For if you dislike them - perhaps you dislike a thing and Allah makes therein much good.

20. But if you want to replace one wife with another and you have given one of them a great amount [in gifts], do not take [back] from it anything. Would you take it in injustice and manifest sin?

21. And how could you take it while you have gone in unto each other and they have taken from you a solemn covenant?

22. And do not marry those [women] whom your fathers married, except what has already occurred. Indeed, it was an immorality and hateful [to Allah] and was evil as a way.

23. Prohibited to you [for marriage] are your mothers, your daughters, your sisters, your father's sisters, your mother's sisters, your brother's daughters, your sister's daughters, your [milk] mothers who nursed you, your sisters through nursing, your wives' mothers, and your step-daughters under your guardianship [born] of your wives unto whom you have gone in. But if you have not gone in unto them, there is no sin upon you. And [also prohibited are] the wives of your sons who are from your [own] loins, and that you take [in marriage] two sisters simultaneously, except for what has already occurred. Indeed, Allah is ever Forgiving and Merciful.

24. And [also prohibited to you are all] married women except those your right hands possess. [This is] the decree of Allah upon you. And lawful to you are [all others] beyond these, [provided] that you seek them [in marriage] with [gifts from] your property, desiring chastity, not unlawful sexual intercourse. So for whatever you enjoy [of marriage] from them, give them their due compensation as an obligation. And there is no blame upon you for what you mutually agree to beyond the obligation. Indeed, Allah is ever Knowing and Wise.

25. And whoever among you cannot [find] the means to marry free, believing women, then [he may marry] from those whom your right hands possess of believing slave girls. And Allah is most knowing about your faith. You [believers] are of one another. So marry them with the permission of their people and give them their due compensation according to what is acceptable. [They should be] chaste, neither [of] those who commit unlawful

intercourse randomly nor those who take [secret] lovers. But once they are sheltered in marriage, if they should commit adultery, then for them is half the punishment for free [unmarried] women. This [allowance] is for him among you who fears sin, but to be patient is better for you. And Allah is Forgiving and Merciful.

26. Allah wants to make clear to you [the lawful from the unlawful] and guide you to the [good] practices of those before you and to accept your repentance. And Allah is Knowing and Wise.

27. Allah wants to accept your repentance, but those who follow [their] passions want you to digress [into] a great deviation.

28. And Allah wants to lighten for you [your difficulties]; and mankind was created weak.

29. O you who have believed, do not consume one another's wealth unjustly but only [in lawful] business by mutual consent. And do not kill yourselves [or one another]. Indeed, Allah is to you ever Merciful.

30. And whoever does that in aggression and injustice - then We will drive him into a Fire. And that, for Allah, is [always] easy.

31. If you avoid the major sins which you are forbidden, We will remove from you your lesser sins and admit you to a noble entrance [into Paradise].

32. And do not wish for that by which Allah has made some of you exceed others. For men is a share of what they have earned, and for women is a share of what they have earned. And ask Allah of his bounty. Indeed Allah is ever, of all things, Knowing.

33. And for all, We have made heirs to what is left by parents and relatives. And to those whom your oaths have bound [to you] - give them their share. Indeed Allah is ever, over all things, a Witness.

34. Men are in charge of women by [right of] what Allah has given one over the other and what they spend [for maintenance] from their wealth. So righteous women are devoutly obedient, guarding in [the husband's] absence what Allah would have them guard. But those [wives] from whom you fear arrogance - [first] advise them; [then if they persist], forsake them in bed; and [finally], strike them. But if they obey you [once more], seek no means against them. Indeed, Allah is ever Exalted and Grand.

35. And if you fear dissension between the two, send an arbitrator

from his people and an arbitrator from her people. If they both desire reconciliation, Allah will cause it between them. Indeed, Allah is ever Knowing and Acquainted [with all things].

36. Worship Allah and associate nothing with Him, and to parents do good, and to relatives, orphans, the needy, the near neighbor, the neighbor farther away, the companion at your side, the traveler, and those whom your right hands possess. Indeed, Allah does not like those who are self-deluding and boastful.

37. Who are stingy and enjoin upon [other] people stinginess and conceal what Allah has given them of His bounty - and We have prepared for the disbelievers a humiliating punishment -

38. And [also] those who spend of their wealth to be seen by the people and believe not in Allah nor in the Last Day. And he to whom Satan is a companion - then evil is he as a companion.

39. And what [harm would come] upon them if they believed in Allah and the Last Day and spent out of what Allah provided for them? And Allah is ever, about them, Knowing.

40. Indeed, Allah does not do injustice, [even] as much as an atom's weight; while if there is a good deed, He multiplies it and gives from Himself a great reward.

41. So how [will it be] when We bring from every nation a witness and we bring you, [O Muhammad] against these [people] as a witness?

42. That Day, those who disbelieved and disobeyed the Messenger will wish they could be covered by the earth. And they will not conceal from Allah a [single] statement.

43. O you who have believed, do not approach prayer while you are intoxicated until you know what you are saying or in a state of janabah, except those passing through [a place of prayer], until you have washed [your whole body]. And if you are ill or on a journey or one of you comes from the place of relieving himself or you have contacted women and find no water, then seek clean earth and wipe over your faces and your hands [with it]. Indeed, Allah is ever Pardoning and Forgiving.

44. Have you not seen those who were given a portion of the Scripture, purchasing error [in exchange for it] and wishing you would lose the way?

45. And Allah is most knowing of your enemies; and sufficient is Allah as an ally, and sufficient is Allah as a helper.

46. Among the Jews are those who distort words from their [proper] usages and say, "We hear and disobey" and "Hear but be not heard" and "Ra'ina," twisting their tongues and defaming the religion. And if they had said [instead], "We hear and obey" and "Wait for us [to understand]," it would have been better for them and more suitable. But Allah has cursed them for their disbelief, so they believe not, except for a few.

47. O you who were given the Scripture, believe in what We have sent down [to Muhammad], confirming that which is with you, before We obliterate faces and turn them toward their backs or curse them as We cursed the sabbath-breakers. And ever is the decree of Allah accomplished.

48. Indeed, Allah does not forgive association with Him, but He forgives what is less than that for whom He wills. And he who associates others with Allah has certainly fabricated a tremendous sin.

49. Have you not seen those who claim themselves to be pure? Rather, Allah purifies whom He wills, and injustice is not done to them, [even] as much as a thread [inside a date seed].

50. Look how they invent about Allah untruth, and sufficient is that as a manifest sin.

51. Have you not seen those who were given a portion of the Scripture, who believe in superstition and false objects of worship and say about the disbelievers, "These are better guided than the believers as to the way"?

52. Those are the ones whom Allah has cursed; and he whom Allah curses - never will you find for him a helper.

53. Or have they a share of dominion? Then [if that were so], they would not give the people [even as much as] the speck on a date seed.

54. Or do they envy people for what Allah has given them of His bounty? But we had already given the family of Abraham the Scripture and wisdom and conferred upon them a great kingdom.

55. And some among them believed in it, and some among them were averse to it. And sufficient is Hell as a blaze.

56. Indeed, those who disbelieve in Our verses - We will drive them

into a Fire. Every time their skins are roasted through We will replace them with other skins so they may taste the punishment. Indeed, Allah is ever Exalted in Might and Wise.

57. But those who believe and do righteous deeds - We will admit them to gardens beneath which rivers flow, wherein they abide forever. For them therein are purified spouses, and We will admit them to deepening shade.

58. Indeed, Allah commands you to render trusts to whom they are due and when you judge between people to judge with justice. Excellent is that which Allah instructs you. Indeed, Allah is ever Hearing and Seeing.

59. O you who have believed, obey Allah and obey the Messenger and those in authority among you. And if you disagree over anything, refer it to Allah and the Messenger, if you should believe in Allah and the Last Day. That is the best [way] and best in result.

60. Have you not seen those who claim to have believed in what was revealed to you, [O Muhammad], and what was revealed before you? They wish to refer legislation to Taghut, while they were commanded to reject it; and Satan wishes to lead them far astray.

61. And when it is said to them, "Come to what Allah has revealed and to the Messenger," you see the hypocrites turning away from you in aversion.

62. So how [will it be] when disaster strikes them because of what their hands have put forth and then they come to you swearing by Allah, "We intended nothing but good conduct and accommodation."

63. Those are the ones of whom Allah knows what is in their hearts, so turn away from them but admonish them and speak to them a far-reaching word.

64. And We did not send any messenger except to be obeyed by permission of Allah. And if, when they wronged themselves, they had come to you, [O Muhammad], and asked forgiveness of Allah and the Messenger had asked forgiveness for them, they would have found Allah Accepting of repentance and Merciful.

65. But no, by your Lord, they will not [truly] believe until they make you, [O Muhammad], judge concerning that over which they dispute among themselves and then find within themselves no

discomfort from what you have judged and submit in [full, willing] submission.

66. And if We had decreed upon them, "Kill yourselves" or "Leave your homes," they would not have done it, except for a few of them. But if they had done what they were instructed, it would have been better for them and a firmer position [for them in faith].

67. And then We would have given them from Us a great reward.

68. And We would have guided them to a straight path.

69. And whoever obeys Allah and the Messenger - those will be with the ones upon whom Allah has bestowed favor of the prophets, the steadfast affirmers of truth, the martyrs and the righteous. And excellent are those as companions.

70. That is the bounty from Allah, and sufficient is Allah as Knower.

71. O you who have believed, take your precaution and [either] go forth in companies or go forth all together.

72. And indeed, there is among you he who lingers behind; and if disaster strikes you, he says, "Allah has favored me in that I was not present with them."

73. But if bounty comes to you from Allah, he will surely say, as if there had never been between you and him any affection. "Oh, I wish I had been with them so I could have attained a great attainment."

74. So let those fight in the cause of Allah who sell the life of this world for the Hereafter. And he who fights in the cause of Allah and is killed or achieves victory - We will bestow upon him a great reward.

75. And what is [the matter] with you that you fight not in the cause of Allah and [for] the oppressed among men, women, and children who say, "Our Lord, take us out of this city of oppressive people and appoint for us from Yourself a protector and appoint for us from Yourself a helper?"

76. Those who believe fight in the cause of Allah, and those who disbelieve fight in the cause of Taghut. So fight against the allies of Satan. Indeed, the plot of Satan has ever been weak.

77. Have you not seen those who were told, "Restrain your hands [from fighting] and establish prayer and give zakah"? But then when fighting was ordained for them, at once a party of them feared men as they fear Allah or with [even] greater fear. They

said, "Our Lord, why have You decreed upon us fighting? If only You had postponed [it for] us for a short time." Say, The enjoyment of this world is little, and the Hereafter is better for he who fears Allah. And injustice will not be done to you, [even] as much as a thread [inside a date seed]."

78. Wherever you may be, death will overtake you, even if you should be within towers of lofty construction. But if good comes to them, they say, "This is from Allah "; and if evil befalls them, they say, "This is from you." Say, "All [things] are from Allah." So what is [the matter] with those people that they can hardly understand any statement?

79. What comes to you of good is from Allah, but what comes to you of evil, [O man], is from yourself. And We have sent you, [O Muhammad], to the people as a messenger, and sufficient is Allah as Witness.

80. He who obeys the Messenger has obeyed Allah; but those who turn away - We have not sent you over them as a guardian.

81. And they say, "[We pledge] obedience." But when they leave you, a group of them spend the night determining to do other than what you say. But Allah records what they plan by night. So leave them alone and rely upon Allah. And sufficient is Allah as Disposer of affairs.

82. Then do they not reflect upon the Qur'an? If it had been from [any] other than Allah, they would have found within it much contradiction.

83. And when there comes to them information about [public] security or fear, they spread it around. But if they had referred it back to the Messenger or to those of authority among them, then the ones who [can] draw correct conclusions from it would have known about it. And if not for the favor of Allah upon you and His mercy, you would have followed Satan, except for a few.

84. So fight, [O Muhammad], in the cause of Allah; you are not held responsible except for yourself. And encourage the believers [to join you] that perhaps Allah will restrain the [military] might of those who disbelieve. And Allah is greater in might and stronger in [exemplary] punishment.

85. Whoever intercedes for a good cause will have a reward therefrom; and whoever intercedes for an evil cause will have a

burden therefrom. And ever is Allah, over all things, a Keeper.

86. And when you are greeted with a greeting, greet [in return] with one better than it or [at least] return it [in a like manner]. Indeed, Allah is ever, over all things, an Accountant.

87. Allah - there is no deity except Him. He will surely assemble you for [account on] the Day of Resurrection, about which there is no doubt. And who is more truthful than Allah in statement.

88. What is [the matter] with you [that you are] two groups concerning the hypocrites, while Allah has made them fall back [into error and disbelief] for what they earned. Do you wish to guide those whom Allah has sent astray? And he whom Allah sends astray - never will you find for him a way [of guidance].

89. They wish you would disbelieve as they disbelieved so you would be alike. So do not take from among them allies until they emigrate for the cause of Allah. But if they turn away, then seize them and kill them wherever you find them and take not from among them any ally or helper.

90. Except for those who take refuge with a people between yourselves and whom is a treaty or those who come to you, their hearts strained at [the prospect of] fighting you or fighting their own people. And if Allah had willed, He could have given them power over you, and they would have fought you. So if they remove themselves from you and do not fight you and offer you peace, then Allah has not made for you a cause [for fighting] against them.

91. You will find others who wish to obtain security from you and [to] obtain security from their people. Every time they are returned to [the influence of] disbelief, they fall back into it. So if they do not withdraw from you or offer you peace or restrain their hands, then seize them and kill them wherever you overtake them. And those - We have made for you against them a clear authorization.

92. And never is it for a believer to kill a believer except by mistake. And whoever kills a believer by mistake - then the freeing of a believing slave and a compensation payment presented to the deceased's family [is required] unless they give [up their right as] charity. But if the deceased was from a people at war with you and he was a believer - then [only] the freeing of a believing slave; and if he was from a people with whom you

have a treaty - then a compensation payment presented to his family and the freeing of a believing slave. And whoever does not find [one or cannot afford to buy one] - then [instead], a fast for two months consecutively, [seeking] acceptance of repentance from Allah. And Allah is ever Knowing and Wise.

93. But whoever kills a believer intentionally - his recompense is Hell, wherein he will abide eternally, and Allah has become angry with him and has cursed him and has prepared for him a great punishment.

94. O you who have believed, when you go forth [to fight] in the cause of Allah, investigate; and do not say to one who gives you [a greeting of] peace "You are not a believer," aspiring for the goods of worldly life; for with Allah are many acquisitions. You [yourselves] were like that before; then Allah conferred His favor upon you, so investigate. Indeed Allah is ever, with what you do, Acquainted.

95. Not equal are those believers remaining [at home] - other than the disabled - and the mujahideen, [who strive and fight] in the cause of Allah with their wealth and their lives. Allah has preferred the mujahideen through their wealth and their lives over those who remain [behind], by degrees. And to both Allah has promised the best [reward]. But Allah has preferred the mujahideen over those who remain [behind] with a great reward-

96. Degrees [of high position] from Him and forgiveness and mercy. And Allah is ever Forgiving and Merciful.

97. Indeed, those whom the angels take [in death] while wronging themselves - [the angels] will say, "In what [condition] were you?" They will say, "We were oppressed in the land." The angels will say, "Was not the earth of Allah spacious [enough] for you to emigrate therein?" For those, their refuge is Hell - and evil it is as a destination.

98. Except for the oppressed among men, women and children who cannot devise a plan nor are they directed to a way -

99. For those it is expected that Allah will pardon them, and Allah is ever Pardoning and Forgiving.

100. And whoever emigrates for the cause of Allah will find on the earth many [alternative] locations and abundance. And whoever leaves his home as an emigrant to Allah and His Messenger and then death overtakes him - his reward has

already become incumbent upon Allah. And Allah is ever Forgiving and Merciful.

101. And when you travel throughout the land, there is no blame upon you for shortening the prayer, [especially] if you fear that those who disbelieve may disrupt [or attack] you. Indeed, the disbelievers are ever to you a clear enemy.

102. And when you are among them and lead them in prayer, let a group of them stand [in prayer] with you and let them carry their arms. And when they have prostrated, let them be [in position] behind you and have the other group come forward which has not [yet] prayed and let them pray with you, taking precaution and carrying their arms. Those who disbelieve wish that you would neglect your weapons and your baggage so they could come down upon you in one [single] attack. But there is no blame upon you, if you are troubled by rain or are ill, for putting down your arms, but take precaution. Indeed, Allah has prepared for the disbelievers a humiliating punishment.

103. And when you have completed the prayer, remember Allah standing, sitting, or [lying] on your sides. But when you become secure, re-establish [regular] prayer. Indeed, prayer has been decreed upon the believers a decree of specified times.

104. And do not weaken in pursuit of the enemy. If you should be suffering - so are they suffering as you are suffering, but you expect from Allah that which they expect not. And Allah is ever Knowing and Wise.

105. Indeed, We have revealed to you, [O Muhammad], the Book in truth so you may judge between the people by that which Allah has shown you. And do not be for the deceitful an advocate.

106. And seek forgiveness of Allah. Indeed, Allah is ever Forgiving and Merciful.

107. And do not argue on behalf of those who deceive themselves. Indeed, Allah loves not one who is a habitually sinful deceiver.

108. They conceal [their evil intentions and deeds] from the people, but they cannot conceal [them] from Allah, and He is with them [in His knowledge] when they spend the night in such as He does not accept of speech. And ever is Allah, of what they do, encompassing.

109. Here you are - those who argue on their behalf in [this] worldly life - but who will argue with Allah for them on the Day of

Resurrection, or who will [then] be their representative?

110. And whoever does a wrong or wrongs himself but then seeks forgiveness of Allah will find Allah Forgiving and Merciful.

111. And whoever commits a sin only earns it against himself. And Allah is ever Knowing and Wise.

112. But whoever earns an offense or a sin and then blames it on an innocent [person] has taken upon himself a slander and manifest sin.

113. And if it was not for the favor of Allah upon you, [O Muhammad], and His mercy, a group of them would have determined to mislead you. But they do not mislead except themselves, and they will not harm you at all. And Allah has revealed to you the Book and wisdom and has taught you that which you did not know. And ever has the favor of Allah upon you been great.

114. No good is there in much of their private conversation, except for those who enjoin charity or that which is right or conciliation between people. And whoever does that seeking means to the approval of Allah - then We are going to give him a great reward.

115. And whoever opposes the Messenger after guidance has become clear to him and follows other than the way of the believers - We will give him what he has taken and drive him into Hell, and evil it is as a destination.

116. Indeed, Allah does not forgive association with Him, but He forgives what is less than that for whom He wills. And he who associates others with Allah has certainly gone far astray.

117. They call upon instead of Him none but female [deities], and they [actually] call upon none but a rebellious Satan.

118. Whom Allah has cursed. For he had said, "I will surely take from among Your servants a specific portion.

119. And I will mislead them, and I will arouse in them [sinful] desires, and I will command them so they will slit the ears of cattle, and I will command them so they will change the creation of Allah." And whoever takes Satan as an ally instead of Allah has certainly sustained a clear loss.

120. Satan promises them and arouses desire in them. But Satan does not promise them except delusion.

121. The refuge of those will be Hell, and they will not find from it an escape.

122. But the ones who believe and do righteous deeds - We will admit them to gardens beneath which rivers flow, wherein they will abide forever. [It is] the promise of Allah, [which is] truth, and who is more truthful than Allah in statement.

123. Paradise is not [obtained] by your wishful thinking nor by that of the People of the Scripture. Whoever does a wrong will be recompensed for it, and he will not find besides Allah a protector or a helper.

124. And whoever does righteous deeds, whether male or female, while being a believer - those will enter Paradise and will not be wronged, [even as much as] the speck on a date seed.

125. And who is better in religion than one who submits himself to Allah while being a doer of good and follows the religion of Abraham, inclining toward truth? And Allah took Abraham as an intimate friend.

126. And to Allah belongs whatever is in the heavens and whatever is on the earth. And ever is Allah, of all things, encompassing.

127. And they request from you, [O Muhammad], a [legal] ruling concerning women. Say, "Allah gives you a ruling about them and [about] what has been recited to you in the Book concerning the orphan girls to whom you do not give what is decreed for them - and [yet] you desire to marry them - and concerning the oppressed among children and that you maintain for orphans [their rights] in justice." And whatever you do of good - indeed, Allah is ever Knowing of it.

128. And if a woman fears from her husband contempt or evasion, there is no sin upon them if they make terms of settlement between them - and settlement is best. And present in [human] souls is stinginess. But if you do good and fear Allah - then indeed Allah is ever, with what you do, Acquainted.

129. And you will never be able to be equal [in feeling] between wives, even if you should strive [to do so]. So do not incline completely [toward one] and leave another hanging. And if you amend [your affairs] and fear Allah - then indeed, Allah is ever Forgiving and Merciful.

130. But if they separate [by divorce], Allah will enrich each [of them] from His abundance. And ever is Allah Encompassing and Wise.

131. And to Allah belongs whatever is in the heavens and whatever is on the earth. And We have instructed those who were given

the Scripture before you and yourselves to fear Allah. But if you disbelieve - then to Allah belongs whatever is in the heavens and whatever is on the earth. And ever is Allah Free of need and Praiseworthy.

132. And to Allah belongs whatever is in the heavens and whatever is on the earth. And sufficient is Allah as Disposer of affairs.

133. If He wills, He can do away with you, O people, and bring others [in your place]. And ever is Allah competent to do that.

134. Whoever desires the reward of this world - then with Allah is the reward of this world and the Hereafter. And ever is Allah Hearing and Seeing.

135. O you who have believed, be persistently standing firm in justice, witnesses for Allah, even if it be against yourselves or parents and relatives. Whether one is rich or poor, Allah is more worthy of both. So follow not [personal] inclination, lest you not be just. And if you distort [your testimony] or refuse [to give it], then indeed Allah is ever, with what you do, Acquainted.

136. O you who have believed, believe in Allah and His Messenger and the Book that He sent down upon His Messenger and the Scripture which He sent down before. And whoever disbelieves in Allah, His angels, His books, His messengers, and the Last Day has certainly gone far astray.

137. Indeed, those who have believed then disbelieved, then believed, then disbelieved, and then increased in disbelief - never will Allah forgive them, nor will He guide them to a way.

138. Give tidings to the hypocrites that there is for them a painful punishment -

139. Those who take disbelievers as allies instead of the believers. Do they seek with them honor [through power]? But indeed, honor belongs to Allah entirely.

140. And it has already come down to you in the Book that when you hear the verses of Allah [recited], they are denied [by them] and ridiculed; so do not sit with them until they enter into another conversation. Indeed, you would then be like them. Indeed Allah will gather the hypocrites and disbelievers in Hell all together -

141. Those who wait [and watch] you. Then if you gain a victory from Allah, they say, "Were we not with you?" But if the

disbelievers have a success, they say [to them], "Did we not gain the advantage over you, but we protected you from the believers?" Allah will judge between [all of] you on the Day of Resurrection, and never will Allah give the disbelievers over the believers a way [to overcome them].

142. Indeed, the hypocrites [think to] deceive Allah, but He is deceiving them. And when they stand for prayer, they stand lazily, showing [themselves to] the people and not remembering Allah except a little,

143. Wavering between them, [belonging] neither to the believers nor to the disbelievers. And whoever Allah leaves astray - never will you find for him a way.

144. O you who have believed, do not take the disbelievers as allies instead of the believers. Do you wish to give Allah against yourselves a clear case?

145. Indeed, the hypocrites will be in the lowest depths of the Fire - and never will you find for them a helper -

146. Except for those who repent, correct themselves, hold fast to Allah, and are sincere in their religion for Allah, for those will be with the believers. And Allah is going to give the believers a great reward.

147. What would Allah do with your punishment if you are grateful and believe? And ever is Allah Appreciative and Knowing.

148. Allah does not like the public mention of evil except by one who has been wronged. And ever is Allah Hearing and Knowing.

149. If [instead] you show [some] good or conceal it or pardon an offense - indeed, Allah is ever Pardoning and Competent.

150. Indeed, those who disbelieve in Allah and His messengers and wish to discriminate between Allah and His messengers and say, "We believe in some and disbelieve in others," and wish to adopt a way in between -

151. Those are the disbelievers, truly. And We have prepared for the disbelievers a humiliating punishment.

152. But they who believe in Allah and His messengers and do not discriminate between any of them - to those He is going to give their rewards. And ever is Allah Forgiving and Merciful.

153. The People of the Scripture ask you to bring down to them a book from the heaven. But they had asked of Moses [even]

greater than that and said, "Show us Allah outright," so the thunderbolt struck them for their wrongdoing. Then they took the calf [for worship] after clear evidences had come to them, and We pardoned that. And We gave Moses a clear authority.

154. And We raised over them the mount for [refusal of] their covenant; and We said to them, "Enter the gate bowing humbly", and We said to them, "Do not transgress on the sabbath", and We took from them a solemn covenant.

155. And [We cursed them] for their breaking of the covenant and their disbelief in the signs of Allah and their killing of the prophets without right and their saying, "Our hearts are wrapped". Rather, Allah has sealed them because of their disbelief, so they believe not, except for a few.

156. And [We cursed them] for their disbelief and their saying against Mary a great slander,

157. And [for] their saying, "Indeed, we have killed the Messiah, Jesus, the son of Mary, the messenger of Allah." And they did not kill him, nor did they crucify him; but [another] was made to resemble him to them. And indeed, those who differ over it are in doubt about it. They have no knowledge of it except the following of assumption. And they did not kill him, for certain.

158. Rather, Allah raised him to Himself. And ever is Allah Exalted in Might and Wise.

159. And there is none from the People of the Scripture but that he will surely believe in Jesus before his death. And on the Day of Resurrection he will be against them a witness.

160. For wrongdoing on the part of the Jews, We made unlawful for them [certain] good foods which had been lawful to them, and for their averting from the way of Allah many [people],

161. And [for] their taking of usury while they had been forbidden from it, and their consuming of the people's wealth unjustly. And we have prepared for the disbelievers among them a painful punishment.

162. But those firm in knowledge among them and the believers believe in what has been revealed to you, [O Muhammad], and what was revealed before you. And the establishers of prayer [especially] and the givers of zakah and the believers in Allah and the Last Day - those We will give a great reward.

163. Indeed, We have revealed to you, [O Muhammad], as We revealed to Noah and the prophets after him. And we revealed to Abraham, Ishmael, Isaac, Jacob, the Descendants, Jesus, Job, Jonah, Aaron, and Solomon, and to David We gave the book [of Psalms].

164. And [We sent] messengers about whom We have related [their stories] to you before and messengers about whom We have not related to you. And Allah spoke to Moses with [direct] speech.

165. [We sent] messengers as bringers of good tidings and warners so that mankind will have no argument against Allah after the messengers. And ever is Allah Exalted in Might and Wise.

166. But Allah bears witness to that which He has revealed to you. He has sent it down with His knowledge, and the angels bear witness [as well]. And sufficient is Allah as Witness.

167. Indeed, those who disbelieve and avert [people] from the way of Allah have certainly gone far astray.

168. Indeed, those who disbelieve and commit wrong [or injustice] - never will Allah forgive them, nor will He guide them to a path.

169. Except the path of Hell; they will abide therein forever. And that, for Allah, is [always] easy.

170. O Mankind, the Messenger has come to you with the truth from your Lord, so believe; it is better for you. But if you disbelieve - then indeed, to Allah belongs whatever is in the heavens and earth. And ever is Allah Knowing and Wise.

171. O People of the Scripture, do not commit excess in your religion or say about Allah except the truth. The Messiah, Jesus, the son of Mary, was but a messenger of Allah and His word which He directed to Mary and a soul [created at a command] from Him. So believe in Allah and His messengers. And do not say, "Three"; desist - it is better for you. Indeed, Allah is but one God. Exalted is He above having a son. To Him belongs whatever is in the heavens and whatever is on the earth. And sufficient is Allah as Disposer of affairs.

172. Never would the Messiah disdain to be a servant of Allah, nor would the angels near [to Him]. And whoever disdains His worship and is arrogant - He will gather them to Himself all together.

173. And as for those who believed and did righteous deeds, He

will give them in full their rewards and grant them extra from His bounty. But as for those who disdained and were arrogant, He will punish them with a painful punishment, and they will not find for themselves besides Allah any protector or helper.

174. O mankind, there has come to you a conclusive proof from your Lord, and We have sent down to you a clear light.

175. So those who believe in Allah and hold fast to Him - He will admit them to mercy from Himself and bounty and guide them to Himself on a straight path.

176. They request from you a [legal] ruling. Say, "Allah gives you a ruling concerning one having neither descendants nor ascendants [as heirs]." If a man dies, leaving no child but [only] a sister, she will have half of what he left. And he inherits from her if she [dies and] has no child. But if there are two sisters [or more], they will have two-thirds of what he left. If there are both brothers and sisters, the male will have the share of two females. Allah makes clear to you [His law], lest you go astray. And Allah is Knowing of all things.

| Verses: 120 | **Surah 05 Al-Maaidah** | Madani |

In the name of Allah, the Entirely Merciful, the Especially Merciful.

01. O you who have believed, fulfill [all] contracts. Lawful for you are the animals of grazing livestock except for that which is recited to you [in this Qur'an] - hunting not being permitted while you are in the state of ihram. Indeed, Allah ordains what He intends.

02. O you who have believed, do not violate the rites of Allah or [the sanctity of] the sacred month or [neglect the marking of] the sacrificial animals and garlanding [them] or [violate the safety of] those coming to the Sacred House seeking bounty from their Lord and [His] approval. But when you come out of ihram, then [you may] hunt. And do not let the hatred of a people for having obstructed you from al-Masjid al-Haram lead you to transgress. And cooperate in righteousness and piety, but do not cooperate in sin and aggression. And fear Allah; indeed, Allah is severe in penalty.

03. Prohibited to you are dead animals, blood, the flesh of swine, and that which has been dedicated to other than Allah, and [those animals] killed by strangling or by a violent blow or by a head-long fall or by the goring of horns, and those from which a wild animal has eaten, except what you [are able to] slaughter

[before its death], and those which are sacrificed on stone altars, and [prohibited is] that you seek decision through divining arrows. That is grave disobedience. This day those who disbelieve have despaired of [defeating] your religion; so fear them not, but fear Me. This day I have perfected for you your religion and completed My favor upon you and have approved for you Islam as religion. But whoever is forced by severe hunger with no inclination to sin - then indeed, Allah is Forgiving and Merciful.

04. They ask you, [O Muhammad], what has been made lawful for them. Say, "Lawful for you are [all] good foods and [game caught by] what you have trained of hunting animals which you train as Allah has taught you. So eat of what they catch for you, and mention the name of Allah upon it, and fear Allah." Indeed, Allah is swift in account.

05. This day [all] good foods have been made lawful, and the food of those who were given the Scripture is lawful for you and your food is lawful for them. And [lawful in marriage are] chaste women from among the believers and chaste women from among those who were given the Scripture before you, when you have given them their due compensation, desiring chastity, not unlawful sexual intercourse or taking [secret] lovers. And whoever denies the faith - his work has become worthless, and he, in the Hereafter, will be among the losers.

06. O you who have believed, when you rise to [perform] prayer, wash your faces and your forearms to the elbows and wipe over your heads and wash your feet to the ankles. And if you are in a state of janabah, then purify yourselves. But if you are ill or on a journey or one of you comes from the place of relieving himself or you have contacted women and do not find water, then seek clean earth and wipe over your faces and hands with it. Allah does not intend to make difficulty for you, but He intends to purify you and complete His favor upon you that you may be grateful.

07. And remember the favor of Allah upon you and His covenant with which He bound you when you said, "We hear and we obey"; and fear Allah. Indeed, Allah is Knowing of that within the breasts.

08. O you who have believed, be persistently standing firm for Allah, witnesses in justice, and do not let the hatred of a people prevent you from being just. Be just; that is nearer to

righteousness. And fear Allah; indeed, Allah is Acquainted with what you do.

09. Allah has promised those who believe and do righteous deeds [that] for them there is forgiveness and great reward.

10. But those who disbelieve and deny Our signs - those are the companions of Hellfire.

11. O you who have believed, remember the favor of Allah upon you when a people determined to extend their hands [in aggression] against you, but He withheld their hands from you; and fear Allah. And upon Allah let the believers rely.

12. And Allah had already taken a covenant from the Children of Israel, and We delegated from among them twelve leaders. And Allah said, "I am with you. If you establish prayer and give zakah and believe in My messengers and support them and loan Allah a goodly loan, I will surely remove from you your misdeeds and admit you to gardens beneath which rivers flow. But whoever of you disbelieves after that has certainly strayed from the soundness of the way."

13. So for their breaking of the covenant We cursed them and made their hearts hard. They distort words from their [proper] usages and have forgotten a portion of that of which they were reminded. And you will still observe deceit among them, except a few of them. But pardon them and overlook [their misdeeds]. Indeed, Allah loves the doers of good.

14. And from those who say, "We are Christians" We took their covenant; but they forgot a portion of that of which they were reminded. So We caused among them animosity and hatred until the Day of Resurrection. And Allah is going to inform them about what they used to do.

15. O People of the Scripture, there has come to you Our Messenger making clear to you much of what you used to conceal of the Scripture and overlooking much. There has come to you from Allah a light and a clear Book.

16. By which Allah guides those who pursue His pleasure to the ways of peace and brings them out from darknesses into the light, by His permission, and guides them to a straight path.

17. They have certainly disbelieved who say that Allah is Christ, the son of Mary. Say, "Then who could prevent Allah at all if He had intended to destroy Christ, the son of Mary, or his mother or

everyone on the earth?" And to Allah belongs the dominion of the heavens and the earth and whatever is between them. He creates what He wills, and Allah is over all things competent.

18. But the Jews and the Christians say, "We are the children of Allah and His beloved." Say, "Then why does He punish you for your sins?" Rather, you are human beings from among those He has created. He forgives whom He wills, and He punishes whom He wills. And to Allah belongs the dominion of the heavens and the earth and whatever is between them, and to Him is the [final] destination.

19. O People of the Scripture, there has come to you Our Messenger to make clear to you [the religion] after a period [of suspension] of messengers, lest you say, "There came not to us any bringer of good tidings or a warner." But there has come to you a bringer of good tidings and a warner. And Allah is over all things competent.

20. And [mention, O Muhammad], when Moses said to his people, "O my people, remember the favor of Allah upon you when He appointed among you prophets and made you possessors and gave you that which He had not given anyone among the worlds.

21. O my people, enter the Holy Land which Allah has assigned to you and do not turn back [from fighting in Allah's cause] and [thus] become losers."

22. They said, "O Moses, indeed within it is a people of tyrannical strength, and indeed, we will never enter it until they leave it; but if they leave it, then we will enter."

23. Said two men from those who feared [to disobey] upon whom Allah had bestowed favor, "Enter upon them through the gate, for when you have entered it, you will be predominant. And upon Allah rely, if you should be believers."

24. They said, "O Moses, indeed we will not enter it, ever, as long as they are within it; so go, you and your Lord, and fight. Indeed, we are remaining right here."

25. [Moses] said, "My Lord, indeed I do not possess except myself and my brother, so part us from the defiantly disobedient people."

26. [Allah] said, "Then indeed, it is forbidden to them for forty years [in which] they will wander throughout the land. So do not grieve over the defiantly disobedient people."

27. And recite to them the story of Adam's two sons, in truth, when they both offered a sacrifice [to Allah], and it was accepted from one of them but was not accepted from the other. Said [the latter], "I will surely kill you." Said [the former], "Indeed, Allah only accepts from the righteous [who fear Him].

28. If you should raise your hand against me to kill me - I shall not raise my hand against you to kill you. Indeed, I fear Allah, Lord of the worlds.

29. Indeed I want you to obtain [thereby] my sin and your sin so you will be among the companions of the Fire. And that is the recompense of wrongdoers."

30. And his soul permitted to him the murder of his brother, so he killed him and became among the losers.

31. Then Allah sent a crow searching in the ground to show him how to hide the disgrace of his brother. He said, "O woe to me! Have I failed to be like this crow and hide the body of my brother?" And he became of the regretful.

32. Because of that, We decreed upon the Children of Israel that whoever kills a soul unless for a soul or for corruption [done] in the land - it is as if he had slain mankind entirely. And whoever saves one - it is as if he had saved mankind entirely. And our messengers had certainly come to them with clear proofs. Then indeed many of them, [even] after that, throughout the land, were transgressors.

33. Indeed, the penalty for those who wage war against Allah and His Messenger and strive upon earth [to cause] corruption is none but that they be killed or crucified or that their hands and feet be cut off from opposite sides or that they be exiled from the land. That is for them a disgrace in this world; and for them in the Hereafter is a great punishment,

34. Except for those who return [repenting] before you apprehend them. And know that Allah is Forgiving and Merciful.

35. O you who have believed, fear Allah and seek the means [of nearness] to Him and strive in His cause that you may succeed.

36. Indeed, those who disbelieve - if they should have all that is in the earth and the like of it with it by which to ransom themselves from the punishment of the Day of Resurrection, it will not be accepted from them, and for them is a painful punishment

37. They will wish to get out of the Fire, but never are they to emerge therefrom, and for them is an enduring punishment.

38. [As for] the thief, the male and the female, amputate their hands in recompense for what they committed as a deterrent [punishment] from Allah. And Allah is Exalted in Might and Wise.

39. But whoever repents after his wrongdoing and reforms, indeed, Allah will turn to him in forgiveness. Indeed, Allah is Forgiving and Merciful.

40. Do you not know that to Allah belongs the dominion of the heavens and the earth? He punishes whom He wills and forgives whom He wills, and Allah is over all things competent.

41. Messenger, let them not grieve you who hasten into disbelief of those who say, "We believe" with their mouths, but their hearts believe not, and from among the Jews. [They are] avid listeners to falsehood, listening to another people who have not come to you. They distort words beyond their [proper] usages, saying "If you are given this, take it; but if you are not given it, then beware." But he for whom Allah intends fitnah - never will you possess [power to do] for him a thing against Allah. Those are the ones for whom Allah does not intend to purify their hearts. For them in this world is disgrace, and for them in the Hereafter is a great punishment.

42. [They are] avid listeners to falsehood, devourers of [what is] unlawful. So if they come to you, [O Muhammad], judge between them or turn away from them. And if you turn away from them - never will they harm you at all. And if you judge, judge between them with justice. Indeed, Allah loves those who act justly.

43. But how is it that they come to you for judgement while they have the Torah, in which is the judgement of Allah? Then they turn away, [even] after that; but those are not [in fact] believers.

44. Indeed, We sent down the Torah, in which was guidance and light. The prophets who submitted [to Allah] judged by it for the Jews, as did the rabbis and scholars by that with which they were entrusted of the Scripture of Allah, and they were witnesses thereto. So do not fear the people but fear Me, and do not exchange My verses for a small price. And whoever does not judge by what Allah has revealed - then it is those who are the disbelievers.

45. And We ordained for them therein a life for a life, an eye for an

eye, a nose for a nose, an ear for an ear, a tooth for a tooth, and for wounds is legal retribution. But whoever gives [up his right as] charity, it is an expiation for him. And whoever does not judge by what Allah has revealed - then it is those who are the wrongdoers.

46. And We sent, following in their footsteps, Jesus, the son of Mary, confirming that which came before him in the Torah; and We gave him the Gospel, in which was guidance and light and confirming that which preceded it of the Torah as guidance and instruction for the righteous.

47. And let the People of the Gospel judge by what Allah has revealed therein. And whoever does not judge by what Allah has revealed - then it is those who are the defiantly disobedient.

48. And We have revealed to you, [O Muhammad], the Book in truth, confirming that which preceded it of the Scripture and as a criterion over it. So judge between them by what Allah has revealed and do not follow their inclinations away from what has come to you of the truth. To each of you We prescribed a law and a method. Had Allah willed, He would have made you one nation [united in religion], but [He intended] to test you in what He has given you; so race to [all that is] good. To Allah is your return all together, and He will [then] inform you concerning that over which you used to differ.

49. And judge, [O Muhammad], between them by what Allah has revealed and do not follow their inclinations and beware of them, lest they tempt you away from some of what Allah has revealed to you. And if they turn away - then know that Allah only intends to afflict them with some of their [own] sins. And indeed, many among the people are defiantly disobedient.

50. Then is it the judgement of [the time of] ignorance they desire? But who is better than Allah in judgement for a people who are certain [in faith].

51. O you who have believed, do not take the Jews and the Christians as allies. They are [in fact] allies of one another. And whoever is an ally to them among you - then indeed, he is [one] of them. Indeed, Allah guides not the wrongdoing people.

52. So you see those in whose hearts is disease hastening into [association with] them, saying, "We are afraid a misfortune may strike us." But perhaps Allah will bring conquest or a decision from Him, and they will become, over what they have been concealing within themselves, regretful.

53. And those who believe will say, "Are these the ones who swore by Allah their strongest oaths that indeed they were with you?" Their deeds have become worthless, and they have become losers.

54. O you who have believed, whoever of you should revert from his religion - Allah will bring forth [in place of them] a people He will love and who will love Him [who are] humble toward the believers, powerful against the disbelievers; they strive in the cause of Allah and do not fear the blame of a critic. That is the favor of Allah; He bestows it upon whom He wills. And Allah is all-Encompassing and Knowing.

55. Your ally is none but Allah and [therefore] His Messenger and those who have believed - those who establish prayer and give zakah, and they bow [in worship].

56. And whoever is an ally of Allah and His Messenger and those who have believed - indeed, the party of Allah - they will be the predominant.

57. O you who have believed, take not those who have taken your religion in ridicule and amusement among the ones who were given the Scripture before you nor the disbelievers as allies. And fear Allah, if you should [truly] be believers.

58. And when you call to prayer, they take it in ridicule and amusement. That is because they are a people who do not use reason.

59. Say, "O People of the Scripture, do you resent us except [for the fact] that we have believed in Allah and what was revealed to us and what was revealed before and because most of you are defiantly disobedient?"

60. Say, "Shall I inform you of [what is] worse than that as penalty from Allah? [It is that of] those whom Allah has cursed and with whom He became angry and made of them apes and pigs and slaves of Taghut. Those are worse in position and further astray from the sound way."

61. And when they come to you, they say, "We believe." But they have entered with disbelief [in their hearts], and they have certainly left with it. And Allah is most knowing of what they were concealing.

62. And you see many of them hastening into sin and aggression and the devouring of [what is] unlawful. How wretched is what they have been doing.

63. Why do the rabbis and religious scholars not forbid them from saying what is sinful and devouring what is unlawful? How wretched is what they have been practicing.

64. And the Jews say, "The hand of Allah is chained." Chained are their hands, and cursed are they for what they say. Rather, both His hands are extended; He spends however He wills. And that which has been revealed to you from your Lord will surely increase many of them in transgression and disbelief. And We have cast among them animosity and hatred until the Day of Resurrection. Every time they kindled the fire of war [against you], Allah extinguished it. And they strive throughout the land [causing] corruption, and Allah does not like corrupters.

65. And if only the People of the Scripture had believed and feared Allah, We would have removed from them their misdeeds and admitted them to Gardens of Pleasure.

66. And if only they upheld [the law of] the Torah, the Gospel, and what has been revealed to them from their Lord, they would have consumed [provision] from above them and from beneath their feet. Among them are a moderate community, but many of them - evil is that which they do.

67. O Messenger, announce that which has been revealed to you from your Lord, and if you do not, then you have not conveyed His message. And Allah will protect you from the people. Indeed, Allah does not guide the disbelieving people.

68. Say, "O People of the Scripture, you are [standing] on nothing until you uphold [the law of] the Torah, the Gospel, and what has been revealed to you from your Lord." And that which has been revealed to you from your Lord will surely increase many of them in transgression and disbelief. So do not grieve over the disbelieving people.

69. Indeed, those who have believed [in Prophet Muhammad] and those [before Him] who were Jews or Sabeans or Christians - those [among them] who believed in Allah and the Last Day and did righteousness - no fear will there be concerning them, nor will they grieve.

70. We had already taken the covenant of the Children of Israel and had sent to them messengers. Whenever there came to them a messenger with what their souls did not desire, a party [of messengers] they denied, and another party they killed.

71. And they thought there would be no [resulting] punishment, so they became blind and deaf. Then Allah turned to them in forgiveness; then [again] many of them became blind and deaf. And Allah is Seeing of what they do.

72. They have certainly disbelieved who say, "Allah is the Messiah, the son of Mary" while the Messiah has said, "O Children of Israel, worship Allah, my Lord and your Lord." Indeed, he who associates others with Allah - Allah has forbidden him Paradise, and his refuge is the Fire. And there are not for the wrongdoers any helpers.

73. They have certainly disbelieved who say, "Allah is the third of three." And there is no god except one God. And if they do not desist from what they are saying, there will surely afflict the disbelievers among them a painful punishment.

74. So will they not repent to Allah and seek His forgiveness? And Allah is Forgiving and Merciful.

75. The Messiah, son of Mary, was not but a messenger; [other] messengers have passed on before him. And his mother was a supporter of truth. They both used to eat food. Look how We make clear to them the signs; then look how they are deluded.

76. Say, "Do you worship besides Allah that which holds for you no [power of] harm or benefit while it is Allah who is the Hearing, the Knowing?"

77. Say, "O People of the Scripture, do not exceed limits in your religion beyond the truth and do not follow the inclinations of a people who had gone astray before and misled many and have strayed from the soundness of the way."

78. Cursed were those who disbelieved among the Children of Israel by the tongue of David and of Jesus, the son of Mary. That was because they disobeyed and [habitually] transgressed.

79. They used not to prevent one another from wrongdoing that they did. How wretched was that which they were doing.

80. You see many of them becoming allies of those who disbelieved. How wretched is that which they have put forth for themselves in that Allah has become angry with them, and in the punishment they will abide eternally.

81. And if they had believed in Allah and the Prophet and in what was revealed to him, they would not have taken them as allies; but many of them are defiantly disobedient.

82. You will surely find the most intense of the people in animosity toward the believers [to be] the Jews and those who associate others with Allah; and you will find the nearest of them in affection to the believers those who say, "We are Christians." That is because among them are priests and monks and because they are not arrogant.

83. And when they hear what has been revealed to the Messenger, you see their eyes overflowing with tears because of what they have recognized of the truth. They say, "Our Lord, we have believed, so register us among the witnesses.

84. And why should we not believe in Allah and what has come to us of the truth? And we aspire that our Lord will admit us [to Paradise] with the righteous people."

85. So Allah rewarded them for what they said with gardens [in Paradise] beneath which rivers flow, wherein they abide eternally. And that is the reward of doers of good.

86. But those who disbelieved and denied Our signs - they are the companions of Hellfire.

87. O you who have believed, do not prohibit the good things which Allah has made lawful to you and do not transgress. Indeed, Allah does not like transgressors.

88. And eat of what Allah has provided for you [which is] lawful and good. And fear Allah, in whom you are believers.

89. Allah will not impose blame upon you for what is meaningless in your oaths, but He will impose blame upon you for [breaking] what you intended of oaths. So its expiation is the feeding of ten needy people from the average of that which you feed your [own] families or clothing them or the freeing of a slave. But whoever cannot find [or afford it] - then a fast of three days [is required]. That is the expiation for oaths when you have sworn. But guard your oaths. Thus does Allah make clear to you His verses that you may be grateful.

90. O you who have believed, indeed, intoxicants, gambling, [sacrificing on] stone alters [to other than Allah], and divining arrows are but defilement from the work of Satan, so avoid it that you may be successful.

91. Satan only wants to cause between you animosity and hatred through intoxicants and gambling and to avert you from the remembrance of Allah and from prayer. So will you not desist?

92. And obey Allah and obey the Messenger and beware. And if you turn away - then know that upon Our Messenger is only [the responsibility for] clear notification.

93. There is not upon those who believe and do righteousness [any] blame concerning what they have eaten [in the past] if they [now] fear Allah and believe and do righteous deeds, and then fear Allah and believe, and then fear Allah and do good; and Allah loves the doers of good.

94. O you who have believed, Allah will surely test you through something of the game that your hands and spears [can] reach, that Allah may make evident those who fear Him unseen. And whoever transgresses after that - for him is a painful punishment.

95. O you who have believed, do not kill game while you are in the state of ihram. And whoever of you kills it intentionally - the penalty is an equivalent from sacrificial animals to what he killed, as judged by two just men among you as an offering [to Allah] delivered to the Ka'bah, or an expiation: the feeding of needy people or the equivalent of that in fasting, that he may taste the consequence of his deed. Allah has pardoned what is past; but whoever returns [to violation], then Allah will take retribution from him. And Allah is Exalted in Might and Owner of Retribution.

96. Lawful to you is game from the sea and its food as provision for you and the travelers, but forbidden to you is game from the land as long as you are in the state of ihram. And fear Allah to whom you will be gathered.

97. Allah has made the Ka'bah, the Sacred House, standing for the people and [has sanctified] the sacred months and the sacrificial animals and the garlands [by which they are identified]. That is so you may know that Allah knows what is in the heavens and what is in the earth and that Allah is Knowing of all things.

98. Know that Allah is severe in penalty and that Allah is Forgiving and Merciful.

99. Not upon the Messenger is [responsibility] except [for] notification. And Allah knows whatever you reveal and whatever you conceal.

100. Say, "Not equal are the evil and the good, although the abundance of evil might impress you." So fear Allah, O you of understanding, that you may be successful.

101. O you who have believed, do not ask about things which, if they are shown to you, will distress you. But if you ask about

them while the Qur'an is being revealed, they will be shown to you. Allah has pardoned that which is past; and Allah is Forgiving and Forbearing.

102. A people asked such [questions] before you; then they became thereby disbelievers.

103. Allah has not appointed [such innovations as] bahirah or sa'ibah or wasilah or ham. But those who disbelieve invent falsehood about Allah, and most of them do not reason.

104. And when it is said to them, "Come to what Allah has revealed and to the Messenger," they say, "Sufficient for us is that upon which we found our fathers." Even though their fathers knew nothing, nor were they guided?

105. O you who have believed, upon you is [responsibility for] yourselves. Those who have gone astray will not harm you when you have been guided. To Allah is you return all together; then He will inform you of what you used to do.

106. O you who have believed, testimony [should be taken] among you when death approaches one of you at the time of bequest - [that of] two just men from among you or two others from outside if you are traveling through the land and the disaster of death should strike you. Detain them after the prayer and let them both swear by Allah if you doubt [their testimony, saying], "We will not exchange our oath for a price, even if he should be a near relative, and we will not withhold the testimony of Allah. Indeed, we would then be of the sinful."

107. But if it is found that those two were guilty of perjury, let two others stand in their place [who are] foremost [in claim] from those who have a lawful right. And let them swear by Allah, "Our testimony is truer than their testimony, and we have not transgressed. Indeed, we would then be of the wrongdoers."

108. That is more likely that they will give testimony according to its [true] objective, or [at least] they would fear that [other] oaths might be taken after their oaths. And fear Allah and listen; and Allah does not guide the defiantly disobedient people.

109. [Be warned of] the Day when Allah will assemble the messengers and say, "What was the response you received?" They will say, "We have no knowledge. Indeed, it is You who is Knower of the unseen"

110. [The Day] when Allah will say, "O Jesus, Son of Mary, remember My favor upon you and upon your mother when I supported you with the Pure Spirit and you spoke to the people in the cradle and in maturity; and [remember] when I taught you writing and wisdom and the Torah and the Gospel; and when you designed from clay [what was] like the form of a bird with My permission, then you breathed into it, and it became a bird with My permission; and you healed the blind and the leper with My permission; and when you brought forth the dead with My permission; and when I restrained the Children of Israel from [killing] you when you came to them with clear proofs and those who disbelieved among them said, "This is not but obvious magic."

111. And [remember] when I inspired to the disciples, "Believe in Me and in My messenger Jesus." They said, "We have believed, so bear witness that indeed we are Muslims [in submission to Allah]."

112. [And remember] when the disciples said, "O Jesus, Son of Mary, can your Lord send down to us a table [spread with food] from the heaven? [Jesus] said," Fear Allah, if you should be believers."

113. They said, "We wish to eat from it and let our hearts be reassured and know that you have been truthful to us and be among its witnesses."

114. Said Jesus, the son of Mary, "O Allah, our Lord, send down to us a table [spread with food] from the heaven to be for us a festival for the first of us and the last of us and a sign from You. And provide for us, and You are the best of providers."

115. Allah said, "Indeed, I will sent it down to you, but whoever disbelieves afterwards from among you - then indeed will I punish him with a punishment by which I have not punished anyone among the worlds."

116. And [beware the Day] when Allah will say, "O Jesus, Son of Mary, did you say to the people, 'Take me and my mother as deities besides Allah?'" He will say, "Exalted are You! It was not for me to say that to which I have no right. If I had said it, You would have known it. You know what is within myself, and I do not know what is within Yourself. Indeed, it is You who is Knower of the unseen.

117. I said not to them except what You commanded me - to worship Allah, my Lord and your Lord. And I was a witness over them as

long as I was among them; but when You took me up, You were the Observer over them, and You are, over all things, Witness.

118. If You should punish them - indeed they are Your servants; but if You forgive them - indeed it is You who is the Exalted in Might, the Wise.

119. Allah will say, "This is the Day when the truthful will benefit from their truthfulness." For them are gardens [in Paradise] beneath which rivers flow, wherein they will abide forever, Allah being pleased with them, and they with Him. That is the great attainment.

120. To Allah belongs the dominion of the heavens and the earth and whatever is within them. And He is over all things competent.

| Verses: 165 | Surah 06 Al-An'aam | Makki |

In the name of Allah, the Entirely Merciful, the Especially Merciful.

01. [All] praise is [due] to Allah, who created the heavens and the earth and made the darkness and the light. Then those who disbelieve equate [others] with their Lord.

02. It is He who created you from clay and then decreed a term and a specified time [known] to Him; then [still] you are in dispute.

03. And He is Allah, [the only deity] in the heavens and the earth. He knows your secret and what you make public, and He knows that which you earn.

04. And no sign comes to them from the signs of their Lord except that they turn away therefrom.

05. For they had denied the truth when it came to them, but there is going to reach them the news of what they used to ridicule.

06. Have they not seen how many generations We destroyed before them which We had established upon the earth as We have not established you? And We sent [rain from] the sky upon them in showers and made rivers flow beneath them; then We destroyed them for their sins and brought forth after them a generation of others.

07. And even if We had sent down to you, [O Muhammad], a written scripture on a page and they touched it with their hands, the disbelievers would say, "This is not but obvious magic."

08. And they say, "Why was there not sent down to him an angel?" But if We had sent down an angel, the matter would have been decided; then they would not be reprieved.

09. And if We had made him an angel, We would have made him [appear as] a man, and We would have covered them with that in which they cover themselves.

10. And already were messengers ridiculed before you, but those who mocked them were enveloped by that which they used to ridicule.

11. Say, "Travel through the land; then observe how was the end of the deniers."

12. Say, "To whom belongs whatever is in the heavens and earth?" Say, "To Allah." He has decreed upon Himself mercy. He will surely assemble you for the Day of Resurrection, about which there is no doubt. Those who will lose themselves [that Day] do not believe.

13. And to Him belongs that which reposes by night and by day, and He is the Hearing, the Knowing.

14. Say, "Is it other than Allah I should take as a protector, Creator of the heavens and the earth, while it is He who feeds and is not fed?" Say, [O Muhammad], "Indeed, I have been commanded to be the first [among you] who submit [to Allah] and [was commanded], 'Do not ever be of the polytheists.' "

15. Say, "Indeed I fear, if I should disobey my Lord, the punishment of a tremendous Day."

16. He from whom it is averted that Day - [Allah] has granted him mercy. And that is the clear attainment.

17. And if Allah should touch you with adversity, there is no remover of it except Him. And if He touches you with good - then He is over all things competent.

18. And He is the subjugator over His servants. And He is the Wise, the Acquainted [with all].

19. Say, "What thing is greatest in testimony?" Say, "Allah is witness between me and you. And this Qur'an was revealed to me that I may warn you thereby and whomever it reaches. Do you [truly] testify that with Allah there are other deities?" Say, "I will not testify [with you]." Say, "Indeed, He is but one God, and indeed, I am free of what you associate [with Him]."

20. Those to whom We have given the Scripture recognize it as they

recognize their [own] sons. Those who will lose themselves [in the Hereafter] do not believe.

21. And who is more unjust than one who invents about Allah a lie or denies His verses? Indeed, the wrongdoers will not succeed.

22. And [mention, O Muhammad], the Day We will gather them all together; then We will say to those who associated others with Allah, "Where are your 'partners' that you used to claim [with Him]?"

23. Then there will be no [excuse upon] examination except they will say, "By Allah, our Lord, we were not those who associated."

24. See how they will lie about themselves. And lost from them will be what they used to invent.

25. And among them are those who listen to you, but We have placed over their hearts coverings, lest they understand it, and in their ears deafness. And if they should see every sign, they will not believe in it. Even when they come to you arguing with you, those who disbelieve say, "This is not but legends of the former peoples."

26. And they prevent [others] from him and are [themselves] remote from him. And they do not destroy except themselves, but they perceive [it] not.

27. If you could but see when they are made to stand before the Fire and will say, "Oh, would that we could be returned [to life on earth] and not deny the signs of our Lord and be among the believers."

28. But what they concealed before has [now] appeared to them. And even if they were returned, they would return to that which they were forbidden; and indeed, they are liars.

29. And they say, "There is none but our worldly life, and we will not be resurrected."

30. If you could but see when they will be made to stand before their Lord. He will say, "Is this not the truth?" They will say, "Yes, by our Lord." He will [then] say, "So taste the punishment because you used to disbelieve."

31. Those will have lost who deny the meeting with Allah, until when the Hour [of resurrection] comes upon them unexpectedly, they will say, "Oh, [how great is] our regret over what we neglected concerning it," while they bear their burdens on their backs. Unquestionably, evil is that which they bear.

32. And the worldly life is not but amusement and diversion; but the home of the Hereafter is best for those who fear Allah, so will you not reason?
33. We know that you, [O Muhammad], are saddened by what they say. And indeed, they do not call you untruthful, but it is the verses of Allah that the wrongdoers reject.
34. And certainly were messengers denied before you, but they were patient over [the effects of] denial, and they were harmed until Our victory came to them. And none can alter the words of Allah. And there has certainly come to you some information about the [previous] messengers.
35. And if their evasion is difficult for you, then if you are able to seek a tunnel into the earth or a stairway into the sky to bring them a sign, [then do so]. But if Allah had willed, He would have united them upon guidance. So never be of the ignorant.
36. Only those who hear will respond. But the dead - Allah will resurrect them; then to Him they will be returned.
37. And they say, "Why has a sign not been sent down to him from his Lord?" Say, "Indeed, Allah is Able to send down a sign, but most of them do not know."
38. And there is no creature on [or within] the earth or bird that flies with its wings except [that they are] communities like you. We have not neglected in the Register a thing. Then unto their Lord they will be gathered.
39. But those who deny Our verses are deaf and dumb within darknesses. Whomever Allah wills - He leaves astray; and whomever He wills - He puts him on a straight path.
40. Say, "Have you considered: if there came to you the punishment of Allah or there came to you the Hour - is it other than Allah you would invoke, if you should be truthful?"
41. No, it is Him [alone] you would invoke, and He would remove that for which you invoked Him if He willed, and you would forget what you associate [with Him].
42. And We have already sent [messengers] to nations before you, [O Muhammad]; then We seized them with poverty and hardship that perhaps they might humble themselves [to Us].
43. Then why, when Our punishment came to them, did they not humble themselves? But their hearts became hardened, and Satan made attractive to them that which they were doing.

44. So when they forgot that by which they had been reminded, We opened to them the doors of every [good] thing until, when they rejoiced in that which they were given, We seized them suddenly, and they were [then] in despair.

45. So the people that committed wrong were eliminated. And praise to Allah, Lord of the worlds.

46. Say, "Have you considered: if Allah should take away your hearing and your sight and set a seal upon your hearts, which deity other than Allah could bring them [back] to you?" Look how we diversify the verses; then they [still] turn away.

47. Say, "Have you considered: if the punishment of Allah should come to you unexpectedly or manifestly, will any be destroyed but the wrongdoing people?"

48. And We send not the messengers except as bringers of good tidings and warners. So whoever believes and reforms - there will be no fear concerning them, nor will they grieve.

49. But those who deny Our verses - the punishment will touch them for their defiant disobedience.

50. Say, [O Muhammad], "I do not tell you that I have the depositories [containing the provision] of Allah or that I know the unseen, nor do I tell you that I am an angel. I only follow what is revealed to me." Say, "Is the blind equivalent to the seeing? Then will you not give thought?"

51. And warn by the Qur'an those who fear that they will be gathered before their Lord - for them besides Him will be no protector and no intercessor - that they might become righteous.

52. And do not send away those who call upon their Lord morning and afternoon, seeking His countenance. Not upon you is anything of their account and not upon them is anything of your account. So were you to send them away, you would [then] be of the wrongdoers.

53. And thus We have tried some of them through others that the disbelievers might say, "Is it these whom Allah has favored among us?" Is not Allah most knowing of those who are grateful?

54. And when those come to you who believe in Our verses, say, "Peace be upon you. Your Lord has decreed upon Himself mercy: that any of you who does wrong out of ignorance and then repents after that and corrects himself - indeed, He is Forgiving and Merciful."

55. And thus do We detail the verses, and [thus] the way of the criminals will become evident.
56. Say, "Indeed, I have been forbidden to worship those you invoke besides Allah." Say, "I will not follow your desires, for I would then have gone astray, and I would not be of the [rightly] guided."
57. Say, "Indeed, I am on clear evidence from my Lord, and you have denied it. I do not have that for which you are impatient. The decision is only for Allah. He relates the truth, and He is the best of deciders."
58. Say, "If I had that for which you are impatient, the matter would have been decided between me and you, but Allah is most knowing of the wrongdoers."
59. And with Him are the keys of the unseen; none knows them except Him. And He knows what is on the land and in the sea. Not a leaf falls but that He knows it. And no grain is there within the darknesses of the earth and no moist or dry [thing] but that it is [written] in a clear record.
60. And it is He who takes your souls by night and knows what you have committed by day. Then He revives you therein that a specified term may be fulfilled. Then to Him will be your return; then He will inform you about what you used to do.
61. And He is the subjugator over His servants, and He sends over you guardian-angels until, when death comes to one of you, Our messengers take him, and they do not fail [in their duties].
62. Then they His servants are returned to Allah, their true Lord. Unquestionably, His is the judgement, and He is the swiftest of accountants.
63. Say, "Who rescues you from the darknesses of the land and sea [when] you call upon Him imploring [aloud] and privately, 'If He should save us from this [crisis], we will surely be among the thankful.' "
64. Say, "It is Allah who saves you from it and from every distress; then you [still] associate others with Him."
65. Say, "He is the [one] Able to send upon you affliction from above you or from beneath your feet or to confuse you [so you become] sects and make you taste the violence of one another." Look how We diversify the signs that they might understand.
66. But your people have denied it while it is the truth. Say, "I am not over you a manager."

67. For every happening is a finality; and you are going to know.

68. And when you see those who engage in [offensive] discourse concerning Our verses, then turn away from them until they enter into another conversation. And if Satan should cause you to forget, then do not remain after the reminder with the wrongdoing people.

69. And those who fear Allah are not held accountable for the disbelievers at all, but [only for] a reminder - that perhaps they will fear Him.

70. And leave those who take their religion as amusement and diversion and whom the worldly life has deluded. But remind with the Qur'an, lest a soul be given up to destruction for what it earned; it will have other than Allah no protector and no intercessor. And if it should offer every compensation, it would not be taken from it. Those are the ones who are given to destruction for what they have earned. For them will be a drink of scalding water and a painful punishment because they used to disbelieve.

71. Say, "Shall we invoke instead of Allah that which neither benefits us nor harms us and be turned back on our heels after Allah has guided us? [We would then be] like one whom the devils enticed [to wander] upon the earth confused, [while] he has companions inviting him to guidance, [calling], 'Come to us.' " Say, "Indeed, the guidance of Allah is the [only] guidance; and we have been commanded to submit to the Lord of the worlds.

72. And to establish prayer and fear Him." And it is He to whom you will be gathered.

73. And it is He who created the heavens and earth in truth. And the day He says, "Be," and it is, His word is the truth. And His is the dominion [on] the Day the Horn is blown. [He is] Knower of the unseen and the witnessed; and He is the Wise, the Acquainted.

74. And [mention, O Muhammad], when Abraham said to his father Azar, "Do you take idols as deities? Indeed, I see you and your people to be in manifest error."

75. And thus did We show Abraham the realm of the heavens and the earth that he would be among the certain [in faith]

76. So when the night covered him [with darkness], he saw a star. He said, "This is my lord." But when it set, he said, "I like not those that disappear."

77. And when he saw the moon rising, he said, "This is my lord." But when it set, he said, "Unless my Lord guides me, I will surely be among the people gone astray."

78. And when he saw the sun rising, he said, "This is my lord; this is greater." But when it set, he said, "O my people, indeed I am free from what you associate with Allah.

79. Indeed, I have turned my face toward He who created the heavens and the earth, inclining toward truth, and I am not of those who associate others with Allah."

80. And his people argued with him. He said, "Do you argue with me concerning Allah while He has guided me? And I fear not what you associate with Him [and will not be harmed] unless my Lord should will something. My Lord encompasses all things in knowledge; then will you not remember?

81. And how should I fear what you associate while you do not fear that you have associated with Allah that for which He has not sent down to you any authority? So which of the two parties has more right to security, if you should know?

82. They who believe and do not mix their belief with injustice - those will have security, and they are [rightly] guided.

83. And that was Our [conclusive] argument which We gave Abraham against his people. We raise by degrees whom We will. Indeed, your Lord is Wise and Knowing.

84. And We gave to Abraham, Isaac and Jacob - all [of them] We guided. And Noah, We guided before; and among his descendants, David and Solomon and Job and Joseph and Moses and Aaron. Thus do We reward the doers of good.

85. And Zechariah and John and Jesus and Elias - and all were of the righteous.

86. And Ishmael and Elisha and Jonah and Lot - and all [of them] We preferred over the worlds.

87. And [some] among their fathers and their descendants and their brothers - and We chose them and We guided them to a straight path.

88. That is the guidance of Allah by which He guides whomever He wills of His servants. But if they had associated others with Allah, then worthless for them would be whatever they were doing.

89. Those are the ones to whom We gave the Scripture and authority

and prophethood. But if the disbelievers deny it, then We have entrusted it to a people who are not therein disbelievers.

90. Those are the ones whom Allah has guided, so from their guidance take an example. Say, "I ask of you for this message no payment. It is not but a reminder for the worlds."

91. And they did not appraise Allah with true appraisal when they said, "Allah did not reveal to a human being anything." Say, "Who revealed the Scripture that Moses brought as light and guidance to the people? You [Jews] make it into pages, disclosing [some of] it and concealing much. And you were taught that which you knew not - neither you nor your fathers." Say, "Allah [revealed it]." Then leave them in their [empty] discourse, amusing themselves.

92. And this is a Book which We have sent down, blessed and confirming what was before it, that you may warn the Mother of Cities and those around it. Those who believe in the Hereafter believe in it, and they are maintaining their prayers.

93. And who is more unjust than one who invents a lie about Allah or says, "It has been inspired to me," while nothing has been inspired to him, and one who says, "I will reveal [something] like what Allah revealed." And if you could but see when the wrongdoers are in the overwhelming pangs of death while the angels extend their hands, [saying], "Discharge your souls! Today you will be awarded the punishment of [extreme] humiliation for what you used to say against Allah other than the truth and [that] you were, toward His verses, being arrogant."

94. [It will be said to them], "And you have certainly come to Us alone as We created you the first time, and you have left whatever We bestowed upon you behind you. And We do not see with you your 'intercessors' which you claimed that they were among you associates [of Allah]. It has [all] been severed between you, and lost from you is what you used to claim."

95. Indeed, Allah is the cleaver of grain and date seeds. He brings the living out of the dead and brings the dead out of the living. That is Allah; so how are you deluded?

96. [He is] the cleaver of daybreak and has made the night for rest and the sun and moon for calculation. That is the determination of the Exalted in Might, the Knowing.

97. And it is He who placed for you the stars that you may be guided by them through the darknesses of the land and sea. We have

detailed the signs for a people who know.

98. And it is He who produced you from one soul and [gave you] a place of dwelling and of storage. We have detailed the signs for a people who understand.

99. And it is He who sends down rain from the sky, and We produce thereby the growth of all things. We produce from it greenery from which We produce grains arranged in layers. And from the palm trees - of its emerging fruit are clusters hanging low. And [We produce] gardens of grapevines and olives and pomegranates, similar yet varied. Look at [each of] its fruit when it yields and [at] its ripening. Indeed in that are signs for a people who believe.

100. But they have attributed to Allah partners - the jinn, while He has created them - and have fabricated for Him sons and daughters. Exalted is He and high above what they describe

101. [He is] Originator of the heavens and the earth. How could He have a son when He does not have a companion and He created all things? And He is, of all things, Knowing.

102. That is Allah, your Lord; there is no deity except Him, the Creator of all things, so worship Him. And He is Disposer of all things.

103. Vision perceives Him not, but He perceives [all] vision; and He is the Subtle, the Acquainted.

104. There has come to you enlightenment from your Lord. So whoever will see does so for [the benefit of] his soul, and whoever is blind [does harm] against it. And [say], "I am not a guardian over you."

105. And thus do We diversify the verses so the disbelievers will say, "You have studied," and so We may make the Qur'an clear for a people who know.

106. Follow, [O Muhammad], what has been revealed to you from your Lord - there is no deity except Him - and turn away from those who associate others with Allah.

107. But if Allah had willed, they would not have associated. And We have not appointed you over them as a guardian, nor are you a manager over them.

108. And do not insult those they invoke other than Allah, lest they insult Allah in enmity without knowledge. Thus We have made pleasing to every community their deeds. Then to their Lord is their return, and He will inform them about what they used to do.

109. And they swear by Allah their strongest oaths that if a sign came to them, they would surely believe in it. Say, "The signs are only with Allah." And what will make you perceive that even if a sign came, they would not believe.

110. And We will turn away their hearts and their eyes just as they refused to believe in it the first time. And We will leave them in their transgression, wandering blindly.

111. And even if We had sent down to them the angels [with the message] and the dead spoke to them [of it] and We gathered together every [created] thing in front of them, they would not believe unless Allah should will. But most of them, [of that], are ignorant.

112. And thus We have made for every prophet an enemy - devils from mankind and jinn, inspiring to one another decorative speech in delusion. But if your Lord had willed, they would not have done it, so leave them and that which they invent.

113. And [it is] so the hearts of those who disbelieve in the Hereafter will incline toward it and that they will be satisfied with it and that they will commit that which they are committing.

114. [Say], "Then is it other than Allah I should seek as judge while it is He who has revealed to you the Book explained in detail?" And those to whom We [previously] gave the Scripture know that it is sent down from your Lord in truth, so never be among the doubters.

115. And the word of your Lord has been fulfilled in truth and in justice. None can alter His words, and He is the Hearing, the Knowing.

116. And if you obey most of those upon the earth, they will mislead you from the way of Allah. They follow not except assumption, and they are not but falsifying.

117. Indeed, your Lord is most knowing of who strays from His way, and He is most knowing of the [rightly] guided.

118. So eat of that [meat] upon which the name of Allah has been mentioned, if you are believers in His verses.

119. And why should you not eat of that upon which the name of Allah has been mentioned while He has explained in detail to you what He has forbidden you, excepting that to which you are compelled. And indeed do many lead [others] astray through their [own] inclinations without knowledge. Indeed, your Lord - He is most knowing of the transgressors.

120. And leave what is apparent of sin and what is concealed thereof. Indeed, those who earn [blame for] sin will be recompensed for that which they used to commit.

121. And do not eat of that upon which the name of Allah has not been mentioned, for indeed, it is grave disobedience. And indeed do the devils inspire their allies [among men] to dispute with you. And if you were to obey them, indeed, you would be associators [of others with Him].

122. And is one who was dead and We gave him life and made for him light by which to walk among the people like one who is in darkness, never to emerge therefrom? Thus it has been made pleasing to the disbelievers that which they were doing.

123. And thus We have placed within every city the greatest of its criminals to conspire therein. But they conspire not except against themselves, and they perceive [it] not.

124. And when a sign comes to them, they say, "Never will we believe until we are given like that which was given to the messengers of Allah." Allah is most knowing of where He places His message. There will afflict those who committed crimes debasement before Allah and severe punishment for what they used to conspire.

125. So whoever Allah wants to guide - He expands his breast to [contain] Islam; and whoever He wants to misguide - He makes his breast tight and constricted as though he were climbing into the sky. Thus does Allah place defilement upon those who do not believe.

126. And this is the path of your Lord, [leading] straight. We have detailed the verses for a people who remember.

127. For them will be the Home of Peace with their Lord. And He will be their protecting friend because of what they used to do.

128. And [mention, O Muhammad], the Day when He will gather them together [and say], "O company of jinn, you have [misled] many of mankind." And their allies among mankind will say, "Our Lord, some of us made use of others, and we have [now] reached our term, which you appointed for us." He will say, "The Fire is your residence, wherein you will abide eternally, except for what Allah wills. Indeed, your Lord is Wise and Knowing."

129. And thus will We make some of the wrongdoers allies of others for what they used to earn.

130. "O company of jinn and mankind, did there not come to you messengers from among you, relating to you My verses and warning you of the meeting of this Day of yours?" They will say, "We bear witness against ourselves"; and the worldly life had deluded them, and they will bear witness against themselves that they were disbelievers.

131. That is because your Lord would not destroy the cities for wrongdoing while their people were unaware.

132. And for all are degrees from what they have done. And your Lord is not unaware of what they do.

133. And your Lord is the Free of need, the possessor of mercy. If He wills, he can do away with you and give succession after you to whomever He wills, just as He produced you from the descendants of another people.

134. Indeed, what you are promised is coming, and you will not cause failure [to Allah].

135. Say, "O my people, work according to your position; [for] indeed, I am working. And you are going to know who will have succession in the home. Indeed, the wrongdoers will not succeed.

136. And the polytheists assign to Allah from that which He created of crops and livestock a share and say, "This is for Allah," by their claim, "and this is for our partners [associated with Him]." But what is for their "partners" does not reach Allah, while what is for Allah - this reaches their "partners." Evil is that which they rule.

137. And likewise, to many of the polytheists their partners have made [to seem] pleasing the killing of their children in order to bring about their destruction and to cover them with confusion in their religion. And if Allah had willed, they would not have done so. So leave them and that which they invent.

138. And they say, "These animals and crops are forbidden; no one may eat from them except whom we will," by their claim. And there are those [camels] whose backs are forbidden [by them] and those upon which the name of Allah is not mentioned - [all of this] an invention of untruth about Him. He will punish them for what they were inventing.

139. And they say, "What is in the bellies of these animals is exclusively for our males and forbidden to our females. But if it is [born] dead, then all of them have shares therein." He will punish them for their description. Indeed, He is Wise and Knowing.

140. Those will have lost who killed their children in foolishness without knowledge and prohibited what Allah had provided for them, inventing untruth about Allah. They have gone astray and were not [rightly] guided.

141. And He it is who causes gardens to grow, [both] trellised and untrellised, and palm trees and crops of different [kinds of] food and olives and pomegranates, similar and dissimilar. Eat of [each of] its fruit when it yields and give its due [zakah] on the day of its harvest. And be not excessive. Indeed, He does not like those who commit excess.

142. And of the grazing livestock are carriers [of burdens] and those [too] small. Eat of what Allah has provided for you and do not follow the footsteps of Satan. Indeed, he is to you a clear enemy.

143. [They are] eight mates - of the sheep, two and of the goats, two. Say, "Is it the two males He has forbidden or the two females or that which the wombs of the two females contain? Inform me with knowledge, if you should be truthful."

144. And of the camels, two and of the cattle, two. Say, "Is it the two males He has forbidden or the two females or that which the wombs of the two females contain? Or were you witnesses when Allah charged you with this? Then who is more unjust than one who invents a lie about Allah to mislead the people by [something] other than knowledge? Indeed, Allah does not guide the wrongdoing people."

145. Say, "I do not find within that which was revealed to me [anything] forbidden to one who would eat it unless it be a dead animal or blood spilled out or the flesh of swine - for indeed, it is impure - or it be [that slaughtered in] disobedience, dedicated to other than Allah. But whoever is forced [by necessity], neither desiring [it] nor transgressing [its limit], then indeed, your Lord is Forgiving and Merciful."

146. And to those who are Jews We prohibited every animal of uncloven hoof; and of the cattle and the sheep We prohibited to them their fat, except what adheres to their backs or the entrails or what is joined with bone. [By] that We repaid them for their injustice. And indeed, We are truthful.

147. So if they deny you, [O Muhammad], say, "Your Lord is the possessor of vast mercy; but His punishment cannot be repelled from the people who are criminals."

148. Those who associated with Allah will say, "If Allah had willed, we would not have associated [anything] and neither would our fathers, nor would we have prohibited anything." Likewise did those before deny until they tasted Our punishment. Say, "Do you have any knowledge that you can produce for us? You follow not except assumption, and you are not but falsifying."

149. Say, "With Allah is the far-reaching argument. If He had willed, He would have guided you all."

150. Say, [O Muhammad], "Bring forward your witnesses who will testify that Allah has prohibited this." And if they testify, do not testify with them. And do not follow the desires of those who deny Our verses and those who do not believe in the Hereafter, while they equate [others] with their Lord.

151. Say, "Come, I will recite what your Lord has prohibited to you. [He commands] that you not associate anything with Him, and to parents, good treatment, and do not kill your children out of poverty; We will provide for you and them. And do not approach immoralities - what is apparent of them and what is concealed. And do not kill the soul which Allah has forbidden [to be killed] except by [legal] right. This has He instructed you that you may use reason."

152. And do not approach the orphan's property except in a way that is best until he reaches maturity. And give full measure and weight in justice. We do not charge any soul except [with that within] its capacity. And when you testify, be just, even if [it concerns] a near relative. And the covenant of Allah fulfill. This has He instructed you that you may remember.

153. And, [moreover], this is My path, which is straight, so follow it; and do not follow [other] ways, for you will be separated from His way. This has He instructed you that you may become righteous.

154. Then We gave Moses the Scripture, making complete [Our favor] upon the one who did good and as a detailed explanation of all things and as guidance and mercy that perhaps in [the matter of] the meeting with their Lord they would believe.

155. And this [Qur'an] is a Book We have revealed [which is] blessed, so follow it and fear Allah that you may receive mercy.

156. [We revealed it] lest you say, "The Scripture was only sent down to two groups before us, but we were of their study unaware,"

157. Or lest you say, "If only the Scripture had been revealed to us, we would have been better guided than they." So there has [now] come to you a clear evidence from your Lord and a guidance and mercy. Then who is more unjust than one who denies the verses of Allah and turns away from them? We will recompense those who turn away from Our verses with the worst of punishment for their having turned away.

158. Do they [then] wait for anything except that the angels should come to them or your Lord should come or that there come some of the signs of your Lord? The Day that some of the signs of your Lord will come no soul will benefit from its faith as long as it had not believed before or had earned through its faith some good. Say, "Wait. Indeed, we [also] are waiting."

159. Indeed, those who have divided their religion and become sects - you, [O Muhammad], are not [associated] with them in anything. Their affair is only [left] to Allah; then He will inform them about what they used to do.

160. Whoever comes [on the Day of Judgement] with a good deed will have ten times the like thereof [to his credit], and whoever comes with an evil deed will not be recompensed except the like thereof; and they will not be wronged.

161. Say, "Indeed, my Lord has guided me to a straight path - a correct religion - the way of Abraham, inclining toward truth. And he was not among those who associated others with Allah."

162. Say, "Indeed, my prayer, my rites of sacrifice, my living and my dying are for Allah, Lord of the worlds.

163. No partner has He. And this I have been commanded, and I am the first [among you] of the Muslims."

164. Say, "Is it other than Allah I should desire as a lord while He is the Lord of all things? And every soul earns not [blame] except against itself, and no bearer of burdens will bear the burden of another. Then to your Lord is your return, and He will inform you concerning that over which you used to differ."

165. And it is He who has made you successors upon the earth and has raised some of you above others in degrees [of rank] that He may try you through what He has given you. Indeed, your Lord is swift in penalty; but indeed, He is Forgiving and Merciful.

| Verses: 206 | **Surah 07 Al-A'raaf** | Makki |

In the name of Allah, the Entirely Merciful, the Especially Merciful.

01. Alif, Lam, Meem, Sad.

02. [This is] a Book revealed to you, [O Muhammad] - so let there not be in your breast distress therefrom - that you may warn thereby and as a reminder to the believers.

03. Follow, [O mankind], what has been revealed to you from your Lord and do not follow other than Him any allies. Little do you remember.

04. And how many cities have We destroyed, and Our punishment came to them at night or while they were sleeping at noon.

05. And their declaration when Our punishment came to them was only that they said, "Indeed, we were wrongdoers!"

06. Then We will surely question those to whom [a message] was sent, and We will surely question the messengers.

07. Then We will surely relate [their deeds] to them with knowledge, and We were not [at all] absent.

08. And the weighing [of deeds] that Day will be the truth. So those whose scales are heavy - it is they who will be the successful.

09. And those whose scales are light - they are the ones who will lose themselves for what injustice they were doing toward Our verses.

10. And We have certainly established you upon the earth and made for you therein ways of livelihood. Little are you grateful.

11. And We have certainly created you, [O Mankind], and given you [human] form. Then We said to the angels, "Prostrate to Adam"; so they prostrated, except for Iblees. He was not of those who prostrated.

12. [Allah] said, "What prevented you from prostrating when I commanded you?" [Satan] said, "I am better than him. You created me from fire and created him from clay."

13. [Allah] said, "Descend from Paradise, for it is not for you to be arrogant therein. So get out; indeed, you are of the debased."

14. [Satan] said, "Reprieve me until the Day they are resurrected."

15. [Allah] said, "Indeed, you are of those reprieved."

16. [Satan] said, "Because You have put me in error, I will surely sit in wait for them on Your straight path.

17. Then I will come to them from before them and from behind them and on their right and on their left, and You will not find most of them grateful [to You]."
18. [Allah] said, "Get out of Paradise, reproached and expelled. Whoever follows you among them - I will surely fill Hell with you, all together."
19. And "O Adam, dwell, you and your wife, in Paradise and eat from wherever you will but do not approach this tree, lest you be among the wrongdoers."
20. But Satan whispered to them to make apparent to them that which was concealed from them of their private parts. He said, "Your Lord did not forbid you this tree except that you become angels or become of the immortal."
21. And he swore [by Allah] to them, "Indeed, I am to you from among the sincere advisors."
22. So he made them fall, through deception. And when they tasted of the tree, their private parts became apparent to them, and they began to fasten together over themselves from the leaves of Paradise. And their Lord called to them, "Did I not forbid you from that tree and tell you that Satan is to you a clear enemy?"
23. They said, "Our Lord, we have wronged ourselves, and if You do not forgive us and have mercy upon us, we will surely be among the losers."
24. [Allah] said, "Descend, being to one another enemies. And for you on the earth is a place of settlement and enjoyment for a time."
25. He said, "Therein you will live, and therein you will die, and from it you will be brought forth."
26. O children of Adam, We have bestowed upon you clothing to conceal your private parts and as adornment. But the clothing of righteousness - that is best. That is from the signs of Allah that perhaps they will remember.
27. O children of Adam, let not Satan tempt you as he removed your parents from Paradise, stripping them of their clothing to show them their private parts. Indeed, he sees you, he and his tribe, from where you do not see them. Indeed, We have made the devils allies to those who do not believe.
28. And when they commit an immorality, they say, "We found our fathers doing it, and Allah has ordered us to do it." Say, "Indeed,

Allah does not order immorality. Do you say about Allah that which you do not know?"

29. Say, [O Muhammad], "My Lord has ordered justice and that you maintain yourselves [in worship of Him] at every place [or time] of prostration, and invoke Him, sincere to Him in religion." Just as He originated you, you will return [to life] -

30. A group [of you] He guided, and a group deserved [to be in] error. Indeed, they had taken the devils as allies instead of Allah while they thought that they were guided.

31. O children of Adam, take your adornment at every masjid, and eat and drink, but be not excessive. Indeed, He likes not those who commit excess.

32. Say, "Who has forbidden the adornment of Allah which He has produced for His servants and the good [lawful] things of provision?" Say, "They are for those who believe during the worldly life [but] exclusively for them on the Day of Resurrection." Thus do We detail the verses for a people who know.

33. Say, "My Lord has only forbidden immoralities - what is apparent of them and what is concealed - and sin, and oppression without right, and that you associate with Allah that for which He has not sent down authority, and that you say about Allah that which you do not know."

34. And for every nation is a [specified] term. So when their time has come, they will not remain behind an hour, nor will they precede [it].

35. O children of Adam, if there come to you messengers from among you relating to you My verses, then whoever fears Allah and reforms - there will be no fear concerning them, nor will they grieve.

36. But the ones who deny Our verses and are arrogant toward them - those are the companions of the Fire; they will abide therein eternally.

37. And who is more unjust than one who invents about Allah a lie or denies His verses? Those will attain their portion of the decree until when Our messengers come to them to take them in death, they will say, "Where are those you used to invoke besides Allah?" They will say, "They have departed from us," and will bear witness against themselves that they were disbelievers.

38. [Allah] will say, "Enter among nations which had passed on

before you of jinn and mankind into the Fire." Every time a nation enters, it will curse its sister until, when they have all overtaken one another therein, the last of them will say about the first of them "Our Lord, these had misled us, so give them a double punishment of the Fire. He will say, "For each is double, but you do not know."

39. And the first of them will say to the last of them, "Then you had not any favor over us, so taste the punishment for what you used to earn."

40. Indeed, those who deny Our verses and are arrogant toward them - the gates of Heaven will not be opened for them, nor will they enter Paradise until a camel enters into the eye of a needle. And thus do We recompense the criminals.

41. They will have from Hell a bed and over them coverings [of fire]. And thus do We recompense the wrongdoers.

42. But those who believed and did righteous deeds - We charge no soul except [within] its capacity. Those are the companions of Paradise; they will abide therein eternally.

43. And We will have removed whatever is within their breasts of resentment, [while] flowing beneath them are rivers. And they will say, "Praise to Allah, who has guided us to this; and we would never have been guided if Allah had not guided us. Certainly the messengers of our Lord had come with the truth." And they will be called, "This is Paradise, which you have been made to inherit for what you used to do."

44. And the companions of Paradise will call out to the companions of the Fire, "We have already found what our Lord promised us to be true. Have you found what your Lord promised to be true?" They will say, "Yes." Then an announcer will announce among them, "The curse of Allah shall be upon the wrongdoers."

45. Who averted [people] from the way of Allah and sought to make it [seem] deviant while they were, concerning the Hereafter, disbelievers.

46. And between them will be a partition, and on [its] elevations are men who recognize all by their mark. And they call out to the companions of Paradise, "Peace be upon you." They have not [yet] entered it, but they long intensely.

47. And when their eyes are turned toward the companions of the Fire, they say, "Our Lord, do not place us with the wrongdoing people."

48. And the companions of the Elevations will call to men [within Hell] whom they recognize by their mark, saying, "Of no avail to you was your gathering and [the fact] that you were arrogant."

49. [Allah will say], "Are these the ones whom you [inhabitants of Hell] swore that Allah would never offer them mercy? Enter Paradise, [O People of the Elevations]. No fear will there be concerning you, nor will you grieve."

50. And the companions of the Fire will call to the companions of Paradise, "Pour upon us some water or from whatever Allah has provided you." They will say, "Indeed, Allah has forbidden them both to the disbelievers."

51. Who took their religion as distraction and amusement and whom the worldly life deluded." So today We will forget them just as they forgot the meeting of this Day of theirs and for having rejected Our verses.

52. And We had certainly brought them a Book which We detailed by knowledge - as guidance and mercy to a people who believe.

53. Do they await except its result? The Day its result comes those who had ignored it before will say, "The messengers of our Lord had come with the truth, so are there [now] any intercessors to intercede for us or could we be sent back to do other than we used to do?" They will have lost themselves, and lost from them is what they used to invent.

54. Indeed, your Lord is Allah, who created the heavens and earth in six days and then established Himself above the Throne. He covers the night with the day, [another night] chasing it rapidly; and [He created] the sun, the moon, and the stars, subjected by His command. Unquestionably, His is the creation and the command; blessed is Allah, Lord of the worlds.

55. Call upon your Lord in humility and privately; indeed, He does not like transgressors.

56. And cause not corruption upon the earth after its reformation. And invoke Him in fear and aspiration. Indeed, the mercy of Allah is near to the doers of good.

57. And it is He who sends the winds as good tidings before His mercy until, when they have carried heavy rainclouds, We drive them to a dead land and We send down rain therein and bring forth thereby [some] of all the fruits. Thus will We bring forth the dead; perhaps you may be reminded.

58. And the good land - its vegetation emerges by permission of its Lord; but that which is bad - nothing emerges except sparsely, with difficulty. Thus do We diversify the signs for a people who are grateful.

59. We had certainly sent Noah to his people, and he said, "O my people, worship Allah; you have no deity other than Him. Indeed, I fear for you the punishment of a tremendous Day."

60. Said the eminent among his people, "Indeed, we see you in clear error."

61. [Noah] said, "O my people, there is not error in me, but I am a messenger from the Lord of the worlds."

62. I convey to you the messages of my Lord and advise you; and I know from Allah what you do not know.

63. Then do you wonder that there has come to you a reminder from your Lord through a man from among you, that he may warn you and that you may fear Allah so you might receive mercy."

64. But they denied him, so We saved him and those who were with him in the ship. And We drowned those who denied Our signs. Indeed, they were a blind people.

65. And to the 'Aad [We sent] their brother Hud. He said, "O my people, worship Allah; you have no deity other than Him. Then will you not fear Him?"

66. Said the eminent ones who disbelieved among his people, "Indeed, we see you in foolishness, and indeed, we think you are of the liars."

67. [Hud] said, "O my people, there is not foolishness in me, but I am a messenger from the Lord of the worlds."

68. I convey to you the messages of my Lord, and I am to you a trustworthy adviser.

69. Then do you wonder that there has come to you a reminder from your Lord through a man from among you, that he may warn you? And remember when He made you successors after the people of Noah and increased you in stature extensively. So remember the favors of Allah that you might succeed."

70. They said, "Have you come to us that we should worship Allah alone and leave what our fathers have worshipped? Then bring us what you promise us, if you should be of the truthful."

71. [Hud] said, "Already have defilement and anger fallen upon you from your Lord. Do you dispute with me concerning [mere] names you have named them, you and your fathers, for which Allah has not sent down any authority? Then wait; indeed, I am with you among those who wait."

72. So We saved him and those with him by mercy from Us. And We eliminated those who denied Our signs, and they were not [at all] believers.

73. And to the Thamud [We sent] their brother Salih. He said, "O my people, worship Allah; you have no deity other than Him. There has come to you clear evidence from your Lord. This is the she-camel of Allah [sent] to you as a sign. So leave her to eat within Allah's land and do not touch her with harm, lest there seize you a painful punishment.

74. And remember when He made you successors after the 'Aad and settled you in the land, [and] you take for yourselves palaces from its plains and carve from the mountains, homes. Then remember the favors of Allah and do not commit abuse on the earth, spreading corruption."

75. Said the eminent ones who were arrogant among his people to those who were oppressed - to those who believed among them, "Do you [actually] know that Salih is sent from his Lord?" They said, "Indeed we, in that with which he was sent, are believers."

76. Said those who were arrogant, "Indeed we, in that which you have believed, are disbelievers."

77. So they hamstrung the she-camel and were insolent toward the command of their Lord and said, "O Salih, bring us what you promise us, if you should be of the messengers."

78. So the earthquake seized them, and they became within their home [corpses] fallen prone.

79. And he turned away from them and said, "O my people, I had certainly conveyed to you the message of my Lord and advised you, but you do not like advisors."

80. And [We had sent] Lot when he said to his people, "Do you commit such immorality as no one has preceded you with from among the worlds?

81. Indeed, you approach men with desire, instead of women. Rather, you are a transgressing people."

82. But the answer of his people was only that they said, "Evict them from your city! Indeed, they are men who keep themselves pure."

83. So We saved him and his family, except for his wife; she was of those who remained [with the evildoers].

84. And We rained upon them a rain [of stones]. Then see how was the end of the criminals.

85. And to [the people of] Madyan [We sent] their brother Shu'ayb. He said, "O my people, worship Allah; you have no deity other than Him. There has come to you clear evidence from your Lord. So fulfill the measure and weight and do not deprive people of their due and cause not corruption upon the earth after its reformation. That is better for you, if you should be believers.

86. And do not sit on every path, threatening and averting from the way of Allah those who believe in Him, seeking to make it [seem] deviant. And remember when you were few and He increased you. And see how was the end of the corrupters.

87. And if there should be a group among you who has believed in that with which I have been sent and a group that has not believed, then be patient until Allah judges between us. And He is the best of judges."

88. Said the eminent ones who were arrogant among his people, "We will surely evict you, O Shu'ayb, and those who have believed with you from our city, or you must return to our religion." He said, "Even if we were unwilling?"

89. We would have invented against Allah a lie if we returned to your religion after Allah had saved us from it. And it is not for us to return to it except that Allah, our Lord, should will. Our Lord has encompassed all things in knowledge. Upon Allah we have relied. Our Lord, decide between us and our people in truth, and You are the best of those who give decision."

90. Said the eminent ones who disbelieved among his people, "If you should follow Shu'ayb, indeed, you would then be losers."

91. So the earthquake seized them, and they became within their home [corpses] fallen prone.

92. Those who denied Shu'ayb - it was as though they had never resided there. Those who denied Shu'ayb - it was they who were the losers.

93. And he turned away from them and said, "O my people, I had

certainly conveyed to you the messages of my Lord and advised you, so how could I grieve for a disbelieving people?"

94. And We sent to no city a prophet [who was denied] except that We seized its people with poverty and hardship that they might humble themselves [to Allah].

95. Then We exchanged in place of the bad [condition], good, until they increased [and prospered] and said, "Our fathers [also] were touched with hardship and ease." So We seized them suddenly while they did not perceive.

96. And if only the people of the cities had believed and feared Allah, We would have opened upon them blessings from the heaven and the earth; but they denied [the messengers], so We seized them for what they were earning."

97. Then, did the people of the cities feel secure from Our punishment coming to them at night while they were asleep?

98. Or did the people of the cities feel secure from Our punishment coming to them in the morning while they were at play?

99. Then did they feel secure from the plan of Allah? But no one feels secure from the plan of Allah except the losing people.

100. Has it not become clear to those who inherited the earth after its [previous] people that if We willed, We could afflict them for their sins? But We seal over their hearts so they do not hear.

101. Those cities - We relate to you, [O Muhammad], some of their news. And certainly did their messengers come to them with clear proofs, but they were not to believe in that which they had denied before. Thus does Allah seal over the hearts of the disbelievers.

102. And We did not find for most of them any covenant; but indeed, We found most of them defiantly disobedient.

103. Then We sent after them Moses with Our signs to Pharaoh and his establishment, but they were unjust toward them. So see how was the end of the corrupters.

104. And Moses said, "O Pharaoh, I am a messenger from the Lord of the worlds

105. [Who is] obligated not to say about Allah except the truth. I have come to you with clear evidence from your Lord, so send with me the Children of Israel."

106. [Pharaoh] said, "If you have come with a sign, then bring it forth, if you should be of the truthful."

107. So Moses threw his staff, and suddenly it was a serpent, manifest.
108. And he drew out his hand; thereupon it was white [with radiance] for the observers.
109. Said the eminent among the people of Pharaoh, "Indeed, this is a learned magician
110. Who wants to expel you from your land [through magic], so what do you instruct?"
111. They said, "Postpone [the matter of] him and his brother and send among the cities gatherers
112. Who will bring you every learned magician."
113. And the magicians came to Pharaoh. They said, "Indeed for us is a reward if we are the predominant."
114. He said, "Yes, and, [moreover], you will be among those made near [to me]."
115. They said, "O Moses, either you throw [your staff], or we will be the ones to throw [first]."
116. He said, "Throw," and when they threw, they bewitched the eyes of the people and struck terror into them, and they presented a great [feat of] magic.
117. And We inspired to Moses, "Throw your staff," and at once it devoured what they were falsifying.
118. So the truth was established, and abolished was what they were doing.
119. And Pharaoh and his people were overcome right there and became debased.
120. And the magicians fell down in prostration [to Allah].
121. They said, "We have believed in the Lord of the worlds,
122. The Lord of Moses and Aaron."
123. Said Pharaoh, "You believed in him before I gave you permission. Indeed, this is a conspiracy which you conspired in the city to expel therefrom its people. But you are going to know.
124. I will surely cut off your hands and your feet on opposite sides; then I will surely crucify you all."
125. They said, "Indeed, to our Lord we will return.
126. And you do not resent us except because we believed in the signs of our Lord when they came to us. Our Lord, pour upon us patience and let us die as Muslims [in submission to You]."

127. And the eminent among the people of Pharaoh said," Will you leave Moses and his people to cause corruption in the land and abandon you and your gods?" [Pharaoh] said, "We will kill their sons and keep their women alive; and indeed, we are subjugators over them."

128. Said Moses to his people, "Seek help through Allah and be patient. Indeed, the earth belongs to Allah. He causes to inherit it whom He wills of His servants. And the [best] outcome is for the righteous."

129. They said, "We have been harmed before you came to us and after you have come to us." He said, "Perhaps your Lord will destroy your enemy and grant you succession in the land and see how you will do."

130. And We certainly seized the people of Pharaoh with years of famine and a deficiency in fruits that perhaps they would be reminded.

131. But when good came to them, they said, "This is ours [by right]." And if a bad [condition] struck them, they saw an evil omen in Moses and those with him. Unquestionably, their fortune is with Allah, but most of them do not know.

132. And they said, "No matter what sign you bring us with which to bewitch us, we will not be believers in you."

133. So We sent upon them the flood and locusts and lice and frogs and blood as distinct signs, but they were arrogant and were a criminal people.

134. And when the punishment descended upon them, they said, "O Moses, invoke for us your Lord by what He has promised you. If you [can] remove the punishment from us, we will surely believe you, and we will send with you the Children of Israel."

135. But when We removed the punishment from them until a term which they were to reach, then at once they broke their word.

136. So We took retribution from them, and We drowned them in the sea because they denied Our signs and were heedless of them.

137. And We caused the people who had been oppressed to inherit the eastern regions of the land and the western ones, which We had blessed. And the good word of your Lord was fulfilled for the Children of Israel because of what they had patiently endured. And We destroyed [all] that Pharaoh and his people were producing and what they had been building.

138. And We took the Children of Israel across the sea; then they came upon a people intent in devotion to [some] idols of theirs. They said, "O Moses, make for us a god just as they have gods." He said, "Indeed, you are a people behaving ignorantly.

139. Indeed, those [worshippers] - destroyed is that in which they are [engaged], and worthless is whatever they were doing."

140. He said, "Is it other than Allah I should desire for you as a god while He has preferred you over the worlds?"

141. And [recall, O Children of Israel], when We saved you from the people of Pharaoh, [who were] afflicting you with the worst torment - killing your sons and keeping your women alive. And in that was a great trial from your Lord.

142. And We made an appointment with Moses for thirty nights and perfected them by [the addition of] ten; so the term of his Lord was completed as forty nights. And Moses said to his brother Aaron, "Take my place among my people, do right [by them], and do not follow the way of the corrupters."

143. And when Moses arrived at Our appointed time and his Lord spoke to him, he said, "My Lord, show me [Yourself] that I may look at You." [Allah] said, "You will not see Me, but look at the mountain; if it should remain in place, then you will see Me." But when his Lord appeared to the mountain, He rendered it level, and Moses fell unconscious. And when he awoke, he said, "Exalted are You! I have repented to You, and I am the first of the believers."

144. [Allah] said, "O Moses, I have chosen you over the people with My messages and My words [to you]. So take what I have given you and be among the grateful."

145. And We wrote for him on the tablets [something] of all things - instruction and explanation for all things, [saying], "Take them with determination and order your people to take the best of it. I will show you the home of the defiantly disobedient."

146. I will turn away from My signs those who are arrogant upon the earth without right; and if they should see every sign, they will not believe in it. And if they see the way of consciousness, they will not adopt it as a way; but if they see the way of error, they will adopt it as a way. That is because they have denied Our signs and they were heedless of them.

147. Those who denied Our signs and the meeting of the Hereafter -

their deeds have become worthless. Are they recompensed except for what they used to do?

148. And the people of Moses made, after [his departure], from their ornaments a calf - an image having a lowing sound. Did they not see that it could neither speak to them nor guide them to a way? They took it [for worship], and they were wrongdoers.

149. And when regret overcame them and they saw that they had gone astray, they said, "If our Lord does not have mercy upon us and forgive us, we will surely be among the losers."

150. And when Moses returned to his people, angry and grieved, he said, "How wretched is that by which you have replaced me after [my departure]. Were you impatient over the matter of your Lord?" And he threw down the tablets and seized his brother by [the hair of] his head, pulling him toward him. [Aaron] said, "O son of my mother, indeed the people oppressed me and were about to kill me, so let not the enemies rejoice over me and do not place me among the wrongdoing people."

151. [Moses] said, "My Lord, forgive me and my brother and admit us into Your mercy, for You are the most merciful of the merciful."

152. Indeed, those who took the calf [for worship] will obtain anger from their Lord and humiliation in the life of this world, and thus do We recompense the inventors [of falsehood].

153. But those who committed misdeeds and then repented after them and believed - indeed your Lord, thereafter, is Forgiving and Merciful.

154. And when the anger subsided in Moses, he took up the tablets; and in their inscription was guidance and mercy for those who are fearful of their Lord.

155. And Moses chose from his people seventy men for Our appointment. And when the earthquake seized them, he said, "My Lord, if You had willed, You could have destroyed them before and me [as well]. Would You destroy us for what the foolish among us have done? This is not but Your trial by which You send astray whom You will and guide whom You will. You are our Protector, so forgive us and have mercy upon us; and You are the best of forgivers.

156. And decree for us in this world [that which is] good and [also] in the Hereafter; indeed, we have turned back to You." [Allah] said, "My punishment - I afflict with it whom I will, but My mercy

encompasses all things." So I will decree it [especially] for those who fear Me and give zakah and those who believe in Our verses -

157. Those who follow the Messenger, the unlettered prophet, whom they find written in what they have of the Torah and the Gospel, who enjoins upon them what is right and forbids them what is wrong and makes lawful for them the good things and prohibits for them the evil and relieves them of their burden and the shackles which were upon them. So they who have believed in him, honored him, supported him and followed the light which was sent down with him - it is those who will be the successful.

158. Say, [O Muhammad], "O mankind, indeed I am the Messenger of Allah to you all, [from Him] to whom belongs the dominion of the heavens and the earth. There is no deity except Him; He gives life and causes death." So believe in Allah and His Messenger, the unlettered prophet, who believes in Allah and His words, and follow him that you may be guided.

159. And among the people of Moses is a community which guides by truth and by it establishes justice.

160. And We divided them into twelve descendant tribes [as distinct] nations. And We inspired to Moses when his people implored him for water, "Strike with your staff the stone," and there gushed forth from it twelve springs. Every people knew its watering place. And We shaded them with clouds and sent down upon them manna and quails, [saying], "Eat from the good things with which We have provided you." And they wronged Us not, but they were [only] wronging themselves.

161. And [mention, O Muhammad], when it was said to them, "Dwell in this city and eat from it wherever you will and say, 'Relieve us of our burdens,' and enter the gate bowing humbly; We will [then] forgive you your sins. We will increase the doers of good [in goodness and reward]."

162. But those who wronged among them changed [the words] to a statement other than that which had been said to them. So We sent upon them a punishment from the sky for the wrong that they were doing.

163. And ask them about the town that was by the sea - when they transgressed in [the matter of] the sabbath - when their fish came to them openly on their sabbath day, and the day they

had no sabbath they did not come to them. Thus did We give them trial because they were defiantly disobedient.

164. And when a community among them said, "Why do you advise [or warn] a people whom Allah is [about] to destroy or to punish with a severe punishment?" they [the advisors] said, "To be absolved before your Lord and perhaps they may fear Him."

165. And when they forgot that by which they had been reminded, We saved those who had forbidden evil and seized those who wronged, with a wretched punishment, because they were defiantly disobeying.

166. So when they were insolent about that which they had been forbidden, We said to them, "Be apes, despised."

167. And [mention] when your Lord declared that He would surely [continue to] send upon them until the Day of Resurrection those who would afflict them with the worst torment. Indeed, your Lord is swift in penalty; but indeed, He is Forgiving and Merciful.

168. And We divided them throughout the earth into nations. Of them some were righteous, and of them some were otherwise. And We tested them with good [times] and bad that perhaps they would return [to obedience].

169. And there followed them successors who inherited the Scripture [while] taking the commodities of this lower life and saying, "It will be forgiven for us." And if an offer like it comes to them, they will [again] take it. Was not the covenant of the Scripture taken from them that they would not say about Allah except the truth, and they studied what was in it? And the home of the Hereafter is better for those who fear Allah, so will you not use reason?

170. But those who hold fast to the Book and establish prayer - indeed, We will not allow to be lost the reward of the reformers.

171. And [mention] when We raised the mountain above them as if it was a dark cloud and they were certain that it would fall upon them, [and Allah said], "Take what We have given you with determination and remember what is in it that you might fear Allah."

172. And [mention] when your Lord took from the children of Adam - from their loins - their descendants and made them testify of themselves, [saying to them], "Am I not your Lord?" They said,

"Yes, we have testified." [This] - lest you should say on the day of Resurrection, "Indeed, we were of this unaware."

173. Or [lest] you say, "It was only that our fathers associated [others in worship] with Allah before, and we were but descendants after them. Then would You destroy us for what the falsifiers have done?"

174. And thus do We [explain in] detail the verses, and perhaps they will return.

175. And recite to them, [O Muhammad], the news of him to whom we gave [knowledge of] Our signs, but he detached himself from them; so Satan pursued him, and he became of the deviators.

176. And if We had willed, we could have elevated him thereby, but he adhered [instead] to the earth and followed his own desire. So his example is like that of the dog: if you chase him, he pants, or if you leave him, he [still] pants. That is the example of the people who denied Our signs. So relate the stories that perhaps they will give thought.

177. How evil an example [is that of] the people who denied Our signs and used to wrong themselves.

178. Whoever Allah guides - he is the [rightly] guided; and whoever He sends astray - it is those who are the losers.

179. And We have certainly created for Hell many of the jinn and mankind. They have hearts with which they do not understand, they have eyes with which they do not see, and they have ears with which they do not hear. Those are like livestock; rather, they are more astray. It is they who are the heedless.

180. And to Allah belong the best names, so invoke Him by them. And leave [the company of] those who practice deviation concerning His names. They will be recompensed for what they have been doing.

181. And among those We created is a community which guides by truth and thereby establishes justice.

182. But those who deny Our signs - We will progressively lead them [to destruction] from where they do not know.

183. And I will give them time. Indeed, my plan is firm.

184. Then do they not give thought? There is in their companion [Muhammad] no madness. He is not but a clear warner.

185. Do they not look into the realm of the heavens and the earth and everything that Allah has created and [think] that perhaps their appointed time has come near? So in what statement hereafter will they believe?

186. Whoever Allah sends astray - there is no guide for him. And He leaves them in their transgression, wandering blindly.

187. They ask you, [O Muhammad], about the Hour: when is its arrival? Say, "Its knowledge is only with my Lord. None will reveal its time except Him. It lays heavily upon the heavens and the earth. It will not come upon you except unexpectedly." They ask you as if you are familiar with it. Say, "Its knowledge is only with Allah, but most of the people do not know."

188. Say, "I hold not for myself [the power of] benefit or harm, except what Allah has willed. And if I knew the unseen, I could have acquired much wealth, and no harm would have touched me. I am not except a warner and a bringer of good tidings to a people who believe."

189. It is He who created you from one soul and created from it its mate that he might dwell in security with her. And when he covers her, she carries a light burden and continues therein. And when it becomes heavy, they both invoke Allah, their Lord, "If You should give us a good [child], we will surely be among the grateful."

190. But when He gives them a good [child], they ascribe partners to Him concerning that which He has given them. Exalted is Allah above what they associate with Him.

191. Do they associate with Him those who create nothing and they are [themselves] created?

192. And the false deities are unable to [give] them help, nor can they help themselves.

193. And if you [believers] invite them to guidance, they will not follow you. It is all the same for you whether you invite them or you are silent.

194. Indeed, those you [polytheists] call upon besides Allah are servants like you. So call upon them and let them respond to you, if you should be truthful.

195. Do they have feet by which they walk? Or do they have hands by which they strike? Or do they have eyes by which they see? Or do they have ears by which they hear? Say, [O Muhammad], "Call your 'partners' and then conspire against me and give me no respite.

196. Indeed, my protector is Allah, who has sent down the Book; and He is an ally to the righteous.

197. And those you call upon besides Him are unable to help you, nor can they help themselves."

198. And if you invite them to guidance, they do not hear; and you see them looking at you while they do not see.

199. Take what is given freely, enjoin what is good, and turn away from the ignorant.

200. And if an evil suggestion comes to you from Satan, then seek refuge in Allah. Indeed, He is Hearing and Knowing.

201. Indeed, those who fear Allah - when an impulse touches them from Satan, they remember [Him] and at once they have insight.

202. But their brothers - the devils increase them in error; then they do not stop short.

203. And when you, [O Muhammad], do not bring them a sign, they say, "Why have you not contrived it?" Say, "I only follow what is revealed to me from my Lord. This [Qur'an] is enlightenment from your Lord and guidance and mercy for a people who believe."

204. So when the Qur'an is recited, then listen to it and pay attention that you may receive mercy.

205. And remember your Lord within yourself in humility and in fear without being apparent in speech - in the mornings and the evenings. And do not be among the heedless.

206. Indeed, those who are near your Lord are not prevented by arrogance from His worship, and they exalt Him, and to Him they prostrate.

| Verses: 75 | **Surah 08 Al-Anfaal** | Madani |

In the name of Allah, the Entirely Merciful, the Especially Merciful.

01. They ask you, [O Muhammad], about the bounties [of war]. Say, "The [decision concerning] bounties is for Allah and the Messenger." So fear Allah and amend that which is between you and obey Allah and His Messenger, if you should be believers.

02. The believers are only those who, when Allah is mentioned, their hearts become fearful, and when His verses are recited to them, it increases them in faith; and upon their Lord they rely -

03. The ones who establish prayer, and from what We have provided them, they spend.

04. Those are the believers, truly. For them are degrees [of high position] with their Lord and forgiveness and noble provision.

05. [It is] just as when your Lord brought you out of your home [for the battle of Badr] in truth, while indeed, a party among the believers were unwilling,

06. Arguing with you concerning the truth after it had become clear, as if they were being driven toward death while they were looking on.

07. [Remember, O believers], when Allah promised you one of the two groups - that it would be yours - and you wished that the unarmed one would be yours. But Allah intended to establish the truth by His words and to eliminate the disbelievers

08. That He should establish the truth and abolish falsehood, even if the criminals disliked it.

09. [Remember] when you asked help of your Lord, and He answered you, "Indeed, I will reinforce you with a thousand from the angels, following one another."

10. And Allah made it not but good tidings and so that your hearts would be assured thereby. And victory is not but from Allah. Indeed, Allah is Exalted in Might and Wise.

11. [Remember] when He overwhelmed you with drowsiness [giving] security from Him and sent down upon you from the sky, rain by which to purify you and remove from you the evil [suggestions] of Satan and to make steadfast your hearts and plant firmly thereby your feet.

12. [Remember] when your Lord inspired to the angels, "I am with

you, so strengthen those who have believed. I will cast terror into the hearts of those who disbelieved, so strike [them] upon the necks and strike from them every fingertip."

13. That is because they opposed Allah and His Messenger. And whoever opposes Allah and His Messenger - indeed, Allah is severe in penalty.

14. "That [is yours], so taste it." And indeed for the disbelievers is the punishment of the Fire.

15. O you who have believed, when you meet those who disbelieve advancing [for battle], do not turn to them your backs [in flight].

16. And whoever turns his back to them on such a day, unless swerving [as a strategy] for war or joining [another] company, has certainly returned with anger [upon him] from Allah, and his refuge is Hell - and wretched is the destination.

17. And you did not kill them, but it was Allah who killed them. And you threw not, [O Muhammad], when you threw, but it was Allah who threw that He might test the believers with a good test. Indeed, Allah is Hearing and Knowing.

18. That [is so], and [also] that Allah will weaken the plot of the disbelievers.

19. If you [disbelievers] seek the victory - the defeat has come to you. And if you desist [from hostilities], it is best for you; but if you return [to war], We will return, and never will you be availed by your [large] company at all, even if it should increase; and [that is] because Allah is with the believers.

20. O you who have believed, obey Allah and His Messenger and do not turn from him while you hear [his order].

21. And do not be like those who say, "We have heard," while they do not hear.

22. Indeed, the worst of living creatures in the sight of Allah are the deaf and dumb who do not use reason.

23. Had Allah known any good in them, He would have made them hear. And if He had made them hear, they would [still] have turned away, while they were refusing.

24. O you who have believed, respond to Allah and to the Messenger when he calls you to that which gives you life. And know that Allah intervenes between a man and his heart and that to Him you will be gathered.

25. And fear a trial which will not strike those who have wronged among you exclusively, and know that Allah is severe in penalty.

26. And remember when you were few and oppressed in the land, fearing that people might abduct you, but He sheltered you, supported you with His victory, and provided you with good things - that you might be grateful.

27. O you who have believed, do not betray Allah and the Messenger or betray your trusts while you know [the consequence].

28. And know that your properties and your children are but a trial and that Allah has with Him a great reward.

29. O you who have believed, if you fear Allah, He will grant you a criterion and will remove from you your misdeeds and forgive you. And Allah is the possessor of great bounty.

30. And [remember, O Muhammad], when those who disbelieved plotted against you to restrain you or kill you or evict you [from Makkah]. But they plan, and Allah plans. And Allah is the best of planners.

31. And when Our verses are recited to them, they say, "We have heard. If we willed, we could say [something] like this. This is not but legends of the former peoples."

32. And [remember] when they said, "O Allah, if this should be the truth from You, then rain down upon us stones from the sky or bring us a painful punishment."

33. But Allah would not punish them while you, [O Muhammad], are among them, and Allah would not punish them while they seek forgiveness.

34. But why should Allah not punish them while they obstruct [people] from al-Masjid al- Haram and they were not [fit to be] its guardians? Its [true] guardians are not but the righteous, but most of them do not know.

35. And their prayer at the House was not except whistling and handclapping. So taste the punishment for what you disbelieved.

36. Indeed, those who disbelieve spend their wealth to avert [people] from the way of Allah. So they will spend it; then it will be for them a [source of] regret; then they will be overcome. And those who have disbelieved - unto Hell they will be gathered.

37. [This is] so that Allah may distinguish the wicked from the good and place the wicked some of them upon others and heap them

all together and put them into Hell. It is those who are the losers.

38. Say to those who have disbelieved [that] if they cease, what has previously occurred will be forgiven for them. But if they return [to hostility] - then the precedent of the former [rebellious] peoples has already taken place.

39. And fight them until there is no fitnah and [until] the religion, all of it, is for Allah. And if they cease - then indeed, Allah is Seeing of what they do.

40. But if they turn away - then know that Allah is your protector. Excellent is the protector, and Excellent is the helper.

41. And know that anything you obtain of war booty - then indeed, for Allah is one fifth of it and for the Messenger and for [his] near relatives and the orphans, the needy, and the [stranded] traveler, if you have believed in Allah and in that which We sent down to Our Servant on the day of criterion - the day when the two armies met. And Allah, over all things, is competent.

42. [Remember] when you were on the near side of the valley, and they were on the farther side, and the caravan was lower [in position] than you. If you had made an appointment [to meet], you would have missed the appointment. But [it was] so that Allah might accomplish a matter already destined - that those who perished [through disbelief] would perish upon evidence and those who lived [in faith] would live upon evidence; and indeed, Allah is Hearing and Knowing.

43. [Remember, O Muhammad], when Allah showed them to you in your dream as few; and if He had shown them to you as many, you [believers] would have lost courage and would have disputed in the matter [of whether to fight], but Allah saved [you from that]. Indeed, He is Knowing of that within the breasts.

44. And [remember] when He showed them to you, when you met, as few in your eyes, and He made you [appear] as few in their eyes so that Allah might accomplish a matter already destined. And to Allah are [all] matters returned.

45. O you who have believed, when you encounter a company [from the enemy forces], stand firm and remember Allah much that you may be successful.

46. And obey Allah and His Messenger, and do not dispute and [thus] lose courage and [then] your strength would depart; and be patient. Indeed, Allah is with the patient.

47. And do not be like those who came forth from their homes insolently and to be seen by people and avert [them] from the way of Allah. And Allah is encompassing of what they do.

48. And [remember] when Satan made their deeds pleasing to them and said, "No one can overcome you today from among the people, and indeed, I am your protector." But when the two armies sighted each other, he turned on his heels and said, "Indeed, I am disassociated from you. Indeed, I see what you do not see; indeed I fear Allah. And Allah is severe in penalty."

49. [Remember] when the hypocrites and those in whose hearts was disease said, "Their religion has deluded those [Muslims]." But whoever relies upon Allah - then indeed, Allah is Exalted in Might and Wise.

50. And if you could but see when the angels take the souls of those who disbelieved... They are striking their faces and their backs and [saying], "Taste the punishment of the Burning Fire.

51. That is for what your hands have put forth [of evil] and because Allah is not ever unjust to His servants."

52. [Theirs is] like the custom of the people of Pharaoh and of those before them. They disbelieved in the signs of Allah, so Allah seized them for their sins. Indeed, Allah is Powerful and severe in penalty.

53. That is because Allah would not change a favor which He had bestowed upon a people until they change what is within themselves. And indeed, Allah is Hearing and Knowing.

54. [Theirs is] like the custom of the people of Pharaoh and of those before them. They denied the signs of their Lord, so We destroyed them for their sins, and We drowned the people of Pharaoh. And all [of them] were wrongdoers.

55. Indeed, the worst of living creatures in the sight of Allah are those who have disbelieved, and they will not [ever] believe -

56. The ones with whom you made a treaty but then they break their pledge every time, and they do not fear Allah.

57. So if you, [O Muhammad], gain dominance over them in war, disperse by [means of] them those behind them that perhaps they will be reminded.

58. If you [have reason to] fear from a people betrayal, throw [their treaty] back to them, [putting you] on equal terms. Indeed, Allah does not like traitors.

59. And let not those who disbelieve think they will escape. Indeed, they will not cause failure [to Allah].

60. And prepare against them whatever you are able of power and of steeds of war by which you may terrify the enemy of Allah and your enemy and others besides them whom you do not know [but] whom Allah knows. And whatever you spend in the cause of Allah will be fully repaid to you, and you will not be wronged.

61. And if they incline to peace, then incline to it [also] and rely upon Allah. Indeed, it is He who is the Hearing, the Knowing.

62. But if they intend to deceive you - then sufficient for you is Allah. It is He who supported you with His help and with the believers

63. And brought together their hearts. If you had spent all that is in the earth, you could not have brought their hearts together; but Allah brought them together. Indeed, He is Exalted in Might and Wise.

64. O Prophet, sufficient for you is Allah and for whoever follows you of the believers.

65. O Prophet, urge the believers to battle. If there are among you twenty [who are] steadfast, they will overcome two hundred. And if there are among you one hundred [who are] steadfast, they will overcome a thousand of those who have disbelieved because they are a people who do not understand.

66. Now, Allah has lightened [the hardship] for you, and He knows that among you is weakness. So if there are from you one hundred [who are] steadfast, they will overcome two hundred. And if there are among you a thousand, they will overcome two thousand by permission of Allah. And Allah is with the steadfast.

67. It is not for a prophet to have captives [of war] until he inflicts a massacre [upon Allah's enemies] in the land. Some Muslims desire the commodities of this world, but Allah desires [for you] the Hereafter. And Allah is Exalted in Might and Wise.

68. If not for a decree from Allah that preceded, you would have been touched for what you took by a great punishment.

69. So consume what you have taken of war booty [as being] lawful and good, and fear Allah. Indeed, Allah is Forgiving and Merciful.

70. O Prophet, say to whoever is in your hands of the captives, "If Allah knows [any] good in your hearts, He will give you [something] better than what was taken from you, and He will forgive you; and Allah is Forgiving and Merciful."

71. But if they intend to betray you - then they have already betrayed Allah before, and He empowered [you] over them. And Allah is Knowing and Wise.

72. Indeed, those who have believed and emigrated and fought with their wealth and lives in the cause of Allah and those who gave shelter and aided - they are allies of one another. But those who believed and did not emigrate - for you there is no guardianship of them until they emigrate. And if they seek help of you for the religion, then you must help, except against a people between yourselves and whom is a treaty. And Allah is Seeing of what you do.

73. And those who disbelieved are allies of one another. If you do not do so, there will be fitnah on earth and great corruption.

74. But those who have believed and emigrated and fought in the cause of Allah and those who gave shelter and aided - it is they who are the believers, truly. For them is forgiveness and noble provision.

75. And those who believed after [the initial emigration] and emigrated and fought with you - they are of you. But those of [blood] relationship are more entitled [to inheritance] in the decree of Allah. Indeed, Allah is Knowing of all things.

| Verses: 129 | Surah 09 At-Tawbah | Madani |

01. [This is a declaration of] disassociation, from Allah and His Messenger, to those with whom you had made a treaty among the polytheists.

02. So travel freely, [O disbelievers], throughout the land [during] four months but know that you cannot cause failure to Allah and that Allah will disgrace the disbelievers.

03. And [it is] an announcement from Allah and His Messenger to the people on the day of the greater pilgrimage that Allah is disassociated from the disbelievers, and [so is] His Messenger. So if you repent, that is best for you; but if you turn away - then know that you will not cause failure to Allah. And give tidings to those who disbelieve of a painful punishment.

04. Excepted are those with whom you made a treaty among the polytheists and then they have not been deficient toward you in anything or supported anyone against you; so complete for them their treaty until their term [has ended]. Indeed, Allah

loves the righteous [who fear Him].

05. And when the sacred months have passed, then kill the polytheists wherever you find them and capture them and besiege them and sit in wait for them at every place of ambush. But if they should repent, establish prayer, and give zakah, let them [go] on their way. Indeed, Allah is Forgiving and Merciful.

06. And if any one of the polytheists seeks your protection, then grant him protection so that he may hear the words of Allah. Then deliver him to his place of safety. That is because they are a people who do not know.

07. How can there be for the polytheists a treaty in the sight of Allah and with His Messenger, except for those with whom you made a treaty at al-Masjid al-Haram? So as long as they are upright toward you, be upright toward them. Indeed, Allah loves the righteous [who fear Him].

08. How [can there be a treaty] while, if they gain dominance over you, they do not observe concerning you any pact of kinship or covenant of protection? They satisfy you with their mouths, but their hearts refuse [compliance], and most of them are defiantly disobedient.

09. They have exchanged the signs of Allah for a small price and averted [people] from His way. Indeed, it was evil that they were doing.

10. They do not observe toward a believer any pact of kinship or covenant of protection. And it is they who are the transgressors.

11. But if they repent, establish prayer, and give zakah, then they are your brothers in religion; and We detail the verses for a people who know.

12. And if they break their oaths after their treaty and defame your religion, then fight the leaders of disbelief, for indeed, there are no oaths [sacred] to them; [fight them that] they might cease.

13. Would you not fight a people who broke their oaths and determined to expel the Messenger, and they had begun [the attack upon] you the first time? Do you fear them? But Allah has more right that you should fear Him, if you are [truly] believers.

14. Fight them; Allah will punish them by your hands and will disgrace them and give you victory over them and satisfy the breasts of a believing people

15. And remove the fury in the believers' hearts. And Allah turns in forgiveness to whom He wills; and Allah is Knowing and Wise.

16. Do you think that you will be left [as you are] while Allah has not yet made evident those among you who strive [for His cause] and do not take other than Allah, His Messenger and the believers as intimates? And Allah is Acquainted with what you do.

17. It is not for the polytheists to maintain the mosques of Allah [while] witnessing against themselves with disbelief. [For] those, their deeds have become worthless, and in the Fire they will abide eternally.

18. The mosques of Allah are only to be maintained by those who believe in Allah and the Last Day and establish prayer and give zakah and do not fear except Allah, for it is expected that those will be of the [rightly] guided.

19. Have you made the providing of water for the pilgrim and the maintenance of al-Masjid al-Haram equal to [the deeds of] one who believes in Allah and the Last Day and strives in the cause of Allah? They are not equal in the sight of Allah. And Allah does not guide the wrongdoing people.

20. The ones who have believed, emigrated and striven in the cause of Allah with their wealth and their lives are greater in rank in the sight of Allah. And it is those who are the attainers [of success].

21. Their Lord gives them good tidings of mercy from Him and approval and of gardens for them wherein is enduring pleasure.

22. [They will be] abiding therein forever. Indeed, Allah has with Him a great reward.

23. O you who have believed, do not take your fathers or your brothers as allies if they have preferred disbelief over belief. And whoever does so among you - then it is those who are the wrongdoers.

24. Say, [O Muhammad], "If your fathers, your sons, your brothers, your wives, your relatives, wealth which you have obtained, commerce wherein you fear decline, and dwellings with which you are pleased are more beloved to you than Allah and His Messenger and jihad in His cause, then wait until Allah executes His command. And Allah does not guide the defiantly disobedient people."

25. Allah has already given you victory in many regions and [even] on the day of Hunayn, when your great number pleased you, but it did not avail you at all, and the earth was confining for you with its vastness; then you turned back, fleeing.

26. Then Allah sent down His tranquillity upon His Messenger and

upon the believers and sent down soldiers angels whom you did not see and punished those who disbelieved. And that is the recompense of the disbelievers.

27. Then Allah will accept repentance after that for whom He wills; and Allah is Forgiving and Merciful.

28. O you who have believed, indeed the polytheists are unclean, so let them not approach al-Masjid al-Haram after this, their [final] year. And if you fear privation, Allah will enrich you from His bounty if He wills. Indeed, Allah is Knowing and Wise.

29. Fight those who do not believe in Allah or in the Last Day and who do not consider unlawful what Allah and His Messenger have made unlawful and who do not adopt the religion of truth from those who were given the Scripture - [fight] until they give the jizyah willingly while they are humbled.

30. The Jews say, "Ezra is the son of Allah "; and the Christians say, "The Messiah is the son of Allah." That is their statement from their mouths; they imitate the saying of those who disbelieved [before them]. May Allah destroy them; how are they deluded?

31. They have taken their scholars and monks as lords besides Allah, and [also] the Messiah, the son of Mary. And they were not commanded except to worship one God; there is no deity except Him. Exalted is He above whatever they associate with Him.

32. They want to extinguish the light of Allah with their mouths, but Allah refuses except to perfect His light, although the disbelievers dislike it.

33. It is He who has sent His Messenger with guidance and the religion of truth to manifest it over all religion, although they who associate others with Allah dislike it.

34. O you who have believed, indeed many of the scholars and the monks devour the wealth of people unjustly and avert [them] from the way of Allah. And those who hoard gold and silver and spend it not in the way of Allah - give them tidings of a painful punishment.

35. The Day when it will be heated in the fire of Hell and seared therewith will be their foreheads, their flanks, and their backs, [it will be said], "This is what you hoarded for yourselves, so taste what you used to hoard."

36. Indeed, the number of months with Allah is twelve [lunar] months in the register of Allah [from] the day He created the heavens and the earth; of these, four are sacred. That is the correct religion, so

do not wrong yourselves during them. And fight against the disbelievers collectively as they fight against you collectively. And know that Allah is with the righteous [who fear Him].

37. Indeed, the postponing [of restriction within sacred months] is an increase in disbelief by which those who have disbelieved are led [further] astray. They make it lawful one year and unlawful another year to correspond to the number made unlawful by Allah and [thus] make lawful what Allah has made unlawful. Made pleasing to them is the evil of their deeds; and Allah does not guide the disbelieving people.

38. O you who have believed, what is [the matter] with you that, when you are told to go forth in the cause of Allah, you adhere heavily to the earth? Are you satisfied with the life of this world rather than the Hereafter? But what is the enjoyment of worldly life compared to the Hereafter except a [very] little.

39. If you do not go forth, He will punish you with a painful punishment and will replace you with another people, and you will not harm Him at all. And Allah is over all things competent.

40. If you do not aid the Prophet - Allah has already aided him when those who disbelieved had driven him out [of Makkah] as one of two, when they were in the cave and he said to his companion, "Do not grieve; indeed Allah is with us." And Allah sent down his tranquillity upon him and supported him with angels you did not see and made the word of those who disbelieved the lowest, while the word of Allah - that is the highest. And Allah is Exalted in Might and Wise.

41. Go forth, whether light or heavy, and strive with your wealth and your lives in the cause of Allah. That is better for you, if you only knew.

42. Had it been an easy gain and a moderate trip, the hypocrites would have followed you, but distant to them was the journey. And they will swear by Allah, "If we were able, we would have gone forth with you," destroying themselves [through false oaths], and Allah knows that indeed they are liars.

43. May Allah pardon you, [O Muhammad]; why did you give them permission [to remain behind]? [You should not have] until it was evident to you who were truthful and you knew [who were] the liars.

44. Those who believe in Allah and the Last Day would not ask permission of you to be excused from striving with their wealth and their lives. And Allah is Knowing of those who fear Him.

45. Only those would ask permission of you who do not believe in Allah and the Last Day and whose hearts have doubted, and they, in their doubt, are hesitating.

46. And if they had intended to go forth, they would have prepared for it [some] preparation. But Allah disliked their being sent, so He kept them back, and they were told, "Remain [behind] with those who remain."

47. Had they gone forth with you, they would not have increased you except in confusion, and they would have been active among you, seeking [to cause] you fitnah. And among you are avid listeners to them. And Allah is Knowing of the wrongdoers.

48. They had already desired dissension before and had upset matters for you until the truth came and the ordinance of Allah appeared, while they were averse.

49. And among them is he who says, "Permit me [to remain at home] and do not put me to trial." Unquestionably, into trial they have fallen. And indeed, Hell will encompass the disbelievers.

50. If good befalls you, it distresses them; but if disaster strikes you, they say, "We took our matter [in hand] before," and turn away while they are rejoicing.

51. Say, "Never will we be struck except by what Allah has decreed for us; He is our protector." And upon Allah let the believers rely.

52. Say, "Do you await for us except one of the two best things while we await for you that Allah will afflict you with punishment from Himself or at our hands? So wait; indeed we, along with you, are waiting."

53. Say, "Spend willingly or unwillingly; never will it be accepted from you. Indeed, you have been a defiantly disobedient people."

54. And what prevents their expenditures from being accepted from them but that they have disbelieved in Allah and in His Messenger and that they come not to prayer except while they are lazy and that they do not spend except while they are unwilling.

55. So let not their wealth or their children impress you. Allah only intends to punish them through them in worldly life and that their souls should depart [at death] while they are disbelievers.

56. And they swear by Allah that they are from among you while they are not from among you; but they are a people who are afraid.

57. If they could find a refuge or some caves or any place to enter [and hide], they would turn to it while they run heedlessly.

58. And among them are some who criticize you concerning the [distribution of] charities. If they are given from them, they approve; but if they are not given from them, at once they become angry.

59. If only they had been satisfied with what Allah and His Messenger gave them and said, "Sufficient for us is Allah; Allah will give us of His bounty, and [so will] His Messenger; indeed, we are desirous toward Allah," [it would have been better for them].

60. Zakah expenditures are only for the poor and for the needy and for those employed to collect [zakah] and for bringing hearts together [for Islam] and for freeing captives [or slaves] and for those in debt and for the cause of Allah and for the [stranded] traveler - an obligation [imposed] by Allah. And Allah is Knowing and Wise.

61. And among them are those who abuse the Prophet and say, "He is an ear." Say, "[It is] an ear of goodness for you that believes in Allah and believes the believers and [is] a mercy to those who believe among you." And those who abuse the Messenger of Allah - for them is a painful punishment.

62. They swear by Allah to you [Muslims] to satisfy you. But Allah and His Messenger are more worthy for them to satisfy, if they should be believers.

63. Do they not know that whoever opposes Allah and His Messenger - that for him is the fire of Hell, wherein he will abide eternally? That is the great disgrace.

64. They hypocrites are apprehensive lest a surah be revealed about them, informing them of what is in their hearts. Say, "Mock [as you wish]; indeed, Allah will expose that which you fear."

65. And if you ask them, they will surely say, "We were only conversing and playing." Say, "Is it Allah and His verses and His Messenger that you were mocking?"

66. Make no excuse; you have disbelieved after your belief. If We pardon one faction of you - We will punish another faction because they were criminals.

67. The hypocrite men and hypocrite women are of one another. They enjoin what is wrong and forbid what is right and close their hands. They have forgotten Allah, so He has forgotten them [accordingly]. Indeed, the hypocrites - it is they who are the defiantly disobedient.

68. Allah has promised the hypocrite men and hypocrite women and the disbelievers the fire of Hell, wherein they will abide eternally. It is sufficient for them. And Allah has cursed them, and for them is an enduring punishment.

69. [You disbelievers are] like those before you; they were stronger than you in power and more abundant in wealth and children. They enjoyed their portion [of worldly enjoyment], and you have enjoyed your portion as those before you enjoyed their portion, and you have engaged [in vanities] like that in which they engaged. [It is] those whose deeds have become worthless in this world and in the Hereafter, and it is they who are the losers.

70. Has there not reached them the news of those before them - the people of Noah and [the tribes of] 'Aad and Thamud and the people of Abraham and the companions of Madyan and the towns overturned? Their messengers came to them with clear proofs. And Allah would never have wronged them, but they were wronging themselves.

71. The believing men and believing women are allies of one another. They enjoin what is right and forbid what is wrong and establish prayer and give zakah and obey Allah and His Messenger. Those - Allah will have mercy upon them. Indeed, Allah is Exalted in Might and Wise.

72. Allah has promised the believing men and believing women gardens beneath which rivers flow, wherein they abide eternally, and pleasant dwellings in gardens of perpetual residence; but approval from Allah is greater. It is that which is the great attainment.

73. O Prophet, fight against the disbelievers and the hypocrites and be harsh upon them. And their refuge is Hell, and wretched is the destination.

74. They swear by Allah that they did not say [anything against the Prophet] while they had said the word of disbelief and disbelieved after their [pretense of] Islam and planned that which they were not to attain. And they were not resentful except [for the fact] that Allah and His Messenger had enriched them of His bounty. So if they repent, it is better for them; but if they turn away, Allah will punish them with a painful punishment in this world and the Hereafter. And there will not be for them on earth any protector or helper.

75. And among them are those who made a covenant with Allah,

[saying], "If He should give us from His bounty, we will surely spend in charity, and we will surely be among the righteous."

76. But when he gave them from His bounty, they were stingy with it and turned away while they refused.

77. So He penalized them with hypocrisy in their hearts until the Day they will meet Him - because they failed Allah in what they promised Him and because they [habitually] used to lie.

78. Did they not know that Allah knows their secrets and their private conversations and that Allah is the Knower of the unseen?

79. Those who criticize the contributors among the believers concerning [their] charities and [criticize] the ones who find nothing [to spend] except their effort, so they ridicule them - Allah will ridicule them, and they will have a painful punishment.

80. Ask forgiveness for them, [O Muhammad], or do not ask forgiveness for them. If you should ask forgiveness for them seventy times - never will Allah forgive them. That is because they disbelieved in Allah and His Messenger, and Allah does not guide the defiantly disobedient people.

81. Those who remained behind rejoiced in their staying [at home] after [the departure of] the Messenger of Allah and disliked to strive with their wealth and their lives in the cause of Allah and said, "Do not go forth in the heat." Say, "The fire of Hell is more intensive in heat" - if they would but understand.

82. So let them laugh a little and [then] weep much as recompense for what they used to earn.

83. If Allah should return you to a faction of them [after the expedition] and then they ask your permission to go out [to battle], say, "You will not go out with me, ever, and you will never fight with me an enemy. Indeed, you were satisfied with sitting [at home] the first time, so sit [now] with those who stay behind."

84. And do not pray [the funeral prayer, O Muhammad], over any of them who has died - ever - or stand at his grave. Indeed, they disbelieved in Allah and His Messenger and died while they were defiantly disobedient.

85. And let not their wealth and their children impress you. Allah only intends to punish them through them in this world and that their souls should depart [at death] while they are disbelievers.

86. And when a surah was revealed [enjoining them] to believe in Allah and to fight with His Messenger, those of wealth among

them asked your permission [to stay back] and said, "Leave us to be with them who sit [at home]."

87. They were satisfied to be with those who stay behind, and their hearts were sealed over, so they do not understand.
88. But the Messenger and those who believed with him fought with their wealth and their lives. Those will have [all that is] good, and it is those who are the successful.
89. Allah has prepared for them gardens beneath which rivers flow, wherein they will abide eternally. That is the great attainment.
90. And those with excuses among the bedouins came to be permitted [to remain], and they who had lied to Allah and His Messenger sat [at home]. There will strike those who disbelieved among them a painful punishment.
91. There is not upon the weak or upon the ill or upon those who do not find anything to spend any discomfort when they are sincere to Allah and His Messenger. There is not upon the doers of good any cause [for blame]. And Allah is Forgiving and Merciful.
92. Nor [is there blame] upon those who, when they came to you that you might give them mounts, you said, "I can find nothing for you to ride upon." They turned back while their eyes overflowed with tears out of grief that they could not find something to spend [for the cause of Allah].
93. The cause [for blame] is only upon those who ask permission of you while they are rich. They are satisfied to be with those who stay behind, and Allah has sealed over their hearts, so they do not know.
94. They will make excuses to you when you have returned to them. Say, "Make no excuse - never will we believe you. Allah has already informed us of your news. And Allah will observe your deeds, and [so will] His Messenger; then you will be taken back to the Knower of the unseen and the witnessed, and He will inform you of what you used to do."
95. They will swear by Allah to you when you return to them that you would leave them alone. So leave them alone; indeed they are evil; and their refuge is Hell as recompense for what they had been earning.
96. They swear to you so that you might be satisfied with them. But if you should be satisfied with them - indeed, Allah is not satisfied with a defiantly disobedient people.

97. The bedouins are stronger in disbelief and hypocrisy and more likely not to know the limits of what [laws] Allah has revealed to His Messenger. And Allah is Knowing and Wise.

98. And among the bedouins are some who consider what they spend as a loss and await for you turns of misfortune. Upon them will be a misfortune of evil. And Allah is Hearing and Knowing.

99. But among the bedouins are some who believe in Allah and the Last Day and consider what they spend as means of nearness to Allah and of [obtaining] invocations of the Messenger. Unquestionably, it is a means of nearness for them. Allah will admit them to His mercy. Indeed, Allah is Forgiving and Merciful.

100. And the first forerunners [in the faith] among the Muhajireen and the Ansar and those who followed them with good conduct - Allah is pleased with them and they are pleased with Him, and He has prepared for them gardens beneath which rivers flow, wherein they will abide forever. That is the great attainment.

101. And among those around you of the bedouins are hypocrites, and [also] from the people of Madinah. They have become accustomed to hypocrisy. You, [O Muhammad], do not know them, [but] We know them. We will punish them twice [in this world]; then they will be returned to a great punishment.

102. And [there are] others who have acknowledged their sins. They had mixed a righteous deed with another that was bad. Perhaps Allah will turn to them in forgiveness. Indeed, Allah is Forgiving and Merciful.

103. Take, [O, Muhammad], from their wealth a charity by which you purify them and cause them increase, and invoke [Allah's blessings] upon them. Indeed, your invocations are reassurance for them. And Allah is Hearing and Knowing.

104. Do they not know that it is Allah who accepts repentance from His servants and receives charities and that it is Allah who is the Accepting of repentance, the Merciful?

105. And say, "Do [as you will], for Allah will see your deeds, and [so, will] His Messenger and the believers. And you will be returned to the Knower of the unseen and the witnessed, and He will inform you of what you used to do."

106. And [there are] others deferred until the command of Allah - whether He will punish them or whether He will forgive them. And Allah is Knowing and Wise.

107. And [there are] those [hypocrites] who took for themselves a mosque for causing harm and disbelief and division among the believers and as a station for whoever had warred against Allah and His Messenger before. And they will surely swear, "We intended only the best." And Allah testifies that indeed they are liars.

108. Do not stand [for prayer] within it - ever. A mosque founded on righteousness from the first day is more worthy for you to stand in. Within it are men who love to purify themselves; and Allah loves those who purify themselves.

109. Then is one who laid the foundation of his building on righteousness [with fear] from Allah and [seeking] His approval better or one who laid the foundation of his building on the edge of a bank about to collapse, so it collapsed with him into the fire of Hell? And Allah does not guide the wrongdoing people.

110. Their building which they built will not cease to be a [cause of] skepticism in their hearts until their hearts are stopped. And Allah is Knowing and Wise.

111. Indeed, Allah has purchased from the believers their lives and their properties [in exchange] for that they will have Paradise. They fight in the cause of Allah, so they kill and are killed. [It is] a true promise [binding] upon Him in the Torah and the Gospel and the Qur'an. And who is truer to his covenant than Allah? So rejoice in your transaction which you have contracted. And it is that which is the great attainment.

112. [Such believers are] the repentant, the worshippers, the praisers [of Allah], the travelers [for His cause], those who bow and prostrate [in prayer], those who enjoin what is right and forbid what is wrong, and those who observe the limits [set by] Allah. And give good tidings to the believers.

113. It is not for the Prophet and those who have believed to ask forgiveness for the polytheists, even if they were relatives, after it has become clear to them that they are companions of Hellfire.

114. And the request of forgiveness of Abraham for his father was only because of a promise he had made to him. But when it became apparent to Abraham that his father was an enemy to Allah, he disassociated himself from him. Indeed was Abraham compassionate and patient.

115. And Allah would not let a people stray after He has guided

them until He makes clear to them what they should avoid. Indeed, Allah is Knowing of all things.

116. Indeed, to Allah belongs the dominion of the heavens and the earth; He gives life and causes death. And you have not besides Allah any protector or any helper.

117. Allah has already forgiven the Prophet and the Muhajireen and the Ansar who followed him in the hour of difficulty after the hearts of a party of them had almost inclined [to doubt], and then He forgave them. Indeed, He was to them Kind and Merciful.

118. And [He also forgave] the three who were left behind [and regretted their error] to the point that the earth closed in on them in spite of its vastness and their souls confined them and they were certain that there is no refuge from Allah except in Him. Then He turned to them so they could repent. Indeed, Allah is the Accepting of repentance, the Merciful.

119. O you who have believed, fear Allah and be with those who are true.

120. It was not [proper] for the people of Madinah and those surrounding them of the bedouins that they remain behind after [the departure of] the Messenger of Allah or that they prefer themselves over his self. That is because they are not afflicted by thirst or fatigue or hunger in the cause of Allah, nor do they tread on any ground that enrages the disbelievers, nor do they inflict upon an enemy any infliction but that is registered for them as a righteous deed. Indeed, Allah does not allow to be lost the reward of the doers of good.

121. Nor do they spend an expenditure, small or large, or cross a valley but that it is registered for them that Allah may reward them for the best of what they were doing.

122. And it is not for the believers to go forth [to battle] all at once. For there should separate from every division of them a group [remaining] to obtain understanding in the religion and warn their people when they return to them that they might be cautious.

123. O you who have believed, fight those adjacent to you of the disbelievers and let them find in you harshness. And know that Allah is with the righteous.

124. And whenever a surah is revealed, there are among the hypocrites those who say, "Which of you has this increased faith?" As for those who believed, it has increased them in faith, while they are rejoicing.

125. But as for those in whose hearts is disease, it has [only] increased them in evil [in addition] to their evil. And they will have died while they are disbelievers.

126. Do they not see that they are tried every year once or twice but then they do not repent nor do they remember?

127. And whenever a surah is revealed, they look at each other, [saying], "Does anyone see you?" and then they dismiss themselves. Allah has dismissed their hearts because they are a people who do not understand.

128. There has certainly come to you a Messenger from among yourselves. Grievous to him is what you suffer; [he is] concerned over you and to the believers is kind and merciful.

129. But if they turn away, [O Muhammad], say, "Sufficient for me is Allah; there is no deity except Him. On Him I have relied, and He is the Lord of the Great Throne."

Surah 10 Yunus

Verses: 109 | Makki

In the name of Allah, the Entirely Merciful, the Especially Merciful.

01. Alif, Lam, Ra. These are the verses of the wise Book

02. Have the people been amazed that We revealed [revelation] to a man from among them, [saying], "Warn mankind and give good tidings to those who believe that they will have a [firm] precedence of honor with their Lord"? [But] the disbelievers say, "Indeed, this is an obvious magician."

03. Indeed, your Lord is Allah, who created the heavens and the earth in six days and then established Himself above the Throne, arranging the matter [of His creation]. There is no intercessor except after His permission. That is Allah, your Lord, so worship Him. Then will you not remember?

04. To Him is your return all together. [It is] the promise of Allah [which is] truth. Indeed, He begins the [process of] creation and then repeats it that He may reward those who have believed and done righteous deeds, in justice. But those who disbelieved will have a drink of scalding water and a painful punishment for what they used to deny.

05. It is He who made the sun a shining light and the moon a derived light and determined for it phases - that you may know the number of years and account [of time]. Allah has not created this except in truth. He details the signs for a people who know.

06. Indeed, in the alternation of the night and the day and [in] what Allah has created in the heavens and the earth are signs for a people who fear Allah

07. Indeed, those who do not expect the meeting with Us and are satisfied with the life of this world and feel secure therein and those who are heedless of Our signs

08. For those their refuge will be the Fire because of what they used to earn.

09. Indeed, those who have believed and done righteous deeds - their Lord will guide them because of their faith. Beneath them rivers will flow in the Gardens of Pleasure

10. Their call therein will be, "Exalted are You, O Allah," and their greeting therein will be, "Peace." And the last of their call will be, "Praise to Allah, Lord of the worlds!"

11. And if Allah was to hasten for the people the evil [they invoke] as He hastens for them the good, their term would have been ended for them. But We leave the ones who do not expect the meeting with Us, in their transgression, wandering blindly

12. And when affliction touches man, he calls upon Us, whether lying on his side or sitting or standing; but when We remove from him his affliction, he continues [in disobedience] as if he had never called upon Us to [remove] an affliction that touched him. Thus is made pleasing to the transgressors that which they have been doing

13. And We had already destroyed generations before you when they wronged, and their messengers had come to them with clear proofs, but they were not to believe. Thus do We recompense the criminal people

14. Then We made you successors in the land after them so that We may observe how you will do.

15. And when Our verses are recited to them as clear evidences, those who do not expect the meeting with Us say, "Bring us a Qur'an other than this or change it." Say, [O Muhammad], "It is not for me to change it on my own accord. I only follow what is revealed to me. Indeed I fear, if I should disobey my Lord, the punishment of a tremendous Day."

16. Say, "If Allah had willed, I would not have recited it to you, nor would He have made it known to you, for I had remained among you a lifetime before it. Then will you not reason?"

17. So who is more unjust than he who invents a lie about Allah or denies His signs? Indeed, the criminals will not succeed

18. And they worship other than Allah that which neither harms them nor benefits them, and they say, "These are our intercessors with Allah " Say, "Do you inform Allah of something He does not know in the heavens or on the earth?" Exalted is He and high above what they associate with Him

19. And mankind was not but one community [united in religion], but [then] they differed. And if not for a word that preceded from your Lord, it would have been judged between them [immediately] concerning that over which they differ.

20. And they say, "Why is a sign not sent down to him from his Lord?" So say, "The unseen is only for Allah [to administer], so wait; indeed, I am with you among those who wait."

21. And when We give the people a taste of mercy after adversity has touched them, at once they conspire against Our verses. Say, "Allah is swifter in strategy." Indeed, Our messengers record that which you conspire

22. It is He who enables you to travel on land and sea until, when you are in ships and they sail with them by a good wind and they rejoice therein, there comes a storm wind and the waves come upon them from everywhere and they assume that they are surrounded, supplicating Allah, sincere to Him in religion, "If You should save us from this, we will surely be among the thankful."

23. But when He saves them, at once they commit injustice upon the earth without right. O mankind, your injustice is only against yourselves, [being merely] the enjoyment of worldly life. Then to Us is your return, and We will inform you of what you used to do.

24. The example of [this] worldly life is but like rain which We have sent down from the sky that the plants of the earth absorb - [those] from which men and livestock eat - until, when the earth has taken on its adornment and is beautified and its people suppose that they have capability over it, there comes to it Our command by night or by day, and We make it as a harvest, as if it had not flourished yesterday. Thus do We explain in detail the signs for a people who give thought.

25. And Allah invites to the Home of Peace and guides whom He wills to a straight path

26. For them who have done good is the best [reward] and extra. No

darkness will cover their faces, nor humiliation. Those are companions of Paradise; they will abide therein eternally

27. But they who have earned [blame for] evil doings - the recompense of an evil deed is its equivalent, and humiliation will cover them. They will have from Allah no protector. It will be as if their faces are covered with pieces of the night - so dark [are they]. Those are the companions of the Fire; they will abide therein eternally.

28. And [mention, O Muhammad], the Day We will gather them all together - then We will say to those who associated others with Allah, "[Remain in] your place, you and your 'partners.' " Then We will separate them, and their "partners" will say, "You did not used to worship us,

29. And sufficient is Allah as a witness between us and you that we were of your worship unaware."

30. There, [on that Day], every soul will be put to trial for what it did previously, and they will be returned to Allah, their master, the Truth, and lost from them is whatever they used to invent.

31. Say, "Who provides for you from the heaven and the earth? Or who controls hearing and sight and who brings the living out of the dead and brings the dead out of the living and who arranges [every] matter?" They will say, "Allah," so say, "Then will you not fear Him?"

32. For that is Allah, your Lord, the Truth. And what can be beyond truth except error? So how are you averted?

33. Thus the word of your Lord has come into effect upon those who defiantly disobeyed - that they will not believe.

34. Say, "Are there of your 'partners' any who begins creation and then repeats it?" Say, "Allah begins creation and then repeats it, so how are you deluded?"

35. Say, "Are there of your 'partners' any who guides to the truth?" Say, "Allah guides to the truth. So is He who guides to the truth more worthy to be followed or he who guides not unless he is guided? Then what is [wrong] with you - how do you judge?"

36. And most of them follow not except assumption. Indeed, assumption avails not against the truth at all. Indeed, Allah is Knowing of what they do.

37. And it was not [possible] for this Qur'an to be produced by other

than Allah, but [it is] a confirmation of what was before it and a detailed explanation of the [former] Scripture, about which there is no doubt, from the Lord of the worlds.

38. Or do they say [about the Prophet], "He invented it?" Say, "Then bring forth a surah like it and call upon [for assistance] whomever you can besides Allah, if you should be truthful."

39. Rather, they have denied that which they encompass not in knowledge and whose interpretation has not yet come to them. Thus did those before them deny. Then observe how was the end of the wrongdoers.

40. And of them are those who believe in it, and of them are those who do not believe in it. And your Lord is most knowing of the corrupters

41. And if they deny you, [O Muhammad], then say, "For me are my deeds, and for you are your deeds. You are disassociated from what I do, and I am disassociated from what you do."

42. And among them are those who listen to you. But can you cause the deaf to hear, although they will not use reason?

43. And among them are those who look at you. But can you guide the blind although they will not [attempt to] see?

44. Indeed, Allah does not wrong the people at all, but it is the people who are wronging themselves.

45. And on the Day when He will gather them, [it will be] as if they had not remained [in the world] but an hour of the day, [and] they will know each other. Those will have lost who denied the meeting with Allah and were not guided

46. And whether We show you some of what We promise them, [O Muhammad], or We take you in death, to Us is their return; then, [either way], Allah is a witness concerning what they are doing

47. And for every nation is a messenger. So when their messenger comes, it will be judged between them in justice, and they will not be wronged

48. And they say, "When is [the fulfillment of] this promise, if you should be truthful?"

49. Say, "I possess not for myself any harm or benefit except what Allah should will. For every nation is a [specified] term. When their time has come, then they will not remain behind an hour, nor will they precede [it]."

50. Say, "Have you considered: if His punishment should come to

you by night or by day - for which [aspect] of it would the criminals be impatient?"

51. Then is it that when it has [actually] occurred you will believe in it? Now? And you were [once] for it impatient

52. Then it will be said to those who had wronged, "Taste the punishment of eternity; are you being recompensed except for what you used to earn?"

53. And they ask information of you, [O Muhammad], "Is it true?" Say, "Yes, by my Lord. Indeed, it is truth; and you will not cause failure [to Allah]."

54. And if each soul that wronged had everything on earth, it would offer it in ransom. And they will confide regret when they see the punishment; and they will be judged in justice, and they will not be wronged

55. Unquestionably, to Allah belongs whatever is in the heavens and the earth. Unquestionably, the promise of Allah is truth, but most of them do not know

56. He gives life and causes death, and to Him you will be returned

57. O mankind, there has to come to you instruction from your Lord and healing for what is in the breasts and guidance and mercy for the believers.

58. Say, "In the bounty of Allah and in His mercy - in that let them rejoice; it is better than what they accumulate."

59. Say, "Have you seen what Allah has sent down to you of provision of which you have made [some] lawful and [some] unlawful?" Say, "Has Allah permitted you [to do so], or do you invent [something] about Allah?"

60. And what will be the supposition of those who invent falsehood about Allah on the Day of Resurrection? Indeed, Allah is full of bounty to the people, but most of them are not grateful."

61. And, [O Muhammad], you are not [engaged] in any matter or recite any of the Qur'an and you [people] do not do any deed except that We are witness over you when you are involved in it. And not absent from your Lord is any [part] of an atom's weight within the earth or within the heaven or [anything] smaller than that or greater but that it is in a clear register.

62. Unquestionably, [for] the allies of Allah there will be no fear concerning them, nor will they grieve

63. Those who believed and were fearing Allah

64. For them are good tidings in the worldly life and in the Hereafter. No change is there in the words of Allah. That is what is the great attainment.

65. And let not their speech grieve you. Indeed, honor [due to power] belongs to Allah entirely. He is the Hearing, the Knowing.

66. Unquestionably, to Allah belongs whoever is in the heavens and whoever is on the earth. And those who invoke other than Allah do not [actually] follow [His] "partners." They follow not except assumption, and they are not but falsifying

67. It is He who made for you the night to rest therein and the day, giving sight. Indeed in that are signs for a people who listen.

68. They have said, "Allah has taken a son." Exalted is He; He is the [one] Free of need. To Him belongs whatever is in the heavens and whatever is in the earth. You have no authority for this [claim]. Do you say about Allah that which you do not know?

69. Say, "Indeed, those who invent falsehood about Allah will not succeed."

70. [For them is brief] enjoyment in this world; then to Us is their return; then We will make them taste the severe punishment because they used to disbelieve

71. And recite to them the news of Noah, when he said to his people, "O my people, if my residence and my reminding of the signs of Allah has become burdensome upon you - then I have relied upon Allah. So resolve upon your plan and [call upon] your associates. Then let not your plan be obscure to you. Then carry it out upon me and do not give me respite.

72. And if you turn away [from my advice] then no payment have I asked of you. My reward is only from Allah, and I have been commanded to be of the Muslims."

73. And they denied him, so We saved him and those with him in the ship and made them successors, and We drowned those who denied Our signs. Then see how was the end of those who were warned.

74. Then We sent after him messengers to their peoples, and they came to them with clear proofs. But they were not to believe in that which they had denied before. Thus We seal over the hearts of the transgressors

75. Then We sent after them Moses and Aaron to Pharaoh and his establishment with Our signs, but they behaved arrogantly and were a criminal people

76. So when there came to them the truth from Us, they said, "Indeed, this is obvious magic."

77. Moses said, "Do you say [thus] about the truth when it has come to you? Is this magic? But magicians will not succeed."

78. They said, "Have you come to us to turn us away from that upon which we found our fathers and so that you two may have grandeur in the land? And we are not believers in you."

79. And Pharaoh said, "Bring to me every learned magician."

80. So when the magicians came, Moses said to them, "Throw down whatever you will throw."

81. And when they had thrown, Moses said, "What you have brought is [only] magic. Indeed, Allah will expose its worthlessness. Indeed, Allah does not amend the work of corrupters.

82. And Allah will establish the truth by His words, even if the criminals dislike it."

83. But no one believed Moses, except [some] youths among his people, for fear of Pharaoh and his establishment that they would persecute them. And indeed, Pharaoh was haughty within the land, and indeed, he was of the transgressors

84. And Moses said, "O my people, if you have believed in Allah, then rely upon Him, if you should be Muslims."

85. So they said, "Upon Allah do we rely. Our Lord, make us not [objects of] trial for the wrongdoing people

86. And save us by Your mercy from the disbelieving people."

87. And We inspired to Moses and his brother, "Settle your people in Egypt in houses and make your houses [facing the] qiblah and establish prayer and give good tidings to the believers."

88. And Moses said, "Our Lord, indeed You have given Pharaoh and his establishment splendor and wealth in the worldly life, our Lord, that they may lead [men] astray from Your way. Our Lord, obliterate their wealth and harden their hearts so that they will not believe until they see the painful punishment."

89. [Allah] said, "Your supplication has been answered." So remain on a right course and follow not the way of those who do not know."

90. And We took the Children of Israel across the sea, and Pharaoh and his soldiers pursued them in tyranny and enmity until, when drowning overtook him, he said, "I believe that there is no deity except that in whom the Children of Israel believe, and I am of the Muslims."

91. Now? And you had disobeyed [Him] before and were of the corrupters?

92. So today We will save you in body that you may be to those who succeed you a sign. And indeed, many among the people, of Our signs, are heedless

93. And We had certainty settled the Children of Israel in an agreeable settlement and provided them with good things. And they did not differ until [after] knowledge had come to them. Indeed, your Lord will judge between them on the Day of Resurrection concerning that over which they used to differ

94. So if you are in doubt, [O Muhammad], about that which We have revealed to you, then ask those who have been reading the Scripture before you. The truth has certainly come to you from your Lord, so never be among the doubters.

95. And never be of those who deny the signs of Allah and [thus] be among the losers.

96. Indeed, those upon whom the word of your Lord has come into effect will not believe,

97. Even if every sign should come to them, until they see the painful punishment.

98. Then has there not been a [single] city that believed so its faith benefited it except the people of Jonah? When they believed, We removed from them the punishment of disgrace in worldly life and gave them enjoyment for a time.

99. And had your Lord willed, those on earth would have believed - all of them entirely. Then, [O Muhammad], would you compel the people in order that they become believers?

100. And it is not for a soul to believe except by permission of Allah, and He will place defilement upon those who will not use reason.

101. Say, "Observe what is in the heavens and earth." But of no avail will be signs or warners to a people who do not believe

102. So do they wait except for like [what occurred in] the days of those who passed on before them? Say, "Then wait; indeed, I am with you among those who wait."

103. Then We will save our messengers and those who have believed. Thus, it is an obligation upon Us that We save the believers

104. Say, [O Muhammad], "O people, if you are in doubt as to my religion - then I do not worship those which you worship besides Allah; but I worship Allah, who causes your death. And I have been commanded to be of the believers

105. And [commanded], 'Direct your face toward the religion, inclining to truth, and never be of those who associate others with Allah;

106. And do not invoke besides Allah that which neither benefits you nor harms you, for if you did, then indeed you would be of the wrongdoers.'"

107. And if Allah should touch you with adversity, there is no remover of it except Him; and if He intends for you good, then there is no repeller of His bounty. He causes it to reach whom He wills of His servants. And He is the Forgiving, the Merciful

108. Say, "O mankind, the truth has come to you from your Lord, so whoever is guided is only guided for [the benefit of] his soul, and whoever goes astray only goes astray [in violation] against it. And I am not over you a manager."

109. And follow what is revealed to you, [O Muhammad], and be patient until Allah will judge. And He is the best of judges.

Verses: 123	Surah 11 Hud	Makki

In the name of Allah, the Entirely Merciful, the Especially Merciful.

01. Alif, Lam, Ra. [This is] a Book whose verses are perfected and then presented in detail from [one who is] Wise and Acquainted.

02. [Through a messenger, saying], "Do not worship except Allah. Indeed, I am to you from Him a warner and a bringer of good tidings,"

03. And [saying], "Seek forgiveness of your Lord and repent to Him, [and] He will let you enjoy a good provision for a specified term and give every doer of favor his favor. But if you turn away, then indeed, I fear for you the punishment of a great Day.

04. To Allah is your return, and He is over all things competent."

05. Unquestionably, they the disbelievers turn away their breasts to hide themselves from Him. Unquestionably, [even] when they cover themselves in their clothing, Allah knows what they conceal and what they declare. Indeed, He is Knowing of that within the breasts.

06. **And there is no creature on earth but that upon Allah is its provision, and He knows its place of dwelling and place of** storage. All is in a clear register.

07. And it is He who created the heavens and the earth in six days - and His Throne had been upon water - that He might test you as to which of you is best in deed. But if you say, "Indeed, you are resurrected after death," those who disbelieve will surely say, "This is not but obvious magic."

08. And if We hold back from them the punishment for a limited time, they will surely say, "What detains it?" Unquestionably, on the Day it comes to them, it will not be averted from them, and they will be enveloped by what they used to ridicule.

09. And if We give man a taste of mercy from Us and then We withdraw it from him, indeed, he is despairing and ungrateful.

10. But if We give him a taste of favor after hardship has touched him, he will surely say, "Bad times have left me." Indeed, he is exultant and boastful -

11. Except for those who are patient and do righteous deeds; those will have forgiveness and great reward.

12. Then would you possibly leave [out] some of what is revealed to you, or is your breast constrained by it because they say, "Why has there not been sent down to him a treasure or come with him an angel?" But you are only a warner. And Allah is Disposer of all things.

13. Or do they say, "He invented it"? Say, "Then bring ten surahs like it that have been invented and call upon [for assistance] whomever you can besides Allah, if you should be truthful."

14. And if they do not respond to you - then know that the Qur'an was revealed with the knowledge of Allah and that there is no deity except Him. Then, would you [not] be Muslims?

15. Whoever desires the life of this world and its adornments - We fully repay them for their deeds therein, and they therein will not be deprived.

16. Those are the ones for whom there is not in the Hereafter but the Fire. And lost is what they did therein, and worthless is what they used to do.

17. So is one who [stands] upon a clear evidence from his Lord [like the aforementioned]? And a witness from Him follows it, and

before it was the Scripture of Moses to lead and as mercy. Those [believers in the former revelations] believe in the Qur'an. But whoever disbelieves in it from the [various] factions - the Fire is his promised destination. So be not in doubt about it. Indeed, it is the truth from your Lord, but most of the people do not believe.

18. And who is more unjust than he who invents a lie about Allah? Those will be presented before their Lord, and the witnesses will say, "These are the ones who lied against their Lord." Unquestionably, the curse of Allah is upon the wrongdoers.

19. Who averted [people] from the way of Allah and sought to make it [seem] deviant while they, concerning the Hereafter, were disbelievers.

20. Those were not causing failure [to Allah] on earth, nor did they have besides Allah any protectors. For them the punishment will be multiplied. They were not able to hear, nor did they see.

21. Those are the ones who will have lost themselves, and lost from them is what they used to invent.

22. Assuredly, it is they in the Hereafter who will be the greatest losers.

23. Indeed, they who have believed and done righteous deeds and humbled themselves to their Lord - those are the companions of Paradise; they will abide eternally therein.

24. The example of the two parties is like the blind and deaf, and the seeing and hearing. Are they equal in comparison? Then, will you not remember?

25. And We had certainly sent Noah to his people, [saying], "Indeed, I am to you a clear warner

26. That you not worship except Allah. Indeed, I fear for you the punishment of a painful day."

27. So the eminent among those who disbelieved from his people said, "We do not see you but as a man like ourselves, and we do not see you followed except by those who are the lowest of us [and] at first suggestion. And we do not see in you over us any merit; rather, we think you are liars."

28. He said, "O my people have you considered: if I should be upon clear evidence from my Lord while He has given me mercy from Himself but it has been made unapparent to you, should we force it upon you while you are averse to it?

29. And O my people, I ask not of you for it any wealth. My reward is

not but from Allah. And I am not one to drive away those who have believed. Indeed, they will meet their Lord, but I see that you are a people behaving ignorantly.

30. And O my people, who would protect me from Allah if I drove them away? Then will you not be reminded?

31. And I do not tell you that I have the depositories [containing the provision] of Allah or that I know the unseen, nor do I tell you that I am an angel, nor do I say of those upon whom your eyes look down that Allah will never grant them any good. Allah is most knowing of what is within their souls. Indeed, I would then be among the wrongdoers."

32. They said, "O Noah, you have disputed us and been frequent in dispute of us. So bring us what you threaten us, if you should be of the truthful."

33. He said, "Allah will only bring it to you if He wills, and you will not cause [Him] failure.

34. And my advice will not benefit you - although I wished to advise you - If Allah should intend to put you in error. He is your Lord, and to Him you will be returned."

35. Or do they say [about Prophet Muhammad], "He invented it"? Say, "If I have invented it, then upon me is [the consequence of] my crime; but I am innocent of what [crimes] you commit."

36. And it was revealed to Noah that, "No one will believe from your people except those who have already believed, so do not be distressed by what they have been doing.

37. And construct the ship under Our observation and Our inspiration and do not address Me concerning those who have wronged; indeed, they are [to be] drowned."

38. And he constructed the ship, and whenever an assembly of the eminent of his people passed by him, they ridiculed him. He said, "If you ridicule us, then we will ridicule you just as you ridicule.

39. And you are going to know who will get a punishment that will disgrace him [on earth] and upon whom will descend an enduring punishment [in the Hereafter]."

40. [So it was], until when Our command came and the oven overflowed, We said, "Load upon the ship of each [creature] two mates and your family, except those about whom the word has preceded, and [include] whoever has believed." But none had believed with him, except a few.

41. And [Noah] said, "Embark therein; in the name of Allah is its course and its anchorage. Indeed, my Lord is Forgiving and Merciful."

42. And it sailed with them through waves like mountains, and Noah called to his son who was apart [from them], "O my son, come aboard with us and be not with the disbelievers."

43. [But] he said, "I will take refuge on a mountain to protect me from the water." [Noah] said, "There is no protector today from the decree of Allah, except for whom He gives mercy." And the waves came between them, and he was among the drowned.

44. And it was said, "O earth, swallow your water, and O sky, withhold [your rain]." And the water subsided, and the matter was accomplished, and the ship came to rest on the [mountain of] Judiyy. And it was said, "Away with the wrongdoing people."

45. And Noah called to his Lord and said, "My Lord, indeed my son is of my family; and indeed, Your promise is true; and You are the most just of judges!"

46. He said, "O Noah, indeed he is not of your family; indeed, he is [one whose] work was other than righteous, so ask Me not for that about which you have no knowledge. Indeed, I advise you, lest you be among the ignorant."

47. [Noah] said, "My Lord, I seek refuge in You from asking that of which I have no knowledge. And unless You forgive me and have mercy upon me, I will be among the losers."

48. It was said, "O Noah, disembark in security from Us and blessings upon you and upon nations [descending] from those with you. But other nations [of them] We will grant enjoyment; then there will touch them from Us a painful punishment."

49. That is from the news of the unseen which We reveal to you, [O Muhammad]. You knew it not, neither you nor your people, before this. So be patient; indeed, the [best] outcome is for the righteous.

50. And to 'Aad [We sent] their brother Hud. He said, "O my people, worship Allah; you have no deity other than Him. You are not but inventors [of falsehood].

51. my people, I do not ask you for it any reward. My reward is only from the one who created me. Then will you not reason?

52. And O my people, ask forgiveness of your Lord and then repent to Him. He will send [rain from] the sky upon you in showers and increase you in strength [added] to your strength. And do not turn away, [being] criminals."

53. They said, "O Hud, you have not brought us clear evidence, and we are not ones to leave our gods on your say-so. Nor are we believers in you.
54. We only say that some of our gods have possessed you with evil." He said, "Indeed, I call Allah to witness, and witness [yourselves] that I am free from whatever you associate with Allah
55. Other than Him. So plot against me all together; then do not give me respite.
56. Indeed, I have relied upon Allah, my Lord and your Lord. There is no creature but that He holds its forelock. Indeed, my Lord is on a path [that is] straight."
57. But if they turn away, [say], "I have already conveyed that with which I was sent to you. My Lord will give succession to a people other than you, and you will not harm Him at all. Indeed my Lord is, over all things, Guardian."
58. And when Our command came, We saved Hud and those who believed with him, by mercy from Us; and We saved them from a harsh punishment.
59. And that was 'Aad, who rejected the signs of their Lord and disobeyed His messengers and followed the order of every obstinate tyrant.
60. And they were [therefore] followed in this world with a curse and [as well] on the Day of Resurrection. Unquestionably, 'Aad denied their Lord; then away with 'Aad, the people of Hud.
61. And to Thamud [We sent] their brother Salih. He said, "O my people, worship Allah; you have no deity other than Him. He has produced you from the earth and settled you in it, so ask forgiveness of Him and then repent to Him. Indeed, my Lord is near and responsive."
62. They said, "O Salih, you were among us a man of promise before this. Do you forbid us to worship what our fathers worshipped? And indeed we are, about that to which you invite us, in disquieting doubt."
63. He said, "O my people, have you considered: if I should be upon clear evidence from my Lord and He has given me mercy from Himself, who would protect me from Allah if I disobeyed Him? So you would not increase me except in loss.
64. And O my people, this is the she-camel of Allah - [she is] to you a sign. So let her feed upon Allah's earth and do not touch her

with harm, or you will be taken by an impending punishment."

65. But they hamstrung her, so he said, "Enjoy yourselves in your homes for three days. That is a promise not to be denied."

66. So when Our command came, We saved Salih and those who believed with him, by mercy from Us, and [saved them] from the disgrace of that day. Indeed, it is your Lord who is the Powerful, the Exalted in Might.

67. And the shriek seized those who had wronged, and they became within their homes [corpses] fallen prone

68. As if they had never prospered therein. Unquestionably, Thamud denied their Lord; then, away with Thamud.

69. And certainly did Our messengers come to Abraham with good tidings; they said, "Peace." He said, "Peace," and did not delay in bringing [them] a roasted calf.

70. But when he saw their hands not reaching for it, he distrusted them and felt from them apprehension. They said, "Fear not. We have been sent to the people of Lot."

71. And his Wife was standing, and she smiled. Then We gave her good tidings of Isaac and after Isaac, Jacob.

72. She said, "Woe to me! Shall I give birth while I am an old woman and this, my husband, is an old man? Indeed, this is an amazing thing!"

73. They said, "Are you amazed at the decree of Allah? May the mercy of Allah and His blessings be upon you, people of the house. Indeed, He is Praiseworthy and Honorable."

74. And when the fright had left Abraham and the good tidings had reached him, he began to argue with Us concerning the people of Lot.

75. Indeed, Abraham was forbearing, grieving and [frequently] returning [to Allah].

76. [The angels said], "O Abraham, give up this [plea]. Indeed, the command of your Lord has come, and indeed, there will reach them a punishment that cannot be repelled."

77. And when Our messengers, [the angels], came to Lot, he was anguished for them and felt for them great discomfort and said, "This is a trying day."

78. And his people came hastening to him, and before [this] they had been doing evil deeds. He said, "O my people, these are my daughters; they are purer for you. So fear Allah and do

not disgrace me concerning my guests. Is there not among you a man of reason?"

79. They said, "You have already known that we have not concerning your daughters any claim, and indeed, you know what we want."

80. He said, "If only I had against you some power or could take refuge in a strong support."

81. The angels said, "O Lot, indeed we are messengers of your Lord; [therefore], they will never reach you. So set out with your family during a portion of the night and let not any among you look back - except your wife; indeed, she will be struck by that which strikes them. Indeed, their appointment is [for] the morning. Is not the morning near?"

82. So when Our command came, We made the highest part [of the city] its lowest and rained upon them stones of layered hard clay, [which were]

83. Marked from your Lord. And Allah's punishment is not from the wrongdoers [very] far.

84. And to Madyan [We sent] their brother Shu'ayb. He said, "O my people, worship Allah; you have no deity other than Him. And do not decrease from the measure and the scale. Indeed, I see you in prosperity, but indeed, I fear for you the punishment of an all-encompassing Day.

85. And O my people, give full measure and weight in justice and do not deprive the people of their due and do not commit abuse on the earth, spreading corruption.

86. What remains [lawful] from Allah is best for you, if you would be believers. But I am not a guardian over you."

87. They said, "O Shu'ayb, does your prayer command you that we should leave what our fathers worship or not do with our wealth what we please? Indeed, you are the forbearing, the discerning!"

88. He said, "O my people, have you considered: if I am upon clear evidence from my Lord and He has provided me with a good provision from Him...? And I do not intend to differ from you in that which I have forbidden you; I only intend reform as much as I am able. And my success is not but through Allah. Upon him I have relied, and to Him I return.

89. And O my people, let not [your] dissension from me cause you to

be struck by that similar to what struck the people of Noah or the people of Hud or the people of Salih. And the people of Lot are not from you far away.

90. And ask forgiveness of your Lord and then repent to Him. Indeed, my Lord is Merciful and Affectionate."

91. They said, "O Shu'ayb, we do not understand much of what you say, and indeed, we consider you among us as weak. And if not for your family, we would have stoned you [to death]; and you are not to us one respected."

92. He said, "O my people, is my family more respected for power by you than Allah? But you put Him behind your backs [in neglect]. Indeed, my Lord is encompassing of what you do.

93. And O my people, work according to your position; indeed, I am working. You are going to know to whom will come a punishment that will disgrace him and who is a liar. So watch; indeed, I am with you a watcher, [awaiting the outcome]."

94. And when Our command came, We saved Shu'ayb and those who believed with him, by mercy from Us. And the shriek seized those who had wronged, and they became within their homes [corpses] fallen prone

95. As if they had never prospered therein. Then, away with Madyan as Thamud was taken away.

96. And We did certainly send Moses with Our signs and a clear authority

97. To Pharaoh and his establishment, but they followed the command of Pharaoh, and the command of Pharaoh was not [at all] discerning.

98. He will precede his people on the Day of Resurrection and lead them into the Fire; and wretched is the place to which they are led.

99. And they were followed in this [world] with a curse and on the Day of Resurrection. And wretched is the gift which is given.

100. That is from the news of the cities, which We relate to you; of them, some are [still] standing and some are [as] a harvest [mowed down].

101. And We did not wrong them, but they wronged themselves. And they were not availed at all by their gods which they invoked other than Allah when there came the command of your Lord. And they did not increase them in other than ruin.

102. And thus is the seizure of your Lord when He seizes the cities while they are committing wrong. Indeed, His seizure is painful and severe.

103. Indeed in that is a sign for those who fear the punishment of the Hereafter. That is a Day for which the people will be collected, and that is a Day [which will be] witnessed.

104. And We do not delay it except for a limited term.

105. The Day it comes no soul will speak except by His permission. And among them will be the wretched and the prosperous.

106. As for those who were [destined to be] wretched, they will be in the Fire. For them therein is [violent] exhaling and inhaling.

107. [They will be] abiding therein as long as the heavens and the earth endure, except what your Lord should will. Indeed, your Lord is an effecter of what He intends.

108. And as for those who were [destined to be] prosperous, they will be in Paradise, abiding therein as long as the heavens and the earth endure, except what your Lord should will - a bestowal uninterrupted.

109. So do not be in doubt, [O Muhammad], as to what these [polytheists] are worshipping. They worship not except as their fathers worshipped before. And indeed, We will give them their share undiminished.

110. And We had certainly given Moses the Scripture, but it came under disagreement. And if not for a word that preceded from your Lord, it would have been judged between them. And indeed they are, concerning the Qur'an, in disquieting doubt.

111. And indeed, each [of the believers and disbelievers] - your Lord will fully compensate them for their deeds. Indeed, He is Acquainted with what they do.

112. So remain on a right course as you have been commanded, [you] and those who have turned back with you [to Allah], and do not transgress. Indeed, He is Seeing of what you do.

113. And do not incline toward those who do wrong, lest you be touched by the Fire, and you would not have other than Allah any protectors; then you would not be helped.

114. And establish prayer at the two ends of the day and at the approach of the night. Indeed, good deeds do away with misdeeds. That is a reminder for those who remember.

115. And be patient, for indeed, Allah does not allow to be lost the reward of those who do good.

116. So why were there not among the generations before you those of enduring discrimination forbidding corruption on earth - except a few of those We saved from among them? But those who wronged pursued what luxury they were given therein, and they were criminals.

117. And your Lord would not have destroyed the cities unjustly while their people were reformers.

118. And if your Lord had willed, He could have made mankind one community; but they will not cease to differ.

119. Except whom your Lord has given mercy, and for that He created them. But the word of your Lord is to be fulfilled that, "I will surely fill Hell with jinn and men all together."

120. And each [story] We relate to you from the news of the messengers is that by which We make firm your heart. And there has come to you, in this, the truth and an instruction and a reminder for the believers.

121. And say to those who do not believe, "Work according to your position; indeed, we are working.

122. And wait, indeed, we are waiting."

123. And to Allah belong the unseen [aspects] of the heavens and the earth and to Him will be returned the matter, all of it, so worship Him and rely upon Him. And your Lord is not unaware of that which you do.

| Verses: 111 | **Surah 12 Yusuf** | Makki |

In the name of Allah, the Entirely Merciful, the Especially Merciful.

01. Alif, Lam, Ra. These are the verses of the clear Book.

02. Indeed, We have sent it down as an Arabic Qur'an that you might understand.

03. We relate to you, [O Muhammad], the best of stories in what We have revealed to you of this Qur'an although you were, before it, among the unaware.

04. [Of these stories mention] when Joseph said to his father, "O my father, indeed I have seen [in a dream] eleven stars and the sun and the moon; I saw them prostrating to me."

05. He said, "O my son, do not relate your vision to your brothers or they will contrive against you a plan. Indeed Satan, to man, is a manifest enemy.

06. And thus will your Lord choose you and teach you the interpretation of narratives and complete His favor upon you and upon the family of Jacob, as He completed it upon your fathers before, Abraham and Isaac. Indeed, your Lord is Knowing and Wise."

07. Certainly were there in Joseph and his brothers signs for those who ask,

08. When they said, "Joseph and his brother are more beloved to our father than we, while we are a clan. Indeed, our father is in clear error.

09. Kill Joseph or cast him out to [another] land; the countenance of your father will [then] be only for you, and you will be after that a righteous people."

10. Said a speaker among them, "Do not kill Joseph but throw him into the bottom of the well; some travelers will pick him up - if you would do [something]."

11. They said, "O our father, why do you not entrust us with Joseph while indeed, we are to him sincere counselors?

12. Send him with us tomorrow that he may eat well and play. And indeed, we will be his guardians.

13. [Jacob] said, "Indeed, it saddens me that you should take him, and I fear that a wolf would eat him while you are of him unaware."

14. They said, "If a wolf should eat him while we are a [strong] clan, indeed, we would then be losers."

15. So when they took him [out] and agreed to put him into the bottom of the well... But We inspired to him, "You will surely inform them [someday] about this affair of theirs while they do not perceive [your identity]."

16. And they came to their father at night, weeping.

17. They said, "O our father, indeed we went racing each other and left Joseph with our possessions, and a wolf ate him. But you would not believe us, even if we were truthful."

18. And they brought upon his shirt false blood. [Jacob] said, "Rather, your souls have enticed you to something, so patience is most fitting. And Allah is the one sought for help against that which you describe."

19. And there came a company of travelers; then they sent their water drawer, and he let down his bucket. He said, "Good news! Here is a boy." And they concealed him, [taking him] as merchandise; and Allah was knowing of what they did.
20. And they sold him for a reduced price - a few dirhams - and they were, concerning him, of those content with little.
21. And the one from Egypt who bought him said to his wife, "Make his residence comfortable. Perhaps he will benefit us, or we will adopt him as a son." And thus, We established Joseph in the land that We might teach him the interpretation of events. And Allah is predominant over His affair, but most of the people do not know.
22. And when Joseph reached maturity, We gave him judgment and knowledge. And thus We reward the doers of good.
23. And she, in whose house he was, sought to seduce him. She closed the doors and said, "Come, you." He said, "[I seek] the refuge of Allah. Indeed, he is my master, who has made good my residence. Indeed, wrongdoers will not succeed."
24. And she certainly determined [to seduce] him, and he would have inclined to her had he not seen the proof of his Lord. And thus [it was] that We should avert from him evil and immorality. Indeed, he was of Our chosen servants.
25. And they both raced to the door, and she tore his shirt from the back, and they found her husband at the door. She said, "What is the recompense of one who intended evil for your wife but that he be imprisoned or a painful punishment?"
26. [Joseph] said, "It was she who sought to seduce me." And a witness from her family testified. "If his shirt is torn from the front, then she has told the truth, and he is of the liars.
27. But if his shirt is torn from the back, then she has lied, and he is of the truthful."
28. So when her husband saw his shirt torn from the back, he said, "Indeed, it is of the women's plan. Indeed, your plan is great.
29. Joseph, ignore this. And, [my wife], ask forgiveness for your sin. Indeed, you were of the sinful."
30. And women in the city said, "The wife of al-'Azeez is seeking to seduce her slave boy; he has impassioned her with love. Indeed, we see her [to be] in clear error."

31. So when she heard of their scheming, she sent for them and prepared for them a banquet and gave each one of them a knife and said [to Joseph], "Come out before them." And when they saw him, they greatly admired him and cut their hands and said, "Perfect is Allah! This is not a man; this is none but a noble angel."

32. She said, "That is the one about whom you blamed me. And I certainly sought to seduce him, but he firmly refused; and if he will not do what I order him, he will surely be imprisoned and will be of those debased."

33. He said, "My Lord, prison is more to my liking than that to which they invite me. And if You do not avert from me their plan, I might incline toward them and [thus] be of the ignorant."

34. So his Lord responded to him and averted from him their plan. Indeed, He is the Hearing, the Knowing.

35. Then it appeared to them after they had seen the signs that al-'Azeez should surely imprison him for a time.

36. And there entered the prison with him two young men. One of them said, "Indeed, I have seen myself [in a dream] pressing wine." The other said, "Indeed, I have seen myself carrying upon my head [some] bread, from which the birds were eating. Inform us of its interpretation; indeed, we see you to be of those who do good."

37. He said, "You will not receive food that is provided to you except that I will inform you of its interpretation before it comes to you. That is from what my Lord has taught me. Indeed, I have left the religion of a people who do not believe in Allah, and they, in the Hereafter, are disbelievers.

38. And I have followed the religion of my fathers, Abraham, Isaac and Jacob. And it was not for us to associate anything with Allah. That is from the favor of Allah upon us and upon the people, but most of the people are not grateful.

39. [my] two companions of prison, are separate lords better or Allah, the One, the Prevailing?

40. You worship not besides Him except [mere] names you have named them, you and your fathers, for which Allah has sent down no authority. Legislation is not but for Allah. He has commanded that you worship not except Him. That is the correct religion, but most of the people do not know.

41. two companions of prison, as for one of you, he will give drink to his master of wine; but as for the other, he will be crucified, and

the birds will eat from his head. The matter has been decreed about which you both inquire."

42. And he said to the one whom he knew would go free, "Mention me before your master." But Satan made him forget the mention [to] his master, and Joseph remained in prison several years.

43. And [subsequently] the king said, "Indeed, I have seen [in a dream] seven fat cows being eaten by seven [that were] lean, and seven green spikes [of grain] and others [that were] dry. O eminent ones, explain to me my vision, if you should interpret visions."

44. They said, "[It is but] a mixture of false dreams, and we are not learned in the interpretation of dreams."

45. But the one who was freed and remembered after a time said, "I will inform you of its interpretation, so send me forth."

46. [He said], "Joseph, O man of truth, explain to us about seven fat cows eaten by seven [that were] lean, and seven green spikes [of grain] and others [that were] dry - that I may return to the people; perhaps they will know [about you]."

47. [Joseph] said, "You will plant for seven years consecutively; and what you harvest leave in its spikes, except a little from which you will eat.

48. Then will come after that seven difficult [years] which will consume what you saved for them, except a little from which you will store.

49. Then will come after that a year in which the people will be given rain and in which they will press [olives and grapes]."

50. And the king said, "Bring him to me." But when the messenger came to him, [Joseph] said, "Return to your master and ask him what is the case of the women who cut their hands. Indeed, my Lord is Knowing of their plan."

51. Said [the king to the women], "What was your condition when you sought to seduce Joseph?" They said, "Perfect is Allah! We know about him no evil." The wife of al-'Azeez said, "Now the truth has become evident. It was I who sought to seduce him, and indeed, he is of the truthful.

52. That is so al-'Azeez will know that I did not betray him in [his] absence and that Allah does not guide the plan of betrayers.

53. And I do not acquit myself. Indeed, the soul is a persistent enjoiner of evil, except those upon which my Lord has mercy. Indeed, my Lord is Forgiving and Merciful."

54. And the king said, "Bring him to me; I will appoint him exclusively for myself." And when he spoke to him, he said, "Indeed, you are today established [in position] and trusted."

55. [Joseph] said, "Appoint me over the storehouses of the land. Indeed, I will be a knowing guardian."

56. And thus We established Joseph in the land to settle therein wherever he willed. We touch with Our mercy whom We will, and We do not allow to be lost the reward of those who do good.

57. And the reward of the Hereafter is better for those who believed and were fearing Allah.

58. And the brothers of Joseph came [seeking food], and they entered upon him; and he recognized them, but he was to them unknown.

59. And when he had furnished them with their supplies, he said, "Bring me a brother of yours from your father. Do not you see that I give full measure and that I am the best of accommodators?

60. But if you do not bring him to me, no measure will there be [hereafter] for you from me, nor will you approach me."

61. They said, "We will attempt to dissuade his father from [keeping] him, and indeed, we will do [it]."

62. And [Joseph] said to his servants, "Put their merchandise into their saddlebags so they might recognize it when they have gone back to their people that perhaps they will [again] return."

63. So when they returned to their father, they said, "O our father, [further] measure has been denied to us, so send with us our brother [that] we will be given measure. And indeed, we will be his guardians."

64. He said, "Should I entrust you with him except [under coercion] as I entrusted you with his brother before? But Allah is the best guardian, and He is the most merciful of the merciful."

65. And when they opened their baggage, they found their merchandise returned to them. They said, "O our father, what [more] could we desire? This is our merchandise returned to us. And we will obtain supplies for our family and protect our brother and obtain an increase of a camel's load; that is an easy measurement."

66. [Jacob] said, "Never will I send him with you until you give me a promise by Allah that you will bring him [back] to me, unless you should be surrounded by enemies." And when they had given their promise, he said, "Allah, over what we say, is Witness."

67. And he said, "O my sons, do not enter from one gate but enter from different gates; and I cannot avail you against [the decree of] Allah at all. The decision is only for Allah; upon Him I have relied, and upon Him let those who would rely [indeed] rely."

68. And when they entered from where their father had ordered them, it did not avail them against Allah at all except [it was] a need within the soul of Jacob, which he satisfied. And indeed, he was a possessor of knowledge because of what We had taught him, but most of the people do not know.

69. And when they entered upon Joseph, he took his brother to himself; he said, "Indeed, I am your brother, so do not despair over what they used to do [to me]."

70. So when he had furnished them with their supplies, he put the [gold measuring] bowl into the bag of his brother. Then an announcer called out, "O caravan, indeed you are thieves."

71. They said while approaching them, "What is it you are missing?"

72. They said, "We are missing the measure of the king. And for he who produces it is [the reward of] a camel's load, and I am responsible for it."

73. They said, "By Allah, you have certainly known that we did not come to cause corruption in the land, and we have not been thieves."

74. The accusers said, "Then what would be its recompense if you should be liars?"

75. [The brothers] said, "Its recompense is that he in whose bag it is found - he [himself] will be its recompense. Thus do we recompense the wrongdoers."

76. So he began [the search] with their bags before the bag of his brother; then he extracted it from the bag of his brother. Thus did We plan for Joseph. He could not have taken his brother within the religion of the king except that Allah willed. We raise in degrees whom We will, but over every possessor of knowledge is one [more] knowing.

77. They said, "If he steals - a brother of his has stolen before." But Joseph kept it within himself and did not reveal it to them. He

said, "You are worse in position, and Allah is most knowing of what you describe."

78. They said, "O 'Azeez, indeed he has a father [who is] an old man, so take one of us in place of him. Indeed, we see you as a doer of good."

79. He said, "[I seek] the refuge of Allah [to prevent] that we take except him with whom we found our possession. Indeed, we would then be unjust."

80. So when they had despaired of him, they secluded themselves in private consultation. The eldest of them said, "Do you not know that your father has taken upon you an oath by Allah and [that] before you failed in [your duty to] Joseph? So I will never leave [this] land until my father permits me or Allah decides for me, and He is the best of judges.

81. Return to your father and say, "O our father, indeed your son has stolen, and we did not testify except to what we knew. And we were not witnesses of the unseen,

82. And ask the city in which we were and the caravan in which we came - and indeed, we are truthful,"

83. [Jacob] said, "Rather, your souls have enticed you to something, so patience is most fitting. Perhaps Allah will bring them to me all together. Indeed it is He who is the Knowing, the Wise."

84. And he turned away from them and said, "Oh, my sorrow over Joseph," and his eyes became white from grief, for he was [of that] a suppressor.

85. They said, "By Allah, you will not cease remembering Joseph until you become fatally ill or become of those who perish."

86. He said, "I only complain of my suffering and my grief to Allah, and I know from Allah that which you do not know.

87. my sons, go and find out about Joseph and his brother and despair not of relief from Allah. Indeed, no one despairs of relief from Allah except the disbelieving people."

88. So when they entered upon Joseph, they said, "O 'Azeez, adversity has touched us and our family, and we have come with goods poor in quality, but give us full measure and be charitable to us. Indeed, Allah rewards the charitable."

89. He said, "Do you know what you did with Joseph and his brother when you were ignorant?"

90. They said, "Are you indeed Joseph?" He said "I am Joseph, and this is my brother. Allah has certainly favored us. Indeed, he who fears Allah and is patient, then indeed, Allah does not allow to be lost the reward of those who do good."

91. They said, "By Allah, certainly has Allah preferred you over us, and indeed, we have been sinners."

92. He said, "No blame will there be upon you today. Allah will forgive you; and He is the most merciful of the merciful."

93. Take this, my shirt, and cast it over the face of my father; he will become seeing. And bring me your family, all together."

94. And when the caravan departed [from Egypt], their father said, "Indeed, I find the smell of Joseph [and would say that he was alive] if you did not think me weakened in mind."

95. They said, "By Allah, indeed you are in your [same] old error."

96. And when the bearer of good tidings arrived, he cast it over his face, and he returned [once again] seeing. He said, "Did I not tell you that I know from Allah that which you do not know?"

97. They said, "O our father, ask for us forgiveness of our sins; indeed, we have been sinners."

98. He said, "I will ask forgiveness for you from my Lord. Indeed, it is He who is the Forgiving, the Merciful."

99. And when they entered upon Joseph, he took his parents to himself and said, "Enter Egypt, Allah willing, safe [and secure]."

100. And he raised his parents upon the throne, and they bowed to him in prostration. And he said, "O my father, this is the explanation of my vision of before. My Lord has made it reality. And He was certainly good to me when He took me out of prison and brought you [here] from bedouin life after Satan had induced [estrangement] between me and my brothers. Indeed, my Lord is Subtle in what He wills. Indeed, it is He who is the Knowing, the Wise.

101. My Lord, You have given me [something] of sovereignty and taught me of the interpretation of dreams. Creator of the heavens and earth, You are my protector in this world and in the Hereafter. Cause me to die a Muslim and join me with the righteous."

102. That is from the news of the unseen which We reveal, [O Muhammad], to you. And you were not with them when they put together their plan while they conspired.

103. And most of the people, although you strive [for it], are not believers.

104. And you do not ask of them for it any payment. It is not except a reminder to the worlds.

105. And how many a sign within the heavens and earth do they pass over while they, therefrom, are turning away.

106. And most of them believe not in Allah except while they associate others with Him.

107. Then do they feel secure that there will not come to them an overwhelming [aspect] of the punishment of Allah or that the Hour will not come upon them suddenly while they do not perceive?

108. Say, "This is my way; I invite to Allah with insight, I and those who follow me. And exalted is Allah; and I am not of those who associate others with Him."

109. And We sent not before you [as messengers] except men to whom We revealed from among the people of cities. So have they not traveled through the earth and observed how was the end of those before them? And the home of the Hereafter is best for those who fear Allah; then will you not reason?

110. [They continued] until, when the messengers despaired and were certain that they had been denied, there came to them Our victory, and whoever We willed was saved. And Our punishment cannot be repelled from the people who are criminals.

111. There was certainly in their stories a lesson for those of understanding. Never was the Qur'an a narration invented, but a confirmation of what was before it and a detailed explanation of all things and guidance and mercy for a people who believe.

| Verses: 43 | Surah 13 Ar-R'ad | Makki |

In the name of Allah, the Entirely Merciful, the Especially Merciful.

01. Alif, Lam, Meem, Ra. These are the verses of the Book; and what has been revealed to you from your Lord is the truth, but most of the people do not believe.

02. It is Allah who erected the heavens without pillars that you [can] see; then He established Himself above the Throne and made subject the sun and the moon, each running [its course] for a specified term. He arranges [each] matter; He details the signs that you may, of the meeting with your Lord, be certain.

03. And it is He who spread the earth and placed therein firmly set mountains and rivers; and from all of the fruits He made therein two mates; He causes the night to cover the day. Indeed in that are signs for a people who give thought.

04. And within the land are neighboring plots and gardens of grapevines and crops and palm trees, [growing] several from a root or otherwise, watered with one water; but We make some of them exceed others in [quality of] fruit. Indeed in that are signs for a people who reason.

05. And if you are astonished, [O Muhammad] - then astonishing is their saying, "When we are dust, will we indeed be [brought] into a new creation?" Those are the ones who have disbelieved in their Lord, and those will have shackles upon their necks, and those are the companions of the Fire; they will abide therein eternally.

06. They impatiently urge you to bring about evil before good, while there has already occurred before them similar punishments [to what they demand]. And indeed, your Lord is full of forgiveness for the people despite their wrongdoing, and indeed, your Lord is severe in penalty.

07. And those who disbelieved say, "Why has a sign not been sent down to him from his Lord?" You are only a warner, and for every people is a guide.

08. Allah knows what every female carries and what the wombs lose [prematurely] or exceed. And everything with Him is by due measure.

09. [He is] Knower of the unseen and the witnessed, the Grand, the Exalted.

10. It is the same [to Him] concerning you whether one conceals [his] speech or one publicizes it and whether one is hidden by night or conspicuous [among others] by day.

11. For each one are successive [angels] before and behind him who protect him by the decree of Allah. Indeed, Allah will not change the condition of a people until they change what is in themselves. And when Allah intends for a people ill, there is no repelling it. And there is not for them besides Him any patron.

12. It is He who shows you lightening, [causing] fear and aspiration, and generates the heavy clouds.

13. And the thunder exalts [Allah] with praise of Him - and the angels [as well] from fear of Him - and He sends thunderbolts

and strikes therewith whom He wills while they dispute about Allah; and He is severe in assault.

14. To Him [alone] is the supplication of truth. And those they call upon besides Him do not respond to them with a thing, except as one who stretches his hands toward water [from afar, calling it] to reach his mouth, but it will not reach it [thus]. And the supplication of the disbelievers is not but in error [i.e. futility].

15. And to Allah prostrates whoever is within the heavens and the earth, willingly or by compulsion, and their shadows [as well] in the mornings and the afternoons.

16. Say, "Who is Lord of the heavens and earth?" Say, "Allah." Say, "Have you then taken besides Him allies not possessing [even] for themselves any benefit or any harm?" Say, "Is the blind equivalent to the seeing? Or is darkness equivalent to light? Or have they attributed to Allah partners who created like His creation so that the creation [of each] seemed similar to them?" Say, "Allah is the Creator of all things, and He is the One, the Prevailing."

17. He sends down from the sky, rain, and valleys flow according to their capacity, and the torrent carries a rising foam. And from that [ore] which they heat in the fire, desiring adornments and utensils, is a foam like it. Thus Allah presents [the example of] truth and falsehood. As for the foam, it vanishes, [being] cast off; but as for that which benefits the people, it remains on the earth. Thus does Allah present examples.

18. For those who have responded to their Lord is the best [reward], but those who did not respond to Him - if they had all that is in the earth entirely and the like of it with it, they would [attempt to] ransom themselves thereby. Those will have the worst account, and their refuge is Hell, and wretched is the resting place.

19. Then is he who knows that what has been revealed to you from your Lord is the truth like one who is blind? They will only be reminded who are people of understanding -

20. Those who fulfill the covenant of Allah and do not break the contract,

21. And those who join that which Allah has ordered to be joined and fear their Lord and are afraid of the evil of [their] account,

22. And those who are patient, seeking the countenance of their Lord, and establish prayer and spend from what We have provided for them secretly and publicly and prevent evil with good - those will have the good consequence of [this] home -

23. Gardens of perpetual residence; they will enter them with whoever were righteous among their fathers, their spouses and their descendants. And the angels will enter upon them from every gate, [saying],

24. "Peace be upon you for what you patiently endured. And excellent is the final home."

25. But those who break the covenant of Allah after contracting it and sever that which Allah has ordered to be joined and spread corruption on earth - for them is the curse, and they will have the worst home.

26. Allah extends provision for whom He wills and restricts [it]. And they rejoice in the worldly life, while the worldly life is not, compared to the Hereafter, except [brief] enjoyment.

27. And those who disbelieved say, "Why has a sign not been sent down to him from his Lord?" Say, [O Muhammad], "Indeed, Allah leaves astray whom He wills and guides to Himself whoever turns back [to Him] -

28. Those who have believed and whose hearts are assured by the remembrance of Allah. Unquestionably, by the remembrance of Allah hearts are assured."

29. Those who have believed and done righteous deeds - a good state is theirs and a good return.

30. Thus have We sent you to a community before which [other] communities have passed on so you might recite to them that which We revealed to you, while they disbelieve in the Most Merciful. Say, "He is my Lord; there is no deity except Him. Upon Him I rely, and to Him is my return."

31. And if there was any qur'an by which the mountains would be removed or the earth would be broken apart or the dead would be made to speak, [it would be this Qur'an], but to Allah belongs the affair entirely. Then have those who believed not accepted that had Allah willed, He would have guided the people, all of them? And those who disbelieve do not cease to be struck, for what they have done, by calamity - or it will descend near their home - until there comes the promise of Allah. Indeed, Allah does not fail in [His] promise.

32. And already were [other] messengers ridiculed before you, and I extended the time of those who disbelieved; then I seized them, and how [terrible] was My penalty.

33. Then is He who is a maintainer of every soul, [knowing] what it has earned, [like any other]? But to Allah they have attributed partners. Say, "Name them. Or do you inform Him of that which He knows not upon the earth or of what is apparent of speech?" Rather, their [own] plan has been made attractive to those who disbelieve, and they have been averted from the way. And whomever Allah leaves astray - there will be for him no guide.

34. For them will be punishment in the life of [this] world, and the punishment of the Hereafter is more severe. And they will not have from Allah any protector.

35. The example of Paradise, which the righteous have been promised, is [that] beneath it rivers flow. Its fruit is lasting, and its shade. That is the consequence for the righteous, and the consequence for the disbelievers is the Fire.

36. And [the believers among] those to whom We have given the [previous] Scripture rejoice at what has been revealed to you, [O Muhammad], but among the [opposing] factions are those who deny part of it. Say, "I have only been commanded to worship Allah and not associate [anything] with Him. To Him I invite, and to Him is my return."

37. And thus We have revealed it as an Arabic legislation. And if you should follow their inclinations after what has come to you of knowledge, you would not have against Allah any ally or any protector.

38. And We have already sent messengers before you and assigned to them wives and descendants. And it was not for a messenger to come with a sign except by permission of Allah. For every term is a decree.

39. Allah eliminates what He wills or confirms, and with Him is the Mother of the Book.

40. And whether We show you part of what We promise them or take you in death, upon you is only the [duty of] notification, and upon Us is the account.

41. Have they not seen that We set upon the land, reducing it from its borders? And Allah decides; there is no adjuster of His decision. And He is swift in account.

42. And those before them had plotted, but to Allah belongs the plan entirely. He knows what every soul earns, and the disbelievers will know for whom is the final home.

43. And those who have disbelieved say, "You are not a messenger." Say, [O Muhammad], "Sufficient is Allah as Witness between me and you, and [the witness of] whoever has knowledge of the Scripture."

Surah 14 Ibrahim

Verses: 52 — Makki

In the name of Allah, the Entirely Merciful, the Especially Merciful.

01. Alif, Lam, Ra. [This is] a Book which We have revealed to you, [O Muhammad], that you might bring mankind out of darknesses into the light by permission of their Lord - to the path of the Exalted in Might, the Praiseworthy -

02. Allah, to whom belongs whatever is in the heavens and whatever is on the earth. And woe to the disbelievers from a severe punishment

03. The ones who prefer the worldly life over the Hereafter and avert [people] from the way of Allah, seeking to make it (seem) deviant. Those are in extreme error.

04. And We did not send any messenger except [speaking] in the language of his people to state clearly for them, and Allah sends astray [thereby] whom He wills and guides whom He wills. And He is the Exalted in Might, the Wise.

05. And We certainly sent Moses with Our signs, [saying], "Bring out your people from darknesses into the light and remind them of the days of Allah." Indeed in that are signs for everyone patient and grateful.

06. And [recall, O Children of Israel], when Moses said to His people, "Remember the favor of Allah upon you when He saved you from the people of Pharaoh, who were afflicting you with the worst torment and were slaughtering your [newborn] sons and keeping your females alive. And in that was a great trial from your Lord.

07. And [remember] when your Lord proclaimed, 'If you are grateful, I will surely increase you [in favor]; but if you deny, indeed, My punishment is severe.' "

08. And Moses said, "If you should disbelieve, you and whoever is on the earth entirely - indeed, Allah is Free of need and Praiseworthy."

09. Has there not reached you the news of those before you - the people of Noah and 'Aad and Thamud and those after them?

No one knows them but Allah. Their messengers brought them clear proofs, but they returned their hands to their mouths and said, "Indeed, we disbelieve in that with which you have been sent, and indeed we are, about that to which you invite us, in disquieting doubt."

10. Their messengers said, "Can there be doubt about Allah, Creator of the heavens and earth? He invites you that He may forgive you of your sins, and He delays your death for a specified term." They said, "You are not but men like us who wish to avert us from what our fathers were worshipping. So bring us a clear authority."

11. Their messengers said to them, "We are only men like you, but Allah confers favor upon whom He wills of His servants. It has never been for us to bring you evidence except by permission of Allah. And upon Allah let the believers rely.

12. And why should we not rely upon Allah while He has guided us to our [good] ways. And we will surely be patient against whatever harm you should cause us. And upon Allah let those who would rely [indeed] rely."

13. And those who disbelieved said to their messengers, "We will surely drive you out of our land, or you must return to our religion." So their Lord inspired to them, "We will surely destroy the wrongdoers.

14. And We will surely cause you to dwell in the land after them. That is for he who fears My position and fears My threat."

15. And they requested victory from Allah, and disappointed, [therefore], was every obstinate tyrant.

16. Before him is Hell, and he will be given a drink of purulent water.

17. He will gulp it but will hardly [be able to] swallow it. And death will come to him from everywhere, but he is not to die. And before him is a massive punishment.

18. The example of those who disbelieve in their Lord is [that] their deeds are like ashes which the wind blows forcefully on a stormy day; they are unable [to keep] from what they earned a [single] thing. That is what is extreme error.

19. Have you not seen that Allah created the heavens and the earth in truth? If He wills, He can do away with you and produce a new creation.

20. And that is not difficult for Allah.

21. And they will come out [for judgement] before Allah all together, and the weak will say to those who were arrogant, "Indeed, we were your followers, so can you avail us anything against the punishment of Allah?" They will say, "If Allah had guided us, we would have guided you. It is all the same for us whether we show intolerance or are patient: there is for us no place of escape."

22. And Satan will say when the matter has been concluded, "Indeed, Allah had promised you the promise of truth. And I promised you, but I betrayed you. But I had no authority over you except that I invited you, and you responded to me. So do not blame me; but blame yourselves. I cannot be called to your aid, nor can you be called to my aid. Indeed, I deny your association of me [with Allah] before. Indeed, for the wrongdoers is a painful punishment."

23. And those who believed and did righteous deeds will be admitted to gardens beneath which rivers flow, abiding eternally therein by permission of their Lord; and their greeting therein will be, "Peace!"

24. Have you not considered how Allah presents an example, [making] a good word like a good tree, whose root is firmly fixed and its branches [high] in the sky?

25. It produces its fruit all the time, by permission of its Lord. And Allah presents examples for the people that perhaps they will be reminded.

26. And the example of a bad word is like a bad tree, uprooted from the surface of the earth, not having any stability.

27. Allah keeps firm those who believe, with the firm word, in worldly life and in the Hereafter. And Allah sends astray the wrongdoers. And Allah does what He wills.

28. Have you not considered those who exchanged the favor of Allah for disbelief and settled their people [in] the home of ruin?

29. [It is] Hell, which they will [enter to] burn, and wretched is the settlement.

30. And they have attributed to Allah equals to mislead [people] from His way. Say, "Enjoy yourselves, for indeed, your destination is the Fire."

31. [O Muhammad], tell My servants who have believed to establish prayer and spend from what We have provided them, secretly

and publicly, before a Day comes in which there will be no exchange, nor any friendships.

32. It is Allah who created the heavens and the earth and sent down rain from the sky and produced thereby some fruits as provision for you and subjected for you the ships to sail through the sea by His command and subjected for you the rivers.

33. And He subjected for you the sun and the moon, continuous [in orbit], and subjected for you the night and the day.

34. And He gave you from all you asked of Him. And if you should count the favor of Allah, you could not enumerate them. Indeed, mankind is [generally] most unjust and ungrateful.

35. And [mention, O Muhammad], when Abraham said, "My Lord, make this city [Makkah] secure and keep me and my sons away from worshipping idols.

36. My Lord, indeed they have led astray many among the people. So whoever follows me - then he is of me; and whoever disobeys me - indeed, You are [yet] Forgiving and Merciful.

37. Our Lord, I have settled some of my descendants in an uncultivated valley near Your sacred House, our Lord, that they may establish prayer. So make hearts among the people incline toward them and provide for them from the fruits that they might be grateful.

38. Our Lord, indeed You know what we conceal and what we declare, and nothing is hidden from Allah on the earth or in the heaven.

39. Praise to Allah, who has granted to me in old age Ishmael and Isaac. Indeed, my Lord is the Hearer of supplication.

40. My Lord, make me an establisher of prayer, and [many] from my descendants. Our Lord, and accept my supplication.

41. Our Lord, forgive me and my parents and the believers the Day the account is established."

42. And never think that Allah is unaware of what the wrongdoers do. He only delays them for a Day when eyes will stare [in horror].

43. Racing ahead, their heads raised up, their glance does not come back to them, and their hearts are void.

44. And, [O Muhammad], warn the people of a Day when the punishment will come to them and those who did wrong will say, "Our Lord, delay us for a short term; we will answer Your call and follow the messengers." [But it will be said], "Had you not sworn, before, that for you there would be no cessation?

45. And you lived among the dwellings of those who wronged themselves, and it had become clear to you how We dealt with them. And We presented for you [many] examples."
46. And they had planned their plan, but with Allah is [recorded] their plan, even if their plan had been [sufficient] to do away with the mountains.
47. So never think that Allah will fail in His promise to His messengers. Indeed, Allah is Exalted in Might and Owner of Retribution.
48. [It will be] on the Day the earth will be replaced by another earth, and the heavens [as well], and all creatures will come out before Allah, the One, the Prevailing.
49. And you will see the criminals that Day bound together in shackles,
50. Their garments of liquid pitch and their faces covered by the Fire.
51. So that Allah will recompense every soul for what it earned. Indeed, Allah is swift in account.
52. This [Qur'an] is notification for the people that they may be warned thereby and that they may know that He is but one God and that those of understanding will be reminded.

| Verses: 99 | Surah 15 Al-Hijr | Makki |

In the name of Allah, the Entirely Merciful, the Especially Merciful.

01. Alif, Lam, Ra. These are the verses of the Book and a clear Qur'an.
02. Perhaps those who disbelieve will wish that they had been Muslims.
03. Let them eat and enjoy themselves and be diverted by [false] hope, for they are going to know.
04. And We did not destroy any city but that for it was a known decree.
05. No nation will precede its term, nor will they remain thereafter.
06. And they say, "O you upon whom the message has been sent down, indeed you are mad.
07. Why do you not bring us the angels, if you should be among the truthful?"
08. We do not send down the angels except with truth; and the disbelievers would not then be reprieved.
09. Indeed, it is We who sent down the Qur'an and indeed, We will be its guardian.
10. And We had certainly sent [messengers] before you, [O Muhammad], among the sects of the former peoples.

11. And no messenger would come to them except that they ridiculed him.
12. Thus do We insert denial into the hearts of the criminals.
13. They will not believe in it, while there has already occurred the precedent of the former peoples.
14. And [even] if We opened to them a gate from the heaven and they continued therein to ascend,
15. They would say, "Our eyes have only been dazzled. Rather, we are a people affected by magic."
16. And We have placed within the heaven great stars and have beautified it for the observers.
17. And We have protected it from every devil expelled [from the mercy of Allah]
18. Except one who steals a hearing and is pursued by a clear burning flame.
19. And the earth - We have spread it and cast therein firmly set mountains and caused to grow therein [something] of every well-balanced thing.
20. And We have made for you therein means of living and [for] those for whom you are not providers.
21. And there is not a thing but that with Us are its depositories, and We do not send it down except according to a known measure.
22. And We have sent the fertilizing winds and sent down water from the sky and given you drink from it. And you are not its retainers.
23. And indeed, it is We who give life and cause death, and We are the Inheritor.
24. And We have already known the preceding [generations] among you, and We have already known the later [ones to come].
25. And indeed, your Lord will gather them; indeed, He is Wise and Knowing.
26. And We did certainly create man out of clay from an altered black mud.
27. And the jinn We created before from scorching fire.
28. And [mention, O Muhammad], when your Lord said to the angels, "I will create a human being out of clay from an altered black mud.

29. And when I have proportioned him and breathed into him of My [created] soul, then fall down to him in prostration."
30. So the angels prostrated - all of them entirely,
31. Except Iblees, he refused to be with those who prostrated.
32. [Allah] said, O Iblees, what is [the matter] with you that you are not with those who prostrate?"
33. He said, "Never would I prostrate to a human whom You created out of clay from an altered black mud."
34. [Allah] said, "Then get out of it, for indeed, you are expelled.
35. And indeed, upon you is the curse until the Day of Recompense."
36. He said, "My Lord, then reprieve me until the Day they are resurrected."
37. [Allah] said, "So indeed, you are of those reprieved
38. Until the Day of the time well-known."
39. [Iblees] said, "My Lord, because You have put me in error, I will surely make [disobedience] attractive to them on earth, and I will mislead them all
40. Except, among them, Your chosen servants."
41. [Allah] said, "This is a path [of return] to Me [that is] straight.
42. Indeed, My servants - no authority will you have over them, except those who follow you of the deviators.
43. And indeed, Hell is the promised place for them all.
44. It has seven gates; for every gate is of them a portion designated."
45. Indeed, the righteous will be within gardens and springs.
46. [Having been told], "Enter it in peace, safe [and secure]."
47. And We will remove whatever is in their breasts of resentment, [so they will be] brothers, on thrones facing each other.
48. No fatigue will touch them therein, nor from it will they [ever] be removed.
49. [O Muhammad], inform My servants that it is I who am the Forgiving, the Merciful.
50. And that it is My punishment which is the painful punishment.
51. And inform them about the guests of Abraham,
52. When they entered upon him and said, "Peace." [Abraham] said, "Indeed, we are fearful of you."

53. [The angels] said, "Fear not. Indeed, we give you good tidings of a learned boy."

54. He said, "Have you given me good tidings although old age has come upon me? Then of what [wonder] do you inform?"

55. They said, "We have given you good tidings in truth, so do not be of the despairing."

56. He said, "And who despairs of the mercy of his Lord except for those astray?"

57. [Abraham] said, "Then what is your business [here], O messengers?"

58. They said, "Indeed, we have been sent to a people of criminals,

59. Except the family of Lot; indeed, we will save them all

60. Except his wife." Allah decreed that she is of those who remain behind.

61. And when the messengers came to the family of Lot,

62. He said, "Indeed, you are people unknown."

63. They said, "But we have come to you with that about which they were disputing,

64. And we have come to you with truth, and indeed, we are truthful.

65. So set out with your family during a portion of the night and follow behind them and let not anyone among you look back and continue on to where you are commanded."

66. And We conveyed to him [the decree] of that matter: that those [sinners] would be eliminated by early morning.

67. And the people of the city came rejoicing.

68. [Lot] said, "Indeed, these are my guests, so do not shame me.

69. And fear Allah and do not disgrace me."

70. They said, "Have we not forbidden you from [protecting] people?"

71. [Lot] said, "These are my daughters - if you would be doers [of lawful marriage]."

72. By your life, [O Muhammad], indeed they were, in their intoxication, wandering blindly.

73. So the shriek seized them at sunrise.

74. And We made the highest part [of the city] its lowest and rained upon them stones of hard clay.

75. Indeed in that are signs for those who discern.
76. And indeed, those cities are [situated] on an established road.
77. Indeed in that is a sign for the believers.
78. And the companions of the thicket were [also] wrongdoers.
79. So We took retribution from them, and indeed, both [cities] are on a clear highway.
80. And certainly did the companions of Thamud deny the messengers.
81. And We gave them Our signs, but from them they were turning away.
82. And they used to carve from the mountains, houses, feeling secure.
83. But the shriek seized them at early morning.
84. So nothing availed them [from] what they used to earn.
85. And We have not created the heavens and earth and that between them except in truth. And indeed, the Hour is coming; so forgive with gracious forgiveness.
86. Indeed, your Lord - He is the Knowing Creator.
87. And We have certainly given you, [O Muhammad], seven of the often repeated [verses] and the great Qur'an.
88. Do not extend your eyes toward that by which We have given enjoyment to [certain] categories of the disbelievers, and do not grieve over them. And lower your wing to the believers
89. And say, "Indeed, I am the clear warner" -
90. Just as We had revealed [scriptures] to the separators
91. Who have made the Qur'an into portions.
92. So by your Lord, We will surely question them all
93. About what they used to do.
94. Then declare what you are commanded and turn away from the polytheists.
95. Indeed, We are sufficient for you against the mockers
96. Who make [equal] with Allah another deity. But they are going to know.
97. And We already know that your breast is constrained by what they say.
98. So exalt [Allah] with praise of your Lord and be of those who prostrate [to Him].
99. And worship your Lord until there comes to you the certainty (death).

| Verses: 128 | **Surah 16 An-Nahl** | Makki |

In the name of Allah, the Entirely Merciful, the Especially Merciful.

01. The command of Allah is coming, so be not impatient for it. Exalted is He and high above what they associate with Him.

02. He sends down the angels, with the inspiration of His command, upon whom He wills of His servants, [telling them], "Warn that there is no deity except Me; so fear Me."

03. He created the heavens and earth in truth. High is He above what they associate with Him.

04. He created man from a sperm-drop; then at once, he is a clear adversary.

05. And the grazing livestock He has created for you; in them is warmth and [numerous] benefits, and from them you eat.

06. And for you in them is [the enjoyment of] beauty when you bring them in [for the evening] and when you send them out [to pasture].

07. And they carry your loads to a land you could not have reached except with difficulty to yourselves. Indeed, your Lord is Kind and Merciful.

08. And [He created] the horses, mules and donkeys for you to ride and [as] adornment. And He creates that which you do not know.

09. And upon Allah is the direction of the [right] way, and among the various paths are those deviating. And if He willed, He could have guided you all.

10. It is He who sends down rain from the sky; from it is drink and from it is foliage in which you pasture [animals].

11. He causes to grow for you thereby the crops, olives, palm trees, grapevines, and from all the fruits. Indeed in that is a sign for a people who give thought.

12. And He has subjected for you the night and day and the sun and moon, and the stars are subjected by His command. Indeed in that are signs for a people who reason.

13. And [He has subjected] whatever He multiplied for you on the earth of varying colors. Indeed in that is a sign for a people who remember.

14. And it is He who subjected the sea for you to eat from it tender meat and to extract from it ornaments which you wear. And you see the ships plowing through it, and [He subjected it] that you may seek of His bounty; and perhaps you will be grateful.
15. And He has cast into the earth firmly set mountains, lest it shift with you, and [made] rivers and roads, that you may be guided,
16. And landmarks. And by the stars they are [also] guided.
17. Then is He who creates like one who does not create? So will you not be reminded?
18. And if you should count the favors of Allah, you could not enumerate them. Indeed, Allah is Forgiving and Merciful.
19. And Allah knows what you conceal and what you declare.
20. And those they invoke other than Allah create nothing, and they [themselves] are created.
21. They are, [in fact], dead, not alive, and they do not perceive when they will be resurrected.
22. Your god is one God. But those who do not believe in the Hereafter - their hearts are disapproving, and they are arrogant.
23. Assuredly, Allah knows what they conceal and what they declare. Indeed, He does not like the arrogant.
24. And when it is said to them, "What has your Lord sent down?" They say, "Legends of the former peoples,"
25. That they may bear their own burdens in full on the Day of Resurrection and some of the burdens of those whom they misguide without knowledge. Unquestionably, evil is that which they bear.
26. Those before them had already plotted, but Allah came at their building from the foundations, so the roof fell upon them from above them, and the punishment came to them from where they did not perceive.
27. Then on the Day of Resurrection He will disgrace them and say, "Where are My 'partners' for whom you used to oppose [the believers]?" Those who were given knowledge will say, "Indeed disgrace, this Day, and evil are upon the disbelievers" -
28. The ones whom the angels take in death [while] wronging themselves, and [who] then offer submission, [saying], "We were not doing any evil." But, yes! Indeed, Allah is Knowing of what you used to do.

29. So enter the gates of Hell to abide eternally therein, and how wretched is the residence of the arrogant.

30. And it will be said to those who feared Allah, "What did your Lord send down?" They will say, "[That which is] good." For those who do good in this world is good; and the home of the Hereafter is better. And how excellent is the home of the righteous -

31. Gardens of perpetual residence, which they will enter, beneath which rivers flow. They will have therein whatever they wish. Thus does Allah reward the righteous -

32. The ones whom the angels take in death, [being] good and pure; [the angels] will say, "Peace be upon you. Enter Paradise for what you used to do."

33. Do the disbelievers await [anything] except that the angels should come to them or there comes the command of your Lord? Thus did those do before them. And Allah wronged them not, but they had been wronging themselves.

34. So they were struck by the evil consequences of what they did and were enveloped by what they used to ridicule.

35. And those who associate others with Allah say, "If Allah had willed, we would not have worshipped anything other than Him, neither we nor our fathers, nor would we have forbidden anything through other than Him." Thus did those do before them. So is there upon the messengers except [the duty of] clear notification?

36. And We certainly sent into every nation a messenger, [saying], "Worship Allah and avoid Taghut." And among them were those whom Allah guided, and among them were those upon whom error was [deservedly] decreed. So proceed through the earth and observe how was the end of the deniers.

37. [Even] if you should strive for their guidance, [O Muhammad], indeed, Allah does not guide those He sends astray, and they will have no helpers.

38. And they swear by Allah their strongest oaths [that] Allah will not resurrect one who dies. But yes - [it is] a true promise [binding] upon Him, but most of the people do not know.

39. [It is] so He will make clear to them [the truth of] that wherein they differ and so those who have disbelieved may know that they were liars.

40. Indeed, Our word to a thing when We intend it is but that We say to it, "Be," and it is.

41. And those who emigrated for [the cause of] Allah after they had been wronged - We will surely settle them in this world in a good place; but the reward of the Hereafter is greater, if only they could know.

42. [They are] those who endured patiently and upon their Lord relied.

43. And We sent not before you except men to whom We revealed [Our message]. So ask the people of the message if you do not know.

44. [We sent them] with clear proofs and written ordinances. And We revealed to you the message that you may make clear to the people what was sent down to them and that they might give thought.

45. Then, do those who have planned evil deeds feel secure that Allah will not cause the earth to swallow them or that the punishment will not come upon them from where they do not perceive?

46. Or that He would not seize them during their [usual] activity, and they could not cause failure?

47. Or that He would not seize them gradually [in a state of dread]? But indeed, your Lord is Kind and Merciful.

48. Have they not considered what things Allah has created? Their shadows incline to the right and to the left, prostrating to Allah, while they are humble.

49. And to Allah prostrates whatever is in the heavens and whatever is on the earth of creatures, and the angels [as well], and they are not arrogant.

50. They fear their Lord above them, and they do what they are commanded.

51. And Allah has said, "Do not take for yourselves two deities. He is but one God, so fear only Me."

52. And to Him belongs whatever is in the heavens and the earth, and to Him is [due] worship constantly. Then is it other than Allah that you fear?

53. And whatever you have of favor - it is from Allah. Then when adversity touches you, to Him you cry for help.

54. Then when He removes the adversity from you, at once a party of you associates others with their Lord

55. So they will deny what We have given them. Then enjoy yourselves, for you are going to know.
56. And they assign to what they do not know a portion of that which We have provided them. By Allah, you will surely be questioned about what you used to invent.
57. And they attribute to Allah daughters - exalted is He - and for them is what they desire.
58. And when one of them is informed of [the birth of] a female, his face becomes dark, and he suppresses grief.
59. He hides himself from the people because of the ill of which he has been informed. Should he keep it in humiliation or bury it in the ground? Unquestionably, evil is what they decide.
60. For those who do not believe in the Hereafter is the description of evil; and for Allah is the highest attribute. And He is Exalted in Might, the Wise.
61. And if Allah were to impose blame on the people for their wrongdoing, He would not have left upon the earth any creature, but He defers them for a specified term. And when their term has come, they will not remain behind an hour, nor will they precede [it].
62. And they attribute to Allah that which they dislike, and their tongues assert the lie that they will have the best [from Him]. Assuredly, they will have the Fire, and they will be [therein] neglected.
63. By Allah, We did certainly send [messengers] to nations before you, but Satan made their deeds attractive to them. And he is the disbelievers' ally today [as well], and they will have a painful punishment.
64. And We have not revealed to you the Book, [O Muhammad], except for you to make clear to them that wherein they have differed and as guidance and mercy for a people who believe.
65. And Allah has sent down rain from the sky and given life thereby to the earth after its lifelessness. Indeed in that is a sign for a people who listen.
66. And indeed, for you in grazing livestock is a lesson. We give you drink from what is in their bellies - between excretion and blood - pure milk, palatable to drinkers.
67. And from the fruits of the palm trees and grapevines you take intoxicant and good provision. Indeed in that is a sign for a people who reason.

68. And your Lord inspired to the bee, "Take for yourself among the mountains, houses, and among the trees and [in] that which they construct.

69. Then eat from all the fruits and follow the ways of your Lord laid down [for you]." There emerges from their bellies a drink, varying in colors, in which there is healing for people. Indeed in that is a sign for a people who give thought.

70. And Allah created you; then He will take you in death. And among you is he who is reversed to the most decrepit [old] age so that he will not know, after [having had] knowledge, a thing. Indeed, Allah is Knowing and Competent.

71. And Allah has favored some of you over others in provision. But those who were favored would not hand over their provision to those whom their right hands possess so they would be equal to them therein. Then is it the favor of Allah they reject?

72. And Allah has made for you from yourselves mates and has made for you from your mates sons and grandchildren and has provided for you from the good things. Then in falsehood do they believe and in the favor of Allah they disbelieve?

73. And they worship besides Allah that which does not possess for them [the power of] provision from the heavens and the earth at all, and [in fact], they are unable.

74. So do not assert similarities to Allah. Indeed, Allah knows and you do not know.

75. Allah presents an example: a slave [who is] owned and unable to do a thing and he to whom We have provided from Us good provision, so he spends from it secretly and publicly. Can they be equal? Praise to Allah! But most of them do not know.

76. And Allah presents an example of two men, one of them dumb and unable to do a thing, while he is a burden to his guardian. Wherever he directs him, he brings no good. Is he equal to one who commands justice, while he is on a straight path?

77. And to Allah belongs the unseen [aspects] of the heavens and the earth. And the command for the Hour is not but as a glance of the eye or even nearer. Indeed, Allah is over all things competent.

78. And Allah has extracted you from the wombs of your mothers not knowing a thing, and He made for you hearing and vision and intellect that perhaps you would be grateful.

79. Do they not see the birds controlled in the atmosphere of the sky? None holds them up except Allah. Indeed in that are signs for a people who believe.

80. And Allah has made for you from your homes a place of rest and made for you from the hides of the animals tents which you find light on your day of travel and your day of encampment; and from their wool, fur and hair is furnishing and enjoyment for a time.

81. And Allah has made for you, from that which He has created, shadows and has made for you from the mountains, shelters and has made for you garments which protect you from the heat and garments which protect you from your [enemy in] battle. Thus does He complete His favor upon you that you might submit [to Him].

82. But if they turn away, [O Muhammad] - then only upon you is [responsibility for] clear notification.

83. They recognize the favor of Allah; then they deny it. And most of them are disbelievers.

84. And [mention] the Day when We will resurrect from every nation a witness. Then it will not be permitted to the disbelievers [to apologize or make excuses], nor will they be asked to appease [Allah].

85. And when those who wronged see the punishment, it will not be lightened for them, nor will they be reprieved.

86. And when those who associated others with Allah see their "partners," they will say," Our Lord, these are our partners [to You] whom we used to invoke besides You." But they will throw at them the statement, "Indeed, you are liars."

87. And they will impart to Allah that Day [their] submission, and lost from them is what they used to invent.

88. Those who disbelieved and averted [others] from the way of Allah - We will increase them in punishment over [their] punishment for what corruption they were causing.

89. And [mention] the Day when We will resurrect among every nation a witness over them from themselves. And We will bring you, [O Muhammad], as a witness over your nation. And We have sent down to you the Book as clarification for all things and as guidance and mercy and good tidings for the Muslims.

90. Indeed, Allah orders justice and good conduct and giving to relatives and forbids immorality and bad conduct and oppression. He admonishes you that perhaps you will be reminded.

91. And fulfill the covenant of Allah when you have taken it, [O believers], and do not break oaths after their confirmation while you have made Allah, over you, a witness. Indeed, Allah knows what you do.

92. And do not be like she who untwisted her spun thread after it was strong [by] taking your oaths as [means of] deceit between you because one community is more plentiful [in number or wealth] than another community. Allah only tries you thereby. And He will surely make clear to you on the Day of Resurrection that over which you used to differ.

93. And if Allah had willed, He could have made you [of] one religion, but He causes to stray whom He wills and guides whom He wills. And you will surely be questioned about what you used to do.

94. And do not take your oaths as [means of] deceit between you, lest a foot slip after it was [once] firm, and you would taste evil [in this world] for what [people] you diverted from the way of Allah, and you would have [in the Hereafter] a great punishment.

95. And do not exchange the covenant of Allah for a small price. Indeed, what is with Allah is best for you, if only you could know.

96. Whatever you have will end, but what Allah has is lasting. And We will surely give those who were patient their reward according to the best of what they used to do.

97. Whoever does righteousness, whether male or female, while he is a believer - We will surely cause him to live a good life, and We will surely give them their reward [in the Hereafter] according to the best of what they used to do.

98. So when you recite the Qur'an, [first] seek refuge in Allah from Satan, the expelled [from His mercy].

99. Indeed, there is for him no authority over those who have believed and rely upon their Lord.

100. His authority is only over those who take him as an ally and those who through him associate others with Allah.

101. And when We substitute a verse in place of a verse - and Allah is most knowing of what He sends down - they say, "You, [O Muhammad], are but an inventor [of lies]." But most of them do not know.

102. Say, [O Muhammad], "The Pure Spirit has brought it down from your Lord in truth to make firm those who believe and as

guidance and good tidings to the Muslims."

103. And We certainly know that they say, "It is only a human being who teaches the Prophet." The tongue of the one they refer to is foreign, and this Qur'an is [in] a clear Arabic language.

104. Indeed, those who do not believe in the verses of Allah - Allah will not guide them, and for them is a painful punishment.

105. They only invent falsehood who do not believe in the verses of Allah, and it is those who are the liars.

106. Whoever disbelieves in Allah after his belief... except for one who is forced [to renounce his religion] while his heart is secure in faith. But those who [willingly] open their breasts to disbelief, upon them is wrath from Allah, and for them is a great punishment;

107. That is because they preferred the worldly life over the Hereafter and that Allah does not guide the disbelieving people.

108. Those are the ones over whose hearts and hearing and vision Allah has sealed, and it is those who are the heedless.

109. Assuredly, it is they, in the Hereafter, who will be the losers.

110. Then, indeed your Lord, to those who emigrated after they had been compelled [to renounce their religion] and thereafter fought [for the cause of Allah] and were patient - indeed, your Lord, after that, is Forgiving and Merciful

111. On the Day when every soul will come disputing for itself, and every soul will be fully compensated for what it did, and they will not be wronged.

112. And Allah presents an example: a city which was safe and secure, its provision coming to it in abundance from every location, but it denied the favors of Allah. So Allah made it taste the envelopment of hunger and fear for what they had been doing.

113. And there had certainly come to them a Messenger from among themselves, but they denied him; so punishment overtook them while they were wrongdoers.

114. Then eat of what Allah has provided for you [which is] lawful and good. And be grateful for the favor of Allah, if it is [indeed] Him that you worship.

115. He has only forbidden to you dead animals, blood, the flesh of swine, and that which has been dedicated to other than Allah. But whoever is forced [by necessity], neither desiring [it] nor transgressing [its limit] - then indeed, Allah is Forgiving and Merciful.

116. And do not say about what your tongues assert of untruth, "This is lawful and this is unlawful," to invent falsehood about Allah. Indeed, those who invent falsehood about Allah will not succeed.

117. [It is but] a brief enjoyment, and they will have a painful punishment.

118. And to those who are Jews We have prohibited that which We related to you before. And We did not wrong them [thereby], but they were wronging themselves.

119. Then, indeed your Lord, to those who have done wrong out of ignorance and then repent after that and correct themselves - indeed, your Lord, thereafter, is Forgiving and Merciful.

120. Indeed, Abraham was a [comprehensive] leader, devoutly obedient to Allah, inclining toward truth, and he was not of those who associate others with Allah.

121. [He was] grateful for His favors. Allah chose him and guided him to a straight path.

122. And We gave him good in this world, and indeed, in the Hereafter he will be among the righteous.

123. Then We revealed to you, [O Muhammad], to follow the religion of Abraham, inclining toward truth; and he was not of those who associate with Allah.

124. The sabbath was only appointed for those who differed over it. And indeed, your Lord will judge between them on the Day of Resurrection concerning that over which they used to differ.

125. Invite to the way of your Lord with wisdom and good instruction, and argue with them in a way that is best. Indeed, your Lord is most knowing of who has strayed from His way, and He is most knowing of who is [rightly] guided.

126. And if you punish [an enemy, O believers], punish with an equivalent of that with which you were harmed. But if you are patient - it is better for those who are patient.

127. And be patient, [O Muhammad], and your patience is not but through Allah. And do not grieve over them and do not be in distress over what they conspire.

128. Indeed, Allah is with those who fear Him and those who are doers of good.

| Verses: 111 | **Surah 17 Al-Israa** | Makki |

In the name of Allah, the Entirely Merciful, the Especially Merciful.

01. Exalted is He who took His Servant by night from al-Masjid al-Haram to al-Masjid al-Aqsa, whose surroundings We have blessed, to show him of Our signs. Indeed, He is the Hearing, the Seeing.

02. And We gave Moses the Scripture and made it a guidance for the Children of Israel that you not take other than Me as Disposer of affairs,

03. descendants of those We carried [in the ship] with Noah. Indeed, he was a grateful servant.

04. And We conveyed to the Children of Israel in the Scripture that, "You will surely cause corruption on the earth twice, and you will surely reach [a degree of] great haughtiness.

05. So when the [time of] promise came for the first of them, We sent against you servants of Ours - those of great military might, and they probed [even] into the homes, and it was a promise fulfilled.

06. Then We gave back to you a return victory over them. And We reinforced you with wealth and sons and made you more numerous in manpower

07. [And said], "If you do good, you do good for yourselves; and if you do evil, [you do it] to yourselves." Then when the final promise came, [We sent your enemies] to sadden your faces and to enter the temple in Jerusalem, as they entered it the first time, and to destroy what they had taken over with [total] destruction.

08. [Then Allah said], "It is expected, [if you repent], that your Lord will have mercy upon you. But if you return [to sin], We will return [to punishment]. And We have made Hell, for the disbelievers, a prison-bed."

09. Indeed, this Qur'an guides to that which is most suitable and gives good tidings to the believers who do righteous deeds that they will have a great reward.

10. And that those who do not believe in the Hereafter - We have prepared for them a painful punishment.

11. And man supplicates for evil as he supplicates for good, and man is ever hasty.

12. And We have made the night and day two signs, and We erased the sign of the night and made the sign of the day visible that you may seek bounty from your Lord and may know the number of years and the account [of time]. And everything We have set out in detail.

13. And [for] every person We have imposed his fate upon his neck, and We will produce for him on the Day of Resurrection a record which he will encounter spread open.

14. [It will be said], "Read your record. Sufficient is yourself against you this Day as accountant."

15. Whoever is guided is only guided for [the benefit of] his soul. And whoever errs only errs against it. And no bearer of burdens will bear the burden of another. And never would We punish until We sent a messenger.

16. And when We intend to destroy a city, We command its affluent but they defiantly disobey therein; so the word comes into effect upon it, and We destroy it with [complete] destruction.

17. And how many have We destroyed from the generations after Noah. And sufficient is your Lord, concerning the sins of His servants, as Acquainted and Seeing.

18. Whoever should desire the immediate - We hasten for him from it what We will to whom We intend. Then We have made for him Hell, which he will [enter to] burn, censured and banished.

19. But whoever desires the Hereafter and exerts the effort due to it while he is a believer - it is those whose effort is ever appreciated [by Allah].

20. To each [category] We extend - to these and to those - from the gift of your Lord. And never has the gift of your Lord been restricted.

21. Look how We have favored [in provision] some of them over others. But the Hereafter is greater in degrees [of difference] and greater in distinction.

22. Do not make [as equal] with Allah another deity and [thereby] become censured and forsaken.

23. And your Lord has decreed that you not worship except Him, and to parents, good treatment. Whether one or both of them reach old age [while] with you, say not to them [so much as], "uff," and do not repel them but speak to them a noble word.

24. And lower to them the wing of humility out of mercy and say, "My

Lord, have mercy upon them as they brought me up [when I was] small."

25. Your Lord is most knowing of what is within yourselves. If you should be righteous [in intention] - then indeed He is ever, to the often returning [to Him], Forgiving.

26. And give the relative his right, and [also] the poor and the traveler, and do not spend wastefully.

27. Indeed, the wasteful are brothers of the devils, and ever has Satan been to his Lord ungrateful.

28. And if you [must] turn away from the needy awaiting mercy from your Lord which you expect, then speak to them a gentle word.

29. And do not make your hand [as] chained to your neck or extend it completely and [thereby] become blamed and insolvent.

30. Indeed, your Lord extends provision for whom He wills and restricts [it]. Indeed He is ever, concerning His servants, Acquainted and Seeing.

31. And do not kill your children for fear of poverty. We provide for them and for you. Indeed, their killing is ever a great sin.

32. And do not approach unlawful sexual intercourse. Indeed, it is ever an immorality and is evil as a way.

33. And do not kill the soul which Allah has forbidden, except by right. And whoever is killed unjustly - We have given his heir authority, but let him not exceed limits in [the matter of] taking life. Indeed, he has been supported [by the law].

34. And do not approach the property of an orphan, except in the way that is best, until he reaches maturity. And fulfill [every] commitment. Indeed, the commitment is ever [that about which one will be] questioned.

35. And give full measure when you measure, and weigh with an even balance. That is the best [way] and best in result.

36. And do not pursue that of which you have no knowledge. Indeed, the hearing, the sight and the heart - about all those [one] will be questioned.

37. And do not walk upon the earth exultantly. Indeed, you will never tear the earth [apart], and you will never reach the mountains in height.

38. All that - its evil is ever, in the sight of your Lord, detested.

39. That is from what your Lord has revealed to you, [O

Muhammad], of wisdom. And, [O mankind], do not make [as equal] with Allah another deity, lest you be thrown into Hell, blamed and banished.

40. Then, has your Lord chosen you for [having] sons and taken from among the angels daughters? Indeed, you say a grave saying.

41. And We have certainly diversified [the contents] in this Qur'an that mankind may be reminded, but it does not increase the disbelievers except in aversion.

42. Say, [O Muhammad], "If there had been with Him [other] gods, as they say, then they [each] would have sought to the Owner of the Throne a way."

43. Exalted is He and high above what they say by great sublimity.

44. The seven heavens and the earth and whatever is in them exalt Him. And there is not a thing except that it exalts [Allah] by His praise, but you do not understand their [way of] exalting. Indeed, He is ever Forbearing and Forgiving.

45. And when you recite the Qur'an, We put between you and those who do not believe in the Hereafter a concealed partition.

46. And We have placed over their hearts coverings, lest they understand it, and in their ears deafness. And when you mention your Lord alone in the Qur'an, they turn back in aversion.

47. We are most knowing of how they listen to it when they listen to you and [of] when they are in private conversation, when the wrongdoers say, "You follow not but a man affected by magic."

48. Look how they strike for you comparisons; but they have strayed, so they cannot [find] a way.

49. And they say, "When we are bones and crumbled particles, will we [truly] be resurrected as a new creation?"

50. Say, "Be you stones or iron

51. Or [any] creation of that which is great within your breasts." And they will say, "Who will restore us?" Say, "He who brought you forth the first time." Then they will nod their heads toward you and say, "When is that?" Say, "Perhaps it will be soon -

52. On the Day He will call you and you will respond with praise of Him and think that you had not remained [in the world] except for a little."

53. And tell My servants to say that which is best. Indeed, Satan

induces [dissension] among them. Indeed Satan is ever, to mankind, a clear enemy.

54. Your Lord is most knowing of you. If He wills, He will have mercy upon you; or if He wills, He will punish you. And We have not sent you, [O Muhammad], over them as a manager.

55. And your Lord is most knowing of whoever is in the heavens and the earth. And We have made some of the prophets exceed others [in various ways], and to David We gave the book [of Psalms].

56. Say, "Invoke those you have claimed [as gods] besides Him, for they do not possess the [ability for] removal of adversity from you or [for its] transfer [to someone else]."

57. Those whom they invoke seek means of access to their Lord, [striving as to] which of them would be nearest, and they hope for His mercy and fear His punishment. Indeed, the punishment of your Lord is ever feared.

58. And there is no city but that We will destroy it before the Day of Resurrection or punish it with a severe punishment. That has ever been in the Register inscribed.

59. And nothing has prevented Us from sending signs except that the former peoples denied them. And We gave Thamud the she-camel as a visible sign, but they wronged her. And We send not the signs except as a warning.

60. And [remember, O Muhammad], when We told you, "Indeed, your Lord has encompassed the people." And We did not make the sight which We showed you except as a trial for the people, as was the accursed tree [mentioned] in the Qur'an. And We threaten them, but it increases them not except in great transgression.

61. And [mention] when We said to the angles, "Prostrate to Adam," and they prostrated, except for Iblees. He said, "Should I prostrate to one You created from clay?"

62. [Iblees] said, "Do You see this one whom You have honored above me? If You delay me until the Day of Resurrection, I will surely destroy his descendants, except for a few."

63. [Allah] said, "Go, for whoever of them follows you, indeed Hell will be the recompense of you - an ample recompense.

64. And incite [to senselessness] whoever you can among them with your voice and assault them with your horses and foot soldiers and become a partner in their wealth and their children and promise them." But Satan does not promise them except delusion.

65. Indeed, over My [believing] servants there is for you no authority. And sufficient is your Lord as Disposer of affairs.

66. It is your Lord who drives the ship for you through the sea that you may seek of His bounty. Indeed, He is ever, to you, Merciful.

67. And when adversity touches you at sea, lost are [all] those you invoke except for Him. But when He delivers you to the land, you turn away [from Him]. And ever is man ungrateful.

68. Then do you feel secure that [instead] He will not cause a part of the land to swallow you or send against you a storm of stones? Then you would not find for yourselves an advocate.

69. Or do you feel secure that He will not send you back into the sea another time and send upon you a hurricane of wind and drown you for what you denied? Then you would not find for yourselves against Us an avenger.

70. And We have certainly honored the children of Adam and carried them on the land and sea and provided for them of the good things and preferred them over much of what We have created, with [definite] preference.

71. [Mention, O Muhammad], the Day We will call forth every people with their record [of deeds]. Then whoever is given his record in his right hand - those will read their records, and injustice will not be done to them, [even] as much as a thread [inside the date seed].

72. And whoever is blind in this [life] will be blind in the Hereafter and more astray in way.

73. And indeed, they were about to tempt you away from that which We revealed to you in order to [make] you invent about Us something else; and then they would have taken you as a friend.

74. And if We had not strengthened you, you would have almost inclined to them a little.

75. Then [if you had], We would have made you taste double [punishment in] life and double [after] death. Then you would not find for yourself against Us a helper.

76. And indeed, they were about to drive you from the land to evict you therefrom. And then [when they do], they will not remain [there] after you, except for a little.

77. [That is Our] established way for those We had sent before you of Our messengers; and you will not find in Our way any alteration.

78. Establish prayer at the decline of the sun [from its meridian] until the darkness of the night and [also] the Qur'an of dawn. Indeed, the recitation of dawn is ever witnessed.
79. And from [part of] the night, pray with it as additional [worship] for you; it is expected that your Lord will resurrect you to a praised station.
80. And say, "My Lord, cause me to enter a sound entrance and to exit a sound exit and grant me from Yourself a supporting authority."
81. And say, "Truth has come, and falsehood has departed. Indeed is falsehood, [by nature], ever bound to depart."
82. And We send down of the Qur'an that which is healing and mercy for the believers, but it does not increase the wrongdoers except in loss.
83. And when We bestow favor upon the disbeliever, he turns away and distances himself; and when evil touches him, he is ever despairing.
84. Say, "Each works according to his manner, but your Lord is most knowing of who is best guided in way."
85. And they ask you, [O Muhammad], about the soul. Say, "The soul is of the affair of my Lord. And mankind have not been given of knowledge except a little."
86. And if We willed, We could surely do away with that which We revealed to you. Then you would not find for yourself concerning it an advocate against Us.
87. Except [We have left it with you] as a mercy from your Lord. Indeed, His favor upon you has ever been great.
88. Say, "If mankind and the jinn gathered in order to produce the like of this Qur'an, they could not produce the like of it, even if they were to each other assistants."
89. And We have certainly diversified for the people in this Qur'an from every [kind] of example, but most of the people refused [anything] except disbelief.
90. And they say, "We will not believe you until you break open for us from the ground a spring.
91. Or [until] you have a garden of palm tress and grapes and make rivers gush forth within them in force [and abundance]
92. Or you make the heaven fall upon us in fragments as you have claimed or you bring Allah and the angels before [us]

93. Or you have a house of gold or you ascend into the sky. And [even then], we will not believe in your ascension until you bring down to us a book we may read." Say, "Exalted is my Lord! Was I ever but a human messenger?"

94. And what prevented the people from believing when guidance came to them except that they said, "Has Allah sent a human messenger?"

95. Say, "If there were upon the earth angels walking securely, We would have sent down to them from the heaven an angel [as a] messenger."

96. Say, "Sufficient is Allah as Witness between me and you. Indeed he is ever, concerning His servants, Acquainted and Seeing."

97. And whoever Allah guides - he is the [rightly] guided; and whoever He sends astray - you will never find for them protectors besides Him, and We will gather them on the Day of Resurrection [fallen] on their faces - blind, dumb and deaf. Their refuge is Hell; every time it subsides We increase them in blazing fire.

98. That is their recompense because they disbelieved in Our verses and said, "When we are bones and crumbled particles, will we [truly] be resurrected [in] a new creation?"

99. Do they not see that Allah, who created the heavens and earth, is [the one] Able to create the likes of them? And He has appointed for them a term, about which there is no doubt. But the wrongdoers refuse [anything] except disbelief.

100. Say [to them], "If you possessed the depositories of the mercy of my Lord, then you would withhold out of fear of spending." And ever has man been stingy.

101. And We had certainly given Moses nine evident signs, so ask the Children of Israel [about] when he came to them and Pharaoh said to him, "Indeed I think, O Moses, that you are affected by magic."

102. [Moses] said, "You have already known that none has sent down these [signs] except the Lord of the heavens and the earth as evidence, and indeed I think, O Pharaoh, that you are destroyed."

103. So he intended to drive them from the land, but We drowned him and those with him all together.

104. And We said after Pharaoh to the Children of Israel, "Dwell in the land, and when there comes the promise of the Hereafter, We will bring you forth in [one] gathering."

105. And with the truth We have sent the Qur'an down, and with the truth it has descended. And We have not sent you, [O Muhammad], except as a bringer of good tidings and a warner.

106. And [it is] a Qur'an which We have separated [by intervals] that you might recite it to the people over a prolonged period. And We have sent it down progressively.

107. Say, "Believe in it or do not believe. Indeed, those who were given knowledge before it - when it is recited to them, they fall upon their faces in prostration,

108. And they say, "Exalted is our Lord! Indeed, the promise of our Lord has been fulfilled."

109. And they fall upon their faces weeping, and the Qur'an increases them in humble submission.

110. Say, "Call upon Allah or call upon the Most Merciful. Whichever [name] you call - to Him belong the best names." And do not recite [too] loudly in your prayer or [too] quietly but seek between that an [intermediate] way.

111. And say, "Praise to Allah, who has not taken a son and has had no partner in [His] dominion and has no [need of a] protector out of weakness; and glorify Him with [great] glorification."

Verses: 110	Surah 18 Al-Kahf	Makki

In the name of Allah, the Entirely Merciful, the Especially Merciful.

01. [All] praise is [due] to Allah, who has sent down upon His Servant the Book and has not made therein any deviance.

02. [He has made it] straight, to warn of severe punishment from Him and to give good tidings to the believers who do righteous deeds that they will have a good reward

03. In which they will remain forever

04. And to warn those who say, "Allah has taken a son."

05. They have no knowledge of it, nor had their fathers. Grave is the word that comes out of their mouths; they speak not except a lie.

06. Then perhaps you would kill yourself through grief over them, [O Muhammad], if they do not believe in this message, [and] out of sorrow.

07. Indeed, We have made that which is on the earth adornment for it that We may test them [as to] which of them is best in deed.

08. And indeed, We will make that which is upon it [into] a barren ground.

09. Or have you thought that the companions of the cave and the inscription were, among Our signs, a wonder?

10. [Mention] when the youths retreated to the cave and said, "Our Lord, grant us from Yourself mercy and prepare for us from our affair right guidance."

11. So We cast [a cover of sleep] over their ears within the cave for a number of years.

12. Then We awakened them that We might show which of the two factions was most precise in calculating what [extent] they had remained in time.

13. It is We who relate to you, [O Muhammad], their story in truth. Indeed, they were youths who believed in their Lord, and We increased them in guidance.

14. And We made firm their hearts when they stood up and said, "Our Lord is the Lord of the heavens and the earth. Never will we invoke besides Him any deity. We would have certainly spoken, then, an excessive transgression.

15. These, our people, have taken besides Him deities. Why do they not bring for [worship of] them a clear authority? And who is more unjust than one who invents about Allah a lie?"

16. [The youths said to one another], "And when you have withdrawn from them and that which they worship other than Allah, retreat to the cave. Your Lord will spread out for you of His mercy and will prepare for you from your affair facility."

17. And [had you been present], you would see the sun when it rose, inclining away from their cave on the right, and when it set, passing away from them on the left, while they were [laying] within an open space thereof. That was from the signs of Allah. He whom Allah guides is the [rightly] guided, but he whom He leaves astray - never will you find for him a protecting guide.

18. And you would think them awake, while they were asleep. And We turned them to the right and to the left, while their dog stretched his forelegs at the entrance. If you had looked at them, you would have turned from them in flight and been filled by them with terror.

19. And similarly, We awakened them that they might question one another. Said a speaker from among them, "How long have you remained [here]?" They said, "We have remained a day or part of a day." They said, "Your Lord is most knowing of how long you remained. So send one of you with this silver coin of yours to the city and let him look to which is the best of food and bring you provision from it and let him be cautious. And let no one be aware of you.

20. Indeed, if they come to know of you, they will stone you or return you to their religion. And never would you succeed, then - ever."

21. And similarly, We caused them to be found that they [who found them] would know that the promise of Allah is truth and that of the Hour there is no doubt. [That was] when they disputed among themselves about their affair and [then] said, "Construct over them a structure. Their Lord is most knowing about them." Said those who prevailed in the matter, "We will surely take [for ourselves] over them a masjid."

22. They will say there were three, the fourth of them being their dog; and they will say there were five, the sixth of them being their dog - guessing at the unseen; and they will say there were seven, and the eighth of them was their dog. Say, [O Muhammad], "My Lord is most knowing of their number. None knows them except a few. So do not argue about them except with an obvious argument and do not inquire about them among [the speculators] from anyone."

23. And never say of anything, "Indeed, I will do that tomorrow,"

24. Except [when adding], "If Allah wills." And remember your Lord when you forget [it] and say, "Perhaps my Lord will guide me to what is nearer than this to right conduct."

25. And they remained in their cave for three hundred years and exceeded by nine.

26. Say, "Allah is most knowing of how long they remained. He has [knowledge of] the unseen [aspects] of the heavens and the earth. How Seeing is He and how Hearing! They have not besides Him any protector, and He shares not His legislation with anyone."

27. And recite, [O Muhammad], what has been revealed to you of the Book of your Lord. There is no changer of His words, and never will you find in other than Him a refuge.

28. And keep yourself patient [by being] with those who call upon their Lord in the morning and the evening, seeking His countenance. And let not your eyes pass beyond them, desiring adornments of the worldly life, and do not obey one whose heart We have made heedless of Our remembrance and who follows his desire and whose affair is ever [in] neglect.

29. And say, "The truth is from your Lord, so whoever wills - let him believe; and whoever wills - let him disbelieve." Indeed, We have prepared for the wrongdoers a fire whose walls will surround them. And if they call for relief, they will be relieved with water like murky oil, which scalds [their] faces. Wretched is the drink, and evil is the resting place.

30. Indeed, those who have believed and done righteous deeds - indeed, We will not allow to be lost the reward of any who did well in deeds.

31. Those will have gardens of perpetual residence; beneath them rivers will flow. They will be adorned therein with bracelets of gold and will wear green garments of fine silk and brocade, reclining therein on adorned couches. Excellent is the reward, and good is the resting place.

32. And present to them an example of two men: We granted to one of them two gardens of grapevines, and We bordered them with palm trees and placed between them [fields of] crops.

33. Each of the two gardens produced its fruit and did not fall short thereof in anything. And We caused to gush forth within them a river.

34. And he had fruit, so he said to his companion while he was conversing with him, "I am greater than you in wealth and mightier in [numbers of] men."

35. And he entered his garden while he was unjust to himself. He said, "I do not think that this will perish - ever.

36. And I do not think the Hour will occur. And even if I should be brought back to my Lord, I will surely find better than this as a return."

37. His companion said to him while he was conversing with him, "Have you disbelieved in He who created you from dust and then from a sperm-drop and then proportioned you [as] a man?

38. But as for me, He is Allah, my Lord, and I do not associate with my Lord anyone.

39. And why did you, when you entered your garden, not say, 'What

Allah willed [has occurred]; there is no power except in Allah '? Although you see me less than you in wealth and children,

40. It may be that my Lord will give me [something] better than your garden and will send upon it a calamity from the sky, and it will become a smooth, dusty ground,

41. Or its water will become sunken [into the earth], so you would never be able to seek it."

42. And his fruits were encompassed [by ruin], so he began to turn his hands about [in dismay] over what he had spent on it, while it had collapsed upon its trellises, and said, "Oh, I wish I had not associated with my Lord anyone."

43. And there was for him no company to aid him other than Allah, nor could he defend himself.

44. There the authority is [completely] for Allah, the Truth. He is best in reward and best in outcome.

45. And present to them the example of the life of this world, [its being] like rain which We send down from the sky, and the vegetation of the earth mingles with it and [then] it becomes dry remnants, scattered by the winds. And Allah is ever, over all things, Perfect in Ability.

46. Wealth and children are [but] adornment of the worldly life. But the enduring good deeds are better to your Lord for reward and better for [one's] hope.

47. And [warn of] the Day when We will remove the mountains and you will see the earth prominent, and We will gather them and not leave behind from them anyone.

48. And they will be presented before your Lord in rows, [and He will say], "You have certainly come to Us just as We created you the first time. But you claimed that We would never make for you an appointment."

49. And the record [of deeds] will be placed [open], and you will see the criminals fearful of that within it, and they will say, "Oh, woe to us! What is this book that leaves nothing small or great except that it has enumerated it?" And they will find what they did present [before them]. And your Lord does injustice to no one.

50. And [mention] when We said to the angels, "Prostrate to Adam," and they prostrated, except for Iblees. He was of the jinn and departed from the command of his Lord. Then will you take him and his

descendants as allies other than Me while they are enemies to you? Wretched it is for the wrongdoers as an exchange.

51. I did not make them witness to the creation of the heavens and the earth or to the creation of themselves, and I would not have taken the misguiders as assistants.

52. And [warn of] the Day when He will say, "Call 'My partners' whom you claimed," and they will invoke them, but they will not respond to them. And We will put between them [a valley of] destruction.

53. And the criminals will see the Fire and will be certain that they are to fall therein. And they will not find from it a way elsewhere.

54. And We have certainly diversified in this Qur'an for the people from every [kind of] example; but man has ever been, most of anything, [prone to] dispute.

55. And nothing has prevented the people from believing when guidance came to them and from asking forgiveness of their Lord except that there [must] befall them the [accustomed] precedent of the former peoples or that the punishment should come [directly] before them.

56. And We send not the messengers except as bringers of good tidings and warners. And those who disbelieve dispute by [using] falsehood to [attempt to] invalidate thereby the truth and have taken My verses, and that of which they are warned, in ridicule.

57. And who is more unjust than one who is reminded of the verses of his Lord but turns away from them and forgets what his hands have put forth? Indeed, We have placed over their hearts coverings, lest they understand it, and in their ears deafness. And if you invite them to guidance - they will never be guided, then - ever.

58. And your Lord is the Forgiving, full of mercy. If He were to impose blame upon them for what they earned, He would have hastened for them the punishment. Rather, for them is an appointment from which they will never find an escape.

59. And those cities - We destroyed them when they wronged, and We made for their destruction an appointed time.

60. And [mention] when Moses said to his servant, "I will not cease [traveling] until I reach the junction of the two seas or continue for a long period."

61. But when they reached the junction between them, they forgot their fish, and it took its course into the sea, slipping away.

62. So when they had passed beyond it, [Moses] said to his boy, "Bring us our morning meal. We have certainly suffered in this, our journey, [much] fatigue."

63. He said, "Did you see when we retired to the rock? Indeed, I forgot [there] the fish. And none made me forget it except Satan - that I should mention it. And it took its course into the sea amazingly".

64. [Moses] said, "That is what we were seeking." So they returned, following their footprints.

65. And they found a servant from among Our servants to whom we had given mercy from us and had taught him from Us a [certain] knowledge.

66. Moses said to him, "May I follow you on [the condition] that you teach me from what you have been taught of sound judgement?"

67. He said, "Indeed, with me you will never be able to have patience.

68. And how can you have patience for what you do not encompass in knowledge?"

69. [Moses] said, "You will find me, if Allah wills, patient, and I will not disobey you in [any] order."

70. He said, "Then if you follow me, do not ask me about anything until I make to you about it mention."

71. So they set out, until when they had embarked on the ship, al-Khidhr tore it open. [Moses] said, "Have you torn it open to drown its people? You have certainly done a grave thing."

72. [Al-Khidhr] said, "Did I not say that with me you would never be able to have patience?"

73. [Moses] said, "Do not blame me for what I forgot and do not cover me in my matter with difficulty."

74. So they set out, until when they met a boy, al-Khidhr killed him. [Moses] said, "Have you killed a pure soul for other than [having killed] a soul? You have certainly done a deplorable thing."

75. [Al-Khidhr] said, "Did I not tell you that with me you would never be able to have patience?"

76. [Moses] said, "If I should ask you about anything after this, then do not keep me as a companion. You have obtained from me an excuse."

77. So they set out, until when they came to the people of a town, they asked its people for food, but they refused to offer them

hospitality. And they found therein a wall about to collapse, so al-Khidhr restored it. [Moses] said, "If you wished, you could have taken for it a payment."

78. [Al-Khidhr] said, "This is parting between me and you. I will inform you of the interpretation of that about which you could not have patience.

79. As for the ship, it belonged to poor people working at sea. So I intended to cause defect in it as there was after them a king who seized every [good] ship by force.

80. And as for the boy, his parents were believers, and we feared that he would overburden them by transgression and disbelief.

81. So we intended that their Lord should substitute for them one better than him in purity and nearer to mercy.

82. And as for the wall, it belonged to two orphan boys in the city, and there was beneath it a treasure for them, and their father had been righteous. So your Lord intended that they reach maturity and extract their treasure, as a mercy from your Lord. And I did it not of my own accord. That is the interpretation of that about which you could not have patience."

83. And they ask you, [O Muhammad], about Dhul-Qarnayn. Say, "I will recite to you about him a report."

84. Indeed We established him upon the earth, and We gave him to everything a way.

85. So he followed a way

86. Until, when he reached the setting of the sun, he found it [as if] setting in a spring of dark mud, and he found near it a people. Allah said, "O Dhul-Qarnayn, either you punish [them] or else adopt among them [a way of] goodness."

87. He said, "As for one who wrongs, we will punish him. Then he will be returned to his Lord, and He will punish him with a terrible punishment.

88. But as for one who believes and does righteousness, he will have a reward of Paradise, and we will speak to him from our command with ease."

89. Then he followed a way

90. Until, when he came to the rising of the sun, he found it rising on a people for whom We had not made against it any shield.

91. Thus. And We had encompassed [all] that he had in knowledge.

92. Then he followed a way
93. Until, when he reached [a pass] between two mountains, he found beside them a people who could hardly understand [his] speech.
94. They said, "O Dhul-Qarnayn, indeed Gog and Magog are [great] corrupters in the land. So may we assign for you an expenditure that you might make between us and them a barrier?"
95. He said, "That in which my Lord has established me is better [than what you offer], but assist me with strength; I will make between you and them a dam.
96. Bring me sheets of iron" - until, when he had leveled [them] between the two mountain walls, he said, "Blow [with bellows]," until when he had made it [like] fire, he said, "Bring me, that I may pour over it molten copper."
97. So Gog and Magog were unable to pass over it, nor were they able [to effect] in it any penetration.
98. [Dhul-Qarnayn] said, "This is a mercy from my Lord; but when the promise of my Lord comes, He will make it level, and ever is the promise of my Lord true."
99. And We will leave them that day surging over each other, and [then] the Horn will be blown, and We will assemble them in [one] assembly.
100. And We will present Hell that Day to the Disbelievers, on display -
101. Those whose eyes had been within a cover [removed] from My remembrance, and they were not able to hear.
102. Then do those who disbelieve think that they can take My servants instead of Me as allies? Indeed, We have prepared Hell for the disbelievers as a lodging.
103. Say, [O Muhammad], "Shall we [believers] inform you of the greatest losers as to [their] deeds?
104. [They are] those whose effort is lost in worldly life, while they think that they are doing well in work."
105. Those are the ones who disbelieve in the verses of their Lord and in [their] meeting Him, so their deeds have become worthless; and We will not assign to them on the Day of Resurrection any importance.
106. That is their recompense - Hell - for what they denied and [because] they took My signs and My messengers in ridicule.

107. Indeed, those who have believed and done righteous deeds - they will have the Gardens of Paradise as a lodging,

108. Wherein they abide eternally. They will not desire from it any transfer.

109. Say, "If the sea were ink for [writing] the words of my Lord, the sea would be exhausted before the words of my Lord were exhausted, even if We brought the like of it as a supplement."

110. Say, "I am only a man like you, to whom has been revealed that your god is one God. So whoever would hope for the meeting with his Lord - let him do righteous work and not associate in the worship of his Lord anyone."

Surah 19 Maryam

Verses: 98 | Makki

In the name of Allah, the Entirely Merciful, the Especially Merciful.

01. Kaf, Ha, Ya, 'Ayn, Sad.

02. [This is] a mention of the mercy of your Lord to His servant Zechariah

03. When he called to his Lord a private supplication.

04. He said, "My Lord, indeed my bones have weakened, and my head has filled with white, and never have I been in my supplication to You, my Lord, unhappy.

05. And indeed, I fear the successors after me, and my wife has been barren, so give me from Yourself an heir

06. Who will inherit me and inherit from the family of Jacob. And make him, my Lord, pleasing [to You]."

07. [He was told], "O Zechariah, indeed We give you good tidings of a boy whose name will be John. We have not assigned to any before [this] name."

08. He said, "My Lord, how will I have a boy when my wife has been barren and I have reached extreme old age?"

09. [An angel] said, "Thus [it will be]; your Lord says, 'It is easy for Me, for I created you before, while you were nothing.' "

10. [Zechariah] said, "My Lord, make for me a sign." He said, "Your sign is that you will not speak to the people for three nights, [being] sound."

11. So he came out to his people from the prayer chamber and signaled to them to exalt [Allah] in the morning and afternoon.

12. [Allah] said, "O John, take the Scripture with determination." And We gave him judgement [while yet] a boy

13. And affection from Us and purity, and he was fearing of Allah

14. And dutiful to his parents, and he was not a disobedient tyrant.

15. And peace be upon him the day he was born and the day he dies and the day he is raised alive.

16. And mention, [O Muhammad], in the Book [the story of] Mary, when she withdrew from her family to a place toward the east.

17. And she took, in seclusion from them, a screen. Then We sent to her Our Angel, and he represented himself to her as a well-proportioned man.

18. She said, "Indeed, I seek refuge in the Most Merciful from you, [so leave me], if you should be fearing of Allah."

19. He said, "I am only the messenger of your Lord to give you [news of] a pure boy."

20. She said, "How can I have a boy while no man has touched me and I have not been unchaste?"

21. He said, "Thus [it will be]; your Lord says, 'It is easy for Me, and We will make him a sign to the people and a mercy from Us. And it is a matter [already] decreed.' "

22. So she conceived him, and she withdrew with him to a remote place.

23. And the pains of childbirth drove her to the trunk of a palm tree. She said, "Oh, I wish I had died before this and was in oblivion, forgotten."

24. But he called her from below her, "Do not grieve; your Lord has provided beneath you a stream.

25. And shake toward you the trunk of the palm tree; it will drop upon you ripe, fresh dates.

26. So eat and drink and be contented. And if you see from among humanity anyone, say, 'Indeed, I have vowed to the Most Merciful abstention, so I will not speak today to [any] man.' "

27. Then she brought him to her people, carrying him. They said, "O Mary, you have certainly done a thing unprecedented.

28. sister of Aaron, your father was not a man of evil, nor was your mother unchaste."

29. So she pointed to him. They said, "How can we speak to one who is in the cradle a child?"

30. [Jesus] said, "Indeed, I am the servant of Allah. He has given me the Scripture and made me a prophet.

31. And He has made me blessed wherever I am and has enjoined upon me prayer and zakah as long as I remain alive

32. And [made me] dutiful to my mother, and He has not made me a wretched tyrant.

33. And peace is on me the day I was born and the day I will die and the day I am raised alive."

34. That is Jesus, the son of Mary - the word of truth about which they are in dispute.

35. It is not [befitting] for Allah to take a son; exalted is He! When He decrees an affair, He only says to it, "Be," and it is.

36. [Jesus said], "And indeed, Allah is my Lord and your Lord, so worship Him. That is a straight path."

37. Then the factions differed [concerning Jesus] from among them, so woe to those who disbelieved - from the scene of a tremendous Day.

38. How [clearly] they will hear and see the Day they come to Us, but the wrongdoers today are in clear error.

39. And warn them, [O Muhammad], of the Day of Regret, when the matter will be concluded; and [yet], they are in [a state of] heedlessness, and they do not believe.

40. Indeed, it is We who will inherit the earth and whoever is on it, and to Us they will be returned.

41. And mention in the Book [the story of] Abraham. Indeed, he was a man of truth and a prophet.

42. [Mention] when he said to his father, "O my father, why do you worship that which does not hear and does not see and will not benefit you at all?

43. my father, indeed there has come to me of knowledge that which has not come to you, so follow me; I will guide you to an even path.

44. my father, do not worship Satan. Indeed Satan has ever been, to the Most Merciful, disobedient.

45. my father, indeed I fear that there will touch you a punishment from the Most Merciful so you would be to Satan a companion [in Hellfire]."

46. [His father] said, "Have you no desire for my gods, O Abraham?

If you do not desist, I will surely stone you, so avoid me a prolonged time."
47. [Abraham] said, "Peace will be upon you. I will ask forgiveness for you of my Lord. Indeed, He is ever gracious to me.
48. And I will leave you and those you invoke other than Allah and will invoke my Lord. I expect that I will not be in invocation to my Lord unhappy."
49. So when he had left them and those they worshipped other than Allah, We gave him Isaac and Jacob, and each [of them] We made a prophet.
50. And We gave them of Our mercy, and we made for them a reputation of high honor.
51. And mention in the Book, Moses. Indeed, he was chosen, and he was a messenger and a prophet.
52. And We called him from the side of the mount at [his] right and brought him near, confiding [to him].
53. And We gave him out of Our mercy his brother Aaron as a prophet.
54. And mention in the Book, Ishmael. Indeed, he was true to his promise, and he was a messenger and a prophet.
55. And he used to enjoin on his people prayer and zakah and was to his Lord pleasing.
56. And mention in the Book, Idrees. Indeed, he was a man of truth and a prophet.
57. And We raised him to a high station.
58. Those were the ones upon whom Allah bestowed favor from among the prophets of the descendants of Adam and of those We carried [in the ship] with Noah, and of the descendants of Abraham and Israel, and of those whom We guided and chose. When the verses of the Most Merciful were recited to them, they fell in prostration and weeping.
59. But there came after them successors who neglected prayer and pursued desires; so they are going to meet evil -
60. Except those who repent, believe and do righteousness; for those will enter Paradise and will not be wronged at all.
61. [Therein are] gardens of perpetual residence which the Most Merciful has promised His servants in the unseen. Indeed, His promise has ever been coming.

62. They will not hear therein any ill speech - only [greetings of] peace - and they will have their provision therein, morning and afternoon.

63. That is Paradise, which We give as inheritance to those of Our servants who were fearing of Allah.

64. [Gabriel said], "And we [angels] descend not except by the order of your Lord. To Him belongs that before us and that behind us and what is in between. And never is your Lord forgetful -

65. Lord of the heavens and the earth and whatever is between them - so worship Him and have patience for His worship. Do you know of any similarity to Him?"

66. And the disbeliever says, "When I have died, am I going to be brought forth alive?"

67. Does man not remember that We created him before, while he was nothing?

68. So by your Lord, We will surely gather them and the devils; then We will bring them to be present around Hell upon their knees.

69. Then We will surely extract from every sect those of them who were worst against the Most Merciful in insolence.

70. Then, surely it is We who are most knowing of those most worthy of burning therein.

71. And there is none of you except he will come to it. This is upon your Lord an inevitability decreed.

72. Then We will save those who feared Allah and leave the wrongdoers within it, on their knees.

73. And when Our verses are recited to them as clear evidences, those who disbelieve say to those who believe, "Which of [our] two parties is best in position and best in association?"

74. And how many a generation have We destroyed before them who were better in possessions and [outward] appearance?

75. Say, "Whoever is in error - let the Most Merciful extend for him an extension [in wealth and time] until, when they see that which they were promised - either punishment [in this world] or the Hour [of resurrection] - they will come to know who is worst in position and weaker in soldiers."

76. And Allah increases those who were guided, in guidance, and the enduring good deeds are better to your Lord for reward and better for recourse.

77. Then, have you seen he who disbelieved in Our verses and said, "I will surely be given wealth and children [in the next life]?"
78. Has he looked into the unseen, or has he taken from the Most Merciful a promise?
79. No! We will record what he says and extend for him from the punishment extensively.
80. And We will inherit him [in] what he mentions, and he will come to Us alone.
81. And they have taken besides Allah [false] deities that they would be for them [a source of] honor.
82. No! Those "gods" will deny their worship of them and will be against them opponents [on the Day of Judgement].
83. Do you not see that We have sent the devils upon the disbelievers, inciting them to [evil] with [constant] incitement?
84. So be not impatient over them. We only count out to them a [limited] number.
85. On the Day We will gather the righteous to the Most Merciful as a delegation
86. And will drive the criminals to Hell in thirst
87. None will have [power of] intercession except he who had taken from the Most Merciful a covenant.
88. And they say, "The Most Merciful has taken [for Himself] a son."
89. You have done an atrocious thing.
90. The heavens almost rupture therefrom and the earth splits open and the mountains collapse in devastation
91. That they attribute to the Most Merciful a son.
92. And it is not appropriate for the Most Merciful that He should take a son.
93. There is no one in the heavens and earth but that he comes to the Most Merciful as a servant.
94. He has enumerated them and counted them a [full] counting.
95. And all of them are coming to Him on the Day of Resurrection alone.
96. Indeed, those who have believed and done righteous deeds - the Most Merciful will appoint for them affection.

97. So, [O Muhammad], We have only made Qur'an easy in the Arabic language that you may give good tidings thereby to the righteous and warn thereby a hostile people.

98. And how many have We destroyed before them of generations? Do you perceive of them anyone or hear from them a sound?

| Verses: 135 | **Surah 20 Taa-Haa** | Makki |

In the name of Allah, the Entirely Merciful, the Especially Merciful.

01. Ta, Ha.
02. We have not sent down to you the Qur'an that you be distressed
03. But only as a reminder for those who fear [Allah] -
04. A revelation from He who created the earth and highest heavens,
05. The Most Merciful [who is] above the Throne established.
06. To Him belongs what is in the heavens and what is on the earth and what is between them and what is under the soil.
07. And if you speak aloud - then indeed, He knows the secret and what is [even] more hidden.
08. Allah - there is no deity except Him. To Him belong the best names.
09. And has the story of Moses reached you? -
10. When he saw a fire and said to his family, "Stay here; indeed, I have perceived a fire; perhaps I can bring you a torch or find at the fire some guidance."
11. And when he came to it, he was called, "O Moses,
12. Indeed, I am your Lord, so remove your sandals. Indeed, you are in the sacred valley of Tuwa.
13. And I have chosen you, so listen to what is revealed [to you].
14. Indeed, I am Allah. There is no deity except Me, so worship Me and establish prayer for My remembrance.
15. Indeed, the Hour is coming - I almost conceal it - so that every soul may be recompensed according to that for which it strives.
16. So do not let one avert you from it who does not believe in it and follows his desire, for you [then] would perish.
17. And what is that in your right hand, O Moses?"
18. He said, "It is my staff; I lean upon it, and I bring down leaves for my sheep and I have therein other uses."

19. [Allah] said, "Throw it down, O Moses."
20. So he threw it down, and thereupon it was a snake, moving swiftly.
21. [Allah] said, "Seize it and fear not; We will return it to its former condition.
22. And draw in your hand to your side; it will come out white without disease - another sign,
23. That We may show you [some] of Our greater signs.
24. Go to Pharaoh. Indeed, he has transgressed."
25. [Moses] said, "My Lord, expand for me my breast [with assurance]
26. And ease for me my task
27. And untie the knot from my tongue
28. That they may understand my speech.
29. And appoint for me a minister from my family -
30. Aaron, my brother.
31. Increase through him my strength
32. And let him share my task
33. That we may exalt You much
34. And remember You much.
35. Indeed, You are of us ever Seeing."
36. [Allah] said, "You have been granted your request, O Moses.
37. And We had already conferred favor upon you another time,
38. When We inspired to your mother what We inspired,
39. [Saying], 'Cast him into the chest and cast it into the river, and the river will throw it onto the bank; there will take him an enemy to Me and an enemy to him.' And I bestowed upon you love from Me that you would be brought up under My eye.
40. [And We favored you] when your sister went and said, 'Shall I direct you to someone who will be responsible for him?' So We restored you to your mother that she might be content and not grieve. And you killed someone, but We saved you from retaliation and tried you with a [severe] trial. And you remained [some] years among the people of Madyan. Then you came [here] at the decreed time, O Moses.
41. And I produced you for Myself.
42. Go, you and your brother, with My signs and do not slacken in My remembrance.

43. Go, both of you, to Pharaoh. Indeed, he has transgressed.
44. And speak to him with gentle speech that perhaps he may be reminded or fear [Allah]."
45. They said, "Our Lord, indeed we are afraid that he will hasten [punishment] against us or that he will transgress."
46. [Allah] said, "Fear not. Indeed, I am with you both; I hear and I see.
47. So go to him and say, 'Indeed, we are messengers of your Lord, so send with us the Children of Israel and do not torment them. We have come to you with a sign from your Lord. And peace will be upon he who follows the guidance.
48. Indeed, it has been revealed to us that the punishment will be upon whoever denies and turns away.' "
49. [Pharaoh] said, "So who is the Lord of you two, O Moses?"
50. He said, "Our Lord is He who gave each thing its form and then guided [it]."
51. [Pharaoh] said, "Then what is the case of the former generations?"
52. [Moses] said, "The knowledge thereof is with my Lord in a record. My Lord neither errs nor forgets."
53. [It is He] who has made for you the earth as a bed [spread out] and inserted therein for you roadways and sent down from the sky, rain and produced thereby categories of various plants.
54. Eat [therefrom] and pasture your livestock. Indeed, in that are signs for those of intelligence.
55. From the earth We created you, and into it We will return you, and from it We will extract you another time.
56. And We certainly showed Pharaoh Our signs - all of them - but he denied and refused.
57. He said, "Have you come to us to drive us out of our land with your magic, O Moses?
58. Then we will surely bring you magic like it, so make between us and you an appointment, which we will not fail to keep and neither will you, in a place assigned."
59. [Moses] said, "Your appointment is on the day of the festival when the people assemble at mid-morning."
60. So Pharaoh went away, put together his plan, and then came [to Moses].

61. Moses said to the magicians summoned by Pharaoh, "Woe to you! Do not invent a lie against Allah or He will exterminate you with a punishment; and he has failed who invents [such falsehood]."
62. So they disputed over their affair among themselves and concealed their private conversation.
63. They said, "Indeed, these are two magicians who want to drive you out of your land with their magic and do away with your most exemplary way.
64. So resolve upon your plan and then come [forward] in line. And he has succeeded today who overcomes."
65. They said, "O Moses, either you throw or we will be the first to throw."
66. He said, "Rather, you throw." And suddenly their ropes and staffs seemed to him from their magic that they were moving [like snakes].
67. And he sensed within himself apprehension, did Moses.
68. Allah said, "Fear not. Indeed, it is you who are superior.
69. And throw what is in your right hand; it will swallow up what they have crafted. What they have crafted is but the trick of a magician, and the magician will not succeed wherever he is."
70. So the magicians fell down in prostration. They said, "We have believed in the Lord of Aaron and Moses."
71. [Pharaoh] said, "You believed him before I gave you permission. Indeed, he is your leader who has taught you magic. So I will surely cut off your hands and your feet on opposite sides, and I will crucify you on the trunks of palm trees, and you will surely know which of us is more severe in [giving] punishment and more enduring."
72. They said, "Never will we prefer you over what has come to us of clear proofs and [over] He who created us. So decree whatever you are to decree. You can only decree for this worldly life.
73. Indeed, we have believed in our Lord that He may forgive us our sins and what you compelled us [to do] of magic. And Allah is better and more enduring."
74. Indeed, whoever comes to his Lord as a criminal - indeed, for him is Hell; he will neither die therein nor live.
75. But whoever comes to Him as a believer having done righteous deeds - for those will be the highest degrees [in position]:

76. Gardens of perpetual residence beneath which rivers flow, wherein they abide eternally. And that is the reward of one who purifies himself.
77. And We had inspired to Moses, "Travel by night with My servants and strike for them a dry path through the sea; you will not fear being overtaken [by Pharaoh] nor be afraid [of drowning]."
78. So Pharaoh pursued them with his soldiers, and there covered them from the sea that which covered them,
79. And Pharaoh led his people astray and did not guide [them].
80. Children of Israel, We delivered you from your enemy, and We made an appointment with you at the right side of the mount, and We sent down to you manna and quails,
81. [Saying], "Eat from the good things with which We have provided you and do not transgress [or oppress others] therein, lest My anger should descend upon you. And he upon whom My anger descends has certainly fallen."
82. But indeed, I am the Perpetual Forgiver of whoever repents and believes and does righteousness and then continues in guidance.
83. [Allah] said, "And what made you hasten from your people, O Moses?"
84. He said, "They are close upon my tracks, and I hastened to You, my Lord, that You be pleased."
85. [Allah] said, "But indeed, We have tried your people after you [departed], and the Samiri has led them astray."
86. So Moses returned to his people, angry and grieved. He said, "O my people, did your Lord not make you a good promise? Then, was the time [of its fulfillment] too long for you, or did you wish that wrath from your Lord descend upon you, so you broke your promise [of obedience] to me?"
87. They said, "We did not break our promise to you by our will, but we were made to carry burdens from the ornaments of the people [of Pharaoh], so we threw them [into the fire], and thus did the Samiri throw."
88. And he extracted for them [the statue of] a calf which had a lowing sound, and they said, "This is your god and the god of Moses, but he forgot."
89. Did they not see that it could not return to them any speech and that it did not possess for them any harm or benefit?

90. And Aaron had already told them before [the return of Moses], "O my people, you are only being tested by it, and indeed, your Lord is the Most Merciful, so follow me and obey my order."

91. They said, "We will never cease being devoted to the calf until Moses returns to us."

92. [Moses] said, "O Aaron, what prevented you, when you saw them going astray,

93. From following me? Then have you disobeyed my order?"

94. [Aaron] said, "O son of my mother, do not seize [me] by my beard or by my head. Indeed, I feared that you would say, 'You caused division among the Children of Israel, and you did not observe [or await] my word.' "

95. [Moses] said, "And what is your case, O Samiri?"

96. He said, "I saw what they did not see, so I took a handful [of dust] from the track of the messenger and threw it, and thus did my soul entice me."

97. [Moses] said, "Then go. And indeed, it is [decreed] for you in [this] life to say, 'No contact.' And indeed, you have an appointment [in the Hereafter] you will not fail to keep. And look at your 'god' to which you remained devoted. We will surely burn it and blow it into the sea with a blast.

98. Your god is only Allah, except for whom there is no deity. He has encompassed all things in knowledge."

99. Thus, [O Muhammad], We relate to you from the news of what has preceded. And We have certainly given you from Us the Qur'an.

100. Whoever turns away from it - then indeed, he will bear on the Day of Resurrection a burden,

101. [Abiding] eternally therein, and evil it is for them on the Day of Resurrection as a load -

102. The Day the Horn will be blown. And We will gather the criminals, that Day, blue-eyed.

103. They will murmur among themselves, "You remained not but ten [days in the world]."

104. We are most knowing of what they say when the best of them in manner will say, "You remained not but one day."

105. And they ask you about the mountains, so say, "My Lord will blow them away with a blast.

106. And He will leave the earth a level plain;

107. You will not see therein a depression or an elevation."
108. That Day, everyone will follow [the call of] the Caller [with] no deviation therefrom, and [all] voices will be stilled before the Most Merciful, so you will not hear except a whisper [of footsteps].
109. That Day, no intercession will benefit except [that of] one to whom the Most Merciful has given permission and has accepted his word.
110. Allah knows what is [presently] before them and what will be after them, but they do not encompass it in knowledge.
111. And [all] faces will be humbled before the Ever-Living, the Sustainer of existence. And he will have failed who carries injustice.
112. But he who does of righteous deeds while he is a believer - he will neither fear injustice nor deprivation.
113. And thus We have sent it down as an Arabic Qur'an and have diversified therein the warnings that perhaps they will avoid [sin] or it would cause them remembrance.
114. So high [above all] is Allah, the Sovereign, the Truth. And, [O Muhammad], do not hasten with [recitation of] the Qur'an before its revelation is completed to you, and say, "My Lord, increase me in knowledge."
115. And We had already taken a promise from Adam before, but he forgot; and We found not in him determination.
116. And [mention] when We said to the angels, "Prostrate to Adam," and they prostrated, except Iblees; he refused.
117. So We said, "O Adam, indeed this is an enemy to you and to your wife. Then let him not remove you from Paradise so you would suffer.
118. Indeed, it is [promised] for you not to be hungry therein or be unclothed.
119. And indeed, you will not be thirsty therein or be hot from the sun."
120. Then Satan whispered to him; he said, "O Adam, shall I direct you to the tree of eternity and possession that will not deteriorate?"
121. And Adam and his wife ate of it, and their private parts became apparent to them, and they began to fasten over themselves from the leaves of Paradise. And Adam disobeyed his Lord and erred.
122. Then his Lord chose him and turned to him in forgiveness and guided [him].
123. [Allah] said, "Descend from Paradise - all, [your descendants]

being enemies to one another. And if there should come to you guidance from Me - then whoever follows My guidance will neither go astray [in the world] nor suffer [in the Hereafter].

124. And whoever turns away from My remembrance - indeed, he will have a depressed life, and We will gather him on the Day of Resurrection blind."

125. He will say, "My Lord, why have you raised me blind while I was [once] seeing?"

126. [Allah] will say, "Thus did Our signs come to you, and you forgot them; and thus will you this Day be forgotten."

127. And thus do We recompense he who transgressed and did not believe in the signs of his Lord. And the punishment of the Hereafter is more severe and more enduring.

128. Then, has it not become clear to them how many generations We destroyed before them as they walk among their dwellings? Indeed in that are signs for those of intelligence.

129. And if not for a word that preceded from your Lord, punishment would have been an obligation [due immediately], and [if not for] a specified term [decreed].

130. So be patient over what they say and exalt [Allah] with praise of your Lord before the rising of the sun and before its setting; and during periods of the night [exalt Him] and at the ends of the day, that you may be satisfied.

131. And do not extend your eyes toward that by which We have given enjoyment to [some] categories of them, [its being but] the splendor of worldly life by which We test them. And the provision of your Lord is better and more enduring.

132. And enjoin prayer upon your family [and people] and be steadfast therein. We ask you not for provision; We provide for you, and the [best] outcome is for [those of] righteousness.

133. And they say, "Why does he not bring us a sign from his Lord?" Has there not come to them evidence of what was in the former scriptures?

134. And if We had destroyed them with a punishment before him, they would have said, "Our Lord, why did You not send to us a messenger so we could have followed Your verses before we were humiliated and disgraced?"

135. Say, "Each [of us] is waiting; so wait. For you will know who are the companions of the sound path and who is guided."

| Verses: 112 | **Surah 21 Al-Anbiyaa** | Makki |

In the name of Allah, the Entirely Merciful, the Especially Merciful.

01. [The time of] their account has approached for the people, while they are in heedlessness turning away.
02. No mention comes to them anew from their Lord except that they listen to it while they are at play
03. With their hearts distracted. And those who do wrong conceal their private conversation, [saying], "Is this [Prophet] except a human being like you? So would you approach magic while you are aware [of it]?"
04. The Prophet said, "My Lord knows whatever is said throughout the heaven and earth, and He is the Hearing, the Knowing."
05. But they say, "[The revelation is but] a mixture of false dreams; rather, he has invented it; rather, he is a poet. So let him bring us a sign just as the previous [messengers] were sent [with miracles]."
06. Not a [single] city which We destroyed believed before them, so will they believe?
07. And We sent not before you, [O Muhammad], except men to whom We revealed [the message], so ask the people of the message if you do not know.
08. And We did not make the prophets forms not eating food, nor were they immortal [on earth].
09. Then We fulfilled for them the promise, and We saved them and whom We willed and destroyed the transgressors.
10. We have certainly sent down to you a Book in which is your mention. Then will you not reason?
11. And how many a city which was unjust have We shattered and produced after it another people.
12. And when its inhabitants perceived Our punishment, at once they fled from it.
13. [Some angels said], "Do not flee but return to where you were given luxury and to your homes - perhaps you will be questioned."
14. They said, "O woe to us! Indeed, we were wrongdoers."
15. And that declaration of theirs did not cease until We made them [as] a harvest [mowed down], extinguished [like a fire].
16. And We did not create the heaven and earth and that between them in play.

17. Had We intended to take a diversion, We could have taken it from [what is] with Us - if [indeed] We were to do so.
18. Rather, We dash the truth upon falsehood, and it destroys it, and thereupon it departs. And for you is destruction from that which you describe.
19. To Him belongs whoever is in the heavens and the earth. And those near Him are not prevented by arrogance from His worship, nor do they tire.
20. They exalt [Him] night and day [and] do not slacken.
21. Or have men taken for themselves gods from the earth who resurrect [the dead]?
22. Had there been within the heavens and earth gods besides Allah, they both would have been ruined. So exalted is Allah, Lord of the Throne, above what they describe.
23. He is not questioned about what He does, but they will be questioned.
24. Or have they taken gods besides Him? Say, [O Muhammad], "Produce your proof. This [Qur'an] is the message for those with me and the message of those before me." But most of them do not know the truth, so they are turning away.
25. And We sent not before you any messenger except that We revealed to him that, "There is no deity except Me, so worship Me."
26. And they say, "The Most Merciful has taken a son." Exalted is He! Rather, they are [but] honored servants.
27. They cannot precede Him in word, and they act by His command.
28. He knows what is [presently] before them and what will be after them, and they cannot intercede except on behalf of one whom He approves. And they, from fear of Him, are apprehensive.
29. And whoever of them should say, "Indeed, I am a god besides Him"- that one We would recompense with Hell. Thus do We recompense the wrongdoers.
30. Have those who disbelieved not considered that the heavens and the earth were a joined entity, and We separated them and made from water every living thing? Then will they not believe?
31. And We placed within the earth firmly set mountains, lest it should shift with them, and We made therein [mountain] passes [as] roads that they might be guided.
32. And We made the sky a protected ceiling, but they, from its signs, are turning away.

33. And it is He who created the night and the day and the sun and the moon; all [heavenly bodies] in an orbit are swimming.

34. And We did not grant to any man before you eternity [on earth]; so if you die - would they be eternal?

35. Every soul will taste death. And We test you with evil and with good as trial; and to Us you will be returned.

36. And when those who disbelieve see you, [O Muhammad], they take you not except in ridicule, [saying], "Is this the one who insults your gods?" And they are, at the mention of the Most Merciful, disbelievers.

37. Man was created of haste. I will show you My signs, so do not impatiently urge Me.

38. And they say, "When is this promise, if you should be truthful?"

39. If those who disbelieved but knew the time when they will not avert the Fire from their faces or from their backs and they will not be aided...

40. Rather, it will come to them unexpectedly and bewilder them, and they will not be able to repel it, nor will they be reprieved.

41. And already were messengers ridiculed before you, but those who mocked them were enveloped by what they used to ridicule.

42. Say, "Who can protect you at night or by day from the Most Merciful?" But they are, from the remembrance of their Lord, turning away.

43. Or do they have gods to defend them other than Us? They are unable [even] to help themselves, nor can they be protected from Us.

44. But, [on the contrary], We have provided good things for these [disbelievers] and their fathers until life was prolonged for them. Then do they not see that We set upon the land, reducing it from its borders? So it is they who will overcome?

45. Say, "I only warn you by revelation." But the deaf do not hear the call when they are warned.

46. And if [as much as] a whiff of the punishment of your Lord should touch them, they would surely say, "O woe to us! Indeed, we have been wrongdoers."

47. And We place the scales of justice for the Day of Resurrection, so no soul will be treated unjustly at all. And if there is [even]

the weight of a mustard seed, We will bring it forth. And sufficient are We as accountant.

48. And We had already given Moses and Aaron the criterion and a light and a reminder for the righteous

49. Who fear their Lord unseen, while they are of the Hour apprehensive.

50. And this [Qur'an] is a blessed message which We have sent down. Then are you with it unacquainted?

51. And We had certainly given Abraham his sound judgement before, and We were of him well-Knowing

52. When he said to his father and his people, "What are these statues to which you are devoted?"

53. They said, "We found our fathers worshippers of them."

54. He said, "You were certainly, you and your fathers, in manifest error."

55. They said, "Have you come to us with truth, or are you of those who jest?"

56. He said, "[No], rather, your Lord is the Lord of the heavens and the earth who created them, and I, to that, am of those who testify.

57. And [I swear] by Allah, I will surely plan against your idols after you have turned and gone away."

58. So he made them into fragments, except a large one among them, that they might return to it [and question].

59. They said, "Who has done this to our gods? Indeed, he is of the wrongdoers."

60. They said, "We heard a young man mention them who is called Abraham."

61. They said, "Then bring him before the eyes of the people that they may testify."

62. They said, "Have you done this to our gods, O Abraham?"

63. He said, "Rather, this - the largest of them - did it, so ask them, if they should [be able to] speak."

64. So they returned to [blaming] themselves and said [to each other], "Indeed, you are the wrongdoers."

65. Then they reversed themselves, [saying], "You have already known that these do not speak!"

66. He said, "Then do you worship instead of Allah that which does not benefit you at all or harm you?

67. Uff to you and to what you worship instead of Allah. Then will you not use reason?"
68. They said, "Burn him and support your gods - if you are to act."
69. Allah said, "O fire, be coolness and safety upon Abraham."
70. And they intended for him harm, but We made them the greatest losers.
71. And We delivered him and Lot to the land which We had blessed for the worlds.
72. And We gave him Isaac and Jacob in addition, and all [of them] We made righteous.
73. And We made them leaders guiding by Our command. And We inspired to them the doing of good deeds, establishment of prayer, and giving of zakah; and they were worshippers of Us.
74. And to Lot We gave judgement and knowledge, and We saved him from the city that was committing wicked deeds. Indeed, they were a people of evil, defiantly disobedient.
75. And We admitted him into Our mercy. Indeed, he was of the righteous.
76. And [mention] Noah, when he called [to Allah] before [that time], so We responded to him and saved him and his family from the great flood.
77. And We saved him from the people who denied Our signs. Indeed, they were a people of evil, so We drowned them, all together.
78. And [mention] David and Solomon, when they judged concerning the field - when the sheep of a people overran it [at night], and We were witness to their judgement.
79. And We gave understanding of the case to Solomon, and to each [of them] We gave judgement and knowledge. And We subjected the mountains to exalt [Us], along with David and [also] the birds. And We were doing [that].
80. And We taught him the fashioning of coats of armor to protect you from your [enemy in] battle. So will you then be grateful?
81. And to Solomon [We subjected] the wind, blowing forcefully, proceeding by his command toward the land which We had blessed. And We are ever, of all things, Knowing.
82. And of the devils were those who dived for him and did work other than that. And We were of them a guardian.

83. And [mention] Job, when he called to his Lord, "Indeed, adversity has touched me, and you are the Most Merciful of the merciful."

84. So We responded to him and removed what afflicted him of adversity. And We gave him [back] his family and the like thereof with them as mercy from Us and a reminder for the worshippers [of Allah].

85. And [mention] Ishmael and Idrees and Dhul-Kifl; all were of the patient.

86. And We admitted them into Our mercy. Indeed, they were of the righteous.

87. And [mention] the man of the fish, when he went off in anger and thought that We would not decree [anything] upon him. And he called out within the darknesses, "There is no deity except You; exalted are You. Indeed, I have been of the wrongdoers."

88. So We responded to him and saved him from the distress. And thus do We save the believers.

89. And [mention] Zechariah, when he called to his Lord, "My Lord, do not leave me alone [with no heir], while you are the best of inheritors."

90. So We responded to him, and We gave to him John, and amended for him his wife. Indeed, they used to hasten to good deeds and supplicate Us in hope and fear, and they were to Us humbly submissive.

91. And [mention] the one who guarded her chastity, so We blew into her [garment] through Our angel [Gabriel], and We made her and her son a sign for the worlds.

92. Indeed this, your religion, is one religion, and I am your Lord, so worship Me.

93. And [yet] they divided their affair among themselves, [but] all to Us will return.

94. So whoever does righteous deeds while he is a believer - no denial will there be for his effort, and indeed We, of it, are recorders.

95. And there is prohibition upon [the people of] a city which We have destroyed that they will [ever] return

96. Until when [the dam of] Gog and Magog has been opened and they, from every elevation, descend

97. And [when] the true promise has approached; then suddenly the eyes of those who disbelieved will be staring [in horror, while they say], "O woe to us; we had been unmindful of this; rather, we were wrongdoers."

98. Indeed, you [disbelievers] and what you worship other than Allah are the firewood of Hell. You will be coming to [enter] it.

99. Had these [false deities] been [actual] gods, they would not have come to it, but all are eternal therein.

100. For them therein is heavy sighing, and they therein will not hear.

101. Indeed, those for whom the best [reward] has preceded from Us - they are from it far removed.

102. They will not hear its sound, while they are, in that which their souls desire, abiding eternally.

103. They will not be grieved by the greatest terror, and the angels will meet them, [saying], "This is your Day which you have been promised" -

104. The Day when We will fold the heaven like the folding of a [written] sheet for the records. As We began the first creation, We will repeat it. [That is] a promise binding upon Us. Indeed, We will do it.

105. And We have already written in the book [of Psalms] after the [previous] mention that the land [of Paradise] is inherited by My righteous servants.

106. Indeed, in this [Qur'an] is notification for a worshipping people.

107. And We have not sent you, [O Muhammad], except as a mercy to the worlds.

108. Say, "It is only revealed to me that your god is but one God; so will you be Muslims [in submission to Him]?"

109. But if they turn away, then say, "I have announced to [all of] you equally. And I know not whether near or far is that which you are promised.

110. Indeed, He knows what is declared of speech, and He knows what you conceal.

111. And I know not; perhaps it is a trial for you and enjoyment for a time."

112. [The Prophet] has said, "My Lord, judge [between us] in truth. And our Lord is the Most Merciful, the one whose help is sought against that which you describe."

| Verses: 78 | **Surah 22 Al-Hajj** | Madani |

In the name of Allah, the Entirely Merciful, the Especially Merciful.

01. O mankind, fear your Lord. Indeed, the convulsion of the [final] Hour is a terrible thing.

02. On the Day you see it every nursing mother will be distracted from that [child] she was nursing, and every pregnant woman will abort her pregnancy, and you will see the people [appearing] intoxicated while they are not intoxicated; but the punishment of Allah is severe.

03. And of the people is he who disputes about Allah without knowledge and follows every rebellious devil.

04. It has been decreed for every devil that whoever turns to him - he will misguide him and will lead him to the punishment of the Blaze.

05. People, if you should be in doubt about the Resurrection, then [consider that] indeed, We created you from dust, then from a sperm-drop, then from a clinging clot, and then from a lump of flesh, formed and unformed - that We may show you. And We settle in the wombs whom We will for a specified term, then We bring you out as a child, and then [We develop you] that you may reach your [time of] maturity. And among you is he who is taken in [early] death, and among you is he who is returned to the most decrepit [old] age so that he knows, after [once having] knowledge, nothing. And you see the earth barren, but when We send down upon it rain, it quivers and swells and grows [something] of every beautiful kind.

06. That is because Allah is the Truth and because He gives life to the dead and because He is over all things competent

07. And [that they may know] that the Hour is coming - no doubt about it - and that Allah will resurrect those in the graves.

08. And of the people is he who disputes about Allah without knowledge or guidance or an enlightening book [from Him],

09. Twisting his neck [in arrogance] to mislead [people] from the way of Allah. For him in the world is disgrace, and We will make him taste on the Day of Resurrection the punishment of the Burning Fire [while it is said],

10. "That is for what your hands have put forth and because Allah is not ever unjust to [His] servants."

11. And of the people is he who worships Allah on an edge. If he is touched by good, he is reassured by it; but if he is struck by trial, he turns on his face [to the other direction]. He has lost [this] world and the Hereafter. That is what is the manifest loss.
12. He invokes instead of Allah that which neither harms him nor benefits him. That is what is the extreme error.
13. He invokes one whose harm is closer than his benefit - how wretched the protector and how wretched the associate.
14. Indeed, Allah will admit those who believe and do righteous deeds to gardens beneath which rivers flow. Indeed, Allah does what He intends.
15. Whoever should think that Allah will not support [Prophet Muhammad] in this world and the Hereafter - let him extend a rope to the ceiling, then cut off [his breath], and let him see: will his effort remove that which enrages [him]?
16. And thus have We sent the Qur'an down as verses of clear evidence and because Allah guides whom He intends.
17. Indeed, those who have believed and those who were Jews and the Sabeans and the Christians and the Magians and those who associated with Allah - Allah will judge between them on the Day of Resurrection. Indeed Allah is, over all things, Witness.
18. Do you not see that to Allah prostrates whoever is in the heavens and whoever is on the earth and the sun, the moon, the stars, the mountains, the trees, the moving creatures and many of the people? But upon many the punishment has been justified. And he whom Allah humiliates - for him there is no bestower of honor. Indeed, Allah does what He wills.
19. These are two adversaries who have disputed over their Lord. But those who disbelieved will have cut out for them garments of fire. Poured upon their heads will be scalding water
20. By which is melted that within their bellies and [their] skins.
21. And for [striking] them are maces of iron.
22. Every time they want to get out of Hellfire from anguish, they will be returned to it, and [it will be said], "Taste the punishment of the Burning Fire!"
23. Indeed, Allah will admit those who believe and do righteous deeds to gardens beneath which rivers flow. They will be adorned therein with bracelets of gold and pearl, and their garments therein will be silk.

24. And they had been guided [in worldly life] to good speech, and they were guided to the path of the Praiseworthy.

25. Indeed, those who have disbelieved and avert [people] from the way of Allah and [from] al-Masjid al-Haram, which We made for the people - equal are the resident therein and one from outside; and [also] whoever intends [a deed] therein of deviation [in religion] or wrongdoing - We will make him taste of a painful punishment.

26. And [mention, O Muhammad], when We designated for Abraham the site of the House, [saying], "Do not associate anything with Me and purify My House for those who perform Tawaf and those who stand [in prayer] and those who bow and prostrate.

27. And proclaim to the people the Hajj [pilgrimage]; they will come to you on foot and on every lean camel; they will come from every distant pass -

28. That they may witness benefits for themselves and mention the name of Allah on known days over what He has provided for them of [sacrificial] animals. So eat of them and feed the miserable and poor.

29. Then let them end their untidiness and fulfill their vows and perform Tawaf around the ancient House."

30. That [has been commanded], and whoever honors the sacred ordinances of Allah - it is best for him in the sight of his Lord. And permitted to you are the grazing livestock, except what is recited to you. So avoid the uncleanliness of idols and avoid false statement,

31. Inclining [only] to Allah, not associating [anything] with Him. And he who associates with Allah - it is as though he had fallen from the sky and was snatched by the birds or the wind carried him down into a remote place.

32. That [is so]. And whoever honors the symbols of Allah - indeed, it is from the piety of hearts.

33. For you the animals marked for sacrifice are benefits for a specified term; then their place of sacrifice is at the ancient House.

34. And for all religion We have appointed a rite [of sacrifice] that they may mention the name of Allah over what He has provided for them of [sacrificial] animals. For your god is one God, so to Him submit. And, [O Muhammad], give good tidings to the humble [before their Lord]

35. Who, when Allah is mentioned, their hearts are fearful, and [to] the patient over what has afflicted them, and the establishers of prayer and those who spend from what We have provided them.

36. And the camels and cattle We have appointed for you as among the symbols of Allah; for you therein is good. So mention the name of Allah upon them when lined up [for sacrifice]; and when they are [lifeless] on their sides, then eat from them and feed the needy and the beggar. Thus have We subjected them to you that you may be grateful.

37. Their meat will not reach Allah, nor will their blood, but what reaches Him is piety from you. Thus have We subjected them to you that you may glorify Allah for that [to] which He has guided you; and give good tidings to the doers of good.

38. Indeed, Allah defends those who have believed. Indeed, Allah does not like everyone treacherous and ungrateful.

39. Permission [to fight] has been given to those who are being fought, because they were wronged. And indeed, Allah is competent to give them victory.

40. [They are] those who have been evicted from their homes without right - only because they say, "Our Lord is Allah." And were it not that Allah checks the people, some by means of others, there would have been demolished monasteries, churches, synagogues, and mosques in which the name of Allah is much mentioned. And Allah will surely support those who support Him. Indeed, Allah is Powerful and Exalted in Might.

41. [And they are] those who, if We give them authority in the land, establish prayer and give zakah and enjoin what is right and forbid what is wrong. And to Allah belongs the outcome of [all] matters.

42. And if they deny you, [O Muhammad] - so, before them, did the people of Noah and 'Aad and Thamud deny [their prophets],

43. And the people of Abraham and the people of Lot

44. And the inhabitants of Madyan. And Moses was denied, so I prolonged enjoyment for the disbelievers; then I seized them, and how [terrible] was My reproach.

45. And how many a city did We destroy while it was committing wrong - so it is [now] fallen into ruin - and [how many] an abandoned well and [how many] a lofty palace.

46. So have they not traveled through the earth and have hearts by which to reason and ears by which to hear? For indeed, it is not

eyes that are blinded, but blinded are the hearts which are within the breasts.

47. And they urge you to hasten the punishment. But Allah will never fail in His promise. And indeed, a day with your Lord is like a thousand years of those which you count.

48. And for how many a city did I prolong enjoyment while it was committing wrong. Then I seized it, and to Me is the [final] destination.

49. Say, "O people, I am only to you a clear warner."

50. And those who have believed and done righteous deeds - for them is forgiveness and noble provision.

51. But the ones who strove against Our verses, [seeking] to cause failure - those are the companions of Hellfire.

52. And We did not send before you any messenger or prophet except that when he spoke [or recited], Satan threw into it [some misunderstanding]. But Allah abolishes that which Satan throws in; then Allah makes precise His verses. And Allah is Knowing and Wise.

53. [That is] so He may make what Satan throws in a trial for those within whose hearts is disease and those hard of heart. And indeed, the wrongdoers are in extreme dissension.

54. And so those who were given knowledge may know that it is the truth from your Lord and [therefore] believe in it, and their hearts humbly submit to it. And indeed is Allah the Guide of those who have believed to a straight path.

55. But those who disbelieve will not cease to be in doubt of it until the Hour comes upon them unexpectedly or there comes to them the punishment of a barren Day.

56. [All] sovereignty that Day is for Allah; He will judge between them. So they who believed and did righteous deeds will be in the Gardens of Pleasure.

57. And they who disbelieved and denied Our signs - for those there will be a humiliating punishment.

58. And those who emigrated for the cause of Allah and then were killed or died - Allah will surely provide for them a good provision. And indeed, it is Allah who is the best of providers.

59. He will surely cause them to enter an entrance with which they will be pleased, and indeed, Allah is Knowing and Forbearing.

60. That [is so]. And whoever responds [to injustice] with the equivalent of that with which he was harmed and then is tyrannized - Allah will surely aid him. Indeed, Allah is Pardoning and Forgiving.

61. That is because Allah causes the night to enter the day and causes the day to enter the night and because Allah is Hearing and Seeing.

62. That is because Allah is the Truth, and that which they call upon other than Him is falsehood, and because Allah is the Most High, the Grand.

63. Do you not see that Allah has sent down rain from the sky and the earth becomes green? Indeed, Allah is Subtle and Acquainted.

64. To Him belongs what is in the heavens and what is on the earth. And indeed, Allah is the Free of need, the Praiseworthy.

65. Do you not see that Allah has subjected to you whatever is on the earth and the ships which run through the sea by His command? And He restrains the sky from falling upon the earth, unless by His permission. Indeed Allah, to the people, is Kind and Merciful.

66. And He is the one who gave you life; then He causes you to die and then will [again] give you life. Indeed, mankind is ungrateful.

67. For every religion We have appointed rites which they perform. So, [O Muhammad], let the disbelievers not contend with you over the matter but invite them to your Lord. Indeed, you are upon straight guidance.

68. And if they dispute with you, then say, "Allah is most knowing of what you do.

69. Allah will judge between you on the Day of Resurrection concerning that over which you used to differ."

70. Do you not know that Allah knows what is in the heaven and earth? Indeed, that is in a Record. Indeed that, for Allah, is easy.

71. And they worship besides Allah that for which He has not sent down authority and that of which they have no knowledge. And there will not be for the wrongdoers any helper.

72. And when Our verses are recited to them as clear evidences, you recognize in the faces of those who disbelieve disapproval. They are almost on the verge of assaulting those who recite to

them Our verses. Say, "Then shall I inform you of [what is] worse than that? [It is] the Fire which Allah has promised those who disbelieve, and wretched is the destination."

73. people, an example is presented, so listen to it. Indeed, those you invoke besides Allah will never create [as much as] a fly, even if they gathered together for that purpose. And if the fly should steal away from them a [tiny] thing, they could not recover it from him. Weak are the pursuer and pursued.

74. They have not appraised Allah with true appraisal. Indeed, Allah is Powerful and Exalted in Might.

75. Allah chooses from the angels messengers and from the people. Indeed, Allah is Hearing and Seeing.

76. He knows what is [presently] before them and what will be after them. And to Allah will be returned [all] matters.

77. O you who have believed, bow and prostrate and worship your Lord and do good - that you may succeed.

78. And strive for Allah with the striving due to Him. He has chosen you and has not placed upon you in the religion any difficulty. [It is] the religion of your father, Abraham. Allah named you "Muslims" before [in former scriptures] and in this [revelation] that the Messenger may be a witness over you and you may be witnesses over the people. So establish prayer and give zakah and hold fast to Allah. He is your protector; and excellent is the protector, and excellent is the helper.

Verses: 118 — Surah 23 Al-Mu'minoon — Makki

In the name of Allah, the Entirely Merciful, the Especially Merciful.

01. Certainly will the believers have succeeded:
02. They who are during their prayer humbly submissive
03. And they who turn away from ill speech
04. And they who are observant of zakah
05. And they who guard their private parts
06. Except from their wives or those their right hands possess, for indeed, they will not be blamed -
07. But whoever seeks beyond that, then those are the transgressors -
08. And they who are to their trusts and their promises attentive
09. And they who carefully maintain their prayers -

10. Those are the inheritors
11. Who will inherit al-Firdaus. They will abide therein eternally.
12. And certainly did We create man from an extract of clay.
13. Then We placed him as a sperm-drop in a firm lodging.
14. Then We made the sperm-drop into a clinging clot, and We made the clot into a lump [of flesh], and We made [from] the lump, bones, and We covered the bones with flesh; then We developed him into another creation. So blessed is Allah, the best of creators.
15. Then indeed, after that you are to die.
16. Then indeed you, on the Day of Resurrection, will be resurrected.
17. And We have created above you seven layered heavens, and never have We been of [Our] creation unaware.
18. And We have sent down rain from the sky in a measured amount and settled it in the earth. And indeed, We are Able to take it away.
19. And We brought forth for you thereby gardens of palm trees and grapevines in which for you are abundant fruits and from which you eat.
20. And [We brought forth] a tree issuing from Mount Sinai which produces oil and food for those who eat.
21. And indeed, for you in livestock is a lesson. We give you drink from that which is in their bellies, and for you in them are numerous benefits, and from them you eat.
22. And upon them and on ships you are carried.
23. And We had certainly sent Noah to his people, and he said, "O my people, worship Allah; you have no deity other than Him; then will you not fear Him?"
24. But the eminent among those who disbelieved from his people said, "This is not but a man like yourselves who wishes to take precedence over you; and if Allah had willed [to send a messenger], He would have sent down angels. We have not heard of this among our forefathers.
25. He is not but a man possessed with madness, so wait concerning him for a time."
26. [Noah] said, "My Lord, support me because they have denied me."
27. So We inspired to him, "Construct the ship under Our observation, and Our inspiration, and when Our command comes and the

oven overflows, put into the ship from each [creature] two mates and your family, except those for whom the decree [of destruction] has proceeded. And do not address Me concerning those who have wronged; indeed, they are to be drowned.

28. And when you have boarded the ship, you and those with you, then say, 'Praise to Allah who has saved us from the wrongdoing people.'

29. And say, 'My Lord, let me land at a blessed landing place, and You are the best to accommodate [us].' "

30. Indeed in that are signs, and indeed, We are ever testing [Our servants].

31. Then We produced after them a generation of others.

32. And We sent among them a messenger from themselves, [saying], "Worship Allah; you have no deity other than Him; then will you not fear Him?"

33. And the eminent among his people who disbelieved and denied the meeting of the Hereafter while We had given them luxury in the worldly life said, "This is not but a man like yourselves. He eats of that from which you eat and drinks of what you drink.

34. And if you should obey a man like yourselves, indeed, you would then be losers.

35. Does he promise you that when you have died and become dust and bones that you will be brought forth [once more]?

36. How far, how far, is that which you are promised.

37. Life is not but our worldly life - we die and live, but we will not be resurrected.

38. He is not but a man who has invented a lie about Allah, and we will not believe him."

39. He said, "My Lord, support me because they have denied me."

40. [Allah] said, "After a little, they will surely become regretful."

41. So the shriek seized them in truth, and We made them as [plant] stubble. Then away with the wrongdoing people.

42. Then We produced after them other generations.

43. No nation will precede its time [of termination], nor will they remain [thereafter].

44. Then We sent Our messengers in succession. Every time there

came to a nation its messenger, they denied him, so We made them follow one another [to destruction], and We made them narrations. So away with a people who do not believe.

45. Then We sent Moses and his brother Aaron with Our signs and a clear authority

46. To Pharaoh and his establishment, but they were arrogant and were a haughty people.

47. They said, "Should we believe two men like ourselves while their people are for us in servitude?"

48. So they denied them and were of those destroyed.

49. And We certainly gave Moses the Scripture that perhaps they would be guided.

50. And We made the son of Mary and his mother a sign and sheltered them within a high ground having level [areas] and flowing water.

51. [Allah said], "O messengers, eat from the good foods and work righteousness. Indeed, I, of what you do, am Knowing.

52. And indeed this, your religion, is one religion, and I am your Lord, so fear Me."

53. But the people divided their religion among them into sects - each faction, in what it has, rejoicing.

54. So leave them in their confusion for a time.

55. Do they think that what We extend to them of wealth and children

56. Is [because] We hasten for them good things? Rather, they do not perceive.

57. Indeed, they who are apprehensive from fear of their Lord

58. And they who believe in the signs of their Lord

59. And they who do not associate anything with their Lord

60. And they who give what they give while their hearts are fearful because they will be returning to their Lord -

61. It is those who hasten to good deeds, and they outstrip [others] therein.

62. And We charge no soul except [with that within] its capacity, and with Us is a record which speaks with truth; and they will not be wronged.

63. But their hearts are covered with confusion over this, and they have [evil] deeds besides disbelief which they are doing,
64. Until when We seize their affluent ones with punishment, at once they are crying [to Allah] for help.
65. Do not cry out today. Indeed, by Us you will not be helped.
66. My verses had already been recited to you, but you were turning back on your heels
67. In arrogance regarding it, conversing by night, speaking evil.
68. Then have they not reflected over the Qur'an, or has there come to them that which had not come to their forefathers?
69. Or did they not know their Messenger, so they are toward him disacknowledging?
70. Or do they say, "In him is madness?" Rather, he brought them the truth, but most of them, to the truth, are averse.
71. But if the Truth had followed their inclinations, the heavens and the earth and whoever is in them would have been ruined. Rather, We have brought them their message, but they, from their message, are turning away.
72. Or do you, [O Muhammad], ask them for payment? But the reward of your Lord is best, and He is the best of providers.
73. And indeed, you invite them to a straight path.
74. But indeed, those who do not believe in the Hereafter are deviating from the path.
75. And even if We gave them mercy and removed what was upon them of affliction, they would persist in their transgression, wandering blindly.
76. And We had gripped them with suffering [as a warning], but they did not yield to their Lord, nor did they humbly supplicate, [and will continue thus]
77. Until when We have opened before them a door of severe punishment, immediately they will be therein in despair.
78. And it is He who produced for you hearing and vision and hearts; little are you grateful.
79. And it is He who has multiplied you throughout the earth, and to Him you will be gathered.
80. And it is He who gives life and causes death, and His is the alternation of the night and the day. Then will you not reason?

81. Rather, they say like what the former peoples said.
82. They said, "When we have died and become dust and bones, are we indeed to be resurrected?
83. We have been promised this, we and our forefathers, before; this is not but legends of the former peoples."
84. Say, [O Muhammad], "To whom belongs the earth and whoever is in it, if you should know?"
85. They will say, "To Allah." Say, "Then will you not remember?"
86. Say, "Who is Lord of the seven heavens and Lord of the Great Throne?"
87. They will say, "[They belong] to Allah." Say, "Then will you not fear Him?"
88. Say, "In whose hand is the realm of all things - and He protects while none can protect against Him - if you should know?"
89. They will say, "[All belongs] to Allah." Say, "Then how are you deluded?"
90. Rather, We have brought them the truth, and indeed they are liars.
91. Allah has not taken any son, nor has there ever been with Him any deity. [If there had been], then each deity would have taken what it created, and some of them would have sought to overcome others. Exalted is Allah above what they describe [concerning Him].
92. [He is] Knower of the unseen and the witnessed, so high is He above what they associate [with Him].
93. Say, [O Muhammad], "My Lord, if You should show me that which they are promised,
94. My Lord, then do not place me among the wrongdoing people."
95. And indeed, We are able to show you what We have promised them.
96. Repel, by [means of] what is best, [their] evil. We are most knowing of what they describe.
97. And say, "My Lord, I seek refuge in You from the incitements of the devils,
98. And I seek refuge in You, my Lord, lest they be present with me."
99. [For such is the state of the disbelievers], until, when death comes to one of them, he says, "My Lord, send me back
100. That I might do righteousness in that which I left behind." No! It is only a word he is saying; and behind them is a barrier until

the Day they are resurrected.

101. So when the Horn is blown, no relationship will there be among them that Day, nor will they ask about one another.

102. And those whose scales are heavy [with good deeds] - it is they who are the successful.

103. But those whose scales are light - those are the ones who have lost their souls, [being] in Hell, abiding eternally.

104. The Fire will sear their faces, and they therein will have taut smiles.

105. [It will be said]. "Were not My verses recited to you and you used to deny them?"

106. They will say, "Our Lord, our wretchedness overcame us, and we were a people astray.

107. Our Lord, remove us from it, and if we were to return [to evil], we would indeed be wrongdoers."

108. He will say, "Remain despised therein and do not speak to Me.

109. Indeed, there was a party of My servants who said, 'Our Lord, we have believed, so forgive us and have mercy upon us, and You are the best of the merciful.'

110. But you took them in mockery to the point that they made you forget My remembrance, and you used to laugh at them.

111. Indeed, I have rewarded them this Day for their patient endurance - that they are the attainers [of success]."

112. [Allah] will say, "How long did you remain on earth in number of years?"

113. They will say, "We remained a day or part of a day; ask those who enumerate."

114. He will say, "You stayed not but a little - if only you had known.

115. Then did you think that We created you uselessly and that to Us you would not be returned?"

116. So exalted is Allah, the Sovereign, the Truth; there is no deity except Him, Lord of the Noble Throne.

117. And whoever invokes besides Allah another deity for which he has no proof - then his account is only with his Lord. Indeed, the disbelievers will not succeed.

118. And, [O Muhammad], say, "My Lord, forgive and have mercy, and You are the best of the merciful."

| Verses: 64 | **Surah 24 An-Noor** | Madani |

In the name of Allah, the Entirely Merciful, the Especially Merciful.

01. [This is] a surah which We have sent down and made [that within it] obligatory and revealed therein verses of clear evidence that you might remember.

02. The [unmarried] woman or [unmarried] man found guilty of sexual intercourse - lash each one of them with a hundred lashes, and do not be taken by pity for them in the religion of Allah, if you should believe in Allah and the Last Day. And let a group of the believers witness their punishment.

03. The fornicator does not marry except a [female] fornicator or polytheist, and none marries her except a fornicator or a polytheist, and that has been made unlawful to the believers.

04. And those who accuse chaste women and then do not produce four witnesses - lash them with eighty lashes and do not accept from them testimony ever after. And those are the defiantly disobedient,

05. Except for those who repent thereafter and reform, for indeed, Allah is Forgiving and Merciful.

06. And those who accuse their wives [of adultery] and have no witnesses except themselves - then the witness of one of them [shall be] four testimonies [swearing] by Allah that indeed, he is of the truthful.

07. And the fifth [oath will be] that the curse of Allah be upon him if he should be among the liars.

08. But it will prevent punishment from her if she gives four testimonies [swearing] by Allah that indeed, he is of the liars.

09. And the fifth [oath will be] that the wrath of Allah be upon her if he was of the truthful.

10. And if not for the favor of Allah upon you and His mercy... and because Allah is Accepting of repentance and Wise.

11. Indeed, those who came with falsehood are a group among you. Do not think it bad for you; rather it is good for you. For every person among them is what [punishment] he has earned from the sin, and he who took upon himself the greater portion thereof - for him is a great punishment.

12. Why, when you heard it, did not the believing men and believing women think good of one another and say, "This is an obvious falsehood"?

13. Why did they [who slandered] not produce for it four witnesses? And when they do not produce the witnesses, then it is they, in the sight of Allah, who are the liars.

14. And if it had not been for the favor of Allah upon you and His mercy in this world and the Hereafter, you would have been touched for that [lie] in which you were involved by a great punishment

15. When you received it with your tongues and said with your mouths that of which you had no knowledge and thought it was insignificant while it was, in the sight of Allah, tremendous.

16. And why, when you heard it, did you not say, "It is not for us to speak of this. Exalted are You, [O Allah]; this is a great slander"?

17. Allah warns you against returning to the likes of this [conduct], ever, if you should be believers.

18. And Allah makes clear to you the verses, and Allah is Knowing and Wise.

19. Indeed, those who like that immorality should be spread [or publicized] among those who have believed will have a painful punishment in this world and the Hereafter. And Allah knows and you do not know.

20. And if it had not been for the favor of Allah upon you and His mercy... and because Allah is Kind and Merciful.

21. O you who have believed, do not follow the footsteps of Satan. And whoever follows the footsteps of Satan - indeed, he enjoins immorality and wrongdoing. And if not for the favor of Allah upon you and His mercy, not one of you would have been pure, ever, but Allah purifies whom He wills, and Allah is Hearing and Knowing.

22. And let not those of virtue among you and wealth swear not to give [aid] to their relatives and the needy and the emigrants for the cause of Allah, and let them pardon and overlook. Would you not like that Allah should forgive you? And Allah is Forgiving and Merciful.

23. Indeed, those who [falsely] accuse chaste, unaware and believing women are cursed in this world and the Hereafter; and they will have a great punishment

24. On a Day when their tongues, their hands and their feet will bear witness against them as to what they used to do.

25. That Day, Allah will pay them in full their deserved recompense, and they will know that it is Allah who is the perfect in justice.

26. Evil words are for evil men, and evil men are [subjected] to evil words. And good words are for good men, and good men are [an object] of good words. Those [good people] are declared innocent of what the slanderers say. For them is forgiveness and noble provision.

27. O you who have believed, do not enter houses other than your own houses until you ascertain welcome and greet their inhabitants. That is best for you; perhaps you will be reminded.

28. And if you do not find anyone therein, do not enter them until permission has been given you. And if it is said to you, "Go back," then go back; it is purer for you. And Allah is Knowing of what you do.

29. There is no blame upon you for entering houses not inhabited in which there is convenience for you. And Allah knows what you reveal and what you conceal.

30. Tell the believing men to reduce [some] of their vision and guard their private parts. That is purer for them. Indeed, Allah is Acquainted with what they do.

31. And tell the believing women to reduce [some] of their vision and guard their private parts and not expose their adornment except that which [necessarily] appears thereof and to wrap [a portion of] their headcovers over their chests and not expose their adornment except to their husbands, their fathers, their husbands' fathers, their sons, their husbands' sons, their brothers, their brothers' sons, their sisters' sons, their women, that which their right hands possess, or those male attendants having no physical desire, or children who are not yet aware of the private aspects of women. And let them not stamp their feet to make known what they conceal of their adornment. And turn to Allah in repentance, all of you, O believers, that you might succeed.

32. And marry the unmarried among you and the righteous among your male slaves and female slaves. If they should be poor, Allah will enrich them from His bounty, and Allah is all-Encompassing and Knowing.

33. But let them who find not [the means for] marriage abstain [from sexual relations] until Allah enriches them from His bounty. And those who seek a contract [for eventual emancipation] from among whom your right hands possess - then make a contract with them if you know there is within them goodness and give them from the wealth of Allah which He has given you. And do

not compel your slave girls to prostitution, if they desire chastity, to seek [thereby] the temporary interests of worldly life. And if someone should compel them, then indeed, Allah is [to them], after their compulsion, Forgiving and Merciful.

34. And We have certainly sent down to you distinct verses and examples from those who passed on before you and an admonition for those who fear Allah.

35. Allah is the Light of the heavens and the earth. The example of His light is like a niche within which is a lamp, the lamp is within glass, the glass as if it were a pearly [white] star lit from [the oil of] a blessed olive tree, neither of the east nor of the west, whose oil would almost glow even if untouched by fire. Light upon light. Allah guides to His light whom He wills. And Allah presents examples for the people, and Allah is Knowing of all things.

36. [Such niches are] in mosques which Allah has ordered to be raised and that His name be mentioned therein; exalting Him within them in the morning and the evenings

37. [Are] men whom neither commerce nor sale distracts from the remembrance of Allah and performance of prayer and giving of zakah. They fear a Day in which the hearts and eyes will [fearfully] turn about -

38. That Allah may reward them [according to] the best of what they did and increase them from His bounty. And Allah gives provision to whom He wills without account.

39. But those who disbelieved - their deeds are like a mirage in a lowland which a thirsty one thinks is water until, when he comes to it, he finds it is nothing but finds Allah before Him, and He will pay him in full his due; and Allah is swift in account.

40. Or [they are] like darknesses within an unfathomable sea which is covered by waves, upon which are waves, over which are clouds - darknesses, some of them upon others. When one puts out his hand [therein], he can hardly see it. And he to whom Allah has not granted light - for him there is no light.

41. Do you not see that Allah is exalted by whomever is within the heavens and the earth and [by] the birds with wings spread [in flight]? Each [of them] has known his [means of] prayer and exalting [Him], and Allah is Knowing of what they do.

42. And to Allah belongs the dominion of the heavens and the earth, and to Allah is the destination.

43. Do you not see that Allah drives clouds? Then He brings them together, then He makes them into a mass, and you see the rain emerge from within it. And He sends down from the sky, mountains [of clouds] within which is hail, and He strikes with it whom He wills and averts it from whom He wills. The flash of its lightening almost takes away the eyesight.

44. Allah alternates the night and the day. Indeed in that is a lesson for those who have vision.

45. Allah has created every [living] creature from water. And of them are those that move on their bellies, and of them are those that walk on two legs, and of them are those that walk on four. Allah creates what He wills. Indeed, Allah is over all things competent.

46. We have certainly sent down distinct verses. And Allah guides whom He wills to a straight path.

47. But the hypocrites say, "We have believed in Allah and in the Messenger, and we obey"; then a party of them turns away after that. And those are not believers.

48. And when they are called to [the words of] Allah and His Messenger to judge between them, at once a party of them turns aside [in refusal].

49. But if the right is theirs, they come to him in prompt obedience.

50. Is there disease in their hearts? Or have they doubted? Or do they fear that Allah will be unjust to them, or His Messenger? Rather, it is they who are the wrongdoers.

51. The only statement of the [true] believers when they are called to Allah and His Messenger to judge between them is that they say, "We hear and we obey." And those are the successful.

52. And whoever obeys Allah and His Messenger and fears Allah and is conscious of Him - it is those who are the attainers.

53. And they swear by Allah their strongest oaths that if you ordered them, they would go forth [in Allah's cause]. Say, "Do not swear. [Such] obedience is known. Indeed, Allah is Acquainted with that which you do."

54. Say, "Obey Allah and obey the Messenger; but if you turn away - then upon him is only that [duty] with which he has been charged, and upon you is that with which you have been charged. And if you obey him, you will be [rightly] guided. And there is not upon the Messenger except the [responsibility for] clear notification."

55. Allah has promised those who have believed among you and done righteous deeds that He will surely grant them succession [to authority] upon the earth just as He granted it to those before them and that He will surely establish for them [therein] their religion which He has preferred for them and that He will surely substitute for them, after their fear, security, [for] they worship Me, not associating anything with Me. But whoever disbelieves after that - then those are the defiantly disobedient.

56. And establish prayer and give zakah and obey the Messenger - that you may receive mercy.

57. Never think that the disbelievers are causing failure [to Allah] upon the earth. Their refuge will be the Fire - and how wretched the destination.

58. O you who have believed, let those whom your right hands possess and those who have not [yet] reached puberty among you ask permission of you [before entering] at three times: before the dawn prayer and when you put aside your clothing [for rest] at noon and after the night prayer. [These are] three times of privacy for you. There is no blame upon you nor upon them beyond these [periods], for they continually circulate among you - some of you, among others. Thus does Allah make clear to you the verses; and Allah is Knowing and Wise.

59. And when the children among you reach puberty, let them ask permission [at all times] as those before them have done. Thus does Allah make clear to you His verses; and Allah is Knowing and Wise.

60. And women of post-menstrual age who have no desire for marriage - there is no blame upon them for putting aside their outer garments [but] not displaying adornment. But to modestly refrain [from that] is better for them. And Allah is Hearing and Knowing.

61. There is not upon the blind [any] constraint nor upon the lame constraint nor upon the ill constraint nor upon yourselves when you eat from your [own] houses or the houses of your fathers or the houses of your mothers or the houses of your brothers or the houses of your sisters or the houses of your father's brothers or the houses of your father's sisters or the houses of your mother's brothers or the houses of your mother's sisters or [from houses] whose keys you possess or [from the house] of your friend. There is no blame upon you whether you eat together or separately. But when you enter houses, give

greetings of peace upon each other - a greeting from Allah, blessed and good. Thus does Allah make clear to you the verses [of ordinance] that you may understand.

62. The believers are only those who believe in Allah and His Messenger and, when they are [meeting] with him for a matter of common interest, do not depart until they have asked his permission. Indeed, those who ask your permission, [O Muhammad] - those are the ones who believe in Allah and His Messenger. So when they ask your permission for something of their affairs, then give permission to whom you will among them and ask forgiveness for them of Allah. Indeed, Allah is Forgiving and Merciful.

63. Do not make [your] calling of the Messenger among yourselves as the call of one of you to another. Already Allah knows those of you who slip away, concealed by others. So let those beware who dissent from the Prophet's order, lest fitnah strike them or a painful punishment.

64. Unquestionably, to Allah belongs whatever is in the heavens and earth. Already He knows that upon which you [stand] and [knows] the Day when they will be returned to Him and He will inform them of what they have done. And Allah is Knowing of all things.

Verses: 77	Surah 25 Al-Furqaan	Makki

In the name of Allah, the Entirely Merciful, the Especially Merciful.

01. Blessed is He who sent down the Criterion upon His Servant that he may be to the worlds a warner -

02. He to whom belongs the dominion of the heavens and the earth and who has not taken a son and has not had a partner in dominion and has created each thing and determined it with [precise] determination.

03. But they have taken besides Him gods which create nothing, while they are created, and possess not for themselves any harm or benefit and possess not [power to cause] death or life or resurrection.

04. And those who disbelieve say, "This [Qur'an] is not except a falsehood he invented, and another people assisted him in it." But they have committed an injustice and a lie.

05. And they say, "Legends of the former peoples which he has written down, and they are dictated to him morning and afternoon."

06. Say, [O Muhammad], "It has been revealed by He who knows [every] secret within the heavens and the earth. Indeed, He is ever Forgiving and Merciful."

07. And they say, "What is this messenger that eats food and walks in the markets? Why was there not sent down to him an angel so he would be with him a warner?

08. Or [why is not] a treasure presented to him [from heaven], or does he [not] have a garden from which he eats?" And the wrongdoers say, "You follow not but a man affected by magic."

09. Look how they strike for you comparisons; but they have strayed, so they cannot [find] a way.

10. Blessed is He who, if He willed, could have made for you [something] better than that - gardens beneath which rivers flow - and could make for you palaces.

11. But they have denied the Hour, and We have prepared for those who deny the Hour a Blaze.

12. When the Hellfire sees them from a distant place, they will hear its fury and roaring.

13. And when they are thrown into a narrow place therein bound in chains, they will cry out thereupon for destruction.

14. [They will be told], "Do not cry this Day for one destruction but cry for much destruction."

15. Say, "Is that better or the Garden of Eternity which is promised to the righteous? It will be for them a reward and destination.

16. For them therein is whatever they wish, [while] abiding eternally. It is ever upon your Lord a promise [worthy to be] requested.

17. And [mention] the Day He will gather them and that which they worship besides Allah and will say, "Did you mislead these, My servants, or did they [themselves] stray from the way?"

18. They will say, "Exalted are You! It was not for us to take besides You any allies. But You provided comforts for them and their fathers until they forgot the message and became a people ruined."

19. So they will deny you, [disbelievers], in what you say, and you cannot avert [punishment] or [find] help. And whoever commits injustice among you - We will make him taste a great punishment.

20. And We did not send before you, [O Muhammad], any of the messengers except that they ate food and walked in the markets. And We have made some of you [people] as trial for others - will you have patience? And ever is your Lord, Seeing.

21. And those who do not expect the meeting with Us say, "Why were not angels sent down to us, or [why] do we [not] see our Lord?" They have certainly become arrogant within themselves and [become] insolent with great insolence.

22. The day they see the angels - no good tidings will there be that day for the criminals, and [the angels] will say, "Prevented and inaccessible."

23. And We will regard what they have done of deeds and make them as dust dispersed.

24. The companions of Paradise, that Day, are [in] a better settlement and better resting place.

25. And [mention] the Day when the heaven will split open with [emerging] clouds, and the angels will be sent down in successive descent.

26. True sovereignty, that Day, is for the Most Merciful. And it will be upon the disbelievers a difficult Day.

27. And the Day the wrongdoer will bite on his hands [in regret] he will say, "Oh, I wish I had taken with the Messenger a way.

28. Oh, woe to me! I wish I had not taken that one as a friend.

29. He led me away from the remembrance after it had come to me. And ever is Satan, to man, a deserter."

30. And the Messenger has said, "O my Lord, indeed my people have taken this Qur'an as [a thing] abandoned."

31. And thus have We made for every prophet an enemy from among the criminals. But sufficient is your Lord as a guide and a helper.

32. And those who disbelieve say, "Why was the Qur'an not revealed to him all at once?" Thus [it is] that We may strengthen thereby your heart. And We have spaced it distinctly.

33. And they do not come to you with an argument except that We bring you the truth and the best explanation.

34. The ones who are gathered on their faces to Hell - those are the worst in position and farthest astray in [their] way.

35. And We had certainly given Moses the Scripture and appointed with him his brother Aaron as an assistant.

36. And We said, "Go both of you to the people who have denied Our signs." Then We destroyed them with [complete] destruction.

37. And the people of Noah - when they denied the messengers, We drowned them, and We made them for mankind a sign. And We

have prepared for the wrongdoers a painful punishment.

38. And [We destroyed] 'Aad and Thamud and the companions of the well and many generations between them.

39. And for each We presented examples [as warnings], and each We destroyed with [total] destruction.

40. And they have already come upon the town which was showered with a rain of evil. So have they not seen it? But they are not expecting resurrection.

41. And when they see you, [O Muhammad], they take you not except in ridicule, [saying], "Is this the one whom Allah has sent as a messenger?

42. He almost would have misled us from our gods had we not been steadfast in [worship of] them." But they are going to know, when they see the punishment, who is farthest astray in [his] way.

43. Have you seen the one who takes as his god his own desire? Then would you be responsible for him?

44. Or do you think that most of them hear or reason? They are not except like livestock. Rather, they are [even] more astray in [their] way.

45. Have you not considered your Lord - how He extends the shadow, and if He willed, He could have made it stationary? Then We made the sun for it an indication.

46. Then We hold it in hand for a brief grasp.

47. And it is He who has made the night for you as clothing and sleep [a means for] rest and has made the day a resurrection.

48. And it is He who sends the winds as good tidings before His mercy, and We send down from the sky pure water

49. That We may bring to life thereby a dead land and give it as drink to those We created of numerous livestock and men.

50. And We have certainly distributed it among them that they might be reminded, but most of the people refuse except disbelief.

51. And if We had willed, We could have sent into every city a warner.

52. So do not obey the disbelievers, and strive against them with the Qur'an a great striving.

53. And it is He who has released [simultaneously] the two seas, one fresh and sweet and one salty and bitter, and He placed between them a barrier and prohibiting partition.

54. And it is He who has created from water a human being and made him [a relative by] lineage and marriage. And ever is your Lord competent [concerning creation].

55. But they worship rather than Allah that which does not benefit them or harm them, and the disbeliever is ever, against his Lord, an assistant [to Satan].

56. And We have not sent you, [O Muhammad], except as a bringer of good tidings and a warner.

57. Say, "I do not ask of you for it any payment - only that whoever wills might take to his Lord a way."

58. And rely upon the Ever-Living who does not die, and exalt [Allah] with His praise. And sufficient is He to be, with the sins of His servants, Acquainted -

59. He who created the heavens and the earth and what is between them in six days and then established Himself above the Throne - the Most Merciful, so ask about Him one well informed.

60. And when it is said to them, "Prostrate to the Most Merciful," they say, "And what is the Most Merciful? Should we prostrate to that which you order us?" And it increases them in aversion.

61. Blessed is He who has placed in the sky great stars and placed therein a [burning] lamp and luminous moon.

62. And it is He who has made the night and the day in succession for whoever desires to remember or desires gratitude.

63. And the servants of the Most Merciful are those who walk upon the earth easily, and when the ignorant address them [harshly], they say [words of] peace,

64. And those who spend [part of] the night to their Lord prostrating and standing [in prayer]

65. And those who say, "Our Lord, avert from us the punishment of Hell. Indeed, its punishment is ever adhering;

66. Indeed, it is evil as a settlement and residence."

67. And [they are] those who, when they spend, do so not excessively or sparingly but are ever, between that, [justly] moderate

68. And those who do not invoke with Allah another deity or kill the soul which Allah has forbidden [to be killed], except by right, and do not commit unlawful sexual intercourse. And whoever should do that will meet a penalty.

69. Multiplied for him is the punishment on the Day of Resurrection, and he will abide therein humiliated -

70. Except for those who repent, believe and do righteous work. For them Allah will replace their evil deeds with good. And ever is Allah Forgiving and Merciful.

71. And he who repents and does righteousness does indeed turn to Allah with [accepted] repentance.

72. And [they are] those who do not testify to falsehood, and when they pass near ill speech, they pass by with dignity.

73. And those who, when reminded of the verses of their Lord, do not fall upon them deaf and blind.

74. And those who say, "Our Lord, grant us from among our wives and offspring comfort to our eyes and make us an example for the righteous."

75. Those will be awarded the Chamber for what they patiently endured, and they will be received therein with greetings and [words of] peace.

76. Abiding eternally therein. Good is the settlement and residence.

77. Say, "What would my Lord care for you if not for your supplication?" For you [disbelievers] have denied, so your denial is going to be adherent.

| Verses: 227 | **Surah 26 Ash-Shu'araa** | Makki |

In the name of Allah, the Entirely Merciful, the Especially Merciful.

01. Ta, Seen, Meem.

02. These are the verses of the clear Book.

03. Perhaps, [O Muhammad], you would kill yourself with grief that they will not be believers.

04. If We willed, We could send down to them from the sky a sign for which their necks would remain humbled.

05. And no revelation comes to them anew from the Most Merciful except that they turn away from it.

06. For they have already denied, but there will come to them the news of that which they used to ridicule.

07. Did they not look at the earth - how much We have produced therein from every noble kind?

08. Indeed in that is a sign, but most of them were not to be believers.
09. And indeed, your Lord - He is the Exalted in Might, the Merciful.
10. And [mention] when your Lord called Moses, [saying], "Go to the wrongdoing people -
11. The people of Pharaoh. Will they not fear Allah?"
12. He said, "My Lord, indeed I fear that they will deny me
13. And that my breast will tighten and my tongue will not be fluent, so send for Aaron.
14. And they have upon me a [claim due to] sin, so I fear that they will kill me."
15. [Allah] said, "No. Go both of you with Our signs; indeed, We are with you, listening.
16. Go to Pharaoh and say, 'We are the messengers of the Lord of the worlds,
17. [Commanded to say], "Send with us the Children of Israel."'"
18. [Pharaoh] said, "Did we not raise you among us as a child, and you remained among us for years of your life?
19. And [then] you did your deed which you did, and you were of the ungrateful."
20. [Moses] said, "I did it, then, while I was of those astray.
21. So I fled from you when I feared you. Then my Lord granted me wisdom and prophethood and appointed me [as one] of the messengers.
22. And is this a favor of which you remind me - that you have enslaved the Children of Israel?"
23. Said Pharaoh, "And what is the Lord of the worlds?"
24. [Moses] said, "The Lord of the heavens and earth and that between them, if you should be convinced."
25. [Pharaoh] said to those around him, "Do you not hear?"
26. [Moses] said, "Your Lord and the Lord of your first forefathers."
27. [Pharaoh] said, "Indeed, your 'messenger' who has been sent to you is mad."
28. [Moses] said, "Lord of the east and the west and that between them, if you were to reason."
29. [Pharaoh] said, "If you take a god other than me, I will surely place you among those imprisoned."

30. [Moses] said, "Even if I brought you proof manifest?"
31. [Pharaoh] said, "Then bring it, if you should be of the truthful."
32. So [Moses] threw his staff, and suddenly it was a serpent manifest.
33. And he drew out his hand; thereupon it was white for the observers.
34. [Pharaoh] said to the eminent ones around him, "Indeed, this is a learned magician.
35. He wants to drive you out of your land by his magic, so what do you advise?"
36. They said, "Postpone [the matter of] him and his brother and send among the cities gatherers
37. Who will bring you every learned, skilled magician."
38. So the magicians were assembled for the appointment of a well-known day.
39. And it was said to the people, "Will you congregate
40. That we might follow the magicians if they are the predominant?"
41. And when the magicians arrived, they said to Pharaoh, "Is there indeed for us a reward if we are the predominant?"
42. He said, "Yes, and indeed, you will then be of those near [to me]."
43. Moses said to them, "Throw whatever you will throw."
44. So they threw their ropes and their staffs and said, "By the might of Pharaoh, indeed it is we who are predominant."
45. Then Moses threw his staff, and at once it devoured what they falsified.
46. So the magicians fell down in prostration [to Allah].
47. They said, "We have believed in the Lord of the worlds,
48. The Lord of Moses and Aaron."
49. [Pharaoh] said, "You believed Moses before I gave you permission. Indeed, he is your leader who has taught you magic, but you are going to know. I will surely cut off your hands and your feet on opposite sides, and I will surely crucify you all."
50. They said, "No harm. Indeed, to our Lord we will return.
51. Indeed, we aspire that our Lord will forgive us our sins because we were the first of the believers."
52. And We inspired to Moses, "Travel by night with My servants; indeed, you will be pursued."

53. Then Pharaoh sent among the cities gatherers
54. [And said], "Indeed, those are but a small band,
55. And indeed, they are enraging us,
56. And indeed, we are a cautious society... "
57. So We removed them from gardens and springs
58. And treasures and honorable station -
59. Thus. And We caused to inherit it the Children of Israel.
60. So they pursued them at sunrise.
61. And when the two companies saw one another, the companions of Moses said, "Indeed, we are to be overtaken!"
62. [Moses] said, "No! Indeed, with me is my Lord; He will guide me."
63. Then We inspired to Moses, "Strike with your staff the sea," and it parted, and each portion was like a great towering mountain.
64. And We advanced thereto the pursuers.
65. And We saved Moses and those with him, all together.
66. Then We drowned the others.
67. Indeed in that is a sign, but most of them were not to be believers.
68. And indeed, your Lord - He is the Exalted in Might, the Merciful.
69. And recite to them the news of Abraham,
70. When he said to his father and his people, "What do you worship?"
71. They said, "We worship idols and remain to them devoted."
72. He said, "Do they hear you when you supplicate?
73. Or do they benefit you, or do they harm?"
74. They said, "But we found our fathers doing thus."
75. He said, "Then do you see what you have been worshipping,
76. You and your ancient forefathers?
77. Indeed, they are enemies to me, except the Lord of the worlds,
78. Who created me, and He [it is who] guides me.
79. And it is He who feeds me and gives me drink.
80. And when I am ill, it is He who cures me
81. And who will cause me to die and then bring me to life
82. And who I aspire that He will forgive me my sin on the Day of Recompense."

83. [And he said], "My Lord, grant me authority and join me with the righteous.
84. And grant me a reputation of honor among later generations.
85. And place me among the inheritors of the Garden of Pleasure.
86. And forgive my father. Indeed, he has been of those astray.
87. And do not disgrace me on the Day they are [all] resurrected -
88. The Day when there will not benefit [anyone] wealth or children
89. But only one who comes to Allah with a sound heart."
90. And Paradise will be brought near [that Day] to the righteous.
91. And Hellfire will be brought forth for the deviators,
92. And it will be said to them, "Where are those you used to worship
93. Other than Allah? Can they help you or help themselves?"
94. So they will be overturned into Hellfire, they and the deviators
95. And the soldiers of Iblees, all together.
96. They will say while they dispute therein,
97. "By Allah, we were indeed in manifest error
98. When we equated you with the Lord of the worlds.
99. And no one misguided us except the criminals.
100. So now we have no intercessors
101. And not a devoted friend.
102. Then if we only had a return [to the world] and could be of the believers... "
103. Indeed in that is a sign, but most of them were not to be believers.
104. And indeed, your Lord - He is the Exalted in Might, the Merciful.
105. The people of Noah denied the messengers
106. When their brother Noah said to them, "Will you not fear Allah?
107. Indeed, I am to you a trustworthy messenger.
108. So fear Allah and obey me.
109. And I do not ask you for it any payment. My payment is only from the Lord of the worlds.
110. So fear Allah and obey me."
111. They said, "Should we believe you while you are followed by the lowest [class of people]?"

112. He said, "And what is my knowledge of what they used to do?
113. Their account is only upon my Lord, if you [could] perceive.
114. And I am not one to drive away the believers.
115. I am only a clear warner."
116. They said, "If you do not desist, O Noah, you will surely be of those who are stoned."
117. He said, "My Lord, indeed my people have denied me.
118. Then judge between me and them with decisive judgement and save me and those with me of the believers."
119. So We saved him and those with him in the laden ship.
120. Then We drowned thereafter the remaining ones.
121. Indeed in that is a sign, but most of them were not to be believers.
122. And indeed, your Lord - He is the Exalted in Might, the Merciful.
123. 'Aad denied the messengers
124. When their brother Hud said to them, "Will you not fear Allah?
125. Indeed, I am to you a trustworthy messenger.
126. So fear Allah and obey me.
127. And I do not ask you for it any payment. My payment is only from the Lord of the worlds.
128. Do you construct on every elevation a sign, amusing yourselves,
129. And take for yourselves palaces and fortresses that you might abide eternally?
130. And when you strike, you strike as tyrants.
131. So fear Allah and obey me.
132. And fear He who provided you with that which you know,
133. Provided you with grazing livestock and children
134. And gardens and springs.
135. Indeed, I fear for you the punishment of a terrible day."
136. They said, "It is all the same to us whether you advise or are not of the advisors.
137. This is not but the custom of the former peoples,
138. And we are not to be punished."
139. And they denied him, so We destroyed them. Indeed in that is a sign, but most of them were not to be believers.

140. And indeed, your Lord - He is the Exalted in Might, the Merciful.
141. Thamud denied the messengers
142. When their brother Salih said to them, "Will you not fear Allah?
143. Indeed, I am to you a trustworthy messenger.
144. So fear Allah and obey me.
145. And I do not ask you for it any payment. My payment is only from the Lord of the worlds.
146. Will you be left in what is here, secure [from death],
147. Within gardens and springs
148. And fields of crops and palm trees with softened fruit?
149. And you carve out of the mountains, homes, with skill.
150. So fear Allah and obey me.
151. And do not obey the order of the transgressors,
152. Who cause corruption in the land and do not amend."
153. They said, "You are only of those affected by magic.
154. You are but a man like ourselves, so bring a sign, if you should be of the truthful."
155. He said, "This is a she-camel. For her is a [time of] drink, and for you is a [time of] drink, [each] on a known day.
156. And do not touch her with harm, lest you be seized by the punishment of a terrible day."
157. But they hamstrung her and so became regretful.
158. And the punishment seized them. Indeed in that is a sign, but most of them were not to be believers.
159. And indeed, your Lord - He is the Exalted in Might, the Merciful.
160. The people of Lot denied the messengers
161. When their brother Lot said to them, "Will you not fear Allah?
162. Indeed, I am to you a trustworthy messenger.
163. So fear Allah and obey me.
164. And I do not ask you for it any payment. My payment is only from the Lord of the worlds.
165. Do you approach males among the worlds
166. And leave what your Lord has created for you as mates? But you are a people transgressing."

167. They said, "If you do not desist, O Lot, you will surely be of those evicted."
168. He said, "Indeed, I am, toward your deed, of those who detest [it].
169. My Lord, save me and my family from [the consequence of] what they do."
170. So We saved him and his family, all,
171. Except an old woman among those who remained behind.
172. Then We destroyed the others.
173. And We rained upon them a rain [of stones], and evil was the rain of those who were warned.
174. Indeed in that is a sign, but most of them were not to be believers.
175. And indeed, your Lord - He is the Exalted in Might, the Merciful.
176. The companions of the thicket denied the messengers
177. When Shu'ayb said to them, "Will you not fear Allah?
178. Indeed, I am to you a trustworthy messenger.
179. So fear Allah and obey me.
180. And I do not ask you for it any payment. My payment is only from the Lord of the worlds.
181. Give full measure and do not be of those who cause loss.
182. And weigh with an even balance.
183. And do not deprive people of their due and do not commit abuse on earth, spreading corruption.
184. And fear He who created you and the former creation."
185. They said, "You are only of those affected by magic.
186. You are but a man like ourselves, and indeed, we think you are among the liars.
187. So cause to fall upon us fragments of the sky, if you should be of the truthful."
188. He said, "My Lord is most knowing of what you do."
189. And they denied him, so the punishment of the day of the black cloud seized them. Indeed, it was the punishment of a terrible day.
190. Indeed in that is a sign, but most of them were not to be believers.
191. And indeed, your Lord - He is the Exalted in Might, the Merciful.
192. And indeed, the Qur'an is the revelation of the Lord of the worlds.
193. The Trustworthy Spirit has brought it down

194. Upon your heart, [O Muhammad] - that you may be of the warners -
195. In a clear Arabic language.
196. And indeed, it is [mentioned] in the scriptures of former peoples.
197. And has it not been a sign to them that it is recognized by the scholars of the Children of Israel?
198. And even if We had revealed it to one among the foreigners
199. And he had recited it to them [perfectly], they would [still] not have been believers in it.
200. Thus have We inserted disbelief into the hearts of the criminals.
201. They will not believe in it until they see the painful punishment.
202. And it will come to them suddenly while they perceive [it] not.
203. And they will say, "May we be reprieved?"
204. So for Our punishment are they impatient?
205. Then have you considered if We gave them enjoyment for years
206. And then there came to them that which they were promised?
207. They would not be availed by the enjoyment with which they were provided.
208. And We did not destroy any city except that it had warners
209. As a reminder; and never have We been unjust.
210. And the devils have not brought the revelation down.
211. It is not allowable for them, nor would they be able.
212. Indeed they, from [its] hearing, are removed.
213. So do not invoke with Allah another deity and [thus] be among the punished.
214. And warn, [O Muhammad], your closest kindred.
215. And lower your wing to those who follow you of the believers.
216. And if they disobey you, then say, "Indeed, I am disassociated from what you are doing."
217. And rely upon the Exalted in Might, the Merciful,
218. Who sees you when you arise
219. And your movement among those who prostrate.
220. Indeed, He is the Hearing, the Knowing.
221. Shall I inform you upon whom the devils descend?

222. They descend upon every sinful liar.
223. They pass on what is heard, and most of them are liars.
224. And the poets - [only] the deviators follow them;
225. Do you not see that in every valley they roam
226. And that they say what they do not do? -
227. Except those [poets] who believe and do righteous deeds and remember Allah often and defend [the Muslims] after they were wronged. And those who have wronged are going to know to what [kind of] return they will be returned.

| Verses: 93 | **Surah 27 An-Naml** | Makki |

In the name of Allah, the Entirely Merciful, the Especially Merciful.

01. Ta, Seen. These are the verses of the Qur'an and a clear Book
02. As guidance and good tidings for the believers
03. Who establish prayer and give zakah, and of the Hereafter they are certain [in faith].
04. Indeed, for those who do not believe in the Hereafter, We have made pleasing to them their deeds, so they wander blindly.
05. Those are the ones for whom there will be the worst of punishment, and in the Hereafter they are the greatest losers.
06. And indeed, [O Muhammad], you receive the Qur'an from one Wise and Knowing.
07. [Mention] when Moses said to his family, "Indeed, I have perceived a fire. I will bring you from there information or will bring you a burning torch that you may warm yourselves."
08. But when he came to it, he was called, "Blessed is whoever is at the fire and whoever is around it. And exalted is Allah, Lord of the worlds.
09. Moses, indeed it is I - Allah, the Exalted in Might, the Wise."
10. And [he was told], "Throw down your staff." But when he saw it writhing as if it were a snake, he turned in flight and did not return. [Allah said], "O Moses, fear not. Indeed, in My presence the messengers do not fear.
11. Otherwise, he who wrongs, then substitutes good after evil - indeed, I am Forgiving and Merciful.
12. And put your hand into the opening of your garment [at the breast]; it will come out white without disease. [These are]

among the nine signs [you will take] to Pharaoh and his people. Indeed, they have been a people defiantly disobedient."

13. But when there came to them Our visible signs, they said, "This is obvious magic."

14. And they rejected them, while their [inner] selves were convinced thereof, out of injustice and haughtiness. So see how was the end of the corrupters.

15. And We had certainly given to David and Solomon knowledge, and they said, "Praise [is due] to Allah, who has favored us over many of His believing servants."

16. And Solomon inherited David. He said, "O people, we have been taught the language of birds, and we have been given from all things. Indeed, this is evident bounty."

17. And gathered for Solomon were his soldiers of the jinn and men and birds, and they were [marching] in rows.

18. Until, when they came upon the valley of the ants, an ant said, "O ants, enter your dwellings that you not be crushed by Solomon and his soldiers while they perceive not."

19. So [Solomon] smiled, amused at her speech, and said, "My Lord, enable me to be grateful for Your favor which You have bestowed upon me and upon my parents and to do righteousness of which You approve. And admit me by Your mercy into [the ranks of] Your righteous servants."

20. And he took attendance of the birds and said, "Why do I not see the hoopoe - or is he among the absent?

21. I will surely punish him with a severe punishment or slaughter him unless he brings me clear authorization."

22. But the hoopoe stayed not long and said, "I have encompassed [in knowledge] that which you have not encompassed, and I have come to you from Sheba with certain news.

23. Indeed, I found [there] a woman ruling them, and she has been given of all things, and she has a great throne.

24. I found her and her people prostrating to the sun instead of Allah, and Satan has made their deeds pleasing to them and averted them from [His] way, so they are not guided,

25. [And] so they do not prostrate to Allah, who brings forth what is hidden within the heavens and the earth and knows what you conceal and what you declare -

26. Allah - there is no deity except Him, Lord of the Great Throne."

27. [Solomon] said, "We will see whether you were truthful or were of the liars.

28. Take this letter of mine and deliver it to them. Then leave them and see what [answer] they will return."

29. She said, "O eminent ones, indeed, to me has been delivered a noble letter.

30. Indeed, it is from Solomon, and indeed, it reads: 'In the name of Allah, the Entirely Merciful, the Especially Merciful,

31. Be not haughty with me but come to me in submission [as Muslims]."

32. She said, "O eminent ones, advise me in my affair. I would not decide a matter until you witness [for] me."

33. They said, "We are men of strength and of great military might, but the command is yours, so see what you will command."

34. She said, "Indeed kings - when they enter a city, they ruin it and render the honored of its people humbled. And thus do they do.

35. But indeed, I will send to them a gift and see with what [reply] the messengers will return."

36. So when they came to Solomon, he said, "Do you provide me with wealth? But what Allah has given me is better than what He has given you. Rather, it is you who rejoice in your gift.

37. Return to them, for we will surely come to them with soldiers that they will be powerless to encounter, and we will surely expel them therefrom in humiliation, and they will be debased."

38. [Solomon] said, "O assembly [of jinn], which of you will bring me her throne before they come to me in submission?"

39. A powerful one from among the jinn said, "I will bring it to you before you rise from your place, and indeed, I am for this [task] strong and trustworthy."

40. Said one who had knowledge from the Scripture, "I will bring it to you before your glance returns to you." And when [Solomon] saw it placed before him, he said, "This is from the favor of my Lord to test me whether I will be grateful or ungrateful. And whoever is grateful - his gratitude is only for [the benefit of] himself. And whoever is ungrateful - then indeed, my Lord is Free of need and Generous."

41. He said, "Disguise for her her throne; we will see whether she will be guided [to truth] or will be of those who is not guided."

42. So when she arrived, it was said [to her], "Is your throne like this?" She said, "[It is] as though it was it." [Solomon said], "And we were given knowledge before her, and we have been Muslims [in submission to Allah].

43. And that which she was worshipping other than Allah had averted her [from submission to Him]. Indeed, she was from a disbelieving people."

44. She was told, "Enter the palace." But when she saw it, she thought it was a body of water and uncovered her shins [to wade through]. He said, "Indeed, it is a palace [whose floor is] made smooth with glass." She said, "My Lord, indeed I have wronged myself, and I submit with Solomon to Allah, Lord of the worlds."

45. And We had certainly sent to Thamud their brother Salih, [saying], "Worship Allah," and at once they were two parties conflicting.

46. He said, "O my people, why are you impatient for evil instead of good? Why do you not seek forgiveness of Allah that you may receive mercy?"

47. They said, "We consider you a bad omen, you and those with you." He said, "Your omen is with Allah. Rather, you are a people being tested."

48. And there were in the city nine family heads causing corruption in the land and not amending [its affairs].

49. They said, "Take a mutual oath by Allah that we will kill him by night, he and his family. Then we will say to his executor, 'We did not witness the destruction of his family, and indeed, we are truthful.' "

50. And they planned a plan, and We planned a plan, while they perceived not.

51. Then look how was the outcome of their plan - that We destroyed them and their people, all.

52. So those are their houses, desolate because of the wrong they had done. Indeed in that is a sign for people who know.

53. And We saved those who believed and used to fear Allah.

54. And [mention] Lot, when he said to his people, "Do you commit immorality while you are seeing?

55. Do you indeed approach men with desire instead of women? Rather, you are a people behaving ignorantly."

56. But the answer of his people was not except that they said, "Expel the family of Lot from your city. Indeed, they are people who keep themselves pure."

57. So We saved him and his family, except for his wife; We destined her to be of those who remained behind.
58. And We rained upon them a rain [of stones], and evil was the rain of those who were warned.
59. Say, [O Muhammad], "Praise be to Allah, and peace upon His servants whom He has chosen. Is Allah better or what they associate with Him?"
60. [More precisely], is He [not best] who created the heavens and the earth and sent down for you rain from the sky, causing to grow thereby gardens of joyful beauty which you could not [otherwise] have grown the trees thereof? Is there a deity with Allah? [No], but they are a people who ascribe equals [to Him].
61. Is He [not best] who made the earth a stable ground and placed within it rivers and made for it firmly set mountains and placed between the two seas a barrier? Is there a deity with Allah? [No], but most of them do not know.
62. Is He [not best] who responds to the desperate one when he calls upon Him and removes evil and makes you inheritors of the earth? Is there a deity with Allah? Little do you remember.
63. Is He [not best] who guides you through the darknesses of the land and sea and who sends the winds as good tidings before His mercy? Is there a deity with Allah? High is Allah above whatever they associate with Him.
64. Is He [not best] who begins creation and then repeats it and who provides for you from the heaven and earth? Is there a deity with Allah? Say, "Produce your proof, if you should be truthful."
65. Say, "None in the heavens and earth knows the unseen except Allah, and they do not perceive when they will be resurrected."
66. Rather, their knowledge is arrested concerning the Hereafter. Rather, they are in doubt about it. Rather, they are, concerning it, blind.
67. And those who disbelieve say, "When we have become dust as well as our forefathers, will we indeed be brought out [of the graves]?
68. We have been promised this, we and our forefathers, before. This is not but legends of the former peoples."
69. Say, [O Muhammad], "Travel through the land and observe how was the end of the criminals."

70. And grieve not over them or be in distress from what they conspire.
71. And they say, "When is [the fulfillment of] this promise, if you should be truthful?"
72. Say, "Perhaps it is close behind you - some of that for which you are impatient.
73. And indeed, your Lord is full of bounty for the people, but most of them do not show gratitude."
74. And indeed, your Lord knows what their breasts conceal and what they declare.
75. And there is nothing concealed within the heaven and the earth except that it is in a clear Register.
76. Indeed, this Qur'an relates to the Children of Israel most of that over which they disagree.
77. And indeed, it is guidance and mercy for the believers.
78. Indeed, your Lord will judge between them by His [wise] judgement. And He is the Exalted in Might, the Knowing.
79. So rely upon Allah; indeed, you are upon the clear truth.
80. Indeed, you will not make the dead hear, nor will you make the deaf hear the call when they have turned their backs retreating.
81. And you cannot guide the blind away from their error. You will only make hear those who believe in Our verses so they are Muslims [submitting to Allah].
82. And when the word befalls them, We will bring forth for them a creature from the earth speaking to them, [saying] that the people were, of Our verses, not certain [in faith].
83. And [warn of] the Day when We will gather from every nation a company of those who deny Our signs, and they will be [driven] in rows
84. Until, when they arrive [at the place of Judgement], He will say, "Did you deny My signs while you encompassed them not in knowledge, or what [was it that] you were doing?"
85. And the decree will befall them for the wrong they did, and they will not [be able to] speak.
86. Do they not see that We made the night that they may rest therein and the day giving sight? Indeed in that are signs for a people who believe.

87. And [warn of] the Day the Horn will be blown, and whoever is in the heavens and whoever is on the earth will be terrified except whom Allah wills. And all will come to Him humbled.

88. And you see the mountains, thinking them rigid, while they will pass as the passing of clouds. [It is] the work of Allah, who perfected all things. Indeed, He is Acquainted with that which you do.

89. Whoever comes [at Judgement] with a good deed will have better than it, and they, from the terror of that Day, will be safe.

90. And whoever comes with an evil deed - their faces will be overturned into the Fire, [and it will be said], "Are you recompensed except for what you used to do?"

91. [Say, O Muhammad], "I have only been commanded to worship the Lord of this city, who made it sacred and to whom [belongs] all things. And I am commanded to be of the Muslims [those who submit to Allah]

92. And to recite the Qur'an." And whoever is guided is only guided for [the benefit of] himself; and whoever strays - say, "I am only [one] of the warners."

93. And say, "[All] praise is [due] to Allah. He will show you His signs, and you will recognize them. And your Lord is not unaware of what you do."

| Verses: 88 | **Surah 28 Al-Qasas** | Makki |

In the name of Allah, the Entirely Merciful, the Especially Merciful.

01. Ta, Seen, Meem.

02. These are the verses of the clear Book.

03. We recite to you from the news of Moses and Pharaoh in truth for a people who believe.

04. Indeed, Pharaoh exalted himself in the land and made its people into factions, oppressing a sector among them, slaughtering their [newborn] sons and keeping their females alive. Indeed, he was of the corrupters.

05. And We wanted to confer favor upon those who were oppressed in the land and make them leaders and make them inheritors

06. And establish them in the land and show Pharaoh and [his minister] Haman and their soldiers through them that which they had feared.

07. And We inspired to the mother of Moses, "Suckle him; but when you fear for him, cast him into the river and do not fear and do not grieve. Indeed, We will return him to you and will make him [one] of the messengers."

08. And the family of Pharaoh picked him up [out of the river] so that he would become to them an enemy and a [cause of] grief. Indeed, Pharaoh and Haman and their soldiers were deliberate sinners.

09. And the wife of Pharaoh said, "[He will be] a comfort of the eye for me and for you. Do not kill him; perhaps he may benefit us, or we may adopt him as a son." And they perceived not.

10. And the heart of Moses' mother became empty [of all else]. She was about to disclose [the matter concerning] him had We not bound fast her heart that she would be of the believers.

11. And she said to his sister, "Follow him"; so she watched him from a distance while they perceived not.

12. And We had prevented from him [all] wet nurses before, so she said, "Shall I direct you to a household that will be responsible for him for you while they are to him [for his upbringing] sincere?"

13. So We restored him to his mother that she might be content and not grieve and that she would know that the promise of Allah is true. But most of the people do not know.

14. And when he attained his full strength and was [mentally] mature, We bestowed upon him judgement and knowledge. And thus do We reward the doers of good.

15. And he entered the city at a time of inattention by its people and found therein two men fighting: one from his faction and one from among his enemy. And the one from his faction called for help to him against the one from his enemy, so Moses struck him and [unintentionally] killed him. [Moses] said, "This is from the work of Satan. Indeed, he is a manifest, misleading enemy."

16. He said, "My Lord, indeed I have wronged myself, so forgive me," and He forgave him. Indeed, He is the Forgiving, the Merciful.

17. He said, "My Lord, for the favor You bestowed upon me, I will never be an assistant to the criminals."

18. And he became inside the city fearful and anticipating [exposure], when suddenly the one who sought his help previous day cried out to him [once again]. Moses said to him, "Indeed, you are an evident, [persistent] deviator."

19. And when he wanted to strike the one who was an enemy to both of them, he said, "O Moses, do you intend to kill me as you killed someone yesterday? You only want to be a tyrant in the land and do not want to be of the amenders."

20. And a man came from the farthest end of the city, running. He said, "O Moses, indeed the eminent ones are conferring over you [intending] to kill you, so leave [the city]; indeed, I am to you of the sincere advisors."

21. So he left it, fearful and anticipating [apprehension]. He said, "My Lord, save me from the wrongdoing people."

22. And when he directed himself toward Madyan, he said, "Perhaps my Lord will guide me to the sound way."

23. And when he came to the well of Madyan, he found there a crowd of people watering [their flocks], and he found aside from them two women driving back [their flocks]. He said, "What is your circumstance?" They said, "We do not water until the shepherds dispatch [their flocks]; and our father is an old man."

24. So he watered [their flocks] for them; then he went back to the shade and said, "My Lord, indeed I am, for whatever good You would send down to me, in need."

25. Then one of the two women came to him walking with shyness. She said, "Indeed, my father invites you that he may reward you for having watered for us." So when he came to him and related to him the story, he said, "Fear not. You have escaped from the wrongdoing people."

26. One of the women said, "O my father, hire him. Indeed, the best one you can hire is the strong and the trustworthy."

27. He said, "Indeed, I wish to wed you one of these, my two daughters, on [the condition] that you serve me for eight years; but if you complete ten, it will be [as a favor] from you. And I do not wish to put you in difficulty. You will find me, if Allah wills, from among the righteous."

28. [Moses] said, "That is [established] between me and you. Whichever of the two terms I complete - there is no injustice to me, and Allah, over what we say, is Witness."

29. And when Moses had completed the term and was traveling with his family, he perceived from the direction of the mount a fire. He said to his family, "Stay here; indeed, I have perceived a

fire. Perhaps I will bring you from there [some] information or burning wood from the fire that you may warm yourselves."

30. But when he came to it, he was called from the right side of the valley in a blessed spot - from the tree, "O Moses, indeed I am Allah, Lord of the worlds."

31. And [he was told], "Throw down your staff." But when he saw it writhing as if it was a snake, he turned in flight and did not return. [Allah said], "O Moses, approach and fear not. Indeed, you are of the secure.

32. Insert your hand into the opening of your garment; it will come out white, without disease. And draw in your arm close to you [as prevention] from fear, for those are two proofs from your Lord to Pharaoh and his establishment. Indeed, they have been a people defiantly disobedient."

33. He said, "My Lord, indeed, I killed from among them someone, and I fear they will kill me.

34. And my brother Aaron is more fluent than me in tongue, so send him with me as support, verifying me. Indeed, I fear that they will deny me."

35. [Allah] said, "We will strengthen your arm through your brother and grant you both supremacy so they will not reach you. [It will be] through Our signs; you and those who follow you will be the predominant."

36. But when Moses came to them with Our signs as clear evidences, they said, "This is not except invented magic, and we have not heard of this [religion] among our forefathers."

37. And Moses said, "My Lord is more knowing [than we or you] of who has come with guidance from Him and to whom will be succession in the home. Indeed, wrongdoers do not succeed."

38. And Pharaoh said, "O eminent ones, I have not known you to have a god other than me. Then ignite for me, O Haman, [a fire] upon the clay and make for me a tower that I may look at the God of Moses. And indeed, I do think he is among the liars."

39. And he was arrogant, he and his soldiers, in the land, without right, and they thought that they would not be returned to Us.

40. So We took him and his soldiers and threw them into the sea. So see how was the end of the wrongdoers.

41. And We made them leaders inviting to the Fire, and on the Day of Resurrection they will not be helped.

42. And We caused to overtake them in this world a curse, and on the Day of Resurrection they will be of the despised.

43. And We gave Moses the Scripture, after We had destroyed the former generations, as enlightenment for the people and guidance and mercy that they might be reminded.

44. And you, [O Muhammad], were not on the western side [of the mount] when We revealed to Moses the command, and you were not among the witnesses [to that].

45. But We produced [many] generations [after Moses], and prolonged was their duration. And you were not a resident among the people of Madyan, reciting to them Our verses, but We were senders [of this message].

46. And you were not at the side of the mount when We called [Moses] but [were sent] as a mercy from your Lord to warn a people to whom no warner had come before you that they might be reminded.

47. And if not that a disaster should strike them for what their hands put forth [of sins] and they would say, "Our Lord, why did You not send us a messenger so we could have followed Your verses and been among the believers?"...

48. But when the truth came to them from Us, they said, "Why was he not given like that which was given to Moses?" Did they not disbelieve in that which was given to Moses before? They said, "[They are but] two works of magic supporting each other, and indeed we are, in both, disbelievers."

49. Say, "Then bring a scripture from Allah which is more guiding than either of them that I may follow it, if you should be truthful."

50. But if they do not respond to you - then know that they only follow their [own] desires. And who is more astray than one who follows his desire without guidance from Allah? Indeed, Allah does not guide the wrongdoing people.

51. And We have [repeatedly] conveyed to them the Qur'an that they might be reminded.

52. Those to whom We gave the Scripture before it - they are believers in it.

53. And when it is recited to them, they say, "We have believed in it; indeed, it is the truth from our Lord. Indeed we were, [even] before it, Muslims [submitting to Allah]."

54. Those will be given their reward twice for what they patiently endured and [because] they avert evil through good, and from what We have provided them they spend.
55. And when they hear ill speech, they turn away from it and say, "For us are our deeds, and for you are your deeds. Peace will be upon you; we seek not the ignorant."
56. Indeed, [O Muhammad], you do not guide whom you like, but Allah guides whom He wills. And He is most knowing of the [rightly] guided.
57. And they say, "If we were to follow the guidance with you, we would be swept from our land." Have we not established for them a safe sanctuary to which are brought the fruits of all things as provision from Us? But most of them do not know.
58. And how many a city have We destroyed that was insolent in its [way of] living, and those are their dwellings which have not been inhabited after them except briefly. And it is We who were the inheritors.
59. And never would your Lord have destroyed the cities until He had sent to their mother a messenger reciting to them Our verses. And We would not destroy the cities except while their people were wrongdoers.
60. And whatever thing you [people] have been given - it is [only for] the enjoyment of worldly life and its adornment. And what is with Allah is better and more lasting; so will you not use reason?
61. Then is he whom We have promised a good promise which he will obtain like he for whom We provided enjoyment of worldly life [but] then he is, on the Day of Resurrection, among those presented [for punishment in Hell]?
62. And [warn of] the Day He will call them and say, "Where are My 'partners' which you used to claim?"
63. Those upon whom the word will have come into effect will say, "Our Lord, these are the ones we led to error. We led them to error just as we were in error. We declare our disassociation [from them] to You. They did not used to worship us."
64. And it will be said, "Invoke your 'partners' " and they will invoke them; but they will not respond to them, and they will see the punishment. If only they had followed guidance!
65. And [mention] the Day He will call them and say, "What did you answer the messengers?"

66. But the information will be unapparent to them that Day, so they will not [be able to] ask one another.

67. But as for one who had repented, believed, and done righteousness, it is promised by Allah that he will be among the successful.

68. And your Lord creates what He wills and chooses; not for them was the choice. Exalted is Allah and high above what they associate with Him.

69. And your Lord knows what their breasts conceal and what they declare.

70. And He is Allah; there is no deity except Him. To Him is [due all] praise in the first [life] and the Hereafter. And His is the [final] decision, and to Him you will be returned.

71. Say, "Have you considered: if Allah should make for you the night continuous until the Day of Resurrection, what deity other than Allah could bring you light? Then will you not hear?"

72. Say, "Have you considered: if Allah should make for you the day continuous until the Day of Resurrection, what deity other than Allah could bring you a night in which you may rest? Then will you not see?"

73. And out of His mercy He made for you the night and the day that you may rest therein and [by day] seek from His bounty and [that] perhaps you will be grateful.

74. And [warn of] the Day He will call them and say, "Where are my 'partners' which you used to claim?"

75. And We will extract from every nation a witness and say, "Produce your proof," and they will know that the truth belongs to Allah, and lost from them is that which they used to invent.

76. Indeed, Qarun was from the people of Moses, but he tyrannized them. And We gave him of treasures whose keys would burden a band of strong men; thereupon his people said to him, "Do not exult. Indeed, Allah does not like the exultant.

77. But seek, through that which Allah has given you, the home of the Hereafter; and [yet], do not forget your share of the world. And do good as Allah has done good to you. And desire not corruption in the land. Indeed, Allah does not like corrupters."

78. He said, "I was only given it because of knowledge I have." Did he not know that Allah had destroyed before him of generations those who were greater than him in power and

greater in accumulation [of wealth]? But the criminals, about their sins, will not be asked.

79. So he came out before his people in his adornment. Those who desired the worldly life said, "Oh, would that we had like what was given to Qarun. Indeed, he is one of great fortune."

80. But those who had been given knowledge said, "Woe to you! The reward of Allah is better for he who believes and does righteousness. And none are granted it except the patient."

81. And We caused the earth to swallow him and his home. And there was for him no company to aid him other than Allah, nor was he of those who [could] defend themselves.

82. And those who had wished for his position the previous day began to say, "Oh, how Allah extends provision to whom He wills of His servants and restricts it! If not that Allah had conferred favor on us, He would have caused it to swallow us. Oh, how the disbelievers do not succeed!"

83. That home of the Hereafter We assign to those who do not desire exaltedness upon the earth or corruption. And the [best] outcome is for the righteous.

84. Whoever comes [on the Day of Judgement] with a good deed will have better than it; and whoever comes with an evil deed - then those who did evil deeds will not be recompensed except [as much as] what they used to do.

85. Indeed, [O Muhammad], He who imposed upon you the Qur'an will take you back to a place of return. Say, "My Lord is most knowing of who brings guidance and who is in clear error."

86. And you were not expecting that the Book would be conveyed to you, but [it is] a mercy from your Lord. So do not be an assistant to the disbelievers.

87. And never let them avert you from the verses of Allah after they have been revealed to you. And invite [people] to your Lord. And never be of those who associate others with Allah.

88. And do not invoke with Allah another deity. There is no deity except Him. Everything will be destroyed except His Face. His is the judgement, and to Him you will be returned.

| Verses: 69 | **Surah 29 Al-Ankaboot** | Makki |

In the name of Allah, the Entirely Merciful, the Especially Merciful.

01. Alif, Lam, Meem

02. Do the people think that they will be left to say, "We believe" and they will not be tried?

03. But We have certainly tried those before them, and Allah will surely make evident those who are truthful, and He will surely make evident the liars.

04. Or do those who do evil deeds think they can outrun Us? Evil is what they judge.

05. Whoever should hope for the meeting with Allah - indeed, the term decreed by Allah is coming. And He is the Hearing, the Knowing.

06. And whoever strives only strives for [the benefit of] himself. Indeed, Allah is free from need of the worlds.

07. And those who believe and do righteous deeds - We will surely remove from them their misdeeds and will surely reward them according to the best of what they used to do.

08. And We have enjoined upon man goodness to parents. But if they endeavor to make you associate with Me that of which you have no knowledge, do not obey them. To Me is your return, and I will inform you about what you used to do.

09. And those who believe and do righteous deeds - We will surely admit them among the righteous [into Paradise].

10. And of the people are some who say, "We believe in Allah," but when one [of them] is harmed for [the cause of] Allah, they consider the trial of the people as [if it were] the punishment of Allah. But if victory comes from your Lord, they say, "Indeed, We were with you." Is not Allah most knowing of what is within the breasts of all creatures?

11. And Allah will surely make evident those who believe, and He will surely make evident the hypocrites.

12. And those who disbelieve say to those who believe, "Follow our way, and we will carry your sins." But they will not carry anything of their sins. Indeed, they are liars.

13. But they will surely carry their [own] burdens and [other] burdens along with their burdens, and they will surely be questioned on the Day of Resurrection about what they used to invent.

14. And We certainly sent Noah to his people, and he remained among them a thousand years minus fifty years, and the flood seized them while they were wrongdoers.

15. But We saved him and the companions of the ship, and We made it a sign for the worlds.

16. And [We sent] Abraham, when he said to his people, "Worship Allah and fear Him. That is best for you, if you should know.

17. You only worship, besides Allah, idols, and you produce a falsehood. Indeed, those you worship besides Allah do not possess for you [the power of] provision. So seek from Allah provision and worship Him and be grateful to Him. To Him you will be returned."

18. And if you [people] deny [the message] - already nations before you have denied. And there is not upon the Messenger except [the duty of] clear notification.

19. Have they not considered how Allah begins creation and then repeats it? Indeed that, for Allah, is easy.

20. Say, [O Muhammad], "Travel through the land and observe how He began creation. Then Allah will produce the final creation. Indeed Allah, over all things, is competent."

21. He punishes whom He wills and has mercy upon whom He wills, and to Him you will be returned.

22. And you will not cause failure [to Allah] upon the earth or in the heaven. And you have not other than Allah any protector or any helper.

23. And the ones who disbelieve in the signs of Allah and the meeting with Him - those have despaired of My mercy, and they will have a painful punishment.

24. And the answer of Abraham's people was not but that they said, "Kill him or burn him," but Allah saved him from the fire. Indeed in that are signs for a people who believe.

25. And [Abraham] said, "You have only taken, other than Allah, idols as [a bond of] affection among you in worldly life. Then on the Day of Resurrection you will deny one another and curse one another, and your refuge will be the Fire, and you will not have any helpers."

26. And Lot believed him. [Abraham] said, "Indeed, I will emigrate to [the service of] my Lord. Indeed, He is the Exalted in Might, the Wise."

27. And We gave to Him Isaac and Jacob and placed in his descendants prophethood and scripture. And We gave him his reward in this world, and indeed, he is in the Hereafter among the righteous.

28. And [mention] Lot, when he said to his people, "Indeed, you commit such immorality as no one has preceded you with from among the worlds.

29. Indeed, you approach men and obstruct the road and commit in your meetings [every] evil." And the answer of his people was not but they said, "Bring us the punishment of Allah, if you should be of the truthful."

30. He said, "My Lord, support me against the corrupting people."

31. And when Our messengers came to Abraham with the good tidings, they said, "Indeed, we will destroy the people of that Lot's city. Indeed, its people have been wrongdoers."

32. [Abraham] said, "Indeed, within it is Lot." They said, "We are more knowing of who is within it. We will surely save him and his family, except his wife. She is to be of those who remain behind."

33. And when Our messengers came to Lot, he was distressed for them and felt for them great discomfort. They said, "Fear not, nor grieve. Indeed, we will save you and your family, except your wife; she is to be of those who remain behind.

34. Indeed, we will bring down on the people of this city punishment from the sky because they have been defiantly disobedient."

35. And We have certainly left of it a sign as clear evidence for a people who use reason.

36. And to Madyan [We sent] their brother Shu'ayb, and he said, "O my people, worship Allah and expect the Last Day and do not commit abuse on the earth, spreading corruption."

37. But they denied him, so the earthquake seized them, and they became within their home [corpses] fallen prone.

38. And [We destroyed] 'Aad and Thamud, and it has become clear to you from their [ruined] dwellings. And Satan had made pleasing to them their deeds and averted them from the path, and they were endowed with perception.

39. And [We destroyed] Qarun and Pharaoh and Haman. And Moses had already come to them with clear evidences, and they were arrogant in the land, but they were not outrunners [of Our punishment].

40. So each We seized for his sin; and among them were those upon whom We sent a storm of stones, and among them were those who were seized by the blast [from the sky], and among them were those whom We caused the earth to swallow, and among them were those whom We drowned. And Allah would not have wronged them, but it was they who were wronging themselves.

41. The example of those who take allies other than Allah is like that of the spider who takes a home. And indeed, the weakest of homes is the home of the spider, if they only knew.

42. Indeed, Allah knows whatever thing they call upon other than Him. And He is the Exalted in Might, the Wise.

43. And these examples We present to the people, but none will understand them except those of knowledge.

44. Allah created the heavens and the earth in truth. Indeed in that is a sign for the believers.

45. ==Recite, [O Muhammad], what has been revealed to you of the Book and establish prayer. Indeed, prayer prohibits immorality== and wrongdoing, and the remembrance of Allah is greater. And Allah knows that which you do.

46. And do not argue with the People of the Scripture except in a way that is best, except for those who commit injustice among them, and say, "We believe in that which has been revealed to us and revealed to you. And our God and your God is one; and we are Muslims [in submission] to Him."

47. And thus We have sent down to you the Qur'an. And those to whom We [previously] gave the Scripture believe in it. And among these [people of Makkah] are those who believe in it. And none reject Our verses except the disbelievers.

48. And you did not recite before it any scripture, nor did you inscribe one with your right hand. Otherwise the falsifiers would have had [cause for] doubt.

49. Rather, the Qur'an is distinct verses [preserved] within the breasts of those who have been given knowledge. And none reject Our verses except the wrongdoers.

50. But they say, "Why are not signs sent down to him from his Lord?" Say, "The signs are only with Allah, and I am only a clear warner."

51. And is it not sufficient for them that We revealed to you the Book

which is recited to them? Indeed in that is a mercy and reminder for a people who believe.

52. Say, "Sufficient is Allah between me and you as Witness. He knows what is in the heavens and earth. And they who have believed in falsehood and disbelieved in Allah - it is those who are the losers."

53. And they urge you to hasten the punishment. And if not for [the decree of] a specified term, punishment would have reached them. But it will surely come to them suddenly while they perceive not.

54. They urge you to hasten the punishment. And indeed, Hell will be encompassing of the disbelievers

55. On the Day the punishment will cover them from above them and from below their feet and it is said, "Taste [the result of] what you used to do."

56. My servants who have believed, indeed My earth is spacious, so worship only Me.

57. Every soul will taste death. Then to Us will you be returned.

58. And those who have believed and done righteous deeds - We will surely assign to them of Paradise [elevated] chambers beneath which rivers flow, wherein they abide eternally. Excellent is the reward of the [righteous] workers

59. Who have been patient and upon their Lord rely.

60. And how many a creature carries not its [own] provision. Allah provides for it and for you. And He is the Hearing, the Knowing.

61. If you asked them, "Who created the heavens and earth and subjected the sun and the moon?" they would surely say, "Allah." Then how are they deluded?

62. Allah extends provision for whom He wills of His servants and restricts for him. Indeed Allah is, of all things, Knowing.

63. And if you asked them, "Who sends down rain from the sky and gives life thereby to the earth after its lifelessness?" they would surely say " Allah." Say, "Praise to Allah "; but most of them do not reason.

64. And this worldly life is not but diversion and amusement. And indeed, the home of the Hereafter - that is the [eternal] life, if only they knew.

65. And when they board a ship, they supplicate Allah, sincere to Him in religion. But when He delivers them to the land, at once they associate others with Him

66. So that they will deny what We have granted them, and they will enjoy themselves. But they are going to know.

67. Have they not seen that We made [Makkah] a safe sanctuary, while people are being taken away all around them? Then in falsehood do they believe, and in the favor of Allah they disbelieve?

68. And who is more unjust than one who invents a lie about Allah or denies the truth when it has come to him? Is there not in Hell a [sufficient] residence for the disbelievers?

69. And those who strive for Us - We will surely guide them to Our ways. And indeed, Allah is with the doers of good.

Surah 30 Ar-Room

Verses: 60 — Makki

In the name of Allah, the Entirely Merciful, the Especially Merciful.

01. Alif, Lam, Meem.

02. The Byzantines have been defeated

03. In the nearest land. But they, after their defeat, will overcome.

04. Within three to nine years. To Allah belongs the command before and after. And that day the believers will rejoice

05. In the victory of Allah. He gives victory to whom He wills, and He is the Exalted in Might, the Merciful.

06. [It is] the promise of Allah. Allah does not fail in His promise, but most of the people do not know.

07. They know what is apparent of the worldly life, but they, of the Hereafter, are unaware.

08. Do they not contemplate within themselves? Allah has not created the heavens and the earth and what is between them except in truth and for a specified term. And indeed, many of the people, in [the matter of] the meeting with their Lord, are disbelievers.

09. Have they not traveled through the earth and observed how was the end of those before them? They were greater than them in power, and they plowed the earth and built it up more than they have built it up, and their messengers came to them with clear evidences. And Allah would not ever have wronged them, but they were wronging themselves.

10. Then the end of those who did evil was the worst [consequence] because they denied the signs of Allah and used to ridicule them.

11. Allah begins creation; then He will repeat it; then to Him you will be returned.

12. And the Day the Hour appears the criminals will be in despair.

13. And there will not be for them among their [alleged] partners any intercessors, and they will [then] be disbelievers in their partners.

14. And the Day the Hour appears - that Day they will become separated.

15. And as for those who had believed and done righteous deeds, they will be in a garden [of Paradise], delighted.

16. But as for those who disbelieved and denied Our verses and the meeting of the Hereafter, those will be brought into the punishment [to remain].

17. So exalted is Allah when you reach the evening and when you reach the morning.

18. And to Him is [due all] praise throughout the heavens and the earth. And [exalted is He] at night and when you are at noon.

19. He brings the living out of the dead and brings the dead out of the living and brings to life the earth after its lifelessness. And thus will you be brought out.

20. And of His signs is that He created you from dust; then, suddenly you were human beings dispersing [throughout the earth].

21. And of His signs is that He created for you from yourselves mates that you may find tranquillity in them; and He placed between you affection and mercy. Indeed in that are signs for a people who give thought.

22. And of His signs is the creation of the heavens and the earth and the diversity of your languages and your colors. Indeed in that are signs for those of knowledge.

23. And of His signs is your sleep by night and day and your seeking of His bounty. Indeed in that are signs for a people who listen.

24. And of His signs is [that] He shows you the lightning [causing] fear and aspiration, and He sends down rain from the sky by which He brings to life the earth after its lifelessness. Indeed in that are signs for a people who use reason.

25. And of His signs is that the heaven and earth remain by His

command. Then when He calls you with a [single] call from the earth, immediately you will come forth.

26. And to Him belongs whoever is in the heavens and earth. All are to Him devoutly obedient.

27. And it is He who begins creation; then He repeats it, and that is [even] easier for Him. To Him belongs the highest attribute in the heavens and earth. And He is the Exalted in Might, the Wise.

28. He presents to you an example from yourselves. Do you have among those whom your right hands possess any partners in what We have provided for you so that you are equal therein [and] would fear them as your fear of one another [within a partnership]? Thus do We detail the verses for a people who use reason.

29. But those who wrong follow their [own] desires without knowledge. Then who can guide one whom Allah has sent astray? And for them there are no helpers.

30. So direct your face toward the religion, inclining to truth. [Adhere to] the fitrah of Allah upon which He has created [all] people. No change should there be in the creation of Allah. That is the correct religion, but most of the people do not know.

31. [Adhere to it], turning in repentance to Him, and fear Him and establish prayer and do not be of those who associate others with Allah

32. [Or] of those who have divided their religion and become sects, every faction rejoicing in what it has.

33. And when adversity touches the people, they call upon their Lord, turning in repentance to Him. Then when He lets them taste mercy from Him, at once a party of them associate others with their Lord,

34. So that they will deny what We have granted them. Then enjoy yourselves, for you are going to know.

35. Or have We sent down to them an authority, and it speaks of what they were associating with Him?

36. And when We let the people taste mercy, they rejoice therein, but if evil afflicts them for what their hands have put forth, immediately they despair.

37. Do they not see that Allah extends provision for whom He wills and restricts [it]? Indeed, in that are signs for a people who believe.

38. So give the relative his right, as well as the needy and the traveler. That is best for those who desire the countenance of Allah, and it is they who will be the successful.

39. And whatever you give for interest to increase within the wealth of people will not increase with Allah. But what you give in zakah, desiring the countenance of Allah - those are the multipliers.

40. Allah is the one who created you, then provided for you, then will cause you to die, and then will give you life. Are there any of your "partners" who does anything of that? Exalted is He and high above what they associate with Him.

41. Corruption has appeared throughout the land and sea by [reason of] what the hands of people have earned so He may let them taste part of [the consequence of] what they have done that perhaps they will return [to righteousness].

42. Say, [O Muhammad], "Travel through the land and observe how was the end of those before. Most of them were associators [of others with Allah].

43. So direct your face toward the correct religion before a Day comes from Allah of which there is no repelling. That Day, they will be divided.

44. Whoever disbelieves - upon him is [the consequence of] his disbelief. And whoever does righteousness - they are for themselves preparing,

45. That He may reward those who have believed and done righteous deeds out of His bounty. Indeed, He does not like the disbelievers.

46. And of His signs is that He sends the winds as bringers of good tidings and to let you taste His mercy and so the ships may sail at His command and so you may seek of His bounty, and perhaps you will be grateful.

47. And We have already sent messengers before you to their peoples, and they came to them with clear evidences; then We took retribution from those who committed crimes, and incumbent upon Us was support of the believers.

48. It is Allah who sends the winds, and they stir the clouds and spread them in the sky however He wills, and He makes them fragments so you see the rain emerge from within them. And when He causes it to fall upon whom He wills of His servants, immediately they rejoice

49. Although they were, before it was sent down upon them - before that, in despair.

50. So observe the effects of the mercy of Allah - how He gives life to the earth after its lifelessness. Indeed, that [same one] will give life to the dead, and He is over all things competent.

51. But if We should send a [bad] wind and they saw [their crops] turned yellow, they would remain thereafter disbelievers.

52. So indeed, you will not make the dead hear, nor will you make the deaf hear the call when they turn their backs, retreating.

53. And you cannot guide the blind away from their error. You will only make hear those who believe in Our verses so they are Muslims [in submission to Allah].

54. Allah is the one who created you from weakness, then made after weakness strength, then made after strength weakness and white hair. He creates what He wills, and He is the Knowing, the Competent.

55. And the Day the Hour appears the criminals will swear they had remained but an hour. Thus they were deluded.

56. But those who were given knowledge and faith will say, "You remained the extent of Allah 's decree until the Day of Resurrection, and this is the Day of Resurrection, but you did not used to know."

57. So that Day, their excuse will not benefit those who wronged, nor will they be asked to appease [Allah].

58. And We have certainly presented to the people in this Qur'an from every [kind of] example. But, [O Muhammad], if you should bring them a sign, the disbelievers will surely say, "You [believers] are but falsifiers."

59. Thus does Allah seal the hearts of those who do not know.

60. So be patient. Indeed, the promise of Allah is truth. And let them not disquiet you who are not certain [in faith].

Verses: 34	**Surah 31 Luqman**	Makki

In the name of Allah, the Entirely Merciful, the Especially Merciful.

01. Alif, Lam, Meem.

02. These are verses of the wise Book,

03. As guidance and mercy for the doers of good

04. Who establish prayer and give zakah, and they, of the Hereafter, are certain [in faith].

05. Those are on [right] guidance from their Lord, and it is those who are the successful.

06. And of the people is he who buys the amusement of speech to mislead [others] from the way of Allah without knowledge and who takes it in ridicule. Those will have a humiliating punishment.

07. And when our verses are recited to him, he turns away arrogantly as if he had not heard them, as if there was in his ears deafness. So give him tidings of a painful punishment.

08. Indeed, those who believe and do righteous deeds - for them are the Gardens of Pleasure.

09. Wherein they abide eternally; [it is] the promise of Allah [which is] truth. And He is the Exalted in Might, the Wise.

10. He created the heavens without pillars that you see and has cast into the earth firmly set mountains, lest it should shift with you, and dispersed therein from every creature. And We sent down rain from the sky and made grow therein [plants] of every noble kind.

11. This is the creation of Allah. So show Me what those other than Him have created. Rather, the wrongdoers are in clear error.

12. And We had certainly given Luqman wisdom [and said], "Be grateful to Allah." And whoever is grateful is grateful for [the benefit of] himself. And whoever denies [His favor] - then indeed, Allah is Free of need and Praiseworthy.

13. And [mention, O Muhammad], when Luqman said to his son while he was instructing him, "O my son, do not associate [anything] with Allah. Indeed, association [with him] is great injustice."

14. And We have enjoined upon man [care] for his parents. His mother carried him, [increasing her] in weakness upon weakness, and his weaning is in two years. Be grateful to Me and to your parents; to Me is the [final] destination.

15. But if they endeavor to make you associate with Me that of which you have no knowledge, do not obey them but accompany them in [this] world with appropriate kindness and follow the way of those who turn back to Me [in repentance]. Then to Me will be your return, and I will inform you about what you used to do.

16. [And Luqman said], "O my son, indeed if wrong should be the weight of a mustard seed and should be within a rock or [anywhere] in the heavens or in the earth, Allah will bring it forth. Indeed, Allah is Subtle and Acquainted.

17. my son, establish prayer, enjoin what is right, forbid what is wrong, and be patient over what befalls you. Indeed, [all] that is of the matters [requiring] determination.

18. And do not turn your cheek [in contempt] toward people and do not walk through the earth exultantly. Indeed, Allah does not like everyone self-deluded and boastful.

19. And be moderate in your pace and lower your voice; indeed, the most disagreeable of sounds is the voice of donkeys."

20. Do you not see that Allah has made subject to you whatever is in the heavens and whatever is in the earth and amply bestowed upon you His favors, [both] apparent and unapparent? But of the people is he who disputes about Allah without knowledge or guidance or an enlightening Book [from Him].

21. And when it is said to them, "Follow what Allah has revealed," they say, "Rather, we will follow that upon which we found our fathers." Even if Satan was inviting them to the punishment of the Blaze?

22. And whoever submits his face to Allah while he is a doer of good - then he has grasped the most trustworthy handhold. And to Allah will be the outcome of [all] matters.

23. And whoever has disbelieved - let not his disbelief grieve you. To Us is their return, and We will inform them of what they did. Indeed, Allah is Knowing of that within the breasts.

24. We grant them enjoyment for a little; then We will force them to a massive punishment.

25. And if you asked them, "Who created the heavens and earth?" they would surely say, "Allah." Say, "[All] praise is [due] to Allah "; but most of them do not know.

26. To Allah belongs whatever is in the heavens and earth. Indeed, Allah is the Free of need, the Praiseworthy.

27. And if whatever trees upon the earth were pens and the sea [was ink], replenished thereafter by seven [more] seas, the words of Allah would not be exhausted. Indeed, Allah is Exalted in Might and Wise.

28. Your creation and your resurrection will not be but as that of a single soul. Indeed, Allah is Hearing and Seeing.

29. Do you not see that Allah causes the night to enter the day and causes the day to enter the night and has subjected the sun and the moon, each running [its course] for a specified term, and that Allah, with whatever you do, is Acquainted?

30. That is because Allah is the Truth, and that what they call upon other than Him is falsehood, and because Allah is the Most High, the Grand.

31. Do you not see that ships sail through the sea by the favor of Allah that He may show you of His signs? Indeed in that are signs for everyone patient and grateful.

32. And when waves come over them like canopies, they supplicate Allah, sincere to Him in religion. But when He delivers them to the land, there are [some] of them who are moderate [in faith]. And none rejects Our signs except everyone treacherous and ungrateful.

33. O mankind, fear your Lord and fear a Day when no father will avail his son, nor will a son avail his father at all. Indeed, the promise of Allah is truth, so let not the worldly life delude you and be not deceived about Allah by the Deceiver.

34. Indeed, Allah [alone] has knowledge of the Hour and sends down the rain and knows what is in the wombs. And no soul perceives what it will earn tomorrow, and no soul perceives in what land it will die. Indeed, Allah is Knowing and Acquainted.

| Verses: 30 | Surah 32 As-Sajdah | Makki |

In the name of Allah, the Entirely Merciful, the Especially Merciful.

01. Alif, Lam, Meem.

02. [This is] the revelation of the Book about which there is no doubt from the Lord of the worlds.

03. Or do they say, "He invented it"? Rather, it is the truth from your Lord, [O Muhammad], that you may warn a people to whom no warner has come before you [so] perhaps they will be guided.

04. It is Allah who created the heavens and the earth and whatever is between them in six days; then He established Himself above the Throne. You have not besides Him any protector or any intercessor; so will you not be reminded?

05. He arranges [each] matter from the heaven to the earth; then it will ascend to Him in a Day, the extent of which is a thousand years of those which you count.

06. That is the Knower of the unseen and the witnessed, the Exalted in Might, the Merciful,

07. Who perfected everything which He created and began the creation of man from clay.

08. Then He made his posterity out of the extract of a liquid disdained.

09. Then He proportioned him and breathed into him from His [created] soul and made for you hearing and vision and hearts; little are you grateful.

10. And they say, "When we are lost within the earth, will we indeed be [recreated] in a new creation?" Rather, they are, in [the matter of] the meeting with their Lord, disbelievers.

11. Say, "The angel of death will take you who has been entrusted with you. Then to your Lord you will be returned."

12. If you could but see when the criminals are hanging their heads before their Lord, [saying], "Our Lord, we have seen and heard, so return us [to the world]; we will work righteousness. Indeed, we are [now] certain."

13. And if We had willed, We could have given every soul its guidance, but the word from Me will come into effect [that] "I will surely fill Hell with jinn and people all together.

14. So taste [punishment] because you forgot the meeting of this, your Day; indeed, We have [accordingly] forgotten you. And taste the punishment of eternity for what you used to do."

15. Only those believe in Our verses who, when they are reminded by them, fall down in prostration and exalt [Allah] with praise of their Lord, and they are not arrogant.

16. They arise from [their] beds; they supplicate their Lord in fear and aspiration, and from what We have provided them, they spend.

17. And no soul knows what has been hidden for them of comfort for eyes as reward for what they used to do.

18. Then is one who was a believer like one who was defiantly disobedient? They are not equal.

19. As for those who believed and did righteous deeds, for them will be the Gardens of Refuge as accommodation for what they used to do.

20. But as for those who defiantly disobeyed, their refuge is the Fire. Every time they wish to emerge from it, they will be returned to

it while it is said to them, "Taste the punishment of the Fire which you used to deny."

21. And we will surely let them taste the nearer punishment short of the greater punishment that perhaps they will repent.

22. And who is more unjust than one who is reminded of the verses of his Lord; then he turns away from them? Indeed We, from the criminals, will take retribution.

23. And We certainly gave Moses the Scripture, so do not be in doubt over his meeting. And we made the Torah guidance for the Children of Israel.

24. And We made from among them leaders guiding by Our command when they were patient and [when] they were certain of Our signs.

25. Indeed, your Lord will judge between them on the Day of Resurrection concerning that over which they used to differ.

26. Has it not become clear to them how many generations We destroyed before them, [as] they walk among their dwellings? Indeed in that are signs; then do they not hear?

27. Have they not seen that We drive the water [in clouds] to barren land and bring forth thereby crops from which their livestock eat and [they] themselves? Then do they not see?

28. And they say, "When will be this conquest, if you should be truthful?"

29. Say, [O Muhammad], "On the Day of Conquest the belief of those who had disbelieved will not benefit them, nor will they be reprieved."

30. So turn away from them and wait. Indeed, they are waiting.

Surah 33 Al-Ahzaab

Verses: 73 — Madani

In the name of Allah, the Entirely Merciful, the Especially Merciful.

01. O Prophet, fear Allah and do not obey the disbelievers and the hypocrites. Indeed, Allah is ever Knowing and Wise.

02. And follow that which is revealed to you from your Lord. Indeed Allah is ever, with what you do, Acquainted.

03. And rely upon Allah; and sufficient is Allah as Disposer of affairs.

04. Allah has not made for a man two hearts in his interior. And He has not made your wives whom you declare unlawful your mothers. And he has not made your adopted sons your [true]

sons. That is [merely] your saying by your mouths, but Allah says the truth, and He guides to the [right] way.

05. Call them by [the names of] their fathers; it is more just in the sight of Allah. But if you do not know their fathers - then they are [still] your brothers in religion and those entrusted to you. And there is no blame upon you for that in which you have erred but [only for] what your hearts intended. And ever is Allah Forgiving and Merciful.

06. The Prophet is more worthy of the believers than themselves, and his wives are [in the position of] their mothers. And those of [blood] relationship are more entitled [to inheritance] in the decree of Allah than the [other] believers and the emigrants, except that you may do to your close associates a kindness [through bequest]. That was in the Book inscribed.

07. And [mention, O Muhammad], when We took from the prophets their covenant and from you and from Noah and Abraham and Moses and Jesus, the son of Mary; and We took from them a solemn covenant.

08. That He may question the truthful about their truth. And He has prepared for the disbelievers a painful punishment.

09. O you who have believed, remember the favor of Allah upon you when armies came to [attack] you and We sent upon them a wind and armies [of angels] you did not see. And ever is Allah, of what you do, Seeing.

10. [Remember] when they came at you from above you and from below you, and when eyes shifted [in fear], and hearts reached the throats and you assumed about Allah [various] assumptions.

11. There the believers were tested and shaken with a severe shaking.

12. And [remember] when the hypocrites and those in whose hearts is disease said, "Allah and His Messenger did not promise us except delusion,"

13. And when a faction of them said, "O people of Yathrib, there is no stability for you [here], so return [home]." And a party of them asked permission of the Prophet, saying, "Indeed, our houses are unprotected," while they were not exposed. They did not intend except to flee.

14. And if they had been entered upon from all its [surrounding] regions and fitnah had been demanded of them, they would have done it and not hesitated over it except briefly.

15. And they had already promised Allah before not to turn their backs and flee. And ever is the promise to Allah [that about which one will be] questioned.
16. Say, [O Muhammad], "Never will fleeing benefit you if you should flee from death or killing; and then [if you did], you would not be given enjoyment [of life] except for a little."
17. Say, "Who is it that can protect you from Allah if He intends for you an ill or intends for you a mercy?" And they will not find for themselves besides Allah any protector or any helper.
18. Already Allah knows the hinderers among you and those [hypocrites] who say to their brothers, "Come to us," and do not go to battle, except for a few,
19. Indisposed toward you. And when fear comes, you see them looking at you, their eyes revolving like one being overcome by death. But when fear departs, they lash you with sharp tongues, indisposed toward [any] good. Those have not believed, so Allah has rendered their deeds worthless, and ever is that, for Allah, easy.
20. They think the companies have not [yet] withdrawn. And if the companies should come [again], they would wish they were in the desert among the bedouins, inquiring [from afar] about your news. And if they should be among you, they would not fight except for a little.
21. There has certainly been for you in the Messenger of Allah an excellent pattern for anyone whose hope is in Allah and the Last Day and [who] remembers Allah often.
22. And when the believers saw the companies, they said, "This is what Allah and His Messenger had promised us, and Allah and His Messenger spoke the truth." And it increased them only in faith and acceptance.
23. Among the believers are men true to what they promised Allah. Among them is he who has fulfilled his vow [to the death], and among them is he who awaits [his chance]. And they did not alter [the terms of their commitment] by any alteration -
24. That Allah may reward the truthful for their truth and punish the hypocrites if He wills or accept their repentance. Indeed, Allah is ever Forgiving and Merciful.
25. And Allah repelled those who disbelieved, in their rage, not having obtained any good. And sufficient was Allah for the believers in battle, and ever is Allah Powerful and Exalted in Might.

26. And He brought down those who supported them among the People of the Scripture from their fortresses and cast terror into their hearts [so that] a party you killed, and you took captive a party.

27. And He caused you to inherit their land and their homes and their properties and a land which you have not trodden. And ever is Allah, over all things, competent.

28. O Prophet, say to your wives, "If you should desire the worldly life and its adornment, then come, I will provide for you and give you a gracious release.

29. But if you should desire Allah and His Messenger and the home of the Hereafter - then indeed, Allah has prepared for the doers of good among you a great reward."

30. wives of the Prophet, whoever of you should commit a clear immorality - for her the punishment would be doubled two fold, and ever is that, for Allah, easy.

31. ==And whoever of you devoutly obeys Allah and His Messenger and does righteousness - We will give her her reward twice; and== We have prepared for her a noble provision.

32. wives of the Prophet, you are not like anyone among women. If you fear Allah, then do not be soft in speech [to men], lest he in whose heart is disease should covet, but speak with appropriate speech.

33. And abide in your houses and do not display yourselves as [was] the display of the former times of ignorance. And establish prayer and give zakah and obey Allah and His Messenger. Allah intends only to remove from you the impurity [of sin], O people of the [Prophet's] household, and to purify you with [extensive] purification.

34. And remember what is recited in your houses of the verses of Allah and wisdom. Indeed, Allah is ever Subtle and Acquainted [with all things].

35. Indeed, the Muslim men and Muslim women, the believing men and believing women, the obedient men and obedient women, the truthful men and truthful women, the patient men and patient women, the humble men and humble women, the charitable men and charitable women, the fasting men and fasting women, the men who guard their private parts and the women who do so, and the men who remember Allah often and the women who do so - for them Allah has prepared forgiveness and a great reward.

36. It is not for a believing man or a believing woman, when Allah and His Messenger have decided a matter, that they should [thereafter] have any choice about their affair. And whoever disobeys Allah and His Messenger has certainly strayed into clear error.

37. And [remember, O Muhammad], when you said to the one on whom Allah bestowed favor and you bestowed favor, "Keep your wife and fear Allah," while you concealed within yourself that which Allah is to disclose. And you feared the people, while Allah has more right that you fear Him. So when Zayd had no longer any need for her, We married her to you in order that there not be upon the believers any discomfort concerning the wives of their adopted sons when they no longer have need of them. And ever is the command of Allah accomplished.

38. There is not to be upon the Prophet any discomfort concerning that which Allah has imposed upon him. [This is] the established way of Allah with those [prophets] who have passed on before. And ever is the command of Allah a destiny decreed.

39. [Allah praises] those who convey the messages of Allah and fear Him and do not fear anyone but Allah. And sufficient is Allah as Accountant.

40. Muhammad is not the father of [any] one of your men, but [he is] the Messenger of Allah and last of the prophets. And ever is Allah, of all things, Knowing.

41. O you who have believed, remember Allah with much remembrance

42. And exalt Him morning and afternoon.

43. It is He who confers blessing upon you, and His angels [ask Him to do so] that He may bring you out from darknesses into the light. And ever is He, to the believers, Merciful.

44. Their greeting the Day they meet Him will be, "Peace." And He has prepared for them a noble reward.

45. O Prophet, indeed We have sent you as a witness and a bringer of good tidings and a warner.

46. And one who invites to Allah, by His permission, and an illuminating lamp.

47. And give good tidings to the believers that they will have from Allah great bounty.

48. And do not obey the disbelievers and the hypocrites but do not harm them, and rely upon Allah. And sufficient is Allah as Disposer of affairs.

49. O You who have believed, when you marry believing women and then divorce them before you have touched them, then there is not for you any waiting period to count concerning them. So provide for them and give them a gracious release.

50. O Prophet, indeed We have made lawful to you your wives to whom you have given their due compensation and those your right hand possesses from what Allah has returned to you [of captives] and the daughters of your paternal uncles and the daughters of your paternal aunts and the daughters of your maternal uncles and the daughters of your maternal aunts who emigrated with you and a believing woman if she gives herself to the Prophet [and] if the Prophet wishes to marry her, [this is] only for you, excluding the [other] believers. We certainly know what We have made obligatory upon them concerning their wives and those their right hands possess, [but this is for you] in order that there will be upon you no discomfort. And ever is Allah Forgiving and Merciful.

51. You, [O Muhammad], may put aside whom you will of them or take to yourself whom you will. And any that you desire of those [wives] from whom you had [temporarily] separated - there is no blame upon you [in returning her]. That is more suitable that they should be content and not grieve and that they should be satisfied with what you have given them - all of them. And Allah knows what is in your hearts. And ever is Allah Knowing and Forbearing.

52. Not lawful to you, [O Muhammad], are [any additional] women after [this], nor [is it] for you to exchange them for [other] wives, even if their beauty were to please you, except what your right hand possesses. And ever is Allah, over all things, an Observer.

53. O you who have believed, do not enter the houses of the Prophet except when you are permitted for a meal, without awaiting its readiness. But when you are invited, then enter; and when you have eaten, disperse without seeking to remain for conversation. Indeed, that [behavior] was troubling the Prophet, and he is shy of [dismissing] you. But Allah is not shy of the truth. And when you ask [his wives] for something, ask them from behind a partition. That is purer for your hearts and their hearts. And it is not [conceivable or lawful] for you to harm the Messenger of Allah or to marry his wives after him, ever. Indeed, that would be in the sight of Allah an enormity.

54. Whether you reveal a thing or conceal it, indeed Allah is ever, of all things, Knowing.

55. There is no blame upon women concerning their fathers or their sons or their brothers or their brothers' sons or their sisters' sons or their women or those their right hands possess. And fear Allah. Indeed Allah is ever, over all things, Witness.

56. Indeed, Allah confers blessing upon the Prophet, and His angels [ask Him to do so]. O you who have believed, ask [Allah to confer] blessing upon him and ask [Allah to grant him] peace.

57. Indeed, those who abuse Allah and His Messenger - Allah has cursed them in this world and the Hereafter and prepared for them a humiliating punishment.

58. And those who harm believing men and believing women for [something] other than what they have earned have certainly born upon themselves a slander and manifest sin.

59. O Prophet, tell your wives and your daughters and the women of the believers to bring down over themselves [part] of their outer garments. That is more suitable that they will be known and not be abused. And ever is Allah Forgiving and Merciful.

60. If the hypocrites and those in whose hearts is disease and those who spread rumors in al-Madinah do not cease, We will surely incite you against them; then they will not remain your neighbors therein except for a little.

61. Accursed wherever they are found, [being] seized and massacred completely.

62. [This is] the established way of Allah with those who passed on before; and you will not find in the way of Allah any change.

63. People ask you concerning the Hour. Say," Knowledge of it is only with Allah. And what may make you perceive? Perhaps the Hour is near."

64. Indeed, Allah has cursed the disbelievers and prepared for them a Blaze.

65. Abiding therein forever, they will not find a protector or a helper.

66. The Day their faces will be turned about in the Fire, they will say, "How we wish we had obeyed Allah and obeyed the Messenger."

67. And they will say, "Our Lord, indeed we obeyed our masters and our dignitaries, and they led us astray from the [right] way.

68. Our Lord, give them double the punishment and curse them with a great curse."

69. O you who have believed, be not like those who abused Moses; then Allah cleared him of what they said. And he, in the sight of Allah, was distinguished.

70. O you who have believed, fear Allah and speak words of appropriate justice.

71. He will [then] amend for you your deeds and forgive you your sins. And whoever obeys Allah and His Messenger has certainly attained a great attainment.

72. Indeed, we offered the Trust to the heavens and the earth and the mountains, and they declined to bear it and feared it; but man [undertook to] bear it. Indeed, he was unjust and ignorant.

73. [It was] so that Allah may punish the hypocrite men and hypocrite women and the men and women who associate others with Him and that Allah may accept repentance from the believing men and believing women. And ever is Allah Forgiving and Merciful.

| Verses: 54 | **Surah 34 Saba** | Makki |

In the name of Allah, the Entirely Merciful, the Especially Merciful.

01. [All] praise is [due] to Allah, to whom belongs whatever is in the heavens and whatever is in the earth, and to Him belongs [all] praise in the Hereafter. And He is the Wise, the Acquainted.

02. He knows what penetrates into the earth and what emerges from it and what descends from the heaven and what ascends therein. And He is the Merciful, the Forgiving.

03. But those who disbelieve say, "The Hour will not come to us." Say, "Yes, by my Lord, it will surely come to you. [Allah is] the Knower of the unseen." Not absent from Him is an atom's weight within the heavens or within the earth or [what is] smaller than that or greater, except that it is in a clear register -

04. That He may reward those who believe and do righteous deeds. Those will have forgiveness and noble provision.

05. But those who strive against Our verses [seeking] to cause failure - for them will be a painful punishment of foul nature.

06. And those who have been given knowledge see that what is revealed to you from your Lord is the truth, and it guides to the path of the Exalted in Might, the Praiseworthy.

07. But those who disbelieve say, "Shall we direct you to a man who will inform you [that] when you have disintegrated in complete disintegration, you will [then] be [recreated] in a new creation?

08. Has he invented about Allah a lie or is there in him madness?" Rather, they who do not believe in the Hereafter will be in the punishment and [are in] extreme error.

09. Then, do they not look at what is before them and what is behind them of the heaven and earth? If We should will, We could cause the earth to swallow them or [could] let fall upon them fragments from the sky. Indeed in that is a sign for every servant turning back [to Allah].

10. And We certainly gave David from Us bounty. [We said], "O mountains, repeat [Our] praises with him, and the birds [as well]." And We made pliable for him iron,

11. [Commanding him], "Make full coats of mail and calculate [precisely] the links, and work [all of you] righteousness. Indeed I, of what you do, am Seeing."

12. And to Solomon [We subjected] the wind - its morning [journey was that of] a month - and its afternoon [journey was that of] a month, and We made flow for him a spring of [liquid] copper. And among the jinn were those who worked for him by the permission of his Lord. And whoever deviated among them from Our command - We will make him taste of the punishment of the Blaze.

13. They made for him what he willed of elevated chambers, statues, bowls like reservoirs, and stationary kettles. [We said], "Work, O family of David, in gratitude." And few of My servants are grateful.

14. And when We decreed for Solomon death, nothing indicated to the jinn his death except a creature of the earth eating his staff. But when he fell, it became clear to the jinn that if they had known the unseen, they would not have remained in humiliating punishment.

15. There was for [the tribe of] Saba' in their dwelling place a sign: two [fields of] gardens on the right and on the left. [They were told], "Eat from the provisions of your Lord and be grateful to Him. A good land [have you], and a forgiving Lord."

16. But they turned away [refusing], so We sent upon them the flood of the dam, and We replaced their two [fields of] gardens with gardens of bitter fruit, tamarisks and something of sparse lote trees.

17. [By] that We repaid them because they disbelieved. And do We [thus] repay except the ungrateful?

18. And We placed between them and the cities which We had blessed [many] visible cities. And We determined between them the [distances of] journey, [saying], "Travel between them by night or day in safety."

19. But [insolently] they said, "Our Lord, lengthen the distance between our journeys," and wronged themselves, so We made them narrations and dispersed them in total dispersion. Indeed in that are signs for everyone patient and grateful.

20. And Iblees had already confirmed through them his assumption, so they followed him, except for a party of believers.

21. And he had over them no authority except [it was decreed] that We might make evident who believes in the Hereafter from who is thereof in doubt. And your Lord, over all things, is Guardian.

22. Say, [O Muhammad], "Invoke those you claim [as deities] besides Allah." They do not possess an atom's weight [of ability] in the heavens or on the earth, and they do not have therein any partnership [with Him], nor is there for Him from among them any assistant.

23. And intercession does not benefit with Him except for one whom He permits. [And those wait] until, when terror is removed from their hearts, they will say [to one another], "What has your Lord said?" They will say, "The truth." And He is the Most High, the Grand.

24. Say, "Who provides for you from the heavens and the earth?" Say, "Allah. And indeed, we or you are either upon guidance or in clear error."

25. Say, "You will not be asked about what we committed, and we will not be asked about what you do."

26. Say, "Our Lord will bring us together; then He will judge between us in truth. And He is the Knowing Judge."

27. Say, "Show me those whom you have attached to Him as partners. No! Rather, He [alone] is Allah, the Exalted in Might, the Wise."

28. And We have not sent you except comprehensively to mankind as a bringer of good tidings and a warner. But most of the people do not know.

29. And they say, "When is this promise, if you should be truthful?"

30. Say, "For you is the appointment of a Day [when] you will not remain thereafter an hour, nor will you precede [it]."

31. And those who disbelieve say, "We will never believe in this Qur'an nor in that before it." But if you could see when the wrongdoers are made to stand before their Lord, refuting each other's words... Those who were oppressed will say to those who were arrogant, "If not for you, we would have been believers."

32. Those who were arrogant will say to those who were oppressed, "Did we avert you from guidance after it had come to you? Rather, you were criminals."

33. Those who were oppressed will say to those who were arrogant, "Rather, [it was your] conspiracy of night and day when you were ordering us to disbelieve in Allah and attribute to Him equals." But they will [all] confide regret when they see the punishment; and We will put shackles on the necks of those who disbelieved. Will they be recompensed except for what they used to do?

34. And We did not send into a city any warner except that its affluent said, "Indeed we, in that with which you were sent, are disbelievers."

35. And they said, "We are more [than the believers] in wealth and children, and we are not to be punished."

36. Say, "Indeed, my Lord extends provision for whom He wills and restricts [it], but most of the people do not know."

37. And it is not your wealth or your children that bring you nearer to Us in position, but it is [by being] one who has believed and done righteousness. For them there will be the double reward for what they did, and they will be in the upper chambers [of Paradise], safe [and secure].

38. And the ones who strive against Our verses to cause [them] failure - those will be brought into the punishment [to remain].

39. Say, "Indeed, my Lord extends provision for whom He wills of His servants and restricts [it] for him. But whatever thing you spend [in His cause] - He will compensate it; and He is the best of providers."

40. And [mention] the Day when He will gather them all and then say to the angels, "Did these [people] used to worship you?"

41. They will say, "Exalted are You! You, [O Allah], are our benefactor not them. Rather, they used to worship the jinn; most of them were believers in them."

42. But today you do not hold for one another [the power of] benefit or harm, and We will say to those who wronged, "Taste the punishment of the Fire, which you used to deny."

43. And when our verses are recited to them as clear evidences, they say, "This is not but a man who wishes to avert you from that which your fathers were worshipping." And they say, "This is not except a lie invented." And those who disbelieve say of the truth when it has come to them, "This is not but obvious magic."

44. And We had not given them any scriptures which they could study, and We had not sent to them before you, [O Muhammad], any warner.

45. And those before them denied, and the people of Makkah have not attained a tenth of what We had given them. But the former peoples denied My messengers, so how [terrible] was My reproach.

46. Say, "I only advise you of one [thing] - that you stand for Allah, [seeking truth] in pairs and individually, and then give thought." There is not in your companion any madness. He is only a warner to you before a severe punishment.

47. Say, "Whatever payment I might have asked of you - it is yours. My payment is only from Allah, and He is, over all things, Witness."

48. Say, "Indeed, my Lord projects the truth. Knower of the unseen."

49. Say, "The truth has come, and falsehood can neither begin [anything] nor repeat [it]."

50. Say, "If I should err, I would only err against myself. But if I am guided, it is by what my Lord reveals to me. Indeed, He is Hearing and near."

51. And if you could see when they are terrified but there is no escape, and they will be seized from a place nearby.

52. And they will [then] say, "We believe in it!" But how for them will be the taking [of faith] from a place far away?

53. And they had already disbelieved in it before and would assault the unseen from a place far away.

54. And prevention will be placed between them and what they desire, as was done with their kind before. Indeed, they were in disquieting denial.

| Verses: 45 | **Surah 35 Faatir** | Makki |

In the name of Allah, the Entirely Merciful, the Especially Merciful.

01. [All] praise is [due] to Allah, Creator of the heavens and the earth, [who] made the angels messengers having wings, two or three or four. He increases in creation what He wills. Indeed, Allah is over all things competent.

02. Whatever Allah grants to people of mercy - none can withhold it; and whatever He withholds - none can release it thereafter. And He is the Exalted in Might, the Wise.

03. O mankind, remember the favor of Allah upon you. Is there any creator other than Allah who provides for you from the heaven and earth? There is no deity except Him, so how are you deluded?

04. And if they deny you, [O Muhammad] - already were messengers denied before you. And to Allah are returned [all] matters.

05. O mankind, indeed the promise of Allah is truth, so let not the worldly life delude you and be not deceived about Allah by the Deceiver.

06. Indeed, Satan is an enemy to you; so take him as an enemy. He only invites his party to be among the companions of the Blaze.

07. Those who disbelieve will have a severe punishment, and those who believe and do righteous deeds will have forgiveness and great reward.

08. Then is one to whom the evil of his deed has been made attractive so he considers it good [like one rightly guided]? For indeed, Allah sends astray whom He wills and guides whom He wills. So do not let yourself perish over them in regret. Indeed, Allah is Knowing of what they do.

09. And it is Allah who sends the winds, and they stir the clouds, and We drive them to a dead land and give life thereby to the earth after its lifelessness. Thus is the resurrection.

10. Whoever desires honor [through power] - then to Allah belongs all honor. To Him ascends good speech, and righteous work raises it. But they who plot evil deeds will have a severe punishment, and the plotting of those - it will perish.

11. And Allah created you from dust, then from a sperm-drop; then He made you mates. And no female conceives nor does she give birth except with His knowledge. And no aged person is granted [additional] life nor is his lifespan lessened but that it is in a register. Indeed, that for Allah is easy.

12. And not alike are the two bodies of water. One is fresh and sweet, palatable for drinking, and one is salty and bitter. And from each you eat tender meat and extract ornaments which you wear, and you see the ships plowing through [them] that you might seek of His bounty; and perhaps you will be grateful.
13. He causes the night to enter the day, and He causes the day to enter the night and has subjected the sun and the moon - each running [its course] for a specified term. That is Allah, your Lord; to Him belongs sovereignty. And those whom you invoke other than Him do not possess [as much as] the membrane of a date seed.
14. If you invoke them, they do not hear your supplication; and if they heard, they would not respond to you. And on the Day of Resurrection they will deny your association. And none can inform you like [one] Acquainted [with all matters].
15. O mankind, you are those in need of Allah, while Allah is the Free of need, the Praiseworthy.
16. If He wills, He can do away with you and bring forth a new creation.
17. And that is for Allah not difficult.
18. And no bearer of burdens will bear the burden of another. And if a heavily laden soul calls [another] to [carry some of] its load, nothing of it will be carried, even if he should be a close relative. You can only warn those who fear their Lord unseen and have established prayer. And whoever purifies himself only purifies himself for [the benefit of] his soul. And to Allah is the [final] destination.
19. Not equal are the blind and the seeing,
20. Nor are the darknesses and the light,
21. Nor are the shade and the heat,
22. And not equal are the living and the dead. Indeed, Allah causes to hear whom He wills, but you cannot make hear those in the graves.
23. You, [O Muhammad], are not but a warner.
24. Indeed, We have sent you with the truth as a bringer of good tidings and a warner. And there was no nation but that there had passed within it a warner.
25. And if they deny you - then already have those before them denied. Their messengers came to them with clear proofs and written ordinances and with the enlightening Scripture.
26. Then I seized the ones who disbelieved, and how [terrible] was My reproach.

27. Do you not see that Allah sends down rain from the sky, and We produce thereby fruits of varying colors? And in the mountains are tracts, white and red of varying shades and [some] extremely black.

28. And among people and moving creatures and grazing livestock are various colors similarly. Only those fear Allah, from among His servants, who have knowledge. Indeed, Allah is Exalted in Might and Forgiving.

29. Indeed, those who recite the Book of Allah and establish prayer and spend [in His cause] out of what We have provided them, secretly and publicly, [can] expect a profit that will never perish -

30. That He may give them in full their rewards and increase for them of His bounty. Indeed, He is Forgiving and Appreciative.

31. And that which We have revealed to you, [O Muhammad], of the Book is the truth, confirming what was before it. Indeed, Allah, of His servants, is Acquainted and Seeing.

32. Then we caused to inherit the Book those We have chosen of Our servants; and among them is he who wrongs himself, and among them is he who is moderate, and among them is he who is foremost in good deeds by permission of Allah. That [inheritance] is what is the great bounty.

33. [For them are] gardens of perpetual residence which they will enter. They will be adorned therein with bracelets of gold and pearls, and their garments therein will be silk.

34. And they will say, "Praise to Allah, who has removed from us [all] sorrow. Indeed, our Lord is Forgiving and Appreciative -

35. He who has settled us in the home of duration out of His bounty. There touches us not in it any fatigue, and there touches us not in it weariness [of mind]."

36. And for those who disbelieve will be the fire of Hell. [Death] is not decreed for them so they may die, nor will its torment be lightened for them. Thus do we recompense every ungrateful one.

37. And they will cry out therein, "Our Lord, remove us; we will do righteousness - other than what we were doing!" But did We not grant you life enough for whoever would remember therein to remember, and the warner had come to you? So taste [the punishment], for there is not for the wrongdoers any helper.

38. Indeed, Allah is Knower of the unseen [aspects] of the heavens and earth. Indeed, He is Knowing of that within the breasts.

39. It is He who has made you successors upon the earth. And whoever disbelieves - upon him will be [the consequence of] his disbelief. And the disbelief of the disbelievers does not increase them in the sight of their Lord except in hatred; and the disbelief of the disbelievers does not increase them except in loss.

40. Say, "Have you considered your 'partners' whom you invoke besides Allah? Show me what they have created from the earth, or have they partnership [with Him] in the heavens? Or have We given them a book so they are [standing] on evidence therefrom? [No], rather, the wrongdoers do not promise each other except delusion."

41. Indeed, Allah holds the heavens and the earth, lest they cease. And if they should cease, no one could hold them [in place] after Him. Indeed, He is Forbearing and Forgiving.

42. And they swore by Allah their strongest oaths that if a warner came to them, they would be more guided than [any] one of the [previous] nations. But when a warner came to them, it did not increase them except in aversion.

43. [Due to] arrogance in the land and plotting of evil; but the evil plot does not encompass except its own people. Then do they await except the way of the former peoples? But you will never find in the way of Allah any change, and you will never find in the way of Allah any alteration.

44. Have they not traveled through the land and observed how was the end of those before them? And they were greater than them in power. But Allah is not to be caused failure by anything in the heavens or on the earth. Indeed, He is ever Knowing and Competent.

45. And if Allah were to impose blame on the people for what they have earned, He would not leave upon the earth any creature. But He defers them for a specified term. And when their time comes, then indeed Allah has ever been, of His servants, Seeing.

| Verses: 83 | **Surah 36 Yaa-Seen** | Makki |

In the name of Allah, the Entirely Merciful, the Especially Merciful.

01. Ya, Seen.
02. By the wise Qur'an.
03. Indeed you, [O Muhammad], are from among the messengers,

04. On a straight path.

05. [This is] a revelation of the Exalted in Might, the Merciful,

06. That you may warn a people whose forefathers were not warned, so they are unaware.

07. Already the word has come into effect upon most of them, so they do not believe.

08. Indeed, We have put shackles on their necks, and they are to their chins, so they are with heads [kept] aloft.

09. And We have put before them a barrier and behind them a barrier and covered them, so they do not see.

10. And it is all the same for them whether you warn them or do not warn them - they will not believe.

11. You can only warn one who follows the message and fears the Most Merciful unseen. So give him good tidings of forgiveness and noble reward.

12. Indeed, it is We who bring the dead to life and record what they have put forth and what they left behind, and all things We have enumerated in a clear register.

13. And present to them an example: the people of the city, when the messengers came to it -

14. When We sent to them two but they denied them, so We strengthened them with a third, and they said, "Indeed, we are messengers to you."

15. They said, "You are not but human beings like us, and the Most Merciful has not revealed a thing. You are only telling lies."

16. They said, "Our Lord knows that we are messengers to you,

17. And we are not responsible except for clear notification."

18. They said, "Indeed, we consider you a bad omen. If you do not desist, we will surely stone you, and there will surely touch you, from us, a painful punishment."

19. They said, "Your omen is with yourselves. Is it because you were reminded? Rather, you are a transgressing people."

20. And there came from the farthest end of the city a man, running. He said, "O my people, follow the messengers.

21. Follow those who do not ask of you [any] payment, and they are [rightly] guided.

22. And why should I not worship He who created me and to whom you will be returned?
23. Should I take other than Him [false] deities [while], if the Most Merciful intends for me some adversity, their intercession will not avail me at all, nor can they save me?
24. Indeed, I would then be in manifest error.
25. Indeed, I have believed in your Lord, so listen to me."
26. It was said, "Enter Paradise." He said, "I wish my people could know
27. Of how my Lord has forgiven me and placed me among the honored."
28. And We did not send down upon his people after him any soldiers from the heaven, nor would We have done so.
29. It was not but one shout, and immediately they were extinguished.
30. How regretful for the servants. There did not come to them any messenger except that they used to ridicule him.
31. Have they not considered how many generations We destroyed before them - that they to them will not return?
32. And indeed, all of them will yet be brought present before Us.
33. And a sign for them is the dead earth. We have brought it to life and brought forth from it grain, and from it they eat.
34. And We placed therein gardens of palm trees and grapevines and caused to burst forth therefrom some springs -
35. That they may eat of His fruit. And their hands have not produced it, so will they not be grateful?
36. Exalted is He who created all pairs - from what the earth grows and from themselves and from that which they do not know.
37. And a sign for them is the night. We remove from it [the light of] day, so they are [left] in darkness.
38. And the sun runs [on course] toward its stopping point. That is the determination of the Exalted in Might, the Knowing.
39. And the moon - We have determined for it phases, until it returns [appearing] like the old date stalk.
40. It is not allowable for the sun to reach the moon, nor does the night overtake the day, but each, in an orbit, is swimming.
41. And a sign for them is that We carried their forefathers in a laden ship.

42. And We created for them from the likes of it that which they ride.
43. And if We should will, We could drown them; then no one responding to a cry would there be for them, nor would they be saved
44. Except as a mercy from Us and provision for a time.
45. But when it is said to them, "Beware of what is before you and what is behind you; perhaps you will receive mercy... "
46. And no sign comes to them from the signs of their Lord except that they are from it turning away.
47. And when it is said to them, "Spend from that which Allah has provided for you," those who disbelieve say to those who believe, "Should we feed one whom, if Allah had willed, He would have fed? You are not but in clear error."
48. And they say, "When is this promise, if you should be truthful?"
49. They do not await except one blast which will seize them while they are disputing.
50. And they will not be able [to give] any instruction, nor to their people can they return.
51. And the Horn will be blown; and at once from the graves to their Lord they will hasten.
52. They will say, "O woe to us! Who has raised us up from our sleeping place?" [The reply will be], "This is what the Most Merciful had promised, and the messengers told the truth."
53. It will not be but one blast, and at once they are all brought present before Us.
54. So today no soul will be wronged at all, and you will not be recompensed except for what you used to do.
55. Indeed the companions of Paradise, that Day, will be amused in [joyful] occupation -
56. They and their spouses - in shade, reclining on adorned couches.
57. For them therein is fruit, and for them is whatever they request [or wish]
58. [And] "Peace," a word from a Merciful Lord.
59. [Then He will say], "But stand apart today, you criminals.
60. Did I not enjoin upon you, O children of Adam, that you not worship Satan - [for] indeed, he is to you a clear enemy -
61. And that you worship [only] Me? This is a straight path.

62. And he had already led astray from among you much of creation, so did you not use reason?
63. This is the Hellfire which you were promised.
64. [Enter to] burn therein today for what you used to deny."
65. That Day, We will seal over their mouths, and their hands will speak to Us, and their feet will testify about what they used to earn.
66. And if We willed, We could have obliterated their eyes, and they would race to [find] the path, and how could they see?
67. And if We willed, We could have deformed them, [paralyzing them] in their places so they would not be able to proceed, nor could they return.
68. And he to whom We grant long life We reverse in creation; so will they not understand?
69. And We did not give Prophet Muhammad, knowledge of poetry, nor is it befitting for him. It is not but a message and a clear Qur'an
70. To warn whoever is alive and justify the word against the disbelievers.
71. Do they not see that We have created for them from what Our hands have made, grazing livestock, and [then] they are their owners?
72. And We have tamed them for them, so some of them they ride, and some of them they eat.
73. And for them therein are [other] benefits and drinks, so will they not be grateful?
74. But they have taken besides Allah [false] deities that perhaps they would be helped.
75. They are not able to help them, and they [themselves] are for them soldiers in attendance.
76. So let not their speech grieve you. Indeed, We know what they conceal and what they declare.
77. Does man not consider that We created him from a [mere] sperm-drop - then at once he is a clear adversary?
78. And he presents for Us an example and forgets his [own] creation. He says, "Who will give life to bones while they are disintegrated?"
79. Say, "He will give them life who produced them the first time; and He is, of all creation, Knowing."
80. [It is] He who made for you from the green tree, fire, and then from it you ignite.

81. Is not He who created the heavens and the earth Able to create the likes of them? Yes, [it is so]; and He is the Knowing Creator.
82. His command is only when He intends a thing that He says to it, "Be," and it is.
83. So exalted is He in whose hand is the realm of all things, and to Him you will be returned.

| Verses: 182 | Surah 37 As-Saaffaat | Makki |

In the name of Allah, the Entirely Merciful, the Especially Merciful.

01. By those [angels] lined up in rows
02. And those who drive [the clouds]
03. And those who recite the message,
04. Indeed, your God is One,
05. Lord of the heavens and the earth and that between them and Lord of the sunrises.
06. Indeed, We have adorned the nearest heaven with an adornment of stars
07. And as protection against every rebellious devil
08. [So] they may not listen to the exalted assembly [of angels] and are pelted from every side,
09. Repelled; and for them is a constant punishment,
10. Except one who snatches [some words] by theft, but they are pursued by a burning flame, piercing [in brightness].
11. Then inquire of them, [O Muhammad], "Are they a stronger [or more difficult] creation or those [others] We have created?" Indeed, We created men from sticky clay.
12. But you wonder, while they mock,
13. And when they are reminded, they remember not.
14. And when they see a sign, they ridicule
15. And say, "This is not but obvious magic.
16. When we have died and become dust and bones, are we indeed to be resurrected?
17. And our forefathers [as well]?"
18. Say, "Yes, and you will be [rendered] contemptible."
19. It will be only one shout, and at once they will be observing.

20. They will say, "O woe to us! This is the Day of Recompense."
21. [They will be told], "This is the Day of Judgement which you used to deny."
22. [The angels will be ordered], "Gather those who committed wrong, their kinds, and what they used to worship
23. Other than Allah, and guide them to the path of Hellfire
24. And stop them; indeed, they are to be questioned."
25. [They will be asked], "What is [wrong] with you? Why do you not help each other?"
26. But they, that Day, are in surrender.
27. And they will approach one another blaming each other.
28. They will say, "Indeed, you used to come at us from the right."
29. The oppressors will say, "Rather, you [yourselves] were not believers,
30. And we had over you no authority, but you were a transgressing people.
31. So the word of our Lord has come into effect upon us; indeed, we will taste [punishment].
32. And we led you to deviation; indeed, we were deviators."
33. So indeed they, that Day, will be sharing in the punishment.
34. Indeed, that is how We deal with the criminals.
35. Indeed they, when it was said to them, "There is no deity but Allah," were arrogant
36. And were saying, "Are we to leave our gods for a mad poet?"
37. Rather, the Prophet has come with the truth and confirmed the [previous] messengers.
38. Indeed, you [disbelievers] will be tasters of the painful punishment,
39. And you will not be recompensed except for what you used to do -
40. But not the chosen servants of Allah.
41. Those will have a provision determined -
42. Fruits; and they will be honored
43. In gardens of pleasure
44. On thrones facing one another.
45. There will be circulated among them a cup [of wine] from a flowing spring,

46. White and delicious to the drinkers;
47. No bad effect is there in it, nor from it will they be intoxicated.
48. And with them will be women limiting [their] glances, with large, [beautiful] eyes,
49. As if they were [delicate] eggs, well-protected.
50. And they will approach one another, inquiring of each other.
51. A speaker among them will say, "Indeed, I had a companion [on earth]
52. Who would say, 'Are you indeed of those who believe
53. That when we have died and become dust and bones, we will indeed be recompensed?'"
54. He will say, "Would you [care to] look?"
55. And he will look and see him in the midst of the Hellfire.
56. He will say, "By Allah, you almost ruined me.
57. If not for the favor of my Lord, I would have been of those brought in [to Hell].
58. Then, are we not to die
59. Except for our first death, and we will not be punished?"
60. Indeed, this is the great attainment.
61. For the like of this let the workers [on earth] work.
62. Is Paradise a better accommodation or the tree of zaqqum?
63. Indeed, We have made it a torment for the wrongdoers.
64. Indeed, it is a tree issuing from the bottom of the Hellfire,
65. Its emerging fruit as if it was heads of the devils.
66. And indeed, they will eat from it and fill with it their bellies.
67. Then indeed, they will have after it a mixture of scalding water.
68. Then indeed, their return will be to the Hellfire.
69. Indeed they found their fathers astray.
70. So they hastened [to follow] in their footsteps.
71. And there had already strayed before them most of the former peoples,
72. And We had already sent among them warners.
73. Then look how was the end of those who were warned -

74. But not the chosen servants of Allah.
75. And Noah had certainly called Us, and [We are] the best of responders.
76. And We saved him and his family from the great affliction.
77. And We made his descendants those remaining [on the earth]
78. And left for him [favorable mention] among later generations:
79. "Peace upon Noah among the worlds."
80. Indeed, We thus reward the doers of good.
81. Indeed, he was of Our believing servants.
82. Then We drowned the disbelievers.
83. And indeed, among his kind was Abraham,
84. When he came to his Lord with a sound heart
85. [And] when he said to his father and his people, "What do you worship?
86. Is it falsehood [as] gods other than Allah you desire?
87. Then what is your thought about the Lord of the worlds?"
88. And he cast a look at the stars
89. And said, "Indeed, I am [about to be] ill."
90. So they turned away from him, departing.
91. Then he turned to their gods and said, "Do you not eat?
92. What is [wrong] with you that you do not speak?"
93. And he turned upon them a blow with [his] right hand.
94. Then the people came toward him, hastening.
95. He said, "Do you worship that which you [yourselves] carve,
96. While Allah created you and that which you do?"
97. They said, "Construct for him a furnace and throw him into the burning fire."
98. And they intended for him a plan, but We made them the most debased.
99. And [then] he said, "Indeed, I will go to [where I am ordered by] my Lord; He will guide me.
100. My Lord, grant me [a child] from among the righteous."
101. So We gave him good tidings of a forbearing boy.

102. And when he reached with him [the age of] exertion, he said, "O my son, indeed I have seen in a dream that I [must] sacrifice you, so see what you think." He said, "O my father, do as you are commanded. You will find me, if Allah wills, of the steadfast."

103. And when they had both submitted and he put him down upon his forehead,

104. We called to him, "O Abraham,

105. You have fulfilled the vision." Indeed, We thus reward the doers of good.

106. Indeed, this was the clear trial.

107. And We ransomed him with a great sacrifice,

108. And We left for him [favorable mention] among later generations:

109. "Peace upon Abraham."

110. Indeed, We thus reward the doers of good.

111. Indeed, he was of Our believing servants.

112. And We gave him good tidings of Isaac, a prophet from among the righteous.

113. And We blessed him and Isaac. But among their descendants is the doer of good and the clearly unjust to himself.

114. And We did certainly confer favor upon Moses and Aaron.

115. And We saved them and their people from the great affliction,

116. And We supported them so it was they who overcame.

117. And We gave them the explicit Scripture,

118. And We guided them on the straight path.

119. And We left for them [favorable mention] among later generations:

120. "Peace upon Moses and Aaron."

121. Indeed, We thus reward the doers of good.

122. Indeed, they were of Our believing servants.

123. And indeed, Elias was from among the messengers,

124. When he said to his people, "Will you not fear Allah?

125. Do you call upon Ba'l and leave the best of creators -

126. Allah, your Lord and the Lord of your first forefathers?"

127. And they denied him, so indeed, they will be brought [for punishment],

128. Except the chosen servants of Allah.
129. And We left for him [favorable mention] among later generations:
130. "Peace upon Elias."
131. Indeed, We thus reward the doers of good.
132. Indeed, he was of Our believing servants.
133. And indeed, Lot was among the messengers.
134. [So mention] when We saved him and his family, all,
135. Except his wife among those who remained [with the evildoers].
136. Then We destroyed the others.
137. And indeed, you pass by them in the morning
138. And at night. Then will you not use reason?
139. And indeed, Jonah was among the messengers.
140. [Mention] when he ran away to the laden ship.
141. And he drew lots and was among the losers.
142. Then the fish swallowed him, while he was blameworthy.
143. And had he not been of those who exalt Allah,
144. He would have remained inside its belly until the Day they are resurrected.
145. But We threw him onto the open shore while he was ill.
146. And We caused to grow over him a gourd vine.
147. And We sent him to [his people of] a hundred thousand or more.
148. And they believed, so We gave them enjoyment [of life] for a time.
149. So inquire of them, [O Muhammad], "Does your Lord have daughters while they have sons?
150. Or did We create the angels as females while they were witnesses?"
151. Unquestionably, it is out of their [invented] falsehood that they say,
152. " Allah has begotten," and indeed, they are liars.
153. Has He chosen daughters over sons?
154. What is [wrong] with you? How do you make judgement?
155. Then will you not be reminded?
156. Or do you have a clear authority?
157. Then produce your scripture, if you should be truthful.

158. And they have claimed between Him and the jinn a lineage, but the jinn have already known that they [who made such claims] will be brought to [punishment].

159. Exalted is Allah above what they describe,

160. Except the chosen servants of Allah [who do not share in that sin].

161. So indeed, you [disbelievers] and whatever you worship,

162. You cannot tempt [anyone] away from Him

163. Except he who is to [enter and] burn in the Hellfire.

164. [The angels say], "There is not among us any except that he has a known position.

165. And indeed, we are those who line up [for prayer].

166. And indeed, we are those who exalt Allah."

167. And indeed, the disbelievers used to say,

168. "If we had a message from [those of] the former peoples,

169. We would have been the chosen servants of Allah."

170. But they disbelieved in it, so they are going to know.

171. And Our word has already preceded for Our servants, the messengers,

172. [That] indeed, they would be those given victory

173. And [that] indeed, Our soldiers will be those who overcome.

174. So, [O Muhammad], leave them for a time.

175. And see [what will befall] them, for they are going to see.

176. Then for Our punishment are they impatient?

177. But when it descends in their territory, then evil is the morning of those who were warned.

178. And leave them for a time.

179. And see, for they are going to see.

180. Exalted is your Lord, the Lord of might, above what they describe.

181. And peace upon the messengers.

182. And praise to Allah, Lord of the worlds.

| Verses: 88 | **Surah 38 Saad** | Makki |

In the name of Allah, the Entirely Merciful, the Especially Merciful.

01. Sad. By the Qur'an containing reminder...
02. But those who disbelieve are in pride and dissension.
03. How many a generation have We destroyed before them, and they [then] called out; but it was not a time for escape.
04. And they wonder that there has come to them a warner from among themselves. And the disbelievers say, "This is a magician and a liar.
05. Has he made the gods [only] one God? Indeed, this is a curious thing."
06. And the eminent among them went forth, [saying], "Continue, and be patient over [the defense of] your gods. Indeed, this is a thing intended.
07. We have not heard of this in the latest religion. This is not but a fabrication.
08. Has the message been revealed to him out of [all of] us?" Rather, they are in doubt about My message. Rather, they have not yet tasted My punishment.
09. Or do they have the depositories of the mercy of your Lord, the Exalted in Might, the Bestower?
10. Or is theirs the dominion of the heavens and the earth and what is between them? Then let them ascend through [any] ways of access.
11. [They are but] soldiers [who will be] defeated there among the companies [of disbelievers].
12. The people of Noah denied before them, and [the tribe of] 'Aad and Pharaoh, the owner of stakes,
13. And [the tribe of] Thamud and the people of Lot and the companions of the thicket. Those are the companies.
14. Each of them denied the messengers, so My penalty was justified.
15. And these [disbelievers] await not but one blast [of the Horn]; for it there will be no delay.
16. And they say, "Our Lord, hasten for us our share [of the punishment] before the Day of Account"
17. Be patient over what they say and remember Our servant,

David, the possessor of strength; indeed, he was one who repeatedly turned back [to Allah].

18. Indeed, We subjected the mountains [to praise] with him, exalting [Allah] in the [late] afternoon and [after] sunrise.

19. And the birds were assembled, all with him repeating [praises].

20. And We strengthened his kingdom and gave him wisdom and discernment in speech.

21. And has there come to you the news of the adversaries, when they climbed over the wall of [his] prayer chamber -

22. When they entered upon David and he was alarmed by them? They said, "Fear not. [We are] two adversaries, one of whom has wronged the other, so judge between us with truth and do not exceed [it] and guide us to the sound path.

23. Indeed this, my brother, has ninety-nine ewes, and I have one ewe; so he said, 'Entrust her to me,' and he overpowered me in speech."

24. [David] said, "He has certainly wronged you in demanding your ewe [in addition] to his ewes. And indeed, many associates oppress one another, except for those who believe and do righteous deeds - and few are they." And David became certain that We had tried him, and he asked forgiveness of his Lord and fell down bowing [in prostration] and turned in repentance [to Allah].

25. So We forgave him that; and indeed, for him is nearness to Us and a good place of return.

26. [We said], "O David, indeed We have made you a successor upon the earth, so judge between the people in truth and do not follow [your own] desire, as it will lead you astray from the way of Allah." Indeed, those who go astray from the way of Allah will have a severe punishment for having forgotten the Day of Account.

27. And We did not create the heaven and the earth and that between them aimlessly. That is the assumption of those who disbelieve, so woe to those who disbelieve from the Fire.

28. Or should we treat those who believe and do righteous deeds like corrupters in the land? Or should We treat those who fear Allah like the wicked?

29. [This is] a blessed Book which We have revealed to you, [O Muhammad], that they might reflect upon its verses and that those of understanding would be reminded.

30. And to David We gave Solomon. An excellent servant, indeed he was one repeatedly turning back [to Allah].

31. [Mention] when there were exhibited before him in the afternoon the poised [standing] racehorses.

32. And he said, "Indeed, I gave preference to the love of good [things] over the remembrance of my Lord until the sun disappeared into the curtain [of darkness]."

33. [He said], "Return them to me," and set about striking [their] legs and necks.

34. And We certainly tried Solomon and placed on his throne a body; then he returned.

35. He said, "My Lord, forgive me and grant me a kingdom such as will not belong to anyone after me. Indeed, You are the Bestower."

36. So We subjected to him the wind blowing by his command, gently, wherever he directed,

37. And [also] the devils [of jinn] - every builder and diver

38. And others bound together in shackles.

39. [We said], "This is Our gift, so grant or withhold without account."

40. And indeed, for him is nearness to Us and a good place of return.

41. And remember Our servant Job, when he called to his Lord, "Indeed, Satan has touched me with hardship and torment."

42. [So he was told], "Strike [the ground] with your foot; this is a [spring for] a cool bath and drink."

43. And We granted him his family and a like [number] with them as mercy from Us and a reminder for those of understanding.

44. [We said], "And take in your hand a bunch [of grass] and strike with it and do not break your oath." Indeed, We found him patient, an excellent servant. Indeed, he was one repeatedly turning back [to Allah].

45. And remember Our servants, Abraham, Isaac and Jacob - those of strength and [religious] vision.

46. Indeed, We chose them for an exclusive quality: remembrance of the home [of the Hereafter].

47. And indeed they are, to Us, among the chosen and outstanding.

48. And remember Ishmael, Elisha and Dhul-Kifl, and all are among the outstanding.

49. This is a reminder. And indeed, for the righteous is a good place of return
50. Gardens of perpetual residence, whose doors will be opened to them.
51. Reclining within them, they will call therein for abundant fruit and drink.
52. And with them will be women limiting [their] glances and of equal age.
53. This is what you, [the righteous], are promised for the Day of Account.
54. Indeed, this is Our provision; for it there is no depletion.
55. This [is so]. But indeed, for the transgressors is an evil place of return -
56. Hell, which they will [enter to] burn, and wretched is the resting place.
57. This - so let them taste it - is scalding water and [foul] purulence.
58. And other [punishments] of its type [in various] kinds.
59. [Its inhabitants will say], "This is a company bursting in with you. No welcome for them. Indeed, they will burn in the Fire."
60. They will say, "Nor you! No welcome for you. You, [our leaders], brought this upon us, and wretched is the settlement."
61. They will say, "Our Lord, whoever brought this upon us - increase for him double punishment in the Fire."
62. And they will say, "Why do we not see men whom we used to count among the worst?
63. Is it [because] we took them in ridicule, or has [our] vision turned away from them?"
64. Indeed, that is truth - the quarreling of the people of the Fire.
65. Say, [O Muhammad], "I am only a warner, and there is not any deity except Allah, the One, the Prevailing.
66. Lord of the heavens and the earth and whatever is between them, the Exalted in Might, the Perpetual Forgiver."
67. Say, "It is great news
68. From which you turn away.
69. I had no knowledge of the exalted assembly [of angels] when they were disputing [the creation of Adam].
70. It has not been revealed to me except that I am a clear warner."
71. [So mention] when your Lord said to the angels, "Indeed, I am going to create a human being from clay.
72. So when I have proportioned him and breathed into him of My [created] soul, then fall down to him in prostration."

73. So the angels prostrated - all of them entirely.
74. Except Iblees; he was arrogant and became among the disbelievers.
75. [Allah] said, "O Iblees, what prevented you from prostrating to that which I created with My hands? Were you arrogant [then], or were you [already] among the haughty?"
76. He said, "I am better than him. You created me from fire and created him from clay."
77. [Allah] said, "Then get out of Paradise, for indeed, you are expelled.
78. And indeed, upon you is My curse until the Day of Recompense."
79. He said, "My Lord, then reprieve me until the Day they are resurrected."
80. [Allah] said, "So indeed, you are of those reprieved
81. Until the Day of the time well-known."
82. [Iblees] said, "By your might, I will surely mislead them all
83. Except, among them, Your chosen servants."
84. [Allah] said, "The truth [is My oath], and the truth I say -
85. [That] I will surely fill Hell with you and those of them that follow you all together."
86. Say, [O Muhammad], "I do not ask you for the Qur'an any payment, and I am not of the pretentious
87. It is but a reminder to the worlds.
88. And you will surely know [the truth of] its information after a time."

Surah 39 Az-Zumar

Verses: 75 — Makki

In the name of Allah, the Entirely Merciful, the Especially Merciful.

01. The revelation of the Qur'an is from Allah, the Exalted in Might, the Wise.
02. Indeed, We have sent down to you the Book, [O Muhammad], in truth. So worship Allah, [being] sincere to Him in religion.
03. Unquestionably, for Allah is the pure religion. And those who take protectors besides Him [say], "We only worship them that they may bring us nearer to Allah in position." Indeed, Allah will judge between them concerning that over which they differ. Indeed, Allah does not guide he who is a liar and [confirmed] disbeliever.
04. If Allah had intended to take a son, He could have chosen from what He creates whatever He willed. Exalted is He; He is Allah, the One, the Prevailing.

05. He created the heavens and earth in truth. He wraps the night over the day and wraps the day over the night and has subjected the sun and the moon, each running [its course] for a specified term. Unquestionably, He is the Exalted in Might, the Perpetual Forgiver.

06. He created you from one soul. Then He made from it its mate, and He produced for you from the grazing livestock eight mates. He creates you in the wombs of your mothers, creation after creation, within three darknesses. That is Allah, your Lord; to Him belongs dominion. There is no deity except Him, so how are you averted?

07. If you disbelieve - indeed, Allah is Free from need of you. And He does not approve for His servants disbelief. And if you are grateful, He approves it for you; and no bearer of burdens will bear the burden of another. Then to your Lord is your return, and He will inform you about what you used to do. Indeed, He is Knowing of that within the breasts.

08. And when adversity touches man, he calls upon his Lord, turning to Him [alone]; then when He bestows on him a favor from Himself, he forgets Him whom he called upon before, and he attributes to Allah equals to mislead [people] from His way. Say, "Enjoy your disbelief for a little; indeed, you are of the companions of the Fire."

09. Is one who is devoutly obedient during periods of the night, prostrating and standing [in prayer], fearing the Hereafter and hoping for the mercy of his Lord, [like one who does not]? Say, "Are those who know equal to those who do not know?" Only they will remember [who are] people of understanding.

10. Say, "O My servants who have believed, fear your Lord. For those who do good in this world is good, and the earth of Allah is spacious. Indeed, the patient will be given their reward without account."

11. Say, [O Muhammad], "Indeed, I have been commanded to worship Allah, [being] sincere to Him in religion.

12. And I have been commanded to be the first [among you] of the Muslims."

13. Say, "Indeed I fear, if I should disobey my Lord, the punishment of a tremendous Day."

14. Say, "Allah [alone] do I worship, sincere to Him in my religion,

15. So worship what you will besides Him." Say, "Indeed, the losers are the ones who will lose themselves and their families on the Day of Resurrection. Unquestionably, that is the manifest loss."

16. They will have canopies of fire above them and below them, canopies. By that Allah threatens His servants. O My servants, then fear Me.

17. But those who have avoided Taghut, lest they worship it, and turned back to Allah - for them are good tidings. So give good tidings to My servants

18. Who listen to speech and follow the best of it. Those are the ones Allah has guided, and those are people of understanding.

19. Then, is one who has deserved the decree of punishment [to be guided]? Then, can you save one who is in the Fire?

20. But those who have feared their Lord - for them are chambers, above them chambers built high, beneath which rivers flow. [This is] the promise of Allah. Allah does not fail in [His] promise.

21. Do you not see that Allah sends down rain from the sky and makes it flow as springs [and rivers] in the earth; then He produces thereby crops of varying colors; then they dry and you see them turned yellow; then He makes them [scattered] debris. Indeed in that is a reminder for those of understanding.

22. So is one whose breast Allah has expanded to [accept] Islam and he is upon a light from his Lord [like one whose heart rejects it]? Then woe to those whose hearts are hardened against the remembrance of Allah. Those are in manifest error.

23. Allah has sent down the best statement: a consistent Book wherein is reiteration. The skins shiver therefrom of those who fear their Lord; then their skins and their hearts relax at the remembrance of Allah. That is the guidance of Allah by which He guides whom He wills. And one whom Allah leaves astray - for him there is no guide.

24. Then is he who will shield with his face the worst of the punishment on the Day of Resurrection [like one secure from it]? And it will be said to the wrongdoers, "Taste what you used to earn."

25. Those before them denied, and punishment came upon them from where they did not perceive.

26. So Allah made them taste disgrace in worldly life. But the punishment of the Hereafter is greater, if they only knew.

27. And We have certainly presented for the people in this Qur'an from every [kind of] example - that they might remember.

28. [It is] an Arabic Qur'an, without any deviance that they might become righteous.

29. Allah presents an example: a slave owned by quarreling partners and another belonging exclusively to one man - are they equal in comparison? Praise be to Allah! But most of them do not know.

30. Indeed, you are to die, and indeed, they are to die.

31. Then indeed you, on the Day of Resurrection, before your Lord, will dispute.

32. So who is more unjust than one who lies about Allah and denies the truth when it has come to him? Is there not in Hell a residence for the disbelievers?

33. And the one who has brought the truth and [they who] believed in it - those are the righteous.

34. They will have whatever they desire with their Lord. That is the reward of the doers of good -

35. That Allah may remove from them the worst of what they did and reward them their due for the best of what they used to do.

36. Is not Allah sufficient for His Servant [Prophet Muhammad]? And [yet], they threaten you with those [they worship] other than Him. And whoever Allah leaves astray - for him there is no guide.

37. And whoever Allah guides - for him there is no misleader. Is not Allah Exalted in Might and Owner of Retribution?

38. And if you asked them, "Who created the heavens and the earth?" they would surely say, "Allah." Say, "Then have you considered what you invoke besides Allah? If Allah intended me harm, are they removers of His harm; or if He intended me mercy, are they withholders of His mercy?" Say, "Sufficient for me is Allah; upon Him [alone] rely the [wise] reliers."

39. Say, "O my people, work according to your position, [for] indeed, I am working; and you are going to know

40. To whom will come a torment disgracing him and on whom will descend an enduring punishment."

41. Indeed, We sent down to you the Book for the people in truth. So whoever is guided - it is for [the benefit of] his soul; and

whoever goes astray only goes astray to its detriment. And you are not a manager over them.

42. Allah takes the souls at the time of their death, and those that do not die [He takes] during their sleep. Then He keeps those for which He has decreed death and releases the others for a specified term. Indeed in that are signs for a people who give thought.

43. Or have they taken other than Allah as intercessors? Say, "Even though they do not possess [power over] anything, nor do they reason?"

44. Say, "To Allah belongs [the right to allow] intercession entirely. To Him belongs the dominion of the heavens and the earth. Then to Him you will be returned."

45. And when Allah is mentioned alone, the hearts of those who do not believe in the Hereafter shrink with aversion, but when those [worshipped] other than Him are mentioned, immediately they rejoice.

46. Say, "O Allah, Creator of the heavens and the earth, Knower of the unseen and the witnessed, You will judge between your servants concerning that over which they used to differ."

47. And if those who did wrong had all that is in the earth entirely and the like of it with it, they would [attempt to] ransom themselves thereby from the worst of the punishment on the Day of Resurrection. And there will appear to them from Allah that which they had not taken into account.

48. And there will appear to them the evils they had earned, and they will be enveloped by what they used to ridicule.

49. And when adversity touches man, he calls upon Us; then when We bestow on him a favor from Us, he says, "I have only been given it because of [my] knowledge." Rather, it is a trial, but most of them do not know.

50. Those before them had already said it, but they were not availed by what they used to earn.

51. And the evil consequences of what they earned struck them. And those who have wronged of these [people] will be afflicted by the evil consequences of what they earned; and they will not cause failure.

52. Do they not know that Allah extends provision for whom He wills and restricts [it]? Indeed in that are signs for a people who believe.

53. Say, "O My servants who have transgressed against themselves [by sinning], do not despair of the mercy of Allah. Indeed, Allah forgives all sins. Indeed, it is He who is the Forgiving, the Merciful."

54. And return [in repentance] to your Lord and submit to Him before the punishment comes upon you; then you will not be helped.

55. And follow the best of what was revealed to you from your Lord before the punishment comes upon you suddenly while you do not perceive,

56. Lest a soul should say, "Oh [how great is] my regret over what I neglected in regard to Allah and that I was among the mockers."

57. Or [lest] it say, "If only Allah had guided me, I would have been among the righteous."

58. Or [lest] it say when it sees the punishment, "If only I had another turn so I could be among the doers of good."

59. But yes, there had come to you My verses, but you denied them and were arrogant, and you were among the disbelievers.

60. And on the Day of Resurrection you will see those who lied about Allah [with] their faces blackened. Is there not in Hell a residence for the arrogant?

61. And Allah will save those who feared Him by their attainment; no evil will touch them, nor will they grieve.

62. Allah is the Creator of all things, and He is, over all things, Disposer of affairs.

63. To Him belong the keys of the heavens and the earth. And they who disbelieve in the verses of Allah - it is those who are the losers.

64. Say, [O Muhammad], "Is it other than Allah that you order me to worship, O ignorant ones?"

65. And it was already revealed to you and to those before you that if you should associate [anything] with Allah, your work would surely become worthless, and you would surely be among the losers."

66. Rather, worship [only] Allah and be among the grateful.

67. They have not appraised Allah with true appraisal, while the earth entirely will be [within] His grip on the Day of Resurrection, and the heavens will be folded in His right hand. Exalted is He and high above what they associate with Him.

68. And the Horn will be blown, and whoever is in the heavens and whoever is on the earth will fall dead except whom Allah

wills. Then it will be blown again, and at once they will be standing, looking on.

69. And the earth will shine with the light of its Lord, and the record [of deeds] will be placed, and the prophets and the witnesses will be brought, and it will be judged between them in truth, and they will not be wronged.

70. And every soul will be fully compensated [for] what it did; and He is most knowing of what they do.

71. And those who disbelieved will be driven to Hell in groups until, when they reach it, its gates are opened and its keepers will say, "Did there not come to you messengers from yourselves, reciting to you the verses of your Lord and warning you of the meeting of this Day of yours?" They will say, "Yes, but the word of punishment has come into effect upon the disbelievers."

72. [To them] it will be said, "Enter the gates of Hell to abide eternally therein, and wretched is the residence of the arrogant."

73. But those who feared their Lord will be driven to Paradise in groups until, when they reach it while its gates have been opened and its keepers say, "Peace be upon you; you have become pure; so enter it to abide eternally therein," [they will enter].

74. And they will say, "Praise to Allah, who has fulfilled for us His promise and made us inherit the earth [so] we may settle in Paradise wherever we will. And excellent is the reward of [righteous] workers."

75. And you will see the angels surrounding the Throne, exalting [Allah] with praise of their Lord. And it will be judged between them in truth, and it will be said, "[All] praise to Allah, Lord of the worlds."

Surah 40 Gaafir

Verses: 85 — Makki

In the name of Allah, the Entirely Merciful, the Especially Merciful.

01. Ha, Meem.

02. The revelation of the Book is from Allah, the Exalted in Might, the Knowing.

03. The forgiver of sin, acceptor of repentance, severe in punishment, owner of abundance. There is no deity except Him; to Him is the destination.

04. No one disputes concerning the signs of Allah except those who disbelieve, so be not deceived by their [uninhibited]

movement throughout the land.

05. The people of Noah denied before them and the [disbelieving] factions after them, and every nation intended [a plot] for their messenger to seize him, and they disputed by [using] falsehood to [attempt to] invalidate thereby the truth. So I seized them, and how [terrible] was My penalty.

06. And thus has the word of your Lord come into effect upon those who disbelieved that they are companions of the Fire.

07. Those [angels] who carry the Throne and those around it exalt [Allah] with praise of their Lord and believe in Him and ask forgiveness for those who have believed, [saying], "Our Lord, You have encompassed all things in mercy and knowledge, so forgive those who have repented and followed Your way and protect them from the punishment of Hellfire.

08. Our Lord, and admit them to gardens of perpetual residence which You have promised them and whoever was righteous among their fathers, their spouses and their offspring. Indeed, it is You who is the Exalted in Might, the Wise.

09. And protect them from the evil consequences [of their deeds]. And he whom You protect from evil consequences that Day - You will have given him mercy. And that is the great attainment."

10. Indeed, those who disbelieve will be addressed, "The hatred of Allah for you was [even] greater than your hatred of yourselves [this Day in Hell] when you were invited to faith, but you refused."

11. They will say, "Our Lord, You made us lifeless twice and gave us life twice, and we have confessed our sins. So is there to an exit any way?"

12. [They will be told], "That is because, when Allah was called upon alone, you disbelieved; but if others were associated with Him, you believed. So the judgement is with Allah, the Most High, the Grand."

13. It is He who shows you His signs and sends down to you from the sky, provision. But none will remember except he who turns back [in repentance].

14. So invoke Allah, [being] sincere to Him in religion, although the disbelievers dislike it.

15. [He is] the Exalted above [all] degrees, Owner of the Throne; He places the inspiration of His command upon whom He wills of His servants to warn of the Day of Meeting.

16. The Day they come forth nothing concerning them will be concealed from Allah. To whom belongs [all] sovereignty this Day? To Allah, the One, the Prevailing.
17. This Day every soul will be recompensed for what it earned. No injustice today! Indeed, Allah is swift in account.
18. And warn them, [O Muhammad], of the Approaching Day, when hearts are at the throats, filled [with distress]. For the wrongdoers there will be no devoted friend and no intercessor [who is] obeyed.
19. He knows that which deceives the eyes and what the breasts conceal.
20. And Allah judges with truth, while those they invoke besides Him judge not with anything. Indeed, Allah - He is the Hearing, the Seeing.
21. Have they not traveled through the land and observed how was the end of those who were before them? They were greater than them in strength and in impression on the land, but Allah seized them for their sins. And they had not from Allah any protector.
22. That was because their messengers were coming to them with clear proofs, but they disbelieved, so Allah seized them. Indeed, He is Powerful and severe in punishment.
23. And We did certainly send Moses with Our signs and a clear authority
24. To Pharaoh, Haman and Qarun; but they said, "[He is] a magician and a liar."
25. And when he brought them the truth from Us, they said, "Kill the sons of those who have believed with him and keep their women alive." But the plan of the disbelievers is not except in error.
26. And Pharaoh said, "Let me kill Moses and let him call upon his Lord. Indeed, I fear that he will change your religion or that he will cause corruption in the land."
27. But Moses said, "Indeed, I have sought refuge in my Lord and your Lord from every arrogant one who does not believe in the Day of Account."
28. And a believing man from the family of Pharaoh who concealed his faith said, "Do you kill a man [merely] because he says, 'My Lord is Allah' while he has brought you clear proofs from your Lord? And if he should be lying, then upon him is [the consequence of] his lie; but if he should be truthful, there will strike you some of what he promises you. Indeed, Allah does not guide one who is a transgressor and a liar.

29. my people, sovereignty is yours today, [your being] dominant in the land. But who would protect us from the punishment of Allah if it came to us?" Pharaoh said, "I do not show you except what I see, and I do not guide you except to the way of right conduct."

30. And he who believed said, "O my people, indeed I fear for you [a fate] like the day of the companies -

31. Like the custom of the people of Noah and of 'Aad and Thamud and those after them. And Allah wants no injustice for [His] servants.

32. And O my people, indeed I fear for you the Day of Calling -

33. The Day you will turn your backs fleeing; there is not for you from Allah any protector. And whoever Allah leaves astray - there is not for him any guide.

34. And Joseph had already come to you before with clear proofs, but you remained in doubt of that which he brought to you, until when he died, you said, 'Never will Allah send a messenger after him.' Thus does Allah leave astray he who is a transgressor and skeptic."

35. Those who dispute concerning the signs of Allah without an authority having come to them - great is hatred [of them] in the sight of Allah and in the sight of those who have believed. Thus does Allah seal over every heart [belonging to] an arrogant tyrant.

36. And Pharaoh said, "O Haman, construct for me a tower that I might reach the ways -

37. The ways into the heavens - so that I may look at the deity of Moses; but indeed, I think he is a liar." And thus was made attractive to Pharaoh the evil of his deed, and he was averted from the [right] way. And the plan of Pharaoh was not except in ruin.

38. And he who believed said, "O my people, follow me, I will guide you to the way of right conduct.

39. my people, this worldly life is only [temporary] enjoyment, and indeed, the Hereafter - that is the home of [permanent] settlement.

40. Whoever does an evil deed will not be recompensed except by the like thereof; but whoever does righteousness, whether male or female, while he is a believer - those will enter Paradise, being given provision therein without account.

41. And O my people, how is it that I invite you to salvation while you invite me to the Fire?

42. You invite me to disbelieve in Allah and associate with Him that

of which I have no knowledge, and I invite you to the Exalted in Might, the Perpetual Forgiver.

43. Assuredly, that to which you invite me has no [response to a] supplication in this world or in the Hereafter; and indeed, our return is to Allah, and indeed, the transgressors will be companions of the Fire.

44. And you will remember what I [now] say to you, and I entrust my affair to Allah. Indeed, Allah is Seeing of [His] servants."

45. So Allah protected him from the evils they plotted, and the people of Pharaoh were enveloped by the worst of punishment -

46. The Fire, they are exposed to it morning and evening. And the Day the Hour appears [it will be said], "Make the people of Pharaoh enter the severest punishment."

47. And [mention] when they will argue within the Fire, and the weak will say to those who had been arrogant, "Indeed, we were [only] your followers, so will you relieve us of a share of the Fire?"

48. Those who had been arrogant will say, "Indeed, all [of us] are in it. Indeed, Allah has judged between the servants."

49. And those in the Fire will say to the keepers of Hell, "Supplicate your Lord to lighten for us a day from the punishment."

50. They will say, "Did there not come to you your messengers with clear proofs?" They will say, "Yes." They will reply, "Then supplicate [yourselves], but the supplication of the disbelievers is not except in error."

51. Indeed, We will support Our messengers and those who believe during the life of this world and on the Day when the witnesses will stand -

52. The Day their excuse will not benefit the wrongdoers, and they will have the curse, and they will have the worst home.

53. And We had certainly given Moses guidance, and We caused the Children of Israel to inherit the Scripture

54. As guidance and a reminder for those of understanding.

55. So be patient, [O Muhammad]. Indeed, the promise of Allah is truth. And ask forgiveness for your sin and exalt [Allah] with praise of your Lord in the evening and the morning.

56. Indeed, those who dispute concerning the signs of Allah without [any] authority having come to them - there is not within their breasts

except pride, [the extent of] which they cannot reach. So seek refuge in Allah. Indeed, it is He who is the Hearing, the Seeing.

57. The creation of the heavens and earth is greater than the creation of mankind, but most of the people do not know.

58. And not equal are the blind and the seeing, nor are those who believe and do righteous deeds and the evildoer. Little do you remember.

59. Indeed, the Hour is coming - no doubt about it - but most of the people do not believe.

60. And your Lord says, "Call upon Me; I will respond to you." Indeed, those who disdain My worship will enter Hell [rendered] contemptible.

61. It is Allah who made for you the night that you may rest therein and the day giving sight. Indeed, Allah is full of bounty to the people, but most of the people are not grateful.

62. That is Allah, your Lord, Creator of all things; there is no deity except Him, so how are you deluded?

63. Thus were those [before you] deluded who were rejecting the signs of Allah.

64. It is Allah who made for you the earth a place of settlement and the sky a ceiling and formed you and perfected your forms and provided you with good things. That is Allah, your Lord; then blessed is Allah, Lord of the worlds.

65. He is the Ever-Living; there is no deity except Him, so call upon Him, [being] sincere to Him in religion. [All] praise is [due] to Allah, Lord of the worlds.

66. Say, [O Muhammad], "Indeed, I have been forbidden to worship those you call upon besides Allah once the clear proofs have come to me from my Lord, and I have been commanded to submit to the Lord of the worlds."

67. It is He who created you from dust, then from a sperm-drop, then from a clinging clot; then He brings you out as a child; then [He develops you] that you reach your [time of] maturity, then [further] that you become elders. And among you is he who is taken in death before [that], so that you reach a specified term; and perhaps you will use reason.

68. He it is who gives life and causes death; and when He decrees a matter, He but says to it, "Be," and it is.

69. Do you not consider those who dispute concerning the signs of Allah - how are they averted?

70. Those who deny the Book and that with which We sent Our messengers - they are going to know,
71. When the shackles are around their necks and the chains; they will be dragged
72. In boiling water; then in the Fire they will be filled [with flame].
73. Then it will be said to them, "Where is that which you used to associate [with Him in worship]
74. Other than Allah?" They will say, "They have departed from us; rather, we did not used to invoke previously anything." Thus does Allah put astray the disbelievers.
75. [The angels will say], "That was because you used to exult upon the earth without right and you used to behave insolently.
76. Enter the gates of Hell to abide eternally therein, and wretched is the residence of the arrogant."
77. So be patient, [O Muhammad]; indeed, the promise of Allah is truth. And whether We show you some of what We have promised them or We take you in death, it is to Us they will be returned.
78. And We have already sent messengers before you. Among them are those [whose stories] We have related to you, and among them are those [whose stories] We have not related to you. And it was not for any messenger to bring a sign [or verse] except by permission of Allah. So when the command of Allah comes, it will be concluded in truth, and the falsifiers will thereupon lose [all].
79. It is Allah who made for you the grazing animals upon which you ride, and some of them you eat.
80. And for you therein are [other] benefits and that you may realize upon them a need which is in your breasts; and upon them and upon ships you are carried.
81. And He shows you His signs. So which of the signs of Allah do you deny?
82. Have they not traveled through the land and observed how was the end of those before them? They were more numerous than themselves and greater in strength and in impression on the land, but they were not availed by what they used to earn.
83. And when their messengers came to them with clear proofs, they [merely] rejoiced in what they had of knowledge, but they were enveloped by what they used to ridicule.

84. And when they saw Our punishment, they said," We believe in Allah alone and disbelieve in that which we used to associate with Him."

85. But never did their faith benefit them once they saw Our punishment. [It is] the established way of Allah which has preceded among His servants. And the disbelievers thereupon lost [all].

| Verses: 54 | **Surah 41 Fussilat** | Makki |

In the name of Allah, the Entirely Merciful, the Especially Merciful.

01. Ha, Meem.

02. [This is] a revelation from the Entirely Merciful, the Especially Merciful-

03. A Book whose verses have been detailed, an Arabic Qur'an for a people who know,

04. As a giver of good tidings and a warner; but most of them turn away, so they do not hear.

05. And they say, "Our hearts are within coverings from that to which you invite us, and in our ears is deafness, and between us and you is a partition, so work; indeed, we are working."

06. Say, O [Muhammad], "I am only a man like you to whom it has been revealed that your god is but one God; so take a straight course to Him and seek His forgiveness." And woe to those who associate others with Allah -

07. Those who do not give zakah, and in the Hereafter they are disbelievers.

08. Indeed, those who believe and do righteous deeds - for them is a reward uninterrupted.

09. Say, "Do you indeed disbelieve in He who created the earth in two days and attribute to Him equals? That is the Lord of the worlds."

10. And He placed on the earth firmly set mountains over its surface, and He blessed it and determined therein its [creatures'] sustenance in four days without distinction - for [the information] of those who ask.

11. Then He directed Himself to the heaven while it was smoke and said to it and to the earth, "Come [into being], willingly or by compulsion." They said, "We have come willingly."

12. And He completed them as seven heavens within two days and inspired in each heaven its command. And We adorned the nearest heaven with lamps and as protection. That is the determination of the Exalted in Might, the Knowing.

13. But if they turn away, then say, "I have warned you of a thunderbolt like the thunderbolt [that struck] 'Aad and Thamud.

14. [That occurred] when the messengers had come to them before them and after them, [saying], "Worship not except Allah." They said, "If our Lord had willed, He would have sent down the angels, so indeed we, in that with which you have been sent, are disbelievers."

15. As for 'Aad, they were arrogant upon the earth without right and said, "Who is greater than us in strength?" Did they not consider that Allah who created them was greater than them in strength? But they were rejecting Our signs.

16. So We sent upon them a screaming wind during days of misfortune to make them taste the punishment of disgrace in the worldly life; but the punishment of the Hereafter is more disgracing, and they will not be helped.

17. And as for Thamud, We guided them, but they preferred blindness over guidance, so the thunderbolt of humiliating punishment seized them for what they used to earn.

18. And We saved those who believed and used to fear Allah.

19. And [mention, O Muhammad], the Day when the enemies of Allah will be gathered to the Fire while they are [driven] assembled in rows,

20. Until, when they reach it, their hearing and their eyes and their skins will testify against them of what they used to do.

21. And they will say to their skins, "Why have you testified against us?" They will say, "We were made to speak by Allah, who has made everything speak; and He created you the first time, and to Him you are returned.

22. And you were not covering yourselves, lest your hearing testify against you or your sight or your skins, but you assumed that Allah does not know much of what you do.

23. And that was your assumption which you assumed about your Lord. It has brought you to ruin, and you have become among the losers."

24. So [even] if they are patient, the Fire is a residence for them; and if they ask to appease [Allah], they will not be of those who are allowed to appease.

25. And We appointed for them companions who made attractive to them what was before them and what was behind them [of sin], and the word has come into effect upon them among nations which had passed on before them of jinn and men. Indeed, they [all] were losers.

26. And those who disbelieve say, "Do not listen to this Qur'an and speak noisily during [the recitation of] it that perhaps you will overcome."

27. But We will surely cause those who disbelieve to taste a severe punishment, and We will surely recompense them for the worst of what they had been doing.

28. That is the recompense of the enemies of Allah - the Fire. For them therein is the home of eternity as recompense for what they, of Our verses, were rejecting.

29. And those who disbelieved will [then] say, "Our Lord, show us those who misled us of the jinn and men [so] we may put them under our feet that they will be among the lowest."

30. Indeed, those who have said, "Our Lord is Allah " and then remained on a right course - the angels will descend upon them, [saying], "Do not fear and do not grieve but receive good tidings of Paradise, which you were promised.

31. We [angels] were your allies in worldly life and [are so] in the Hereafter. And you will have therein whatever your souls desire, and you will have therein whatever you request [or wish]

32. As accommodation from a [Lord who is] Forgiving and Merciful."

33. And who is better in speech than one who invites to Allah and does righteousness and says, "Indeed, I am of the Muslims."

34. And not equal are the good deed and the bad. Repel [evil] by that [deed] which is better; and thereupon the one whom between you and him is enmity [will become] as though he was a devoted friend.

35. But none is granted it except those who are patient, and none is granted it except one having a great portion [of good].

36. And if there comes to you from Satan an evil suggestion, then seek refuge in Allah. Indeed, He is the Hearing, the Knowing.

37. And of His signs are the night and day and the sun and moon. Do not prostrate to the sun or to the moon, but prostate to Allah, who created them, if it should be Him that you worship.

38. But if they are arrogant - then those who are near your Lord exalt Him by night and by day, and they do not become weary.

39. And of His signs is that you see the earth stilled, but when We send down upon it rain, it quivers and grows. Indeed, He who has given it life is the Giver of Life to the dead. Indeed, He is over all things competent.

40. Indeed, those who inject deviation into Our verses are not concealed from Us. So, is he who is cast into the Fire better or he who comes secure on the Day of Resurrection? Do whatever you will; indeed, He is Seeing of what you do.

41. Indeed, those who disbelieve in the message after it has come to them... And indeed, it is a mighty Book.

42. Falsehood cannot approach it from before it or from behind it; [it is] a revelation from a [Lord who is] Wise and Praiseworthy.

43. Nothing is said to you, [O Muhammad], except what was already said to the messengers before you. Indeed, your Lord is a possessor of forgiveness and a possessor of painful penalty.

44. And if We had made it a non-Arabic Qur'an, they would have said, "Why are its verses not explained in detail [in our language]? Is it a foreign [recitation] and an Arab [messenger]?" Say, "It is, for those who believe, a guidance and cure." And those who do not believe - in their ears is deafness, and it is upon them blindness. Those are being called from a distant place.

45. And We had already given Moses the Scripture, but it came under disagreement. And if not for a word that preceded from your Lord, it would have been concluded between them. And indeed they are, concerning the Qur'an, in disquieting doubt.

46. Whoever does righteousness - it is for his [own] soul; and whoever does evil [does so] against it. And your Lord is not ever unjust to [His] servants.

47. To him [alone] is attributed knowledge of the Hour. And fruits emerge not from their coverings nor does a female conceive or give birth except with His knowledge. And the Day He will call to them, "Where are My 'partners'?" they will say, "We announce to You that there is [no longer] among us any witness [to that]."

48. And lost from them will be those they were invoking before, and they will be certain that they have no place of escape.

49. Man is not weary of supplication for good [things], but if evil touches him, he is hopeless and despairing.

50. And if We let him taste mercy from Us after an adversity which has touched him, he will surely say, "This is [due] to me, and I do not think the Hour will occur; and [even] if I should be returned to my Lord, indeed, for me there will be with Him the best." But We will surely inform those who disbelieved about what they did, and We will surely make them taste a massive punishment.

51. And when We bestow favor upon man, he turns away and distances himself; but when evil touches him, then he is full of extensive supplication.

52. Say, "Have you considered: if the Qur'an is from Allah and you disbelieved in it, who would be more astray than one who is in extreme dissension?"

53. We will show them Our signs in the horizons and within themselves until it becomes clear to them that it is the truth. But is it not sufficient concerning your Lord that He is, over all things, a Witness?

54. Unquestionably, they are in doubt about the meeting with their Lord. Unquestionably He is, of all things, encompassing.

| Verses: 53 | **Surah 42 Ash-Shura** | Makki |

In the name of Allah, the Entirely Merciful, the Especially Merciful.

01. Ha, Meem.

02. 'Ayn, Seen, Qaf.

03. Thus has He revealed to you, [O Muhammad], and to those before you - Allah, the Exalted in Might, the Wise.

04. To Him belongs whatever is in the heavens and whatever is in the earth, and He is the Most High, the Most Great.

05. The heavens almost break from above them, and the angels exalt [Allah] with praise of their Lord and ask forgiveness for those on earth. Unquestionably, it is Allah who is the Forgiving, the Merciful.

06. And those who take as allies other than Him - Allah is [yet] Guardian over them; and you, [O Muhammad], are not over them a manager.

07. And thus We have revealed to you an Arabic Qur'an that you may warn the Mother of Cities [Makkah] and those around it and warn of the Day of Assembly, about which there is no doubt. A party will be in Paradise and a party in the Blaze.

08. And if Allah willed, He could have made them [of] one religion, but He admits whom He wills into His mercy. And the wrongdoers have not any protector or helper.

09. Or have they taken protectors [or allies] besides him? But Allah - He is the Protector, and He gives life to the dead, and He is over all things competent.

10. And in anything over which you disagree - its ruling is [to be referred] to Allah. [Say], "That is Allah, my Lord; upon Him I have relied, and to Him I turn back."

11. [He is] Creator of the heavens and the earth. He has made for you from yourselves, mates, and among the cattle, mates; He multiplies you thereby. There is nothing like unto Him, and He is the Hearing, the Seeing.

12. To Him belong the keys of the heavens and the earth. He extends provision for whom He wills and restricts [it]. Indeed He is, of all things, Knowing.

13. He has ordained for you of religion what He enjoined upon Noah and that which We have revealed to you, [O Muhammad], and what We enjoined upon Abraham and Moses and Jesus - to establish the religion and not be divided therein. Difficult for those who associate others with Allah is that to which you invite them. Allah chooses for Himself whom He wills and guides to Himself whoever turns back [to Him].

14. And they did not become divided until after knowledge had come to them - out of jealous animosity between themselves. And if not for a word that preceded from your Lord [postponing the penalty] until a specified time, it would have been concluded between them. And indeed, those who were granted inheritance of the Scripture after them are, concerning it, in disquieting doubt.

15. So to that [religion of Allah] invite, [O Muhammad], and remain on a right course as you are commanded and do not follow their inclinations but say, "I have believed in what Allah has revealed of the Qur'an, and I have been commanded to do justice among you. Allah is our Lord and your Lord. For us are our deeds, and for you your deeds. There is no [need for] argument between us and you. Allah will bring us together, and to Him is the [final] destination."

16. And those who argue concerning Allah after He has been responded to - their argument is invalid with their Lord, and upon them is [His] wrath, and for them is a severe punishment.
17. It is Allah who has sent down the Book in truth and [also] the balance. And what will make you perceive? Perhaps the Hour is near.
18. Those who do not believe in it are impatient for it, but those who believe are fearful of it and know that it is the truth. Unquestionably, those who dispute concerning the Hour are in extreme error.
19. Allah is Subtle with His servants; He gives provisions to whom He wills. And He is the Powerful, the Exalted in Might.
20. Whoever desires the harvest of the Hereafter - We increase for him in his harvest. And whoever desires the harvest of this world - We give him thereof, but there is not for him in the Hereafter any share.
21. Or have they other deities who have ordained for them a religion to which Allah has not consented? But if not for the decisive word, it would have been concluded between them. And indeed, the wrongdoers will have a painful punishment.
22. You will see the wrongdoers fearful of what they have earned, and it will [certainly] befall them. And those who have believed and done righteous deeds will be in lush regions of the gardens [in Paradise] having whatever they will in the presence of their Lord. That is what is the great bounty.
23. It is that of which Allah gives good tidings to His servants who believe and do righteous deeds. Say, [O Muhammad], "I do not ask you for this message any payment [but] only good will through kinship." And whoever commits a good deed - We will increase for him good therein. Indeed, Allah is Forgiving and Appreciative.
24. Or do they say, "He has invented about Allah a lie"? But if Allah willed, He could seal over your heart. And Allah eliminates falsehood and establishes the truth by His words. Indeed, He is Knowing of that within the breasts.
25. And it is He who accepts repentance from his servants and pardons misdeeds, and He knows what you do.
26. And He answers [the supplication of] those who have believed and done righteous deeds and increases [for] them from His bounty. But the disbelievers will have a severe punishment.
27. And if Allah had extended [excessively] provision for His

servants, they would have committed tyranny throughout the earth. But He sends [it] down in an amount which He wills. Indeed He is, of His servants, Acquainted and Seeing.

28. And it is He who sends down the rain after they had despaired and spreads His mercy. And He is the Protector, the Praiseworthy.

29. And of his signs is the creation of the heavens and earth and what He has dispersed throughout them of creatures. And He, for gathering them when He wills, is competent.

30. And whatever strikes you of disaster - it is for what your hands have earned; but He pardons much.

31. And you will not cause failure [to Allah] upon the earth. And you have not besides Allah any protector or helper.

32. And of His signs are the ships in the sea, like mountains.

33. If He willed, He could still the wind, and they would remain motionless on its surface. Indeed in that are signs for everyone patient and grateful.

34. Or He could destroy them for what they earned; but He pardons much.

35. And [that is so] those who dispute concerning Our signs may know that for them there is no place of escape.

36. So whatever thing you have been given - it is but [for] enjoyment of the worldly life. But what is with Allah is better and more lasting for those who have believed and upon their Lord rely

37. And those who avoid the major sins and immoralities, and when they are angry, they forgive,

38. And those who have responded to their lord and established prayer and whose affair is [determined by] consultation among themselves, and from what We have provided them, they spend.

39. And those who, when tyranny strikes them, they defend themselves,

40. And the retribution for an evil act is an evil one like it, but whoever pardons and makes reconciliation - his reward is [due] from Allah. Indeed, He does not like wrongdoers.

41. And whoever avenges himself after having been wronged - those have not upon them any cause [for blame].

42. The cause is only against the ones who wrong the people and tyrannize upon the earth without right. Those will have a painful punishment.

43. And whoever is patient and forgives - indeed, that is of the matters [requiring] determination.

44. And he whom Allah sends astray - for him there is no protector beyond Him. And you will see the wrongdoers, when they see the punishment, saying, "Is there for return [to the former world] any way?"

45. And you will see them being exposed to the Fire, humbled from humiliation, looking from [behind] a covert glance. And those who had believed will say, "Indeed, the [true] losers are the ones who lost themselves and their families on the Day of Resurrection. Unquestionably, the wrongdoers are in an enduring punishment."

46. And there will not be for them any allies to aid them other than Allah. And whoever Allah sends astray - for him there is no way.

47. Respond to your Lord before a Day comes from Allah of which there is no repelling. No refuge will you have that day, nor for you will there be any denial.

48. But if they turn away - then We have not sent you, [O Muhammad], over them as a guardian; upon you is only [the duty of] notification. And indeed, when We let man taste mercy from us, he rejoices in it; but if evil afflicts him for what his hands have put forth, then indeed, man is ungrateful.

49. To Allah belongs the dominion of the heavens and the earth; He creates what he wills. He gives to whom He wills female [children], and He gives to whom He wills males.

50. Or He makes them [both] males and females, and He renders whom He wills barren. Indeed, He is Knowing and Competent.

51. And it is not for any human being that Allah should speak to him except by revelation or from behind a partition or that He sends a messenger to reveal, by His permission, what He wills. Indeed, He is Most High and Wise.

52. And thus We have revealed to you an inspiration of Our command. You did not know what is the Book or [what is] faith, but We have made it a light by which We guide whom We will of Our servants. And indeed, [O Muhammad], you guide to a straight path -

53. The path of Allah, to whom belongs whatever is in the heavens and whatever is on the earth. Unquestionably, to Allah do [all] matters evolve.

| Verses: 89 | **Surah 43 Az-Zukhruf** | Makki |

In the name of Allah, the Entirely Merciful, the Especially Merciful.

01. Ha, Meem.
02. By the clear Book,
03. Indeed, We have made it an Arabic Qur'an that you might understand.
04. And indeed it is, in the Mother of the Book with Us, exalted and full of wisdom.
05. Then should We turn the message away, disregarding you, because you are a transgressing people?
06. And how many a prophet We sent among the former peoples,
07. But there would not come to them a prophet except that they used to ridicule him.
08. And We destroyed greater than them in [striking] power, and the example of the former peoples has preceded.
09. And if you should ask them, "Who has created the heavens and the earth?" they would surely say, "They were created by the Exalted in Might, the Knowing."
10. [The one] who has made for you the earth a bed and made for you upon it roads that you might be guided
11. And who sends down rain from the sky in measured amounts, and We revive thereby a dead land - thus will you be brought forth -
12. And who created the species, all of them, and has made for you of ships and animals those which you mount.
13. That you may settle yourselves upon their backs and then remember the favor of your Lord when you have settled upon them and say. "Exalted is He who has subjected this to us, and we could not have [otherwise] subdued it.
14. And indeed we, to our Lord, will [surely] return."
15. But they have attributed to Him from His servants a portion. Indeed, man is clearly ungrateful.
16. Or has He taken, out of what He has created, daughters and chosen you for [having] sons?
17. And when one of them is given good tidings of that which he attributes to the Most Merciful in comparison, his face becomes dark, and he suppresses grief.

18. So is one brought up in ornaments while being during conflict unevident [attributed to Allah]?
19. And they have made the angels, who are servants of the Most Merciful, females. Did they witness their creation? Their testimony will be recorded, and they will be questioned.
20. And they said, "If the Most Merciful had willed, we would not have worshipped them." They have of that no knowledge. They are not but falsifying.
21. Or have We given them a book before the Qur'an to which they are adhering?
22. Rather, they say, "Indeed, we found our fathers upon a religion, and we are in their footsteps [rightly] guided."
23. And similarly, We did not send before you any warner into a city except that its affluent said, "Indeed, we found our fathers upon a religion, and we are, in their footsteps, following."
24. [Each warner] said, "Even if I brought you better guidance than that [religion] upon which you found your fathers?" They said, "Indeed we, in that with which you were sent, are disbelievers."
25. So we took retribution from them; then see how was the end of the deniers.
26. And [mention, O Muhammad], when Abraham said to his father and his people, "Indeed, I am disassociated from that which you worship
27. Except for He who created me; and indeed, He will guide me."
28. And he made it a word remaining among his descendants that they might return [to it].
29. However, I gave enjoyment to these [people of Makkah] and their fathers until there came to them the truth and a clear Messenger.
30. But when the truth came to them, they said, "This is magic, and indeed we are, concerning it, disbelievers."
31. And they said, "Why was this Qur'an not sent down upon a great man from [one of] the two cities?"
32. Do they distribute the mercy of your Lord? It is We who have apportioned among them their livelihood in the life of this world and have raised some of them above others in degrees [of rank] that they may make use of one another for service. But the mercy of your Lord is better than whatever they accumulate.
33. And if it were not that the people would become one community

[of disbelievers], We would have made for those who disbelieve in the Most Merciful - for their houses - ceilings and stairways of silver upon which to mount

34. And for their houses - doors and couches [of silver] upon which to recline

35. And gold ornament. But all that is not but the enjoyment of worldly life. And the Hereafter with your Lord is for the righteous.

36. And whoever is blinded from remembrance of the Most Merciful - We appoint for him a devil, and he is to him a companion.

37. And indeed, the devils avert them from the way [of guidance] while they think that they are [rightly] guided

38. Until, when he comes to Us [at Judgement], he says [to his companion], "Oh, I wish there was between me and you the distance between the east and west - how wretched a companion."

39. And never will it benefit you that Day, when you have wronged, that you are [all] sharing in the punishment.

40. Then will you make the deaf hear, [O Muhammad], or guide the blind or he who is in clear error?

41. And whether [or not] We take you away [in death], indeed, We will take retribution upon them.

42. Or whether [or not] We show you that which We have promised them, indeed, We are Perfect in Ability.

43. So adhere to that which is revealed to you. Indeed, you are on a straight path.

44. And indeed, it is a remembrance for you and your people, and you [all] are going to be questioned.

45. And ask those We sent before you of Our messengers; have We made besides the Most Merciful deities to be worshipped?

46. And certainly did We send Moses with Our signs to Pharaoh and his establishment, and he said, "Indeed, I am the messenger of the Lord of the worlds."

47. But when he brought them Our signs, at once they laughed at them.

48. And We showed them not a sign except that it was greater than its sister, and We seized them with affliction that perhaps they might return [to faith].

49. And they said [to Moses], "O magician, invoke for us your Lord by what He has promised you. Indeed, we will be guided."

50. But when We removed from them the affliction, at once they broke their word.
51. And Pharaoh called out among his people; he said, "O my people, does not the kingdom of Egypt belong to me, and these rivers flowing beneath me; then do you not see?
52. Or am I [not] better than this one who is insignificant and hardly makes himself clear?
53. Then why have there not been placed upon him bracelets of gold or come with him the angels in conjunction?"
54. So he bluffed his people, and they obeyed him. Indeed, they were [themselves] a people defiantly disobedient [of Allah].
55. And when they angered Us, We took retribution from them and drowned them all.
56. And We made them a precedent and an example for the later peoples.
57. And when the son of Mary was presented as an example, immediately your people laughed aloud.
58. And they said, "Are your gods better, or is he?" They did not present the comparison except for [mere] argument. But, [in fact], they are a people prone to dispute.
59. Jesus was not but a servant upon whom We bestowed favor, and We made him an example for the Children of Israel.
60. And if We willed, We could have made [instead] of you angels succeeding [one another] on the earth.
61. And indeed, Jesus will be [a sign for] knowledge of the Hour, so be not in doubt of it, and follow Me. This is a straight path.
62. And never let Satan avert you. Indeed, he is to you a clear enemy.
63. And when Jesus brought clear proofs, he said, "I have come to you with wisdom and to make clear to you some of that over which you differ, so fear Allah and obey me.
64. Indeed, Allah is my Lord and your Lord, so worship Him. This is a straight path."
65. But the denominations from among them differed [and separated], so woe to those who have wronged from the punishment of a painful Day.
66. Are they waiting except for the Hour to come upon them suddenly while they perceive not?

67. Close friends, that Day, will be enemies to each other, except for the righteous
68. [To whom Allah will say], "O My servants, no fear will there be concerning you this Day, nor will you grieve,
69. [You] who believed in Our verses and were Muslims.
70. Enter Paradise, you and your kinds, delighted."
71. Circulated among them will be plates and vessels of gold. And therein is whatever the souls desire and [what] delights the eyes, and you will abide therein eternally.
72. And that is Paradise which you are made to inherit for what you used to do.
73. For you therein is much fruit from which you will eat.
74. Indeed, the criminals will be in the punishment of Hell, abiding eternally.
75. It will not be allowed to subside for them, and they, therein, are in despair.
76. And We did not wrong them, but it was they who were the wrongdoers.
77. And they will call, "O Malik, let your Lord put an end to us!" He will say, "Indeed, you will remain."
78. We had certainly brought you the truth, but most of you, to the truth, were averse.
79. Or have they devised [some] affair? But indeed, We are devising [a plan].
80. Or do they think that We hear not their secrets and their private conversations? Yes, [We do], and Our messengers are with them recording.
81. Say, [O Muhammad], "If the Most Merciful had a son, then I would be the first of [his] worshippers."
82. Exalted is the Lord of the heavens and the earth, Lord of the Throne, above what they describe.
83. So leave them to converse vainly and amuse themselves until they meet their Day which they are promised.
84. And it is Allah who is [the only] deity in the heaven, and on the earth [the only] deity. And He is the Wise, the Knowing.
85. And blessed is He to whom belongs the dominion of the heavens

and the earth and whatever is between them and with whom is knowledge of the Hour and to whom you will be returned.

86. And those they invoke besides Him do not possess [power of] intercession; but only those who testify to the truth [can benefit], and they know.

87. And if you asked them who created them, they would surely say, "Allah." So how are they deluded?

88. And [Allah acknowledges] his saying, "O my Lord, indeed these are a people who do not believe."

89. So turn aside from them and say, "Peace." But they are going to know.

Surah 44 Ad-Dukhaan

Verses: 59 — Makki

In the name of Allah, the Entirely Merciful, the Especially Merciful.

01. Ha, Meem.
02. By the clear Book,
03. Indeed, We sent it down during a blessed night. Indeed, We were to warn [mankind].
04. On that night is made distinct every precise matter -
05. [Every] matter [proceeding] from Us. Indeed, We were to send [a messenger]
06. As mercy from your Lord. Indeed, He is the Hearing, the Knowing.
07. Lord of the heavens and the earth and that between them, if you would be certain.
08. There is no deity except Him; He gives life and causes death. [He is] your Lord and the Lord of your first forefathers.
09. But they are in doubt, amusing themselves.
10. Then watch for the Day when the sky will bring a visible smoke.
11. Covering the people; this is a painful torment.
12. [They will say], "Our Lord, remove from us the torment; indeed, we are believers."
13. How will there be for them a reminder [at that time]? And there had come to them a clear Messenger.
14. Then they turned away from him and said, "[He was] taught [and is] a madman."

15. Indeed, We will remove the torment for a little. Indeed, you [disbelievers] will return [to disbelief].
16. The Day We will strike with the greatest assault, indeed, We will take retribution.
17. And We had already tried before them the people of Pharaoh, and there came to them a noble messenger,
18. [Saying], "Render to me the servants of Allah. Indeed, I am to you a trustworthy messenger,"
19. And [saying], "Be not haughty with Allah. Indeed, I have come to you with clear authority.
20. And indeed, I have sought refuge in my Lord and your Lord, lest you stone me.
21. But if you do not believe me, then leave me alone."
22. And [finally] he called to his Lord that these were a criminal people.
23. [Allah said], "Then set out with My servants by night. Indeed, you are to be pursued.
24. And leave the sea in stillness. Indeed, they are an army to be drowned."
25. How much they left behind of gardens and springs
26. And crops and noble sites
27. And comfort wherein they were amused.
28. Thus. And We caused to inherit it another people.
29. And the heaven and earth wept not for them, nor were they reprieved.
30. And We certainly saved the Children of Israel from the humiliating torment -
31. From Pharaoh. Indeed, he was a haughty one among the transgressors.
32. And We certainly chose them by knowledge over [all] the worlds.
33. And We gave them of signs that in which there was a clear trial.
34. Indeed, these [disbelievers] are saying,
35. "There is not but our first death, and we will not be resurrected.
36. Then bring [back] our forefathers, if you should be truthful."
37. Are they better or the people of Tubba' and those before them? We destroyed them, [for] indeed, they were criminals.
38. And We did not create the heavens and earth and that between them in play.

39. We did not create them except in truth, but most of them do not know.
40. Indeed, the Day of Judgement is the appointed time for them all -
41. The Day when no relation will avail a relation at all, nor will they be helped -
42. Except those [believers] on whom Allah has mercy. Indeed, He is the Exalted in Might, the Merciful.
43. Indeed, the tree of zaqqum
44. Is food for the sinful.
45. Like murky oil, it boils within bellies
46. Like the boiling of scalding water.
47. [It will be commanded], "Seize him and drag him into the midst of the Hellfire,
48. Then pour over his head from the torment of scalding water."
49. [It will be said], "Taste! Indeed, you are the honored, the noble!
50. Indeed, this is what you used to dispute."
51. Indeed, the righteous will be in a secure place;
52. Within gardens and springs,
53. Wearing [garments of] fine silk and brocade, facing each other.
54. Thus. And We will marry them to fair women with large, [beautiful] eyes.
55. They will call therein for every [kind of] fruit - safe and secure.
56. They will not taste death therein except the first death, and He will have protected them from the punishment of Hellfire
57. As bounty from your Lord. That is what is the great attainment.
58. And indeed, We have eased the Qur'an in your tongue that they might be reminded.
59. So watch, [O Muhammad]; indeed, they are watching [for your end].

Surah 45 Al-Jaathiyah

Verses: 37 — Makki

In the name of Allah, the Entirely Merciful, the Especially Merciful.

01. Ha, Meem.
02. The revelation of the Book is from Allah, the Exalted in Might, the Wise.
03. Indeed, within the heavens and earth are signs for the believers.
04. And in the creation of yourselves and what He disperses of moving creatures are signs for people who are certain [in faith].

05. And [in] the alternation of night and day and [in] what Allah sends down from the sky of provision and gives life thereby to the earth after its lifelessness and [in His] directing of the winds are signs for a people who reason.

06. These are the verses of Allah which We recite to you in truth. Then in what statement after Allah and His verses will they believe?

07. Woe to every sinful liar

08. Who hears the verses of Allah recited to him, then persists arrogantly as if he had not heard them. So give him tidings of a painful punishment.

09. And when he knows anything of Our verses, he takes them in ridicule. Those will have a humiliating punishment.

10. Before them is Hell, and what they had earned will not avail them at all nor what they had taken besides Allah as allies. And they will have a great punishment.

11. This [Qur'an] is guidance. And those who have disbelieved in the verses of their Lord will have a painful punishment of foul nature.

12. It is Allah who subjected to you the sea so that ships may sail upon it by His command and that you may seek of His bounty; and perhaps you will be grateful.

13. And He has subjected to you whatever is in the heavens and whatever is on the earth - all from Him. Indeed in that are signs for a people who give thought.

14. Say, [O Muhammad], to those who have believed that they [should] forgive those who expect not the days of Allah so that He may recompense a people for what they used to earn.

15. Whoever does a good deed - it is for himself; and whoever does evil - it is against the self. Then to your Lord you will be returned.

16. And We did certainly give the Children of Israel the Scripture and judgement and prophethood, and We provided them with good things and preferred them over the worlds.

17. And We gave them clear proofs of the matter [of religion]. And they did not differ except after knowledge had come to them - out of jealous animosity between themselves. Indeed, your Lord will judge between them on the Day of Resurrection concerning that over which they used to differ.

18. Then We put you, [O Muhammad], on an ordained way concerning the matter [of religion]; so follow it and do not follow the inclinations of those who do not know.
19. Indeed, they will never avail you against Allah at all. And indeed, the wrongdoers are allies of one another; but Allah is the protector of the righteous.
20. This [Qur'an] is enlightenment for mankind and guidance and mercy for a people who are certain [in faith].
21. Or do those who commit evils think We will make them like those who have believed and done righteous deeds - [make them] equal in their life and their death? Evil is that which they judge.
22. And Allah created the heavens and earth in truth and so that every soul may be recompensed for what it has earned, and they will not be wronged.
23. Have you seen he who has taken as his god his [own] desire, and Allah has sent him astray due to knowledge and has set a seal upon his hearing and his heart and put over his vision a veil? So who will guide him after Allah? Then will you not be reminded?
24. And they say, "There is not but our worldly life; we die and live, and nothing destroys us except time." And they have of that no knowledge; they are only assuming.
25. And when Our verses are recited to them as clear evidences, their argument is only that they say, "Bring [back] our forefathers, if you should be truthful."
26. Say, "Allah causes you to live, then causes you to die; then He will assemble you for the Day of Resurrection, about which there is no doubt, but most of the people do not know."
27. And to Allah belongs the dominion of the heavens and the earth. And the Day the Hour appears - that Day the falsifiers will lose.
28. And you will see every nation kneeling [from fear]. Every nation will be called to its record [and told], "Today you will be recompensed for what you used to do.
29. This, Our record, speaks about you in truth. Indeed, We were having transcribed whatever you used to do."
30. So as for those who believed and did righteous deeds, their Lord will admit them into His mercy. That is what is the clear attainment.
31. But as for those who disbelieved, [it will be said], "Were not Our verses recited to you, but you were arrogant and became a people of criminals?

32. And when it was said, 'Indeed, the promise of Allah is truth and the Hour [is coming] - no doubt about it,' you said, 'We know not what is the Hour. We assume only assumption, and we are not convinced.' "

33. And the evil consequences of what they did will appear to them, and they will be enveloped by what they used to ridicule.

34. And it will be said, "Today We will forget you as you forgot the meeting of this Day of yours, and your refuge is the Fire, and for you there are no helpers.

35. That is because you took the verses of Allah in ridicule, and worldly life deluded you." So that Day they will not be removed from it, nor will they be asked to appease [Allah].

36. Then, to Allah belongs [all] praise - Lord of the heavens and Lord of the earth, Lord of the worlds.

37. And to Him belongs [all] grandeur within the heavens and the earth, and He is the Exalted in Might, the Wise.

Surah 46 Al-Ahqaaf

Verses: 35 — Makki

In the name of Allah, the Entirely Merciful, the Especially Merciful.

01. Ha, Meem.

02. The revelation of the Book is from Allah, the Exalted in Might, the Wise.

03. We did not create the heavens and earth and what is between them except in truth and [for] a specified term. But those who disbelieve, from that of which they are warned, are turning away.

04. Say, [O Muhammad], "Have you considered that which you invoke besides Allah? Show me what they have created of the earth; or did they have partnership in [creation of] the heavens? Bring me a scripture [revealed] before this or a [remaining] trace of knowledge, if you should be truthful."

05. And who is more astray than he who invokes besides Allah those who will not respond to him until the Day of Resurrection, and they, of their invocation, are unaware.

06. And when the people are gathered [that Day], they [who were invoked] will be enemies to them, and they will be deniers of their worship.

07. And when Our verses are recited to them as clear evidences, those who disbelieve say of the truth when it has come to them, "This is obvious magic."

08. Or do they say, "He has invented it?" Say, "If I have invented it, you will not possess for me [the power of protection] from Allah at all. He is most knowing of that in which you are involved. Sufficient is He as Witness between me and you, and He is the Forgiving the Merciful."

09. Say, "I am not something original among the messengers, nor do I know what will be done with me or with you. I only follow that which is revealed to me, and I am not but a clear warner."

10. Say, "Have you considered: if the Qur'an was from Allah, and you disbelieved in it while a witness from the Children of Israel has testified to something similar and believed while you were arrogant...?" Indeed, Allah does not guide the wrongdoing people.

11. And those who disbelieve say of those who believe, "If it had [truly] been good, they would not have preceded us to it." And when they are not guided by it, they will say, "This is an ancient falsehood."

12. And before it was the scripture of Moses to lead and as a mercy. And this is a confirming Book in an Arabic tongue to warn those who have wronged and as good tidings to the doers of good.

13. Indeed, those who have said, "Our Lord is Allah," and then remained on a right course - there will be no fear concerning them, nor will they grieve.

14. Those are the companions of Paradise, abiding eternally therein as reward for what they used to do.

15. And We have enjoined upon man, to his parents, good treatment. His mother carried him with hardship and gave birth to him with hardship, and his gestation and weaning [period] is thirty months. [He grows] until, when he reaches maturity and reaches [the age of] forty years, he says, "My Lord, enable me to be grateful for Your favor which You have bestowed upon me and upon my parents and to work righteousness of which You will approve and make righteous for me my offspring. Indeed, I have repented to You, and indeed, I am of the Muslims."

16. Those are the ones from whom We will accept the best of what they did and overlook their misdeeds, [their being] among the companions of Paradise. [That is] the promise of truth which they had been promised.

17. But one who says to his parents, "Uff to you; do you promise me that I will be brought forth [from the earth] when generations before me have already passed on [into oblivion]?" while they

call to Allah for help [and to their son], "Woe to you! Believe! Indeed, the promise of Allah is truth." But he says, "This is not but legends of the former people" -

18. Those are the ones upon whom the word has come into effect, [who will be] among nations which had passed on before them of jinn and men. Indeed, they [all] were losers.

19. And for all there are degrees [of reward and punishment] for what they have done, and [it is] so that He may fully compensate them for their deeds, and they will not be wronged.

20. And the Day those who disbelieved are exposed to the Fire [it will be said], "You exhausted your pleasures during your worldly life and enjoyed them, so this Day you will be awarded the punishment of [extreme] humiliation because you were arrogant upon the earth without right and because you were defiantly disobedient."

21. And mention, [O Muhammad], the brother of 'Aad, when he warned his people in the [region of] al-Ahqaf - and warners had already passed on before him and after him - [saying], "Do not worship except Allah. Indeed, I fear for you the punishment of a terrible day."

22. They said, "Have you come to delude us away from our gods? Then bring us what you promise us, if you should be of the truthful."

23. He said, "Knowledge [of its time] is only with Allah, and I convey to you that with which I was sent; but I see you [to be] a people behaving ignorantly."

24. And when they saw it as a cloud approaching their valleys, they said, "This is a cloud bringing us rain!" Rather, it is that for which you were impatient: a wind, within it a painful punishment,

25. Destroying everything by command of its Lord. And they became so that nothing was seen [of them] except their dwellings. Thus do We recompense the criminal people.

26. And We had certainly established them in such as We have not established you, and We made for them hearing and vision and hearts. But their hearing and vision and hearts availed them not from anything [of the punishment] when they were [continually] rejecting the signs of Allah; and they were enveloped by what they used to ridicule.

27. And We have already destroyed what surrounds you of [those] cities, and We have diversified the signs [or verses] that perhaps they might return [from disbelief].

28. Then why did those they took besides Allah as deities by which to approach [Him] not aid them? But they had strayed from them. And that was their falsehood and what they were inventing.

29. And [mention, O Muhammad], when We directed to you a few of the jinn, listening to the Qur'an. And when they attended it, they said, "Listen quietly." And when it was concluded, they went back to their people as warners.

30. They said, "O our people, indeed we have heard a [recited] Book revealed after Moses confirming what was before it which guides to the truth and to a straight path.

31. our people, respond to the Messenger of Allah and believe in him; Allah will forgive for you your sins and protect you from a painful punishment.

32. But he who does not respond to the Caller of Allah will not cause failure [to Him] upon earth, and he will not have besides Him any protectors. Those are in manifest error."

33. Do they not see that Allah, who created the heavens and earth and did not fail in their creation, is able to give life to the dead? Yes. Indeed, He is over all things competent.

34. And the Day those who disbelieved are exposed to the Fire [it will be said], "Is this not the truth?" They will say, "Yes, by our Lord." He will say, "Then taste the punishment because you used to disbelieve."

35. So be patient, [O Muhammad], as were those of determination among the messengers and do not be impatient for them. It will be - on the Day they see that which they are promised - as though they had not remained [in the world] except an hour of a day. [This is] notification. And will [any] be destroyed except the defiantly disobedient people?

| Verses: 38 | **Surah 47 Muhammad** | Madani |

In the name of Allah, the Entirely Merciful, the Especially Merciful.

01. Those who disbelieve and avert [people] from the way of Allah - He will waste their deeds.

02. And those who believe and do righteous deeds and believe in what has been sent down upon Muhammad - and it is the truth from their Lord - He will remove from them their misdeeds and amend their condition.

03. That is because those who disbelieve follow falsehood, and those who believe follow the truth from their Lord. Thus does Allah present to the people their comparisons.

04. So when you meet those who disbelieve [in battle], strike [their] necks until, when you have inflicted slaughter upon them, then secure their bonds, and either [confer] favor afterwards or ransom [them] until the war lays down its burdens. That [is the command]. And if Allah had willed, He could have taken vengeance upon them [Himself], but [He ordered armed struggle] to test some of you by means of others. And those who are killed in the cause of Allah - never will He waste their deeds.

05. He will guide them and amend their condition

06. And admit them to Paradise, which He has made known to them.

07. O you who have believed, if you support Allah, He will support you and plant firmly your feet.

08. But those who disbelieve - for them is misery, and He will waste their deeds.

09. That is because they disliked what Allah revealed, so He rendered worthless their deeds.

10. Have they not traveled through the land and seen how was the end of those before them? Allah destroyed [everything] over them, and for the disbelievers is something comparable.

11. That is because Allah is the protector of those who have believed and because the disbelievers have no protector.

12. Indeed, Allah will admit those who have believed and done righteous deeds to gardens beneath which rivers flow, but those who disbelieve enjoy themselves and eat as grazing livestock eat, and the Fire will be a residence for them.

13. And how many a city was stronger than your city [Makkah] which drove you out? We destroyed them; and there was no helper for them.

14. So is he who is on clear evidence from his Lord like him to whom the evil of his work has been made attractive and they follow their [own] desires?

15. Is the description of Paradise, which the righteous are promised, wherein are rivers of water unaltered, rivers of milk the taste of which never changes, rivers of wine delicious to those who drink, and rivers of purified honey, in which they will have from

all [kinds of] fruits and forgiveness from their Lord, like [that of] those who abide eternally in the Fire and are given to drink scalding water that will sever their intestines?

16. And among them, [O Muhammad], are those who listen to you, until when they depart from you, they say to those who were given knowledge, "What has he said just now?" Those are the ones of whom Allah has sealed over their hearts and who have followed their [own] desires.

17. And those who are guided - He increases them in guidance and gives them their righteousness.

18. Then do they await except that the Hour should come upon them unexpectedly? But already there have come [some of] its indications. Then what good to them, when it has come, will be their remembrance?

19. So know, [O Muhammad], that there is no deity except Allah and ask forgiveness for your sin and for the believing men and believing women. And Allah knows of your movement and your resting place.

20. Those who believe say, "Why has a surah not been sent down? But when a precise surah is revealed and fighting is mentioned therein, you see those in whose hearts is hypocrisy looking at you with a look of one overcome by death. And more appropriate for them [would have been]

21. Obedience and good words. And when the matter [of fighting] was determined, if they had been true to Allah, it would have been better for them.

22. So would you perhaps, if you turned away, cause corruption on earth and sever your [ties of] relationship?

23. Those [who do so] are the ones that Allah has cursed, so He deafened them and blinded their vision.

24. Then do they not reflect upon the Qur'an, or are there locks upon [their] hearts?

25. Indeed, those who reverted back [to disbelief] after guidance had become clear to them - Satan enticed them and prolonged hope for them.

26. That is because they said to those who disliked what Allah sent down, "We will obey you in part of the matter." And Allah knows what they conceal.

27. Then how [will it be] when the angels take them in death, striking their faces and their backs?

28. That is because they followed what angered Allah and disliked [what earns] His pleasure, so He rendered worthless their deeds.

29. Or do those in whose hearts is disease think that Allah would never expose their [feelings of] hatred?

30. And if We willed, We could show them to you, and you would know them by their mark; but you will surely know them by the tone of [their] speech. And Allah knows your deeds.

31. And We will surely test you until We make evident those who strive among you [for the cause of Allah] and the patient, and We will test your affairs.

32. Indeed, those who disbelieved and averted [people] from the path of Allah and opposed the Messenger after guidance had become clear to them - never will they harm Allah at all, and He will render worthless their deeds.

33. O you who have believed, obey Allah and obey the Messenger and do not invalidate your deeds.

34. Indeed, those who disbelieved and averted [people] from the path of Allah and then died while they were disbelievers - never will Allah forgive them.

35. So do not weaken and call for peace while you are superior; and Allah is with you and will never deprive you of [the reward of] your deeds.

36. [This] worldly life is only amusement and diversion. And if you believe and fear Allah, He will give you your rewards and not ask you for your properties.

37. If He should ask you for them and press you, you would withhold, and He would expose your unwillingness.

38. Here you are - those invited to spend in the cause of Allah - but among you are those who withhold [out of greed]. And whoever withholds only withholds [benefit] from himself; and Allah is the Free of need, while you are the needy. And if you turn away, He will replace you with another people; then they will not be the likes of you.

Surah 48 Al-Fath

Verses: 29 | **Madani**

In the name of Allah, the Entirely Merciful, the Especially Merciful.

01. Indeed, We have given you, [O Muhammad], a clear conquest

02. That Allah may forgive for you what preceded of your sin and what will follow and complete His favor upon you and guide you to a straight path

03. And [that] Allah may aid you with a mighty victory.

04. It is He who sent down tranquillity into the hearts of the believers that they would increase in faith along with their [present] faith. And to Allah belong the soldiers of the heavens and the earth, and ever is Allah Knowing and Wise.

05. [And] that He may admit the believing men and the believing women to gardens beneath which rivers flow to abide therein eternally and remove from them their misdeeds - and ever is that, in the sight of Allah, a great attainment -

06. And [that] He may punish the hypocrite men and hypocrite women, and the polytheist men and polytheist women - those who assume about Allah an assumption of evil nature. Upon them is a misfortune of evil nature; and Allah has become angry with them and has cursed them and prepared for them Hell, and evil it is as a destination.

07. And to Allah belong the soldiers of the heavens and the earth. And ever is Allah Exalted in Might and Wise.

08. Indeed, We have sent you as a witness and a bringer of good tidings and a warner

09. That you [people] may believe in Allah and His Messenger and honor him and respect the Prophet and exalt Allah morning and afternoon.

10. Indeed, those who pledge allegiance to you, [O Muhammad] - they are actually pledging allegiance to Allah. The hand of Allah is over their hands. So he who breaks his word only breaks it to the detriment of himself. And he who fulfills that which he has promised Allah - He will give him a great reward.

11. Those who remained behind of the bedouins will say to you, "Our properties and our families occupied us, so ask forgiveness for us." They say with their tongues what is not within their hearts. Say, "Then who could prevent Allah at all if He intended for you harm or intended for you benefit? Rather, ever is Allah, with what you do, Acquainted.

12. But you thought that the Messenger and the believers would never return to their families, ever, and that was made pleasing in your hearts. And you assumed an assumption of evil and became a people ruined."

13. And whoever has not believed in Allah and His Messenger - then indeed, We have prepared for the disbelievers a Blaze.

14. And to Allah belongs the dominion of the heavens and the earth. He forgives whom He wills and punishes whom He wills. And ever is Allah Forgiving and Merciful.

15. Those who remained behind will say when you set out toward the war booty to take it, "Let us follow you." They wish to change the words of Allah. Say, "Never will you follow us. Thus did Allah say before." So they will say, "Rather, you envy us." But [in fact] they were not understanding except a little.

16. Say to those who remained behind of the bedouins, "You will be called to [face] a people of great military might; you may fight them, or they will submit. So if you obey, Allah will give you a good reward; but if you turn away as you turned away before, He will punish you with a painful punishment."

17. There is not upon the blind any guilt or upon the lame any guilt or upon the ill any guilt [for remaining behind]. And whoever obeys Allah and His Messenger - He will admit him to gardens beneath which rivers flow; but whoever turns away - He will punish him with a painful punishment.

18. Certainly was Allah pleased with the believers when they pledged allegiance to you, [O Muhammad], under the tree, and He knew what was in their hearts, so He sent down tranquillity upon them and rewarded them with an imminent conquest

19. And much war booty which they will take. And ever is Allah Exalted in Might and Wise.

20. Allah has promised you much booty that you will take [in the future] and has hastened for you this [victory] and withheld the hands of people from you - that it may be a sign for the believers and [that] He may guide you to a straight path.

21. And [He promises] other [victories] that you were [so far] unable to [realize] which Allah has already encompassed. And ever is Allah, over all things, competent.

22. And if those [Makkans] who disbelieve had fought you, they would have turned their backs [in flight]. Then they would not

find a protector or a helper.

23. [This is] the established way of Allah which has occurred before. And never will you find in the way of Allah any change.

24. And it is He who withheld their hands from you and your hands from them within [the area of] Makkah after He caused you to overcome them. And ever is Allah of what you do, Seeing.

25. They are the ones who disbelieved and obstructed you from al-Masjid al-Haram while the offering was prevented from reaching its place of sacrifice. And if not for believing men and believing women whom you did not know - that you might trample them and there would befall you because of them dishonor without [your] knowledge - [you would have been permitted to enter Makkah]. [This was so] that Allah might admit to His mercy whom He willed. If they had been apart [from them], We would have punished those who disbelieved among them with painful punishment

26. When those who disbelieved had put into their hearts chauvinism - the chauvinism of the time of ignorance. But Allah sent down His tranquillity upon His Messenger and upon the believers and imposed upon them the word of righteousness, and they were more deserving of it and worthy of it. And ever is Allah, of all things, Knowing.

27. Certainly has Allah showed to His Messenger the vision in truth. You will surely enter al-Masjid al-Haram, if Allah wills, in safety, with your heads shaved and [hair] shortened, not fearing [anyone]. He knew what you did not know and has arranged before that a conquest near [at hand].

28. It is He who sent His Messenger with guidance and the religion of truth to manifest it over all religion. And sufficient is Allah as Witness.

29. Muhammad is the Messenger of Allah; and those with him are forceful against the disbelievers, merciful among themselves. You see them bowing and prostrating [in prayer], seeking bounty from Allah and [His] pleasure. Their mark is on their faces from the trace of prostration. That is their description in the Torah. And their description in the Gospel is as a plant which produces its offshoots and strengthens them so they grow firm and stand upon their stalks, delighting the sowers - so that Allah may enrage by them the disbelievers. Allah has promised those who believe and do righteous deeds among them forgiveness and a great reward.

| Verses: 18 | **Surah 49 Al-Hujuraat** | Madani |

In the name of Allah, the Entirely Merciful, the Especially Merciful.

01. O you who have believed, do not put [yourselves] before Allah and His Messenger but fear Allah. Indeed, Allah is Hearing and Knowing.

02. O you who have believed, do not raise your voices above the voice of the Prophet or be loud to him in speech like the loudness of some of you to others, lest your deeds become worthless while you perceive not.

03. Indeed, those who lower their voices before the Messenger of Allah - they are the ones whose hearts Allah has tested for righteousness. For them is forgiveness and great reward.

04. Indeed, those who call you, [O Muhammad], from behind the chambers - most of them do not use reason.

05. And if they had been patient until you [could] come out to them, it would have been better for them. But Allah is Forgiving and Merciful.

06. O you who have believed, if there comes to you a disobedient one with information, investigate, lest you harm a people out of ignorance and become, over what you have done, regretful.

07. And know that among you is the Messenger of Allah. If he were to obey you in much of the matter, you would be in difficulty, but Allah has endeared to you the faith and has made it pleasing in your hearts and has made hateful to you disbelief, defiance and disobedience. Those are the [rightly] guided.

08. [It is] as bounty from Allah and favor. And Allah is Knowing and Wise.

09. And if two factions among the believers should fight, then make settlement between the two. But if one of them oppresses the other, then fight against the one that oppresses until it returns to the ordinance of Allah. And if it returns, then make settlement between them in justice and act justly. Indeed, Allah loves those who act justly.

10. The believers are but brothers, so make settlement between your brothers. And fear Allah that you may receive mercy.

11. O you who have believed, let not a people ridicule [another] people; perhaps they may be better than them; nor let women ridicule [other] women; perhaps they may be better than them. And do not insult one another and do not call each other by [offensive] nicknames. Wretched is the name of disobedience

after [one's] faith. And whoever does not repent - then it is those who are the wrongdoers.

12. O you who have believed, avoid much [negative] assumption. Indeed, some assumption is sin. And do not spy or backbite each other. Would one of you like to eat the flesh of his brother when dead? You would detest it. And fear Allah; indeed, Allah is Accepting of repentance and Merciful.

13. O mankind, indeed We have created you from male and female and made you peoples and tribes that you may know one another. Indeed, the most noble of you in the sight of Allah is the most righteous of you. Indeed, Allah is Knowing and Acquainted.

14. The bedouins say, "We have believed." Say, "You have not [yet] believed; but say [instead], 'We have submitted,' for faith has not yet entered your hearts. And if you obey Allah and His Messenger, He will not deprive you from your deeds of anything. Indeed, Allah is Forgiving and Merciful."

15. The believers are only the ones who have believed in Allah and His Messenger and then doubt not but strive with their properties and their lives in the cause of Allah. It is those who are the truthful.

16. Say, "Would you acquaint Allah with your religion while Allah knows whatever is in the heavens and whatever is on the earth, and Allah is Knowing of all things?"

17. They consider it a favor to you that they have accepted Islam. Say, "Do not consider your Islam a favor to me. Rather, Allah has conferred favor upon you that He has guided you to the faith, if you should be truthful."

18. Indeed, Allah knows the unseen [aspects] of the heavens and the earth. And Allah is Seeing of what you do.

| Verses: 45 | **Surah 50 Qaaf** | Makki |

In the name of Allah, the Entirely Merciful, the Especially Merciful.

01. Qaf. By the honored Qur'an...

02. But they wonder that there has come to them a warner from among themselves, and the disbelievers say, "This is an amazing thing.

03. When we have died and have become dust, [we will return to life]? That is a distant return."

04. We know what the earth diminishes of them, and with Us is a retaining record.

05. But they denied the truth when it came to them, so they are in a confused condition.

06. Have they not looked at the heaven above them - how We structured it and adorned it and [how] it has no rifts?

07. And the earth - We spread it out and cast therein firmly set mountains and made grow therein [something] of every beautiful kind,

08. Giving insight and a reminder for every servant who turns [to Allah].

09. And We have sent down blessed rain from the sky and made grow thereby gardens and grain from the harvest

10. And lofty palm trees having fruit arranged in layers -

11. As provision for the servants, and We have given life thereby to a dead land. Thus is the resurrection.

12. The people of Noah denied before them, and the companions of the well and Thamud

13. And 'Aad and Pharaoh and the brothers of Lot

14. And the companions of the thicket and the people of Tubba'. All denied the messengers, so My threat was justly fulfilled.

15. Did We fail in the first creation? But they are in confusion over a new creation.

16. And We have already created man and know what his soul whispers to him, and We are closer to him than [his] jugular vein

17. When the two receivers receive, seated on the right and on the left.

18. Man does not utter any word except that with him is an observer prepared [to record].

19. And the intoxication of death will bring the truth; that is what you were trying to avoid.

20. And the Horn will be blown. That is the Day of [carrying out] the threat.

21. And every soul will come, with it a driver and a witness.

22. [It will be said], "You were certainly in unmindfulness of this, and We have removed from you your cover, so your sight, this Day, is sharp."

23. And his companion, [the angel], will say, "This [record] is what is with me, prepared."
24. [Allah will say], "Throw into Hell every obstinate disbeliever,
25. Preventer of good, aggressor, and doubter,
26. Who made [as equal] with Allah another deity; then throw him into the severe punishment."
27. His [devil] companion will say, "Our Lord, I did not make him transgress, but he [himself] was in extreme error."
28. [Allah] will say, "Do not dispute before Me, while I had already presented to you the warning.
29. The word will not be changed with Me, and never will I be unjust to the servants."
30. On the Day We will say to Hell, "Have you been filled?" and it will say, "Are there some more,"
31. And Paradise will be brought near to the righteous, not far,
32. [It will be said], "This is what you were promised - for every returner [to Allah] and keeper [of His covenant]
33. Who feared the Most Merciful unseen and came with a heart returning [in repentance].
34. Enter it in peace. This is the Day of Eternity."
35. They will have whatever they wish therein, and with Us is more.
36. And how many a generation before them did We destroy who were greater than them in [striking] power and had explored throughout the lands. Is there any place of escape?
37. Indeed in that is a reminder for whoever has a heart or who listens while he is present [in mind].
38. And We did certainly create the heavens and earth and what is between them in six days, and there touched Us no weariness.
39. So be patient, [O Muhammad], over what they say and exalt [Allah] with praise of your Lord before the rising of the sun and before its setting,
40. And [in part] of the night exalt Him and after prostration.
41. And listen on the Day when the Caller will call out from a place that is near -
42. The Day they will hear the blast [of the Horn] in truth. That is the Day of Emergence [from the graves].

43. Indeed, it is We who give life and cause death, and to Us is the destination
44. On the Day the earth breaks away from them [and they emerge] rapidly; that is a gathering easy for Us.
45. We are most knowing of what they say, and you are not over them a tyrant. But remind by the Qur'an whoever fears My threat.

Surah 51 Adh-Dhaariyat

Verses: 60 | Makki

In the name of Allah, the Entirely Merciful, the Especially Merciful.

01. By those [winds] scattering [dust] dispersing
02. And those [clouds] carrying a load [of water]
03. And those [ships] sailing with ease
04. And those [angels] apportioning [each] matter,
05. Indeed, what you are promised is true.
06. And indeed, the recompense is to occur.
07. By the heaven containing pathways,
08. Indeed, you are in differing speech.
09. Deluded away from the Qur'an is he who is deluded.
10. Destroyed are the falsifiers
11. Who are within a flood [of confusion] and heedless.
12. They ask, "When is the Day of Recompense?"
13. [It is] the Day they will be tormented over the Fire
14. [And will be told], "Taste your torment. This is that for which you were impatient."
15. Indeed, the righteous will be among gardens and springs,
16. Accepting what their Lord has given them. Indeed, they were before that doers of good.
17. They used to sleep but little of the night,
18. And in the hours before dawn they would ask forgiveness,
19. And from their properties was [given] the right of the [needy] petitioner and the deprived.
20. And on the earth are signs for the certain [in faith]
21. And in yourselves. Then will you not see?
22. And in the heaven is your provision and whatever you are promised.

23. Then by the Lord of the heaven and earth, indeed, it is truth - just as [sure as] it is that you are speaking.
24. Has there reached you the story of the honored guests of Abraham? -
25. When they entered upon him and said, "[We greet you with] peace." He answered, "[And upon you] peace, [you are] a people unknown."
26. Then he went to his family and came with a fat [roasted] calf
27. And placed it near them; he said, "Will you not eat?"
28. And he felt from them apprehension. They said, "Fear not," and gave him good tidings of a learned boy.
29. And his wife approached with a cry [of alarm] and struck her face and said, "[I am] a barren old woman!"
30. They said, "Thus has said your Lord; indeed, He is the Wise, the Knowing."
31. [Abraham] said, "Then what is your business [here], O messengers?"
32. They said, "Indeed, we have been sent to a people of criminals
33. To send down upon them stones of clay,
34. Marked in the presence of your Lord for the transgressors."
35. So We brought out whoever was in the cities of the believers.
36. And We found not within them other than a [single] house of Muslims.
37. And We left therein a sign for those who fear the painful punishment.
38. And in Moses [was a sign], when We sent him to Pharaoh with clear authority.
39. But he turned away with his supporters and said," A magician or a madman."
40. So We took him and his soldiers and cast them into the sea, and he was blameworthy.
41. And in 'Aad [was a sign], when We sent against them the barren wind.
42. It left nothing of what it came upon but that it made it like disintegrated ruins.
43. And in Thamud, when it was said to them, "Enjoy yourselves for a time."
44. But they were insolent toward the command of their Lord, so the thunderbolt seized them while they were looking on.

45. And they were unable to arise, nor could they defend themselves.
46. And [We destroyed] the people of Noah before; indeed, they were a people defiantly disobedient.
47. And the heaven We constructed with strength, and indeed, We are [its] expander.
48. And the earth We have spread out, and excellent is the preparer.
49. And of all things We created two mates; perhaps you will remember.
50. So flee to Allah. Indeed, I am to you from Him a clear warner.
51. And do not make [as equal] with Allah another deity. Indeed, I am to you from Him a clear warner.
52. Similarly, there came not to those before them any messenger except that they said, "A magician or a madman."
53. Did they suggest it to them? Rather, they [themselves] are a transgressing people.
54. So leave them, [O Muhammad], for you are not to be blamed.
55. And remind, for indeed, the reminder benefits the believers.
56. And I did not create the jinn and mankind except to worship Me.
57. I do not want from them any provision, nor do I want them to feed Me.
58. Indeed, it is Allah who is the [continual] Provider, the firm possessor of strength.
59. And indeed, for those who have wronged is a portion [of punishment] like the portion of their predecessors, so let them not impatiently urge Me.
60. And woe to those who have disbelieved from their Day which they are promised.

| Verses: 49 | ## Surah 52 At-Tur | Makki |

In the name of Allah, the Entirely Merciful, the Especially Merciful.

01. By the mount
02. And [by] a Book inscribed
03. In parchment spread open
04. And [by] the frequented House
05. And [by] the heaven raised high
06. And [by] the sea filled [with fire],
07. Indeed, the punishment of your Lord will occur.

08. Of it there is no preventer.
09. On the Day the heaven will sway with circular motion
10. And the mountains will pass on, departing -
11. Then woe, that Day, to the deniers,
12. Who are in [empty] discourse amusing themselves.
13. The Day they are thrust toward the fire of Hell with a [violent] thrust, [its angels will say],
14. "This is the Fire which you used to deny.
15. Then is this magic, or do you not see?
16. [Enter to] burn therein; then be patient or impatient - it is all the same for you. You are only being recompensed [for] what you used to do."
17. Indeed, the righteous will be in gardens and pleasure,
18. Enjoying what their Lord has given them, and their Lord protected them from the punishment of Hellfire.
19. [They will be told], "Eat and drink in satisfaction for what you used to do."
20. They will be reclining on thrones lined up, and We will marry them to fair women with large, [beautiful] eyes.
21. And those who believed and whose descendants followed them in faith - We will join with them their descendants, and We will not deprive them of anything of their deeds. Every person, for what he earned, is retained.
22. And We will provide them with fruit and meat from whatever they desire.
23. They will exchange with one another a cup [of wine] wherein [results] no ill speech or commission of sin.
24. There will circulate among them [servant] boys [especially] for them, as if they were pearls well-protected.
25. And they will approach one another, inquiring of each other.
26. They will say, "Indeed, we were previously among our people fearful [of displeasing Allah].
27. So Allah conferred favor upon us and protected us from the punishment of the Scorching Fire.
28. Indeed, we used to supplicate Him before. Indeed, it is He who is the Beneficent, the Merciful."

29. So remind [O Muhammad], for you are not, by the favor of your Lord, a soothsayer or a madman.
30. Or do they say [of you], "A poet for whom we await a misfortune of time?"
31. Say, "Wait, for indeed I am, with you, among the waiters."
32. Or do their minds command them to [say] this, or are they a transgressing people?
33. Or do they say, "He has made it up"? Rather, they do not believe.
34. Then let them produce a statement like it, if they should be truthful.
35. Or were they created by nothing, or were they the creators [of themselves]?
36. Or did they create the heavens and the earth? Rather, they are not certain.
37. Or have they the depositories [containing the provision] of your Lord? Or are they the controllers [of them]?
38. Or have they a stairway [into the heaven] upon which they listen? Then let their listener produce a clear authority.
39. Or has He daughters while you have sons?
40. Or do you, [O Muhammad], ask of them a payment, so they are by debt burdened down?
41. Or have they [knowledge of] the unseen, so they write [it] down?
42. Or do they intend a plan? But those who disbelieve - they are the object of a plan.
43. Or have they a deity other than Allah? Exalted is Allah above whatever they associate with Him.
44. And if they were to see a fragment from the sky falling, they would say, "[It is merely] clouds heaped up."
45. So leave them until they meet their Day in which they will be struck insensible -
46. The Day their plan will not avail them at all, nor will they be helped.
47. And indeed, for those who have wronged is a punishment before that, but most of them do not know.
48. And be patient, [O Muhammad], for the decision of your Lord, for indeed, you are in Our eyes. And exalt [Allah] with praise of your Lord when you arise.
49. And in a part of the night exalt Him and after [the setting of] the stars.

| Verses: 62 | **Surah 53 An-Najm** | Makki |

In the name of Allah, the Entirely Merciful, the Especially Merciful.

01. By the star when it descends,
02. Your companion [Muhammad] has not strayed, nor has he erred,
03. Nor does he speak from [his own] inclination.
04. It is not but a revelation revealed,
05. Taught to him by one intense in strength -
06. One of soundness. And he rose to [his] true form
07. While he was in the higher [part of the] horizon.
08. Then he approached and descended
09. And was at a distance of two bow lengths or nearer.
10. And he revealed to His Servant what he revealed.
11. The heart did not lie [about] what it saw.
12. So will you dispute with him over what he saw?
13. And he certainly saw him in another descent
14. At the Lote Tree of the Utmost Boundary -
15. Near it is the Garden of Refuge -
16. When there covered the Lote Tree that which covered [it].
17. The sight [of the Prophet] did not swerve, nor did it transgress [its limit].
18. He certainly saw of the greatest signs of his Lord.
19. So have you considered al-Lat and al-'Uzza?
20. And Manat, the third - the other one?
21. Is the male for you and for Him the female?
22. That, then, is an unjust division.
23. They are not but [mere] names you have named them - you and your forefathers - for which Allah has sent down no authority. They follow not except assumption and what [their] souls desire, and there has already come to them from their Lord guidance.
24. Or is there for man whatever he wishes?
25. Rather, to Allah belongs the Hereafter and the first [life].
26. And how many angels there are in the heavens whose

intercession will not avail at all except [only] after Allah has permitted [it] to whom He wills and approves.

27. Indeed, those who do not believe in the Hereafter name the angels female names,
28. And they have thereof no knowledge. They follow not except assumption, and indeed, assumption avails not against the truth at all.
29. So turn away from whoever turns his back on Our message and desires not except the worldly life.
30. That is their sum of knowledge. Indeed, your Lord is most knowing of who strays from His way, and He is most knowing of who is guided.
31. And to Allah belongs whatever is in the heavens and whatever is in the earth - that He may recompense those who do evil with [the penalty of] what they have done and recompense those who do good with the best [reward] -
32. Those who avoid the major sins and immoralities, only [committing] slight ones. Indeed, your Lord is vast in forgiveness. He was most knowing of you when He produced you from the earth and when you were fetuses in the wombs of your mothers. So do not claim yourselves to be pure; He is most knowing of who fears Him.
33. Have you seen the one who turned away
34. And gave a little and [then] refrained?
35. Does he have knowledge of the unseen, so he sees?
36. Or has he not been informed of what was in the scriptures of Moses
37. And [of] Abraham, who fulfilled [his obligations] -
38. That no bearer of burdens will bear the burden of another
39. And that there is not for man except that [good] for which he strives
40. And that his effort is going to be seen -
41. Then he will be recompensed for it with the fullest recompense
42. And that to your Lord is the finality
43. And that it is He who makes [one] laugh and weep
44. And that it is He who causes death and gives life
45. And that He creates the two mates - the male and female -
46. From a sperm-drop when it is emitted

47. And that [incumbent] upon Him is the next creation
48. And that it is He who enriches and suffices
49. And that it is He who is the Lord of Sirius
50. And that He destroyed the first [people of] 'Aad
51. And Thamud - and He did not spare [them] -
52. And the people of Noah before. Indeed, it was they who were [even] more unjust and oppressing.
53. And the overturned towns He hurled down
54. And covered them by that which He covered.
55. Then which of the favors of your Lord do you doubt?
56. This [Prophet] is a warner like the former warners.
57. The Approaching Day has approached.
58. Of it, [from those] besides Allah, there is no remover.
59. Then at this statement do you wonder?
60. And you laugh and do not weep
61. While you are proudly sporting?
62. So prostrate to Allah and worship [Him].

Verses: 55	Surah 54 Al-Qamar	Makki

In the name of Allah, the Entirely Merciful, the Especially Merciful.

01. The Hour has come near, and the moon has split [in two].
02. And if they see a miracle, they turn away and say, "Passing magic."
03. And they denied and followed their inclinations. But for every matter is a [time of] settlement.
04. And there has already come to them of information that in which there is deterrence -
05. Extensive wisdom - but warning does not avail [them].
06. So leave them, [O Muhammad]. The Day the Caller calls to something forbidding,
07. Their eyes humbled, they will emerge from the graves as if they were locusts spreading,
08. Racing ahead toward the Caller. The disbelievers will say, "This is a difficult Day."
09. The people of Noah denied before them, and they denied Our servant and said, "A madman," and he was repelled.

10. So he invoked his Lord, "Indeed, I am overpowered, so help."

11. Then We opened the gates of the heaven with rain pouring down

12. And caused the earth to burst with springs, and the waters met for a matter already predestined.

13. And We carried him on a [construction of] planks and nails,

14. Sailing under Our observation as reward for he who had been denied.

15. And We left it as a sign, so is there any who will remember?

16. And how [severe] were My punishment and warning.

17. And We have certainly made the Qur'an easy for remembrance, so is there any who will remember?

18. 'Aad denied; and how [severe] were My punishment and warning.

19. Indeed, We sent upon them a screaming wind on a day of continuous misfortune,

20. Extracting the people as if they were trunks of palm trees uprooted.

21. And how [severe] were My punishment and warning.

22. And We have certainly made the Qur'an easy for remembrance, so is there any who will remember?

23. Thamud denied the warning

24. And said, "Is it one human being among us that we should follow? Indeed, we would then be in error and madness.

25. Has the message been sent down upon him from among us? Rather, he is an insolent liar."

26. They will know tomorrow who is the insolent liar.

27. Indeed, We are sending the she-camel as trial for them, so watch them and be patient.

28. And inform them that the water is shared between them, each [day of] drink attended [by turn].

29. But they called their companion, and he dared and hamstrung [her].

30. And how [severe] were My punishment and warning.

31. Indeed, We sent upon them one blast from the sky, and they became like the dry twig fragments of an [animal] pen.

32. And We have certainly made the Qur'an easy for remembrance, so is there any who will remember?

33. The people of Lot denied the warning.
34. Indeed, We sent upon them a storm of stones, except the family of Lot - We saved them before dawn
35. As favor from us. Thus do We reward he who is grateful.
36. And he had already warned them of Our assault, but they disputed the warning.
37. And they had demanded from him his guests, but We obliterated their eyes, [saying], "Taste My punishment and warning."
38. And there came upon them by morning an abiding punishment.
39. So taste My punishment and warning.
40. And We have certainly made the Qur'an easy for remembrance, so is there any who will remember?
41. And there certainly came to the people of Pharaoh warning.
42. They denied Our signs, all of them, so We seized them with a seizure of one Exalted in Might and Perfect in Ability.
43. Are your disbelievers better than those [former ones], or have you immunity in the scripture?
44. Or do they say, "We are an assembly supporting [each other]"?
45. [Their] assembly will be defeated, and they will turn their backs [in retreat].
46. But the Hour is their appointment [for due punishment], and the Hour is more disastrous and more bitter.
47. Indeed, the criminals are in error and madness.
48. The Day they are dragged into the Fire on their faces [it will be said], "Taste the touch of Saqar."
49. Indeed, all things We created with predestination.
50. And Our command is but one, like a glance of the eye.
51. And We have already destroyed your kinds, so is there any who will remember?
52. And everything they did is in written records.
53. And every small and great [thing] is inscribed.
54. Indeed, the righteous will be among gardens and rivers,
55. In a seat of honor near a Sovereign, Perfect in Ability.

| Verses: 78 | **Surah 55 Ar-Rahmaan** | Madani |

In the name of Allah, the Entirely Merciful, the Especially Merciful.

01. The Most Merciful
02. Taught the Qur'an,
03. Created man,
04. [And] taught him eloquence.
05. The sun and the moon [move] by precise calculation,
06. And the stars and trees prostrate.
07. And the heaven He raised and imposed the balance
08. That you not transgress within the balance.
09. And establish weight in justice and do not make deficient the balance.
10. And the earth He laid [out] for the creatures.
11. Therein is fruit and palm trees having sheaths [of dates]
12. And grain having husks and scented plants.
13. So which of the favors of your Lord would you deny?
14. He created man from clay like [that of] pottery.
15. And He created the jinn from a smokeless flame of fire.
16. So which of the favors of your Lord would you deny?
17. [He is] Lord of the two sunrises and Lord of the two sunsets.
18. So which of the favors of your Lord would you deny?
19. He released the two seas, meeting [side by side];
20. Between them is a barrier [so] neither of them transgresses.
21. So which of the favors of your Lord would you deny?
22. From both of them emerge pearl and coral.
23. So which of the favors of your Lord would you deny?
24. And to Him belong the ships [with sails] elevated in the sea like mountains.
25. So which of the favors of your Lord would you deny?
26. Everyone upon the earth will perish,
27. And there will remain the Face of your Lord, Owner of Majesty and Honor.
28. So which of the favors of your Lord would you deny?

29. Whoever is within the heavens and earth asks Him; every day He is bringing about a matter.
30. So which of the favors of your Lord would you deny?
31. We will attend to you, O prominent beings.
32. So which of the favors of your Lord would you deny?
33. company of jinn and mankind, if you are able to pass beyond the regions of the heavens and the earth, then pass. You will not pass except by authority [from Allah].
34. So which of the favors of your Lord would you deny?
35. There will be sent upon you a flame of fire and smoke, and you will not defend yourselves.
36. So which of the favors of your Lord would you deny?
37. And when the heaven is split open and becomes rose-colored like oil -
38. So which of the favors of your Lord would you deny? -
39. Then on that Day none will be asked about his sin among men or jinn.
40. So which of the favors of your Lord would you deny?
41. The criminals will be known by their marks, and they will be seized by the forelocks and the feet.
42. So which of the favors of your Lord would you deny?
43. This is Hell, which the criminals deny.
44. They will go around between it and scalding water, heated [to the utmost degree].
45. So which of the favors of your Lord would you deny?
46. But for he who has feared the position of his Lord are two gardens -
47. So which of the favors of your Lord would you deny? -
48. Having [spreading] branches.
49. So which of the favors of your Lord would you deny?
50. In both of them are two springs, flowing.
51. So which of the favors of your Lord would you deny?
52. In both of them are of every fruit, two kinds.
53. So which of the favors of your Lord would you deny?
54. [They are] reclining on beds whose linings are of silk brocade, and the fruit of the two gardens is hanging low.

55. So which of the favors of your Lord would you deny?
56. In them are women limiting [their] glances, untouched before them by man or jinni -
57. So which of the favors of your Lord would you deny? -
58. As if they were rubies and coral.
59. So which of the favors of your Lord would you deny?
60. Is the reward for good [anything] but good?
61. So which of the favors of your Lord would you deny?
62. And below them both [in excellence] are two [other] gardens -
63. So which of the favors of your Lord would you deny? -
64. Dark green [in color].
65. So which of the favors of your Lord would you deny?
66. In both of them are two springs, spouting.
67. So which of the favors of your Lord would you deny?
68. In both of them are fruit and palm trees and pomegranates.
69. So which of the favors of your Lord would you deny?
70. In them are good and beautiful women -
71. So which of the favors of your Lord would you deny? -
72. Fair ones reserved in pavilions -
73. So which of the favors of your Lord would you deny? -
74. Untouched before them by man or jinni -
75. So which of the favors of your Lord would you deny? -
76. Reclining on green cushions and beautiful fine carpets.
77. So which of the favors of your Lord would you deny?
78. Blessed is the name of your Lord, Owner of Majesty and Honor.

Surah 56 Al-Waqi'ah

Verses: 96 — Makki

In the name of Allah, the Entirely Merciful, the Especially Merciful.

01. When the Occurrence occurs,
02. There is, at its occurrence, no denial.
03. It will bring down [some] and raise up [others].
04. When the earth is shaken with convulsion
05. And the mountains are broken down, crumbling
06. And become dust dispersing.

07. And you become [of] three kinds:
08. Then the companions of the right - what are the companions of the right?
09. And the companions of the left - what are the companions of the left?
10. And the forerunners, the forerunners -
11. Those are the ones brought near [to Allah]
12. In the Gardens of Pleasure,
13. A [large] company of the former peoples
14. And a few of the later peoples,
15. On thrones woven [with ornament],
16. Reclining on them, facing each other.
17. There will circulate among them young boys made eternal
18. With vessels, pitchers and a cup [of wine] from a flowing spring -
19. No headache will they have therefrom, nor will they be intoxicated -
20. And fruit of what they select
21. And the meat of fowl, from whatever they desire.
22. And [for them are] fair women with large, [beautiful] eyes,
23. The likenesses of pearls well-protected,
24. As reward for what they used to do.
25. They will not hear therein ill speech or commission of sin -
26. Only a saying: "Peace, peace."
27. The companions of the right - what are the companions of the right?
28. [They will be] among lote trees with thorns removed
29. And [banana] trees layered [with fruit]
30. And shade extended
31. And water poured out
32. And fruit, abundant [and varied],
33. Neither limited [to season] nor forbidden,
34. And [upon] beds raised high.
35. Indeed, We have produced the women of Paradise in a [new] creation
36. And made them virgins,
37. Devoted [to their husbands] and of equal age,

38. For the companions of the right [who are]
39. A company of the former peoples
40. And a company of the later peoples.
41. And the companions of the left - what are the companions of the left?
42. [They will be] in scorching fire and scalding water
43. And a shade of black smoke,
44. Neither cool nor beneficial.
45. Indeed they were, before that, indulging in affluence,
46. And they used to persist in the great violation,
47. And they used to say, "When we die and become dust and bones, are we indeed to be resurrected?
48. And our forefathers [as well]?"
49. Say, [O Muhammad], "Indeed, the former and the later peoples
50. Are to be gathered together for the appointment of a known Day."
51. Then indeed you, O those astray [who are] deniers,
52. Will be eating from trees of zaqqum
53. And filling with it your bellies
54. And drinking on top of it from scalding water
55. And will drink as the drinking of thirsty camels.
56. That is their accommodation on the Day of Recompense.
57. We have created you, so why do you not believe?
58. Have you seen that which you emit?
59. Is it you who creates it, or are We the Creator?
60. We have decreed death among you, and We are not to be outdone
61. In that We will change your likenesses and produce you in that [form] which you do not know.
62. And you have already known the first creation, so will you not remember?
63. And have you seen that [seed] which you sow?
64. Is it you who makes it grow, or are We the grower?
65. If We willed, We could make it [dry] debris, and you would remain in wonder,
66. [Saying], "Indeed, we are [now] in debt;
67. Rather, we have been deprived."

68. And have you seen the water that you drink?
69. Is it you who brought it down from the clouds, or is it We who bring it down?
70. If We willed, We could make it bitter, so why are you not grateful?
71. And have you seen the fire that you ignite?
72. Is it you who produced its tree, or are We the producer?
73. We have made it a reminder and provision for the travelers,
74. So exalt the name of your Lord, the Most Great.
75. Then I swear by the setting of the stars,
76. And indeed, it is an oath - if you could know - [most] great.
77. Indeed, it is a noble Qur'an
78. In a Register well-protected;
79. None touch it except the purified.
80. [It is] a revelation from the Lord of the worlds.
81. Then is it to this statement that you are indifferent
82. And make [the thanks for] your provision that you deny [the Provider]?
83. Then why, when the soul at death reaches the throat
84. And you are at that time looking on -
85. And Our angels are nearer to him than you, but you do not see -
86. Then why do you not, if you are not to be recompensed,
87. Bring it back, if you should be truthful?
88. And if the deceased was of those brought near to Allah,
89. Then [for him is] rest and bounty and a garden of pleasure.
90. And if he was of the companions of the right,
91. Then [the angels will say], "Peace for you; [you are] from the companions of the right."
92. But if he was of the deniers [who were] astray,
93. Then [for him is] accommodation of scalding water
94. And burning in Hellfire
95. Indeed, this is the true certainty,
96. So exalt the name of your Lord, the Most Great.

| Verses: 29 | **Surah 57 Al-Hadid** | Madani |

In the name of Allah, the Entirely Merciful, the Especially Merciful.

01. Whatever is in the heavens and earth exalts Allah, and He is the Exalted in Might, the Wise.

02. His is the dominion of the heavens and earth. He gives life and causes death, and He is over all things competent.

03. He is the First and the Last, the Ascendant and the Intimate, and He is, of all things, Knowing.

04. It is He who created the heavens and earth in six days and then established Himself above the Throne. He knows what penetrates into the earth and what emerges from it and what descends from the heaven and what ascends therein; and He is with you wherever you are. And Allah, of what you do, is Seeing.

05. His is the dominion of the heavens and earth. And to Allah are returned [all] matters.

06. He causes the night to enter the day and causes the day to enter the night, and he is Knowing of that within the breasts.

07. Believe in Allah and His Messenger and spend out of that in which He has made you successors. For those who have believed among you and spent, there will be a great reward.

08. And why do you not believe in Allah while the Messenger invites you to believe in your Lord and He has taken your covenant, if you should [truly] be believers?

09. It is He who sends down upon His Servant [Muhammad] verses of clear evidence that He may bring you out from darknesses into the light. And indeed, Allah is to you Kind and Merciful.

10. And why do you not spend in the cause of Allah while to Allah belongs the heritage of the heavens and the earth? Not equal among you are those who spent before the conquest [of Makkah] and fought [and those who did so after it]. Those are greater in degree than they who spent afterwards and fought. But to all Allah has promised the best [reward]. And Allah, with what you do, is Acquainted.

11. Who is it that would loan Allah a goodly loan so He will multiply it for him and he will have a noble reward?

12. On the Day you see the believing men and believing women, their light proceeding before them and on their right, [it will be

said], "Your good tidings today are [of] gardens beneath which rivers flow, wherein you will abide eternally." That is what is the great attainment.

13. On the [same] Day the hypocrite men and hypocrite women will say to those who believed, "Wait for us that we may acquire some of your light." It will be said, "Go back behind you and seek light." And a wall will be placed between them with a door, its interior containing mercy, but on the outside of it is torment.

14. The hypocrites will call to the believers, "Were we not with you?" They will say, "Yes, but you afflicted yourselves and awaited [misfortune for us] and doubted, and wishful thinking deluded you until there came the command of Allah. And the Deceiver deceived you concerning Allah.

15. So today no ransom will be taken from you or from those who disbelieved. Your refuge is the Fire. It is most worthy of you, and wretched is the destination.

16. Has the time not come for those who have believed that their hearts should become humbly submissive at the remembrance of Allah and what has come down of the truth? And let them not be like those who were given the Scripture before, and a long period passed over them, so their hearts hardened; and many of them are defiantly disobedient.

17. Know that Allah gives life to the earth after its lifelessness. We have made clear to you the signs; perhaps you will understand.

18. Indeed, the men who practice charity and the women who practice charity and [they who] have loaned Allah a goodly loan - it will be multiplied for them, and they will have a noble reward.

19. And those who have believed in Allah and His messengers - those are [in the ranks of] the supporters of truth and the martyrs, with their Lord. For them is their reward and their light. But those who have disbelieved and denied Our verses - those are the companions of Hellfire.

20. Know that the life of this world is but amusement and diversion and adornment and boasting to one another and competition in increase of wealth and children - like the example of a rain whose [resulting] plant growth pleases the tillers; then it dries and you see it turned yellow; then it becomes [scattered] debris. And in the Hereafter is severe punishment and forgiveness from Allah and approval. And what is the worldly life except the enjoyment of delusion.

21. Race toward forgiveness from your Lord and a Garden whose width is like the width of the heavens and earth, prepared for those who believed in Allah and His messengers. That is the bounty of Allah which He gives to whom He wills, and Allah is the possessor of great bounty.

22. No disaster strikes upon the earth or among yourselves except that it is in a register before We bring it into being - indeed that, for Allah, is easy -

23. In order that you not despair over what has eluded you and not exult [in pride] over what He has given you. And Allah does not like everyone self-deluded and boastful -

24. [Those] who are stingy and enjoin upon people stinginess. And whoever turns away - then indeed, Allah is the Free of need, the Praiseworthy.

25. We have already sent Our messengers with clear evidences and sent down with them the Scripture and the balance that the people may maintain [their affairs] in justice. And We sent down iron, wherein is great military might and benefits for the people, and so that Allah may make evident those who support Him and His messengers unseen. Indeed, Allah is Powerful and Exalted in Might.

26. And We have already sent Noah and Abraham and placed in their descendants prophethood and scripture; and among them is he who is guided, but many of them are defiantly disobedient.

27. Then We sent following their footsteps Our messengers and followed [them] with Jesus, the son of Mary, and gave him the Gospel. And We placed in the hearts of those who followed him compassion and mercy and monasticism, which they innovated; We did not prescribe it for them except [that they did so] seeking the approval of Allah. But they did not observe it with due observance. So We gave the ones who believed among them their reward, but many of them are defiantly disobedient.

28. O you who have believed, fear Allah and believe in His Messenger; He will [then] give you a double portion of His mercy and make for you a light by which you will walk and forgive you; and Allah is Forgiving and Merciful.

29. [This is] so that the People of the Scripture may know that they are not able [to obtain] anything from the bounty of Allah and that [all] bounty is in the hand of Allah; He gives it to whom He wills. And Allah is the possessor of great bounty.

| Verses: 22 | **Surah 58 Al-Mujaadilah** | Madani |

In the name of Allah, the Entirely Merciful, the Especially Merciful.

01. Certainly has Allah heard the speech of the one who argues with you, [O Muhammad], concerning her husband and directs her complaint to Allah. And Allah hears your dialogue; indeed, Allah is Hearing and Seeing.

02. Those who pronounce thihar among you [to separate] from their wives - they are not [consequently] their mothers. Their mothers are none but those who gave birth to them. And indeed, they are saying an objectionable statement and a falsehood. But indeed, Allah is Pardoning and Forgiving.

03. And those who pronounce thihar from their wives and then [wish to] go back on what they said - then [there must be] the freeing of a slave before they touch one another. That is what you are admonished thereby; and Allah is Acquainted with what you do.

04. And he who does not find [a slave] - then a fast for two months consecutively before they touch one another; and he who is unable - then the feeding of sixty poor persons. That is for you to believe [completely] in Allah and His Messenger; and those are the limits [set by] Allah. And for the disbelievers is a painful punishment.

05. Indeed, those who oppose Allah and His Messenger are abased as those before them were abased. And We have certainly sent down verses of clear evidence. And for the disbelievers is a humiliating punishment.

06. On the Day when Allah will resurrect them all and inform them of what they did. Allah had enumerated it, while they forgot it; and Allah is, over all things, Witness.

07. Have you not considered that Allah knows what is in the heavens and what is on the earth? There is in no private conversation three but that He is the fourth of them, nor are there five but that He is the sixth of them - and no less than that and no more except that He is with them [in knowledge] wherever they are. Then He will inform them of what they did, on the Day of Resurrection. Indeed Allah is, of all things, Knowing.

08. Have you not considered those who were forbidden from private conversation, then they return to that which they were forbidden and converse among themselves about sin and aggression and disobedience to the Messenger? And when they come to you, they greet you with that [word] by which Allah does not greet

you and say among themselves, "Why does Allah not punish us for what we say?" Sufficient for them is Hell, which they will [enter to] burn, and wretched is the destination.

09. O you who have believed, when you converse privately, do not converse about sin and aggression and disobedience to the Messenger but converse about righteousness and piety. And fear Allah, to whom you will be gathered.

10. Private conversation is only from Satan that he may grieve those who have believed, but he will not harm them at all except by permission of Allah. And upon Allah let the believers rely.

11. O you who have believed, when you are told, "Space yourselves" in assemblies, then make space; Allah will make space for you. And when you are told, "Arise," then arise; Allah will raise those who have believed among you and those who were given knowledge, by degrees. And Allah is Acquainted with what you do.

12. O you who have believed, when you [wish to] privately consult the Messenger, present before your consultation a charity. That is better for you and purer. But if you find not [the means] - then indeed, Allah is Forgiving and Merciful.

13. Have you feared to present before your consultation charities? Then when you do not and Allah has forgiven you, then [at least] establish prayer and give zakah and obey Allah and His Messenger. And Allah is Acquainted with what you do.

14. Have you not considered those who make allies of a people with whom Allah has become angry? They are neither of you nor of them, and they swear to untruth while they know [they are lying].

15. Allah has prepared for them a severe punishment. Indeed, it was evil that they were doing.

16. They took their [false] oaths as a cover, so they averted [people] from the way of Allah, and for them is a humiliating punishment.

17. Never will their wealth or their children avail them against Allah at all. Those are the companions of the Fire; they will abide therein eternally

18. On the Day Allah will resurrect them all, and they will swear to Him as they swear to you and think that they are [standing] on something. Unquestionably, it is they who are the liars.

19. Satan has overcome them and made them forget the remembrance of Allah. Those are the party of Satan.

Unquestionably, the party of Satan - they will be the losers.

20. Indeed, the ones who oppose Allah and His Messenger - those will be among the most humbled.

21. Allah has written, "I will surely overcome, I and My messengers." Indeed, Allah is Powerful and Exalted in Might.

22. You will not find a people who believe in Allah and the Last Day having affection for those who oppose Allah and His Messenger, even if they were their fathers or their sons or their brothers or their kindred. Those - He has decreed within their hearts faith and supported them with spirit from Him. And We will admit them to gardens beneath which rivers flow, wherein they abide eternally. Allah is pleased with them, and they are pleased with Him - those are the party of Allah. Unquestionably, the party of Allah - they are the successful.

Surah 59 Al-Hashr

Verses: 24 — Madani

In the name of Allah, the Entirely Merciful, the Especially Merciful.

01. Whatever is in the heavens and whatever is on the earth exalts Allah, and He is the Exalted in Might, the Wise.

02. It is He who expelled the ones who disbelieved among the People of the Scripture from their homes at the first gathering. You did not think they would leave, and they thought that their fortresses would protect them from Allah; but [the decree of] Allah came upon them from where they had not expected, and He cast terror into their hearts [so] they destroyed their houses by their [own] hands and the hands of the believers. So take warning, O people of vision.

03. And if not that Allah had decreed for them evacuation, He would have punished them in [this] world, and for them in the Hereafter is the punishment of the Fire.

04. That is because they opposed Allah and His Messenger. And whoever opposes Allah - then indeed, Allah is severe in penalty.

05. Whatever you have cut down of [their] palm trees or left standing on their trunks - it was by permission of Allah and so He would disgrace the defiantly disobedient.

06. And what Allah restored [of property] to His Messenger from them - you did not spur for it [in an expedition] any horses or camels, but Allah gives His messengers power over whom He wills, and Allah is over all things competent.

07. And what Allah restored to His Messenger from the people of the towns - it is for Allah and for the Messenger and for [his] near relatives and orphans and the [stranded] traveler - so that it will not be a perpetual distribution among the rich from among you. And whatever the Messenger has given you - take; and what he has forbidden you - refrain from. And fear Allah; indeed, Allah is severe in penalty.

08. For the poor emigrants who were expelled from their homes and their properties, seeking bounty from Allah and [His] approval and supporting Allah and His Messenger, [there is also a share]. Those are the truthful.

09. And [also for] those who were settled in al-Madinah and [adopted] the faith before them. They love those who emigrated to them and find not any want in their breasts of what the emigrants were given but give [them] preference over themselves, even though they are in privation. And whoever is protected from the stinginess of his soul - it is those who will be the successful.

10. And [there is a share for] those who came after them, saying, "Our Lord, forgive us and our brothers who preceded us in faith and put not in our hearts [any] resentment toward those who have believed. Our Lord, indeed You are Kind and Merciful."

11. Have you not considered those who practice hypocrisy, saying to their brothers who have disbelieved among the People of the Scripture, "If you are expelled, we will surely leave with you, and we will not obey, in regard to you, anyone - ever; and if you are fought, we will surely aid you." But Allah testifies that they are liars.

12. If they are expelled, they will not leave with them, and if they are fought, they will not aid them. And [even] if they should aid them, they will surely turn their backs; then [thereafter] they will not be aided.

13. You [believers] are more fearful within their breasts than Allah. That is because they are a people who do not understand.

14. They will not fight you all except within fortified cities or from behind walls. Their violence among themselves is severe. You think they are together, but their hearts are diverse. That is because they are a people who do not reason.

15. [Theirs is] like the example of those shortly before them: they tasted the bad consequence of their affair, and they will have a painful punishment.

16. [The hypocrites are] like the example of Satan when he says to man, "Disbelieve." But when he disbelieves, he says, "Indeed, I am disassociated from you. Indeed, I fear Allah, Lord of the worlds."

17. So the outcome for both of them is that they will be in the Fire, abiding eternally therein. And that is the recompense of the wrong-doers.

18. O you who have believed, fear Allah. And let every soul look to what it has put forth for tomorrow - and fear Allah. Indeed, Allah is Acquainted with what you do.

19. And be not like those who forgot Allah, so He made them forget themselves. Those are the defiantly disobedient.

20. Not equal are the companions of the Fire and the companions of Paradise. The companions of Paradise - they are the attainers [of success].

21. If We had sent down this Qur'an upon a mountain, you would have seen it humbled and coming apart from fear of Allah. And these examples We present to the people that perhaps they will give thought.

22. He is Allah, other than whom there is no deity, Knower of the unseen and the witnessed. He is the Entirely Merciful, the Especially Merciful.

23. He is Allah, other than whom there is no deity, the Sovereign, the Pure, the Perfection, the Bestower of Faith, the Overseer, the Exalted in Might, the Compeller, the Superior. Exalted is Allah above whatever they associate with Him.

24. He is Allah, the Creator, the Inventor, the Fashioner; to Him belong the best names. Whatever is in the heavens and earth is exalting Him. And He is the Exalted in Might, the Wise.

| Verses: 13 | **Surah 60 Al-Mumtahanah** | Madani |

In the name of Allah, the Entirely Merciful, the Especially Merciful.

01. O you who have believed, do not take My enemies and your enemies as allies, extending to them affection while they have disbelieved in what came to you of the truth, having driven out the Prophet and yourselves [only] because you believe in Allah, your Lord. If you have come out for jihad in My cause and seeking means to My approval, [take them not as friends]. You confide to them affection, but I am most knowing of what you have concealed and what you have declared. And whoever does it among you has

certainly strayed from the soundness of the way.

02. If they gain dominance over you, they would be to you as enemies and extend against you their hands and their tongues with evil, and they wish you would disbelieve.

03. Never will your relatives or your children benefit you; the Day of Resurrection He will judge between you. And Allah, of what you do, is Seeing.

04. There has already been for you an excellent pattern in Abraham and those with him, when they said to their people, "Indeed, we are disassociated from you and from whatever you worship other than Allah. We have denied you, and there has appeared between us and you animosity and hatred forever until you believe in Allah alone" except for the saying of Abraham to his father, "I will surely ask forgiveness for you, but I have not [power to do] for you anything against Allah. Our Lord, upon You we have relied, and to You we have returned, and to You is the destination.

05. Our Lord, make us not [objects of] torment for the disbelievers and forgive us, our Lord. Indeed, it is You who is the Exalted in Might, the Wise."

06. There has certainly been for you in them an excellent pattern for anyone whose hope is in Allah and the Last Day. And whoever turns away - then indeed, Allah is the Free of need, the Praiseworthy.

07. Perhaps Allah will put, between you and those to whom you have been enemies among them, affection. And Allah is competent, and Allah is Forgiving and Merciful.

08. Allah does not forbid you from those who do not fight you because of religion and do not expel you from your homes - from being righteous toward them and acting justly toward them. Indeed, Allah loves those who act justly.

09. Allah only forbids you from those who fight you because of religion and expel you from your homes and aid in your expulsion - [forbids] that you make allies of them. And whoever makes allies of them, then it is those who are the wrongdoers.

10. O you who have believed, when the believing women come to you as emigrants, examine them. Allah is most knowing as to their faith. And if you know them to be believers, then do not return them to the disbelievers; they are not lawful [wives] for them, nor are they lawful [husbands] for them. But give the

disbelievers what they have spent. And there is no blame upon you if you marry them when you have given them their due compensation. And hold not to marriage bonds with disbelieving women, but ask for what you have spent and let them ask for what they have spent. That is the judgement of Allah; He judges between you. And Allah is Knowing and Wise.

11. And if you have lost any of your wives to the disbelievers and you subsequently obtain [something], then give those whose wives have gone the equivalent of what they had spent. And fear Allah, in whom you are believers.

12. O Prophet, when the believing women come to you pledging to you that they will not associate anything with Allah, nor will they steal, nor will they commit unlawful sexual intercourse, nor will they kill their children, nor will they bring forth a slander they have invented between their arms and legs, nor will they disobey you in what is right - then accept their pledge and ask forgiveness for them of Allah. Indeed, Allah is Forgiving and Merciful.

13. O you who have believed, do not make allies of a people with whom Allah has become angry. They have despaired of [reward in] the Hereafter just as the disbelievers have despaired of [meeting] the inhabitants of the graves.

| Verses: 14 | **Surah 61 As-Saff** | Madani |

In the name of Allah, the Entirely Merciful, the Especially Merciful.

01. Whatever is in the heavens and whatever is on the earth exalts Allah, and He is the Exalted in Might, the Wise.

02. O you who have believed, why do you say what you do not do?

03. Great is hatred in the sight of Allah that you say what you do not do.

04. Indeed, Allah loves those who fight in His cause in a row as though they are a [single] structure joined firmly.

05. And [mention, O Muhammad], when Moses said to his people, "O my people, why do you harm me while you certainly know that I am the messenger of Allah to you?" And when they deviated, Allah caused their hearts to deviate. And Allah does not guide the defiantly disobedient people.

06. And [mention] when Jesus, the son of Mary, said, "O children of Israel, indeed I am the messenger of Allah to you confirming what came before me of the Torah and bringing good tidings of a messenger to come after me, whose name

is Ahmad." But when he came to them with clear evidences, they said, "This is obvious magic."

07. And who is more unjust than one who invents about Allah untruth while he is being invited to Islam. And Allah does not guide the wrongdoing people.

08. They want to extinguish the light of Allah with their mouths, but Allah will perfect His light, although the disbelievers dislike it.

09. It is He who sent His Messenger with guidance and the religion of truth to manifest it over all religion, although those who associate others with Allah dislike it.

10. O you who have believed, shall I guide you to a transaction that will save you from a painful punishment?

11. [It is that] you believe in Allah and His Messenger and strive in the cause of Allah with your wealth and your lives. That is best for you, if you should know.

12. He will forgive for you your sins and admit you to gardens beneath which rivers flow and pleasant dwellings in gardens of perpetual residence. That is the great attainment.

13. And [you will obtain] another [favor] that you love - victory from Allah and an imminent conquest; and give good tidings to the believers.

14. O you who have believed, be supporters of Allah, as when Jesus, the son of Mary, said to the disciples, "Who are my supporters for Allah?" The disciples said, "We are supporters of Allah." And a faction of the Children of Israel believed and a faction disbelieved. So We supported those who believed against their enemy, and they became dominant.

| Verses: 11 | Surah 62 Al-Jumu'ah | Madani |

In the name of Allah, the Entirely Merciful, the Especially Merciful.

01. Whatever is in the heavens and whatever is on the earth is exalting Allah, the Sovereign, the Pure, the Exalted in Might, the Wise.

02. It is He who has sent among the unlettered a Messenger from themselves reciting to them His verses and purifying them and teaching them the Book and wisdom - although they were before in clear error -

03. And [to] others of them who have not yet joined them. And He is the Exalted in Might, the Wise.

04. That is the bounty of Allah, which He gives to whom He wills,

and Allah is the possessor of great bounty.

05. The example of those who were entrusted with the Torah and then did not take it on is like that of a donkey who carries volumes [of books]. Wretched is the example of the people who deny the signs of Allah. And Allah does not guide the wrongdoing people.

06. Say, "O you who are Jews, if you claim that you are allies of Allah, excluding the [other] people, then wish for death, if you should be truthful."

07. But they will not wish for it, ever, because of what their hands have put forth. And Allah is Knowing of the wrongdoers.

08. Say, "Indeed, the death from which you flee - indeed, it will meet you. Then you will be returned to the Knower of the unseen and the witnessed, and He will inform you about what you used to do."

09. O you who have believed, when [the adhan] is called for the prayer on the day of Jumu'ah [Friday], then proceed to the remembrance of Allah and leave trade. That is better for you, if you only knew.

10. And when the prayer has been concluded, disperse within the land and seek from the bounty of Allah, and remember Allah often that you may succeed.

11. But when they saw a transaction or a diversion, [O Muhammad], they rushed to it and left you standing. Say, "What is with Allah is better than diversion and than a transaction, and Allah is the best of providers."

| Verses: 11 | **Surah 63 Al-Munafiqoon** | Madani |

In the name of Allah, the Entirely Merciful, the Especially Merciful.

01. When the hypocrites come to you, [O Muhammad], they say, "We testify that you are the Messenger of Allah." And Allah knows that you are His Messenger, and Allah testifies that the hypocrites are liars.

02. They have taken their oaths as a cover, so they averted [people] from the way of Allah. Indeed, it was evil that they were doing.

03. That is because they believed, and then they disbelieved; so their hearts were sealed over, and they do not understand.

04. And when you see them, their forms please you, and if they speak, you listen to their speech. [They are] as if they were

pieces of wood propped up - they think that every shout is against them. They are the enemy, so beware of them. May Allah destroy them; how are they deluded?

05. And when it is said to them, "Come, the Messenger of Allah will ask forgiveness for you," they turn their heads aside and you see them evading while they are arrogant.

06. It is all the same for them whether you ask forgiveness for them or do not ask forgiveness for them; never will Allah forgive them. Indeed, Allah does not guide the defiantly disobedient people.

07. They are the ones who say, "Do not spend on those who are with the Messenger of Allah until they disband." And to Allah belongs the depositories of the heavens and the earth, but the hypocrites do not understand.

08. They say, "If we return to al-Madinah, the more honored [for power] will surely expel therefrom the more humble." And to Allah belongs [all] honor, and to His Messenger, and to the believers, but the hypocrites do not know.

09. O you who have believed, let not your wealth and your children divert you from remembrance of Allah. And whoever does that - then those are the losers.

10. And spend [in the way of Allah] from what We have provided you before death approaches one of you and he says, "My Lord, if only You would delay me for a brief term so I would give charity and be among the righteous."

11. But never will Allah delay a soul when its time has come. And Allah is Acquainted with what you do.

Surah 64 At-Taghabun

Verses: 18 | Madani

In the name of Allah, the Entirely Merciful, the Especially Merciful.

01. Whatever is in the heavens and whatever is on the earth is exalting Allah. To Him belongs dominion, and to Him belongs [all] praise, and He is over all things competent.

02. It is He who created you, and among you is the disbeliever, and among you is the believer. And Allah, of what you do, is Seeing.

03. He created the heavens and earth in truth and formed you and perfected your forms; and to Him is the [final] destination.

04. He knows what is within the heavens and earth and knows what you conceal and what you declare. And Allah is Knowing of that within the breasts.

05. Has there not come to you the news of those who disbelieved before? So they tasted the bad consequence of their affair, and they will have a painful punishment.

06. That is because their messengers used to come to them with clear evidences, but they said, "Shall human beings guide us?" and disbelieved and turned away. And Allah dispensed [with them]; and Allah is Free of need and Praiseworthy.

07. Those who disbelieve have claimed that they will never be resurrected. Say, "Yes, by my Lord, you will surely be resurrected; then you will surely be informed of what you did. And that, for Allah, is easy."

08. So believe in Allah and His Messenger and the Qur'an which We have sent down. And Allah is Acquainted with what you do.

09. The Day He will assemble you for the Day of Assembly - that is the Day of Deprivation. And whoever believes in Allah and does righteousness - He will remove from him his misdeeds and admit him to gardens beneath which rivers flow, wherein they will abide forever. That is the great attainment.

10. But the ones who disbelieved and denied Our verses - those are the companions of the Fire, abiding eternally therein; and wretched is the destination.

11. No disaster strikes except by permission of Allah. And whoever believes in Allah - He will guide his heart. And Allah is Knowing of all things.

12. And obey Allah and obey the Messenger; but if you turn away - then upon Our Messenger is only [the duty of] clear notification.

13. Allah - there is no deity except Him. And upon Allah let the believers rely.

14. O you who have believed, indeed, among your wives and your children are enemies to you, so beware of them. But if you pardon and overlook and forgive - then indeed, Allah is Forgiving and Merciful.

15. Your wealth and your children are but a trial, and Allah has with Him a great reward.

16. So fear Allah as much as you are able and listen and obey and spend [in the way of Allah]; it is better for your selves. And whoever is protected from the stinginess of his soul - it is those who will be the successful.

17. If you loan Allah a goodly loan, He will multiply it for you and forgive you. And Allah is Most Appreciative and Forbearing.

18. Knower of the unseen and the witnessed, the Exalted in Might, the Wise.

Surah 65 At-Talaaq

Verses: 12 — Madani

In the name of Allah, the Entirely Merciful, the Especially Merciful.

01. O Prophet, when you [Muslims] divorce women, divorce them for [the commencement of] their waiting period and keep count of the waiting period, and fear Allah, your Lord. Do not turn them out of their [husbands'] houses, nor should they [themselves] leave [during that period] unless they are committing a clear immorality. And those are the limits [set by] Allah. And whoever transgresses the limits of Allah has certainly wronged himself. You know not; perhaps Allah will bring about after that a [different] matter.

02. And when they have [nearly] fulfilled their term, either retain them according to acceptable terms or part with them according to acceptable terms. And bring to witness two just men from among you and establish the testimony for [the acceptance of] Allah. That is instructed to whoever should believe in Allah and the Last day. And whoever fears Allah - He will make for him a way out

03. And will provide for him from where he does not expect. And whoever relies upon Allah - then He is sufficient for him. Indeed, Allah will accomplish His purpose. Allah has already set for everything a [decreed] extent.

04. And those who no longer expect menstruation among your women - if you doubt, then their period is three months, and [also for] those who have not menstruated. And for those who are pregnant, their term is until they give birth. And whoever fears Allah - He will make for him of his matter ease.

05. That is the command of Allah, which He has sent down to you; and whoever fears Allah - He will remove for him his misdeeds and make great for him his reward.

06. Lodge them [in a section] of where you dwell out of your means and do not harm them in order to oppress them. And if they should be pregnant, then spend on them until they give birth. And if they breastfeed for you, then give them their payment and confer among yourselves in the acceptable way; but if you are in discord, then there may breastfeed for the father another woman.

07. Let a man of wealth spend from his wealth, and he whose provision is restricted - let him spend from what Allah has given him. Allah does not charge a soul except [according to] what He has given it. Allah will bring about, after hardship, ease.

08. And how many a city was insolent toward the command of its Lord and His messengers, so We took it to severe account and punished it with a terrible punishment.

09. And it tasted the bad consequence of its affair, and the outcome of its affair was loss.

10. Allah has prepared for them a severe punishment; so fear Allah, O you of understanding who have believed. Allah has sent down to you the Qur'an.

11. [He sent] a Messenger [Muhammad] reciting to you the distinct verses of Allah that He may bring out those who believe and do righteous deeds from darknesses into the light. And whoever believes in Allah and does righteousness - He will admit him into gardens beneath which rivers flow to abide therein forever. Allah will have perfected for him a provision.

12. It is Allah who has created seven heavens and of the earth, the like of them. [His] command descends among them so you may know that Allah is over all things competent and that Allah has encompassed all things in knowledge.

Surah 66 At-Tahrim

Verses: 12 — Madani

In the name of Allah, the Entirely Merciful, the Especially Merciful.

01. O Prophet, why do you prohibit [yourself from] what Allah has made lawful for you, seeking the approval of your wives? And Allah is Forgiving and Merciful.

02. Allah has already ordained for you [Muslims] the dissolution of your oaths. And Allah is your protector, and He is the Knowing, the Wise.

03. And [remember] when the Prophet confided to one of his wives a statement; and when she informed [another] of it and Allah showed it to him, he made known part of it and ignored a part. And when he informed her about it, she said, "Who told you this?" He said, "I was informed by the Knowing, the Acquainted."

04. If you two [wives] repent to Allah, [it is best], for your hearts have deviated. But if you cooperate against him - then indeed Allah is

his protector, and Gabriel and the righteous of the believers and the angels, moreover, are [his] assistants.

05. Perhaps his Lord, if he divorced you [all], would substitute for him wives better than you - submitting [to Allah], believing, devoutly obedient, repentant, worshipping, and traveling - [ones] previously married and virgins.

06. O you who have believed, protect yourselves and your families from a Fire whose fuel is people and stones, over which are [appointed] angels, harsh and severe; they do not disobey Allah in what He commands them but do what they are commanded.

07. O you who have disbelieved, make no excuses that Day. You will only be recompensed for what you used to do.

08. O you who have believed, repent to Allah with sincere repentance. Perhaps your Lord will remove from you your misdeeds and admit you into gardens beneath which rivers flow [on] the Day when Allah will not disgrace the Prophet and those who believed with him. Their light will proceed before them and on their right; they will say, "Our Lord, perfect for us our light and forgive us. Indeed, You are over all things competent."

09. O Prophet, strive against the disbelievers and the hypocrites and be harsh upon them. And their refuge is Hell, and wretched is the destination.

10. Allah presents an example of those who disbelieved: the wife of Noah and the wife of Lot. They were under two of Our righteous servants but betrayed them, so those prophets did not avail them from Allah at all, and it was said, "Enter the Fire with those who enter."

11. And Allah presents an example of those who believed: the wife of Pharaoh, when she said, "My Lord, build for me near You a house in Paradise and save me from Pharaoh and his deeds and save me from the wrongdoing people."

12. And [the example of] Mary, the daughter of 'Imran, who guarded her chastity, so We blew into [her garment] through Our angel, and she believed in the words of her Lord and His scriptures and was of the devoutly obedient.

| Verses: 30 | **Surah 67 Al-Mulk** | Makki |

In the name of Allah, the Entirely Merciful, the Especially Merciful.

01. Blessed is He in whose hand is dominion, and He is over all things competent -

02. [He] who created death and life to test you [as to] which of you is best in deed - and He is the Exalted in Might, the Forgiving -

03. [And] who created seven heavens in layers. You do not see in the creation of the Most Merciful any inconsistency. So return [your] vision [to the sky]; do you see any breaks?

04. Then return [your] vision twice again. [Your] vision will return to you humbled while it is fatigued.

05. And We have certainly beautified the nearest heaven with stars and have made [from] them what is thrown at the devils and have prepared for them the punishment of the Blaze.

06. And for those who disbelieved in their Lord is the punishment of Hell, and wretched is the destination.

07. When they are thrown into it, they hear from it a [dreadful] inhaling while it boils up.

08. It almost bursts with rage. Every time a company is thrown into it, its keepers ask them, "Did there not come to you a warner?"

09. They will say," Yes, a warner had come to us, but we denied and said, 'Allah has not sent down anything. You are not but in great error.'"

10. And they will say, "If only we had been listening or reasoning, we would not be among the companions of the Blaze."

11. And they will admit their sin, so [it is] alienation for the companions of the Blaze.

12. Indeed, those who fear their Lord unseen will have forgiveness and great reward.

13. And conceal your speech or publicize it; indeed, He is Knowing of that within the breasts.

14. Does He who created not know, while He is the Subtle, the Acquainted?

15. It is He who made the earth tame for you - so walk among its slopes and eat of His provision - and to Him is the resurrection.

16. Do you feel secure that He who [holds authority] in the heaven would not cause the earth to swallow you and suddenly it would sway?

17. Or do you feel secure that He who [holds authority] in the heaven would not send against you a storm of stones? Then you would know how [severe] was My warning.

18. And already had those before them denied, and how [terrible] was My reproach.

19. Do they not see the birds above them with wings outspread and [sometimes] folded in? None holds them [aloft] except the Most Merciful. Indeed He is, of all things, Seeing.

20. Or who is it that could be an army for you to aid you other than the Most Merciful? The disbelievers are not but in delusion.

21. Or who is it that could provide for you if He withheld His provision? But they have persisted in insolence and aversion.

22. Then is one who walks fallen on his face better guided or one who walks erect on a straight path?

23. Say, "It is He who has produced you and made for you hearing and vision and hearts; little are you grateful."

24. Say, "It is He who has multiplied you throughout the earth, and to Him you will be gathered."

25. And they say, "When is this promise, if you should be truthful?"

26. Say, "The knowledge is only with Allah, and I am only a clear warner."

27. But when they see it approaching, the faces of those who disbelieve will be distressed, and it will be said, "This is that for which you used to call."

28. Say, [O Muhammad], "Have you considered: whether Allah should cause my death and those with me or have mercy upon us, who can protect the disbelievers from a painful punishment?"

29. Say, "He is the Most Merciful; we have believed in Him, and upon Him we have relied. And you will [come to] know who it is that is in clear error."

30. Say, "Have you considered: if your water was to become sunken [into the earth], then who could bring you flowing water?"

| Verses: 52 | **Surah 68 Al-Qalam** | Makki |

In the name of Allah, the Entirely Merciful, the Especially Merciful.

01. Nun. By the pen and what they inscribe,
02. You are not, [O Muhammad], by the favor of your Lord, a madman.
03. And indeed, for you is a reward uninterrupted.
04. And indeed, you are of a great moral character.
05. So you will see and they will see
06. Which of you is the afflicted [by a devil].
07. Indeed, your Lord is most knowing of who has gone astray from His way, and He is most knowing of the [rightly] guided.
08. Then do not obey the deniers.
09. They wish that you would soften [in your position], so they would soften [toward you].
10. And do not obey every worthless habitual swearer
11. [And] scorner, going about with malicious gossip -
12. A preventer of good, transgressing and sinful,
13. Cruel, moreover, and an illegitimate pretender.
14. Because he is a possessor of wealth and children,
15. When Our verses are recited to him, he says, "Legends of the former peoples."
16. We will brand him upon the snout.
17. Indeed, We have tried them as We tried the companions of the garden, when they swore to cut its fruit in the [early] morning
18. Without making exception.
19. So there came upon the garden an affliction from your Lord while they were asleep.
20. And it became as though reaped.
21. And they called one another at morning,
22. [Saying], "Go early to your crop if you would cut the fruit."
23. So they set out, while lowering their voices,
24. [Saying], "There will surely not enter it today upon you [any] poor person."
25. And they went early in determination, [assuming themselves] able.
26. But when they saw it, they said, "Indeed, we are lost;

27. Rather, we have been deprived."
28. The most moderate of them said, "Did I not say to you, 'Why do you not exalt [Allah]?' "
29. They said, "Exalted is our Lord! Indeed, we were wrongdoers."
30. Then they approached one another, blaming each other.
31. They said, "O woe to us; indeed we were transgressors.
32. Perhaps our Lord will substitute for us [one] better than it. Indeed, we are toward our Lord desirous."
33. Such is the punishment [of this world]. And the punishment of the Hereafter is greater, if they only knew.
34. Indeed, for the righteous with their Lord are the Gardens of Pleasure.
35. Then will We treat the Muslims like the criminals?
36. What is [the matter] with you? How do you judge?
37. Or do you have a scripture in which you learn
38. That indeed for you is whatever you choose?
39. Or do you have oaths [binding] upon Us, extending until the Day of Resurrection, that indeed for you is whatever you judge?
40. Ask them which of them, for that [claim], is responsible.
41. Or do they have partners? Then let them bring their partners, if they should be truthful.
42. The Day the shin will be uncovered and they are invited to prostration but the disbelievers will not be able,
43. Their eyes humbled, humiliation will cover them. And they used to be invited to prostration while they were sound.
44. So leave Me, [O Muhammad], with [the matter of] whoever denies the Qur'an. We will progressively lead them [to punishment] from where they do not know.
45. And I will give them time. Indeed, My plan is firm.
46. Or do you ask of them a payment, so they are by debt burdened down?
47. Or have they [knowledge of] the unseen, so they write [it] down?
48. Then be patient for the decision of your Lord, [O Muhammad], and be not like the companion of the fish when he called out while he was distressed.
49. If not that a favor from his Lord overtook him, he would have been thrown onto the naked shore while he was censured.

50. And his Lord chose him and made him of the righteous.
51. And indeed, those who disbelieve would almost make you slip with their eyes when they hear the message, and they say, "Indeed, he is mad."
52. But it is not except a reminder to the worlds.

| Verses: 52 | Surah 69 Al-Haaqqah | Makki |

In the name of Allah, the Entirely Merciful, the Especially Merciful.

01. The Inevitable Reality -
02. What is the Inevitable Reality?
03. And what can make you know what is the Inevitable Reality?
04. Thamud and 'Aad denied the Striking Calamity.
05. So as for Thamud, they were destroyed by the overpowering [blast].
06. And as for 'Aad, they were destroyed by a screaming, violent wind
07. Which Allah imposed upon them for seven nights and eight days in succession, so you would see the people therein fallen as if they were hollow trunks of palm trees.
08. Then do you see of them any remains?
09. And there came Pharaoh and those before him and the overturned cities with sin.
10. And they disobeyed the messenger of their Lord, so He seized them with a seizure exceeding [in severity].
11. Indeed, when the water overflowed, We carried your ancestors in the sailing ship
12. That We might make it for you a reminder and [that] a conscious ear would be conscious of it.
13. Then when the Horn is blown with one blast
14. And the earth and the mountains are lifted and leveled with one blow-
15. Then on that Day, the Resurrection will occur,
16. And the heaven will split [open], for that Day it is infirm.
17. And the angels are at its edges. And there will bear the Throne of your Lord above them, that Day, eight [of them].
18. That Day, you will be exhibited [for judgement]; not hidden among you is anything concealed.
19. So as for he who is given his record in his right hand, he will say, "Here, read my record!

20. Indeed, I was certain that I would be meeting my account."
21. So he will be in a pleasant life -
22. In an elevated garden,
23. Its [fruit] to be picked hanging near.
24. [They will be told], "Eat and drink in satisfaction for what you put forth in the days past."
25. But as for he who is given his record in his left hand, he will say, "Oh, I wish I had not been given my record
26. And had not known what is my account.
27. I wish my death had been the decisive one.
28. My wealth has not availed me.
29. Gone from me is my authority."
30. [Allah will say], "Seize him and shackle him.
31. Then into Hellfire drive him.
32. Then into a chain whose length is seventy cubits insert him."
33. Indeed, he did not used to believe in Allah, the Most Great,
34. Nor did he encourage the feeding of the poor.
35. So there is not for him here this Day any devoted friend
36. Nor any food except from the discharge of wounds;
37. None will eat it except the sinners.
38. So I swear by what you see
39. And what you do not see
40. [That] indeed, the Qur'an is the word of a noble Messenger.
41. And it is not the word of a poet; little do you believe.
42. Nor the word of a soothsayer; little do you remember.
43. [It is] a revelation from the Lord of the worlds.
44. And if Muhammad had made up about Us some [false] sayings,
45. We would have seized him by the right hand;
46. Then We would have cut from him the aorta.
47. And there is no one of you who could prevent [Us] from him.
48. And indeed, the Qur'an is a reminder for the righteous.
49. And indeed, We know that among you are deniers.

50. And indeed, it will be [a cause of] regret upon the disbelievers.
51. And indeed, it is the truth of certainty.
52. So exalt the name of your Lord, the Most Great.

| Verses: 44 | **Surah 70 Al-Ma'aarij** | Makki |

In the name of Allah, the Entirely Merciful, the Especially Merciful.

01. A supplicant asked for a punishment bound to happen
02. To the disbelievers; of it there is no preventer.
03. [It is] from Allah, owner of the ways of ascent.
04. The angels and the Spirit will ascend to Him during a Day the extent of which is fifty thousand years.
05. So be patient with gracious patience.
06. Indeed, they see it [as] distant,
07. But We see it [as] near.
08. On the Day the sky will be like murky oil,
09. And the mountains will be like wool,
10. And no friend will ask [anything of] a friend,
11. They will be shown each other. The criminal will wish that he could be ransomed from the punishment of that Day by his children
12. And his wife and his brother
13. And his nearest kindred who shelter him
14. And whoever is on earth entirely [so] then it could save him.
15. No! Indeed, it is the Flame [of Hell],
16. A remover of exteriors.
17. It invites he who turned his back [on truth] and went away [from obedience]
18. And collected [wealth] and hoarded.
19. Indeed, mankind was created anxious:
20. When evil touches him, impatient,
21. And when good touches him, withholding [of it],
22. Except the observers of prayer -
23. Those who are constant in their prayer

24. And those within whose wealth is a known right
25. For the petitioner and the deprived -
26. And those who believe in the Day of Recompense
27. And those who are fearful of the punishment of their Lord -
28. Indeed, the punishment of their Lord is not that from which one is safe -
29. And those who guard their private parts
30. Except from their wives or those their right hands possess, for indeed, they are not to be blamed -
31. But whoever seeks beyond that, then they are the transgressors -
32. And those who are to their trusts and promises attentive
33. And those who are in their testimonies upright
34. And those who [carefully] maintain their prayer:
35. They will be in gardens, honored.
36. So what is [the matter] with those who disbelieve, hastening [from] before you, [O Muhammad],
37. [To sit] on [your] right and [your] left in separate groups?
38. Does every person among them aspire to enter a garden of pleasure?
39. No! Indeed, We have created them from that which they know.
40. So I swear by the Lord of [all] risings and settings that indeed We are able
41. To replace them with better than them; and We are not to be outdone.
42. So leave them to converse vainly and amuse themselves until they meet their Day which they are promised -
43. The Day they will emerge from the graves rapidly as if they were, toward an erected idol, hastening.
44. Their eyes humbled, humiliation will cover them. That is the Day which they had been promised.

| Verses: 28 | **Surah 71 Nooh** | Makki |

In the name of Allah, the Entirely Merciful, the Especially Merciful.

01. Indeed, We sent Noah to his people, [saying], "Warn your people before there comes to them a painful punishment."
02. He said, "O my people, indeed I am to you a clear warner,

03. [Saying], 'Worship Allah, fear Him and obey me.

04. Allah will forgive you of your sins and delay you for a specified term. Indeed, the time [set by] Allah, when it comes, will not be delayed, if you only knew.' "

05. He said, "My Lord, indeed I invited my people [to truth] night and day.

06. But my invitation increased them not except in flight.

07. And indeed, every time I invited them that You may forgive them, they put their fingers in their ears, covered themselves with their garments, persisted, and were arrogant with [great] arrogance.

08. Then I invited them publicly.

09. Then I announced to them and [also] confided to them secretly

10. And said, 'Ask forgiveness of your Lord. Indeed, He is ever a Perpetual Forgiver.

11. He will send [rain from] the sky upon you in [continuing] showers

12. And give you increase in wealth and children and provide for you gardens and provide for you rivers.

13. What is [the matter] with you that you do not attribute to Allah [due] grandeur

14. While He has created you in stages?

15. Do you not consider how Allah has created seven heavens in layers

16. And made the moon therein a [reflected] light and made the sun a burning lamp?

17. And Allah has caused you to grow from the earth a [progressive] growth.

18. Then He will return you into it and extract you [another] extraction.

19. And Allah has made for you the earth an expanse

20. That you may follow therein roads of passage.' "

21. Noah said, "My Lord, indeed they have disobeyed me and followed him whose wealth and children will not increase him except in loss.

22. And they conspired an immense conspiracy.

23. And said, 'Never leave your gods and never leave Wadd or Suwa' or Yaghuth and Ya'uq and Nasr.

24. And already they have misled many. And, [my Lord], do not increase the wrongdoers except in error."

25. Because of their sins they were drowned and put into the Fire, and they found not for themselves besides Allah [any] helpers.
26. And Noah said, "My Lord, do not leave upon the earth from among the disbelievers an inhabitant.
27. Indeed, if You leave them, they will mislead Your servants and not beget except [every] wicked one and [confirmed] disbeliever.
28. My Lord, forgive me and my parents and whoever enters my house a believer and the believing men and believing women. And do not increase the wrongdoers except in destruction."

Surah 72 Al-Jinn

Verses: 28 | Makki

In the name of Allah, the Entirely Merciful, the Especially Merciful.

01. Say, [O Muhammad], "It has been revealed to me that a group of the jinn listened and said, 'Indeed, we have heard an amazing Qur'an.
02. It guides to the right course, and we have believed in it. And we will never associate with our Lord anyone.
03. And [it teaches] that exalted is the nobleness of our Lord; He has not taken a wife or a son
04. And that our foolish one has been saying about Allah an excessive transgression.
05. And we had thought that mankind and the jinn would never speak about Allah a lie.
06. And there were men from mankind who sought refuge in men from the jinn, so they [only] increased them in burden.
07. And they had thought, as you thought, that Allah would never send anyone [as a messenger].
08. And we have sought [to reach] the heaven but found it filled with powerful guards and burning flames.
09. And we used to sit therein in positions for hearing, but whoever listens now will find a burning flame lying in wait for him.
10. And we do not know [therefore] whether evil is intended for those on earth or whether their Lord intends for them a right course.
11. And among us are the righteous, and among us are [others] not so; we were [of] divided ways.
12. And we have become certain that we will never cause failure to Allah upon earth, nor can we escape Him by flight.

13. And when we heard the guidance, we believed in it. And whoever believes in his Lord will not fear deprivation or burden.
14. And among us are Muslims [in submission to Allah], and among us are the unjust. And whoever has become Muslim - those have sought out the right course.
15. But as for the unjust, they will be, for Hell, firewood.'
16. And [Allah revealed] that if they had remained straight on the way, We would have given them abundant provision
17. So We might test them therein. And whoever turns away from the remembrance of his Lord He will put into arduous punishment.
18. And [He revealed] that the masjids are for Allah, so do not invoke with Allah anyone.
19. And that when the Servant of Allah stood up supplicating Him, they almost became about him a compacted mass."
20. Say, [O Muhammad], "I only invoke my Lord and do not associate with Him anyone."
21. Say, "Indeed, I do not possess for you [the power of] harm or right direction."
22. Say, "Indeed, there will never protect me from Allah anyone [if I should disobey], nor will I find in other than Him a refuge.
23. But [I have for you] only notification from Allah, and His messages." And whoever disobeys Allah and His Messenger - then indeed, for him is the fire of Hell; they will abide therein forever.
24. [The disbelievers continue] until, when they see that which they are promised, then they will know who is weaker in helpers and less in number.
25. Say, "I do not know if what you are promised is near or if my Lord will grant for it a [long] period."
26. [He is] Knower of the unseen, and He does not disclose His [knowledge of the] unseen to anyone
27. Except whom He has approved of messengers, and indeed, He sends before each messenger and behind him observers
28. That he may know that they have conveyed the messages of their Lord; and He has encompassed whatever is with them and has enumerated all things in number.

| Verses: 20 | **Surah 73 Al-Muzzammil** | Makki |

In the name of Allah, the Entirely Merciful, the Especially Merciful.

01. you who wraps himself [in clothing],
02. Arise [to pray] the night, except for a little -
03. Half of it - or subtract from it a little
04. Or add to it, and recite the Qur'an with measured recitation.
05. Indeed, We will cast upon you a heavy word.
06. Indeed, the hours of the night are more effective for concurrence [of heart and tongue] and more suitable for words.
07. Indeed, for you by day is prolonged occupation.
08. And remember the name of your Lord and devote yourself to Him with [complete] devotion.
09. [He is] the Lord of the East and the West; there is no deity except Him, so take Him as Disposer of [your] affairs.
10. And be patient over what they say and avoid them with gracious avoidance.
11. And leave Me with [the matter of] the deniers, those of ease [in life], and allow them respite a little.
12. Indeed, with Us [for them] are shackles and burning fire
13. And food that chokes and a painful punishment -
14. On the Day the earth and the mountains will convulse and the mountains will become a heap of sand pouring down.
15. Indeed, We have sent to you a Messenger as a witness upon you just as We sent to Pharaoh a messenger.
16. But Pharaoh disobeyed the messenger, so We seized him with a ruinous seizure.
17. Then how can you fear, if you disbelieve, a Day that will make the children white- haired?
18. The heaven will break apart therefrom; ever is His promise fulfilled.
19. Indeed, this is a reminder, so whoever wills may take to his Lord a way.
20. Indeed, your Lord knows, [O Muhammad], that you stand [in prayer] almost two thirds of the night or half of it or a third of it, and [so do] a group of those with you. And Allah determines

[the extent of] the night and the day. He has known that you [Muslims] will not be able to do it and has turned to you in forgiveness, so recite what is easy [for you] of the Qur'an. He has known that there will be among you those who are ill and others traveling throughout the land seeking [something] of the bounty of Allah and others fighting for the cause of Allah. So recite what is easy from it and establish prayer and give zakah and loan Allah a goodly loan. And whatever good you put forward for yourselves - you will find it with Allah. It is better and greater in reward. And seek forgiveness of Allah. Indeed, Allah is Forgiving and Merciful.

Verses: 56 — Surah 74 Al-Muddaththir — Makki

In the name of Allah, the Entirely Merciful, the Especially Merciful.

01. you who covers himself [with a garment],
02. Arise and warn
03. And your Lord glorify
04. And your clothing purify
05. And uncleanliness avoid
06. And do not confer favor to acquire more
07. But for your Lord be patient.
08. And when the trumpet is blown,
09. That Day will be a difficult day
10. For the disbelievers - not easy.
11. Leave Me with the one I created alone
12. And to whom I granted extensive wealth
13. And children present [with him]
14. And spread [everything] before him, easing [his life].
15. Then he desires that I should add more.
16. No! Indeed, he has been toward Our verses obstinate.
17. I will cover him with arduous torment.
18. Indeed, he thought and deliberated.
19. So may he be destroyed [for] how he deliberated.
20. Then may he be destroyed [for] how he deliberated.
21. Then he considered [again];

22. Then he frowned and scowled;
23. Then he turned back and was arrogant
24. And said, "This is not but magic imitated [from others].
25. This is not but the word of a human being."
26. I will drive him into Saqar.
27. And what can make you know what is Saqar?
28. It lets nothing remain and leaves nothing [unburned],
29. Blackening the skins.
30. Over it are nineteen [angels].
31. And We have not made the keepers of the Fire except angels. And We have not made their number except as a trial for those who disbelieve - that those who were given the Scripture will be convinced and those who have believed will increase in faith and those who were given the Scripture and the believers will not doubt and that those in whose hearts is hypocrisy and the disbelievers will say, "What does Allah intend by this as an example?" Thus does Allah leave astray whom He wills and guides whom He wills. And none knows the soldiers of your Lord except Him. And mention of the Fire is not but a reminder to humanity.
32. No! By the moon
33. And [by] the night when it departs
34. And [by] the morning when it brightens,
35. Indeed, the Fire is of the greatest [afflictions]
36. As a warning to humanity -
37. To whoever wills among you to proceed or stay behind.
38. Every soul, for what it has earned, will be retained
39. Except the companions of the right,
40. [Who will be] in gardens, questioning each other
41. About the criminals,
42. [And asking them], "What put you into Saqar?"
43. They will say, "We were not of those who prayed,
44. Nor did we used to feed the poor.
45. And we used to enter into vain discourse with those who engaged [in it],

46. And we used to deny the Day of Recompense
47. Until there came to us the certainty."
48. So there will not benefit them the intercession of [any] intercessors.
49. Then what is [the matter] with them that they are, from the reminder, turning away
50. As if they were alarmed donkeys
51. Fleeing from a lion?
52. Rather, every person among them desires that he would be given scriptures spread about.
53. No! But they do not fear the Hereafter.
54. No! Indeed, the Qur'an is a reminder
55. Then whoever wills will remember it.
56. And they will not remember except that Allah wills. He is worthy of fear and adequate for [granting] forgiveness.

Surah 75 Al-Qiyaamah

Verses: 40 — Makki

In the name of Allah, the Entirely Merciful, the Especially Merciful.

01. I swear by the Day of Resurrection
02. And I swear by the reproaching soul [to the certainty of resurrection].
03. Does man think that We will not assemble his bones?
04. Yes. [We are] Able [even] to proportion his fingertips.
05. But man desires to continue in sin.
06. He asks, "When is the Day of Resurrection?"
07. So when vision is dazzled
08. And the moon darkens
09. And the sun and the moon are joined,
10. Man will say on that Day, "Where is the [place of] escape?"
11. No! There is no refuge.
12. To your Lord, that Day, is the [place of] permanence.
13. Man will be informed that Day of what he sent ahead and kept back.
14. Rather, man, against himself, will be a witness,
15. Even if he presents his excuses.
16. Move not your tongue with it, [O Muhammad], to hasten with recitation of the Qur'an.

17. Indeed, upon Us is its collection [in your heart] and [to make possible] its recitation.
18. So when We have recited it [through Gabriel], then follow its recitation.
19. Then upon Us is its clarification [to you].
20. No! But you love the immediate
21. And leave the Hereafter.
22. [Some] faces, that Day, will be radiant,
23. Looking at their Lord.
24. And [some] faces, that Day, will be contorted,
25. Expecting that there will be done to them [something] backbreaking.
26. No! When the soul has reached the collar bones
27. And it is said, "Who will cure [him]?"
28. And the dying one is certain that it is the [time of] separation
29. And the leg is wound about the leg,
30. To your Lord, that Day, will be the procession.
31. And the disbeliever had not believed, nor had he prayed.
32. But [instead], he denied and turned away.
33. And then he went to his people, swaggering [in pride].
34. Woe to you, and woe!
35. Then woe to you, and woe!
36. Does man think that he will be left neglected?
37. Had he not been a sperm from semen emitted?
38. Then he was a clinging clot, and [Allah] created [his form] and proportioned [him]
39. And made of him two mates, the male and the female.
40. Is not that [Creator] Able to give life to the dead?

| Verses: 31 | **Surah 76 Al-Insaan/Ad-Dahr** | Madani |

In the name of Allah, the Entirely Merciful, the Especially Merciful.

01. Has there [not] come upon man a period of time when he was not a thing [even] mentioned?
02. Indeed, We created man from a sperm-drop mixture that We may try him; and We made him hearing and seeing.
03. Indeed, We guided him to the way, be he grateful or be he ungrateful.

04. Indeed, We have prepared for the disbelievers chains and shackles and a blaze.
05. Indeed, the righteous will drink from a cup [of wine] whose mixture is of Kafur,
06. A spring of which the [righteous] servants of Allah will drink; they will make it gush forth in force [and abundance].
07. They [are those who] fulfill [their] vows and fear a Day whose evil will be widespread.
08. And they give food in spite of love for it to the needy, the orphan, and the captive,
09. [Saying], "We feed you only for the countenance of Allah. We wish not from you reward or gratitude.
10. Indeed, We fear from our Lord a Day austere and distressful."
11. So Allah will protect them from the evil of that Day and give them radiance and happiness
12. And will reward them for what they patiently endured [with] a garden [in Paradise] and silk [garments].
13. [They will be] reclining therein on adorned couches. They will not see therein any [burning] sun or [freezing] cold.
14. And near above them are its shades, and its [fruit] to be picked will be lowered in compliance.
15. And there will be circulated among them vessels of silver and cups having been [created] clear [as glass],
16. Clear glasses [made] from silver of which they have determined the measure.
17. And they will be given to drink a cup [of wine] whose mixture is of ginger
18. [From] a fountain within Paradise named Salsabeel.
19. There will circulate among them young boys made eternal. When you see them, you would think them [as beautiful as] scattered pearls.
20. And when you look there [in Paradise], you will see pleasure and great dominion.
21. Upon the inhabitants will be green garments of fine silk and brocade. And they will be adorned with bracelets of silver, and their Lord will give them a purifying drink.

22. [And it will be said], "Indeed, this is for you a reward, and your effort has been appreciated."
23. Indeed, it is We who have sent down to you, [O Muhammad], the Qur'an progressively.
24. So be patient for the decision of your Lord and do not obey from among them a sinner or ungrateful [disbeliever].
25. And mention the name of your Lord [in prayer] morning and evening
26. And during the night prostrate to Him and exalt Him a long [part of the] night.
27. Indeed, these [disbelievers] love the immediate and leave behind them a grave Day.
28. We have created them and strengthened their forms, and when We will, We can change their likenesses with [complete] alteration.
29. Indeed, this is a reminder, so he who wills may take to his Lord a way.
30. And you do not will except that Allah wills. Indeed, Allah is ever Knowing and Wise.
31. He admits whom He wills into His mercy; but the wrongdoers - He has prepared for them a painful punishment.

| Verses: 50 | Surah 77 Al-Mursalaat | Makki |

In the name of Allah, the Entirely Merciful, the Especially Merciful.

01. By those [winds] sent forth in gusts
02. And the winds that blow violently
03. And [by] the winds that spread [clouds]
04. And those [angels] who bring criterion
05. And those [angels] who deliver a message
06. As justification or warning,
07. Indeed, what you are promised is to occur.
08. So when the stars are obliterated
09. And when the heaven is opened
10. And when the mountains are blown away
11. And when the messengers' time has come...
12. For what Day was it postponed?
13. For the Day of Judgement.

14. And what can make you know what is the Day of Judgement?
15. Woe, that Day, to the deniers.
16. Did We not destroy the former peoples?
17. Then We will follow them with the later ones.
18. Thus do We deal with the criminals.
19. Woe, that Day, to the deniers.
20. Did We not create you from a liquid disdained?
21. And We placed it in a firm lodging
22. For a known extent.
23. And We determined [it], and excellent [are We] to determine.
24. Woe, that Day, to the deniers.
25. Have We not made the earth a container
26. Of the living and the dead?
27. And We placed therein lofty, firmly set mountains and have given you to drink sweet water.
28. Woe, that Day, to the deniers.
29. [They will be told], "Proceed to that which you used to deny.
30. Proceed to a shadow [of smoke] having three columns
31. [But having] no cool shade and availing not against the flame."
32. Indeed, it throws sparks [as huge] as a fortress,
33. As if they were yellowish [black] camels.
34. Woe, that Day, to the deniers.
35. This is a Day they will not speak,
36. Nor will it be permitted for them to make an excuse.
37. Woe, that Day, to the deniers.
38. This is the Day of Judgement; We will have assembled you and the former peoples.
39. So if you have a plan, then plan against Me.
40. Woe, that Day, to the deniers.
41. Indeed, the righteous will be among shades and springs
42. And fruits from whatever they desire,
43. [Being told], "Eat and drink in satisfaction for what you used to do."
44. Indeed, We thus reward the doers of good.

45. Woe, that Day, to the deniers.
46. [O disbelievers], eat and enjoy yourselves a little; indeed, you are criminals.
47. Woe, that Day, to the deniers.
48. And when it is said to them, "Bow [in prayer]," they do not bow.
49. Woe, that Day, to the deniers.
50. Then in what statement after the Qur'an will they believe?

Verses: 40	Surah 78 An-Naba	Makki

In the name of Allah, the Entirely Merciful, the Especially Merciful.

01. About what are they asking one another?
02. About the great news -
03. That over which they are in disagreement.
04. No! They are going to know.
05. Then, no! They are going to know.
06. Have We not made the earth a resting place?
07. And the mountains as stakes?
08. And We created you in pairs
09. And made your sleep [a means for] rest
10. And made the night as clothing
11. And made the day for livelihood
12. And constructed above you seven strong [heavens]
13. And made [therein] a burning lamp
14. And sent down, from the rain clouds, pouring water
15. That We may bring forth thereby grain and vegetation
16. And gardens of entwined growth.
17. Indeed, the Day of Judgement is an appointed time -
18. The Day the Horn is blown and you will come forth in multitudes
19. And the heaven is opened and will become gateways
20. And the mountains are removed and will be [but] a mirage.
21. Indeed, Hell has been lying in wait
22. For the transgressors, a place of return,

23. In which they will remain for ages [unending].
24. They will not taste therein [any] coolness or drink
25. Except scalding water and [foul] purulence -
26. An appropriate recompense.
27. Indeed, they were not expecting an account
28. And denied Our verses with [emphatic] denial.
29. But all things We have enumerated in writing.
30. "So taste [the penalty], and never will We increase you except in torment."
31. Indeed, for the righteous is attainment -
32. Gardens and grapevines
33. And full-breasted [companions] of equal age
34. And a full cup.
35. No ill speech will they hear therein or any falsehood -
36. [As] reward from your Lord, [a generous] gift [made due by] account,
37. [From] the Lord of the heavens and the earth and whatever is between them, the Most Merciful. They possess not from Him [authority for] speech.
38. The Day that the Spirit and the angels will stand in rows, they will not speak except for one whom the Most Merciful permits, and he will say what is correct.
39. That is the True Day; so he who wills may take to his Lord a [way of] return.
40. Indeed, We have warned you of a near punishment on the Day when a man will observe what his hands have put forth and the disbeliever will say, "Oh, I wish that I were dust!"

Verses: 46	**Surah 79 An-Naji'aat**	Makki

In the name of Allah, the Entirely Merciful, the Especially Merciful.

01. By those [angels] who extract with violence
02. And [by] those who remove with ease
03. And [by] those who glide [as if] swimming
04. And those who race each other in a race
05. And those who arrange [each] matter,
06. On the Day the blast [of the Horn] will convulse [creation],

07. There will follow it the subsequent [one].
08. Hearts, that Day, will tremble,
09. Their eyes humbled.
10. They are [presently] saying, "Will we indeed be returned to [our] former state [of life]?
11. Even if we should be decayed bones?
12. They say, "That, then, would be a losing return."
13. Indeed, it will be but one shout,
14. And suddenly they will be [alert] upon the earth's surface.
15. Has there reached you the story of Moses? -
16. When his Lord called to him in the sacred valley of Tuwa,
17. "Go to Pharaoh. Indeed, he has transgressed.
18. And say to him, 'Would you [be willing to] purify yourself
19. And let me guide you to your Lord so you would fear [Him]?'"
20. And he showed him the greatest sign,
21. But Pharaoh denied and disobeyed.
22. Then he turned his back, striving.
23. And he gathered [his people] and called out
24. And said, "I am your most exalted lord."
25. So Allah seized him in exemplary punishment for the last and the first [transgression].
26. Indeed in that is a warning for whoever would fear [Allah].
27. Are you a more difficult creation or is the heaven? Allah constructed it.
28. He raised its ceiling and proportioned it.
29. And He darkened its night and extracted its brightness.
30. And after that He spread the earth.
31. He extracted from it its water and its pasture,
32. And the mountains He set firmly
33. As provision for you and your grazing livestock.
34. But when there comes the greatest Overwhelming Calamity -
35. The Day when man will remember that for which he strove,
36. And Hellfire will be exposed for [all] those who see -
37. So as for he who transgressed

38. And preferred the life of the world,
39. Then indeed, Hellfire will be [his] refuge.
40. But as for he who feared the position of his Lord and prevented the soul from [unlawful] inclination,
41. Then indeed, Paradise will be [his] refuge.
42. They ask you, [O Muhammad], about the Hour: when is its arrival?
43. In what [position] are you that you should mention it?
44. To your Lord is its finality.
45. You are only a warner for those who fear it.
46. It will be, on the Day they see it, as though they had not remained [in the world] except for an afternoon or a morning thereof.

| Verses: 42 | **Surah 80 Abasa** | Makki |

In the name of Allah, the Entirely Merciful, the Especially Merciful.

01. The Prophet frowned and turned away
02. Because there came to him the blind man, [interrupting].
03. But what would make you perceive, [O Muhammad], that perhaps he might be purified
04. Or be reminded and the remembrance would benefit him?
05. As for he who thinks himself without need,
06. To him you give attention.
07. And not upon you [is any blame] if he will not be purified.
08. But as for he who came to you striving [for knowledge]
09. While he fears [Allah],
10. From him you are distracted.
11. No! Indeed, these verses are a reminder;
12. So whoever wills may remember it.
13. [It is recorded] in honored sheets,
14. Exalted and purified,
15. [Carried] by the hands of messenger-angels,
16. Noble and dutiful.
17. Cursed is man; how disbelieving is he.
18. From what substance did He create him?
19. From a sperm-drop He created him and destined for him;

20. Then He eased the way for him;
21. Then He causes his death and provides a grave for him.
22. Then when He wills, He will resurrect him.
23. No! Man has not yet accomplished what He commanded him.
24. Then let mankind look at his food -
25. How We poured down water in torrents,
26. Then We broke open the earth, splitting [it with sprouts],
27. And caused to grow within it grain
28. And grapes and herbage
29. And olive and palm trees
30. And gardens of dense shrubbery
31. And fruit and grass -
32. [As] enjoyment for you and your grazing livestock.
33. But when there comes the Deafening Blast
34. On the Day a man will flee from his brother
35. And his mother and his father
36. And his wife and his children,
37. For every man, that Day, will be a matter adequate for him.
38. [Some] faces, that Day, will be bright -
39. Laughing, rejoicing at good news.
40. And [other] faces, that Day, will have upon them dust.
41. Blackness will cover them.
42. Those are the disbelievers, the wicked ones.

| Verses: 29 | **Surah 81 At-Takwir** | Makki |

In the name of Allah, the Entirely Merciful, the Especially Merciful.
01. When the sun is wrapped up [in darkness]
02. And when the stars fall, dispersing,
03. And when the mountains are removed
04. And when full-term she-camels are neglected
05. And when the wild beasts are gathered
06. And when the seas are filled with flame
07. And when the souls are paired

08. And when the girl [who was] buried alive is asked
09. For what sin she was killed
10. And when the pages are made public
11. And when the sky is stripped away
12. And when Hellfire is set ablaze
13. And when Paradise is brought near,
14. A soul will [then] know what it has brought [with it].
15. So I swear by the retreating stars -
16. Those that run [their courses] and disappear -
17. And by the night as it closes in
18. And by the dawn when it breathes
19. [That] indeed, the Qur'an is a word [conveyed by] a noble messenger
20. [Who is] possessed of power and with the Owner of the Throne, secure [in position],
21. Obeyed there [in the heavens] and trustworthy.
22. And your companion is not [at all] mad.
23. And he has already seen Gabriel in the clear horizon.
24. And Muhammad is not a withholder of [knowledge of] the unseen.
25. And the Qur'an is not the word of a devil, expelled [from the heavens].
26. So where are you going?
27. It is not except a reminder to the worlds
28. For whoever wills among you to take a right course.
29. And you do not will except that Allah wills - Lord of the worlds.

| Verses: 19 | **Surah 82 Al-Infitaar** | Makki |

In the name of Allah, the Entirely Merciful, the Especially Merciful.

01. When the sky breaks apart
02. And when the stars fall, scattering,
03. And when the seas are erupted
04. And when the [contents of] graves are scattered,
05. A soul will [then] know what it has put forth and kept back.

06. O mankind, what has deceived you concerning your Lord, the Generous,
07. Who created you, proportioned you, and balanced you?
08. In whatever form He willed has He assembled you.
09. No! But you deny the Recompense.
10. And indeed, [appointed] over you are keepers,
11. Noble and recording;
12. They know whatever you do.
13. Indeed, the righteous will be in pleasure,
14. And indeed, the wicked will be in Hellfire.
15. They will [enter to] burn therein on the Day of Recompense,
16. And never therefrom will they be absent.
17. And what can make you know what is the Day of Recompense?
18. Then, what can make you know what is the Day of Recompense?
19. It is the Day when a soul will not possess for another soul [power to do] a thing; and the command, that Day, is [entirely] with Allah.

Surah 83 Al-Mutaffifin

Verses: 36 — Makki

In the name of Allah, the Entirely Merciful, the Especially Merciful.

01. Woe to those who give less [than due],
02. Who, when they take a measure from people, take in full.
03. But if they give by measure or by weight to them, they cause loss.
04. Do they not think that they will be resurrected
05. For a tremendous Day -
06. The Day when mankind will stand before the Lord of the worlds?
07. No! Indeed, the record of the wicked is in sijjeen.
08. And what can make you know what is sijjeen?
09. It is [their destination recorded in] a register inscribed.
10. Woe, that Day, to the deniers,
11. Who deny the Day of Recompense.
12. And none deny it except every sinful transgressor.

13. When Our verses are recited to him, he says, "Legends of the former peoples."
14. No! Rather, the stain has covered their hearts of that which they were earning.
15. No! Indeed, from their Lord, that Day, they will be partitioned.
16. Then indeed, they will [enter and] burn in Hellfire.
17. Then it will be said [to them], "This is what you used to deny."
18. No! Indeed, the record of the righteous is in 'illiyyun.
19. And what can make you know what is 'illiyyun?
20. It is [their destination recorded in] a register inscribed
21. Which is witnessed by those brought near [to Allah].
22. Indeed, the righteous will be in pleasure
23. On adorned couches, observing.
24. You will recognize in their faces the radiance of pleasure.
25. They will be given to drink [pure] wine [which was] sealed.
26. The last of it is musk. So for this let the competitors compete.
27. And its mixture is of Tasneem,
28. A spring from which those near [to Allah] drink.
29. Indeed, those who committed crimes used to laugh at those who believed.
30. And when they passed by them, they would exchange derisive glances.
31. And when they returned to their people, they would return jesting.
32. And when they saw them, they would say, "Indeed, those are truly lost."
33. But they had not been sent as guardians over them.
34. So Today those who believed are laughing at the disbelievers,
35. On adorned couches, observing.
36. Have the disbelievers [not] been rewarded [this Day] for what they used to do?

| Verses: 25 | **Surah 84 Al-Inshiqaaq** | Makki |

In the name of Allah, the Entirely Merciful, the Especially Merciful.

01. When the sky has split [open]
02. And has responded to its Lord and was obligated [to do so]
03. And when the earth has been extended
04. And has cast out that within it and relinquished [it]
05. And has responded to its Lord and was obligated [to do so] -
06. O mankind, indeed you are laboring toward your Lord with [great] exertion and will meet it.
07. Then as for he who is given his record in his right hand,
08. He will be judged with an easy account
09. And return to his people in happiness.
10. But as for he who is given his record behind his back,
11. He will cry out for destruction
12. And [enter to] burn in a Blaze.
13. Indeed, he had [once] been among his people in happiness;
14. Indeed, he had thought he would never return [to Allah].
15. But yes! Indeed, his Lord was ever of him, Seeing.
16. So I swear by the twilight glow
17. And [by] the night and what it envelops
18. And [by] the moon when it becomes full
19. [That] you will surely experience state after state.
20. So what is [the matter] with them [that] they do not believe,
21. And when the Qur'an is recited to them, they do not prostrate [to Allah]?
22. But those who have disbelieved deny,
23. And Allah is most knowing of what they keep within themselves.
24. So give them tidings of a painful punishment,
25. Except for those who believe and do righteous deeds. For them is a reward uninterrupted.

| Verses: 22 | **Surah 85 Al-Burooj** | Makki |

In the name of Allah, the Entirely Merciful, the Especially Merciful.

01. By the sky containing great stars
02. And [by] the promised Day
03. And [by] the witness and what is witnessed,
04. Cursed were the companions of the trench
05. [Containing] the fire full of fuel,
06. When they were sitting near it
07. And they, to what they were doing against the believers, were witnesses.
08. And they resented them not except because they believed in Allah, the Exalted in Might, the Praiseworthy,
09. To whom belongs the dominion of the heavens and the earth. And Allah, over all things, is Witness.
10. Indeed, those who have tortured the believing men and believing women and then have not repented will have the punishment of Hell, and they will have the punishment of the Burning Fire.
11. Indeed, those who have believed and done righteous deeds will have gardens beneath which rivers flow. That is the great attainment.
12. Indeed, the vengeance of your Lord is severe.
13. Indeed, it is He who originates [creation] and repeats.
14. And He is the Forgiving, the Affectionate,
15. Honorable Owner of the Throne,
16. Effecter of what He intends.
17. Has there reached you the story of the soldiers -
18. [Those of] Pharaoh and Thamud?
19. But they who disbelieve are in [persistent] denial,
20. While Allah encompasses them from behind.
21. But this is an honored Qur'an
22. [Inscribed] in a Preserved Slate.

| Verses: 17 | **Surah 86 At-Taariq** | Makki |

In the name of Allah, the Entirely Merciful, the Especially Merciful.

01. By the sky and the night comer -
02. And what can make you know what is the night comer?
03. It is the piercing star -
04. There is no soul but that it has over it a protector.
05. So let man observe from what he was created.
06. He was created from a fluid, ejected,
07. Emerging from between the backbone and the ribs.
08. Indeed, Allah, to return him [to life], is Able.
09. The Day when secrets will be put on trial,
10. Then man will have no power or any helper.
11. By the sky which returns [rain]
12. And [by] the earth which cracks open,
13. Indeed, the Qur'an is a decisive statement,
14. And it is not amusement.
15. Indeed, they are planning a plan,
16. But I am planning a plan.
17. So allow time for the disbelievers. Leave them awhile.

| Verses: 19 | **Surah 87 Al-A'la** | Makki |

In the name of Allah, the Entirely Merciful, the Especially Merciful.

01. Exalt the name of your Lord, the Most High,
02. Who created and proportioned
03. And who destined and [then] guided
04. And who brings out the pasture
05. And [then] makes it black stubble.
06. We will make you recite, [O Muhammad], and you will not forget,
07. Except what Allah should will. Indeed, He knows what is declared and what is hidden.
08. And We will ease you toward ease.

09. So remind, if the reminder should benefit;
10. He who fears [Allah] will be reminded.
11. But the wretched one will avoid it -
12. [He] who will [enter and] burn in the greatest Fire,
13. Neither dying therein nor living.
14. He has certainly succeeded who purifies himself
15. And mentions the name of his Lord and prays.
16. But you prefer the worldly life,
17. While the Hereafter is better and more enduring.
18. Indeed, this is in the former scriptures,
19. The scriptures of Abraham and Moses.

Surah 88 Al-Ghaashiyah

Verses: 26 | Makki

In the name of Allah, the Entirely Merciful, the Especially Merciful.

01. Has there reached you the report of the Overwhelming [event]?
02. [Some] faces, that Day, will be humbled,
03. Working [hard] and exhausted.
04. They will [enter to] burn in an intensely hot Fire.
05. They will be given drink from a boiling spring.
06. For them there will be no food except from a poisonous, thorny plant
07. Which neither nourishes nor avails against hunger.
08. [Other] faces, that Day, will show pleasure.
09. With their effort [they are] satisfied
10. In an elevated garden,
11. Wherein they will hear no unsuitable speech.
12. Within it is a flowing spring.
13. Within it are couches raised high
14. And cups put in place
15. And cushions lined up
16. And carpets spread around.
17. Then do they not look at the camels - how they are created?

18. And at the sky - how it is raised?
19. And at the mountains - how they are erected?
20. And at the earth - how it is spread out?
21. So remind, [O Muhammad]; you are only a reminder.
22. You are not over them a controller.
23. However, he who turns away and disbelieves -
24. Then Allah will punish him with the greatest punishment.
25. Indeed, to Us is their return.
26. Then indeed, upon Us is their account.

| Verses: 30 | **Surah 89 Al-Fajr** | Makki |

In the name of Allah, the Entirely Merciful, the Especially Merciful.

01. By the dawn
02. And [by] ten nights
03. And [by] the even [number] and the odd
04. And [by] the night when it passes,
05. Is there [not] in [all] that an oath [sufficient] for one of perception?
06. Have you not considered how your Lord dealt with 'Aad -
07. [With] Iram - who had lofty pillars,
08. The likes of whom had never been created in the land?
09. And [with] Thamud, who carved out the rocks in the valley?
10. And [with] Pharaoh, owner of the stakes? -
11. [All of] whom oppressed within the lands
12. And increased therein the corruption.
13. So your Lord poured upon them a scourge of punishment.
14. Indeed, your Lord is in observation.
15. And as for man, when his Lord tries him and [thus] is generous to him and favors him, he says, "My Lord has honored me."
16. But when He tries him and restricts his provision, he says, "My Lord has humiliated me."
17. No! But you do not honor the orphan

18. And you do not encourage one another to feed the poor.
19. And you consume inheritance, devouring [it] altogether,
20. And you love wealth with immense love.
21. No! When the earth has been leveled - pounded and crushed -
22. And your Lord has come and the angels, rank upon rank,
23. And brought [within view], that Day, is Hell - that Day, man will remember, but what good to him will be the remembrance?
24. He will say, "Oh, I wish I had sent ahead [some good] for my life."
25. So on that Day, none will punish [as severely] as His punishment,
26. And none will bind [as severely] as His binding [of the evildoers].
27. [To the righteous it will be said], "O reassured soul,
28. Return to your Lord, well-pleased and pleasing [to Him],
29. And enter among My [righteous] servants
30. And enter My Paradise."

Verses: 20	Surah 90 Al-Balad	Makki

In the name of Allah, the Entirely Merciful, the Especially Merciful.

01. I swear by this city, Makkah -
02. And you, [O Muhammad], are free of restriction in this city -
03. And [by] the father and that which was born [of him],
04. We have certainly created man into hardship.
05. Does he think that never will anyone overcome him?
06. He says, "I have spent wealth in abundance."
07. Does he think that no one has seen him?
08. Have We not made for him two eyes?
09. And a tongue and two lips?
10. And have shown him the two ways?
11. But he has not broken through the difficult pass.
12. And what can make you know what is [breaking through] the difficult pass?
13. It is the freeing of a slave
14. Or feeding on a day of severe hunger

15. An orphan of near relationship
16. Or a needy person in misery
17. And then being among those who believed and advised one another to patience and advised one another to compassion.
18. Those are the companions of the right.
19. But they who disbelieved in Our signs - those are the companions of the left.
20. Over them will be fire closed in.

| Verses: 15 | **Surah 91 Ash-Shams** | Makki |

In the name of Allah, the Entirely Merciful, the Especially Merciful.

01. By the sun and its brightness
02. And [by] the moon when it follows it
03. And [by] the day when it displays it
04. And [by] the night when it covers it
05. And [by] the sky and He who constructed it
06. And [by] the earth and He who spread it
07. And [by] the soul and He who proportioned it
08. And inspired it [with discernment of] its wickedness and its righteousness,
09. He has succeeded who purifies it,
10. And he has failed who instills it [with corruption].
11. Thamud denied [their prophet] by reason of their transgression,
12. When the most wretched of them was sent forth.
13. And the messenger of Allah [Salih] said to them, "[Do not harm] the she-camel of Allah or [prevent her from] her drink."
14. But they denied him and hamstrung her. So their Lord brought down upon them destruction for their sin and made it equal [upon all of them].
15. And He does not fear the consequence thereof.

| Verses: 21 | **Surah 92 Al-Lail** | Makki |

In the name of Allah, the Entirely Merciful, the Especially Merciful.

01. By the night when it covers
02. And [by] the day when it appears
03. And [by] He who created the male and female,
04. Indeed, your efforts are diverse.
05. As for he who gives and fears Allah
06. And believes in the best [reward],
07. We will ease him toward ease.
08. But as for he who withholds and considers himself free of need
09. And denies the best [reward],
10. We will ease him toward difficulty.
11. And what will his wealth avail him when he falls?
12. Indeed, [incumbent] upon Us is guidance.
13. And indeed, to Us belongs the Hereafter and the first [life].
14. So I have warned you of a Fire which is blazing.
15. None will [enter to] burn therein except the most wretched one.
16. Who had denied and turned away.
17. But the righteous one will avoid it -
18. [He] who gives [from] his wealth to purify himself
19. And not [giving] for anyone who has [done him] a favor to be rewarded
20. But only seeking the countenance of his Lord, Most High.
21. And he is going to be satisfied.

| Verses: 11 | **Surah 93 Ad-Dhuhaa** | Makki |

In the name of Allah, the Entirely Merciful, the Especially Merciful.

01. By the morning brightness
02. And [by] the night when it covers with darkness,
03. Your Lord has not taken leave of you, [O Muhammad], nor has He detested [you].

04. And the Hereafter is better for you than the first [life].
05. And your Lord is going to give you, and you will be satisfied.
06. Did He not find you an orphan and give [you] refuge?
07. And He found you lost and guided [you],
08. And He found you poor and made [you] self-sufficient.
09. So as for the orphan, do not oppress [him].
10. And as for the petitioner, do not repel [him].
11. But as for the favor of your Lord, report [it].

Surah 94 Ash-Sharh

Verses: 08 | Makki

In the name of Allah, the Entirely Merciful, the Especially Merciful.

01. Did We not expand for you, [O Muhammad], your breast?
02. And We removed from you your burden
03. Which had weighed upon your back
04. And raised high for you your repute.
05. For indeed, with hardship [will be] ease.
06. Indeed, with hardship [will be] ease.
07. So when you have finished [your duties], then stand up [for worship].
08. And to your Lord direct [your] longing.

Surah 95 At-Tin

Verses: 08 | Makki

In the name of Allah, the Entirely Merciful, the Especially Merciful.

01. By the fig and the olive
02. And [by] Mount Sinai
03. And [by] this secure city [Makkah],
04. We have certainly created man in the best of stature;
05. Then We return him to the lowest of the low,
06. Except for those who believe and do righteous deeds, for they will have a reward uninterrupted.
07. So what yet causes you to deny the Recompense?
08. Is not Allah the most just of judges?

| Verses: 19 | **Surah 96 Al-Alaq** | Makki |

In the name of Allah, the Entirely Merciful, the Especially Merciful.

01. Recite in the name of your Lord who created -
02. Created man from a clinging substance.
03. Recite, and your Lord is the most Generous -
04. Who taught by the pen -
05. Taught man that which he knew not.
06. No! [But] indeed, man transgresses
07. Because he sees himself self-sufficient.
08. Indeed, to your Lord is the return.
09. Have you seen the one who forbids
10. A servant when he prays?
11. Have you seen if he is upon guidance
12. Or enjoins righteousness?
13. Have you seen if he denies and turns away -
14. Does he not know that Allah sees?
15. No! If he does not desist, We will surely drag him by the forelock -
16. A lying, sinning forelock.
17. Then let him call his associates;
18. We will call the angels of Hell.
19. No! Do not obey him. But prostrate and draw near [to Allah].

| Verses: 05 | **Surah 97 Al-Qadr** | Makki |

In the name of Allah, the Entirely Merciful, the Especially Merciful.

01. Indeed, We sent the Qur'an down during the Night of Decree.
02. And what can make you know what is the Night of Decree?
03. The Night of Decree is better than a thousand months.
04. The angels and the Spirit descend therein by permission of their Lord for every matter.
05. Peace it is until the emergence of dawn.

| Verses: 08 | **Surah 98 Al-Bayyinah** | Madani |

In the name of Allah, the Entirely Merciful, the Especially Merciful.

01. Those who disbelieved among the People of the Scripture and the polytheists were not to be parted [from misbelief] until there came to them clear evidence -

02. A Messenger from Allah, reciting purified scriptures

03. Within which are correct writings.

04. Nor did those who were given the Scripture become divided until after there had come to them clear evidence.

05. And they were not commanded except to worship Allah, [being] sincere to Him in religion, inclining to truth, and to establish prayer and to give zakah. And that is the correct religion.

06. Indeed, they who disbelieved among the People of the Scripture and the polytheists will be in the fire of Hell, abiding eternally therein. Those are the worst of creatures.

07. Indeed, they who have believed and done righteous deeds - those are the best of creatures.

08. Their reward with Allah will be gardens of perpetual residence beneath which rivers flow, wherein they will abide forever, Allah being pleased with them and they with Him. That is for whoever has feared his Lord.

| Verses: 08 | **Surah 99 Az-Zalzalah** | Madani |

In the name of Allah, the Entirely Merciful, the Especially Merciful.

01. When the earth is shaken with its [final] earthquake

02. And the earth discharges its burdens

03. And man says, "What is [wrong] with it?" -

04. That Day, it will report its news

05. Because your Lord has commanded it.

06. That Day, the people will depart separated [into categories] to be shown [the result of] their deeds.

07. So whoever does an atom's weight of good will see it,

08. And whoever does an atom's weight of evil will see it.

| Verses: 11 | **Surah 100 Al-Aadiyaat** | Makki |

In the name of Allah, the Entirely Merciful, the Especially Merciful.

01. By the racers, panting,

02. And the producers of sparks [when] striking

03. And the chargers at dawn,

04. Stirring up thereby [clouds of] dust,

05. Arriving thereby in the center collectively,

06. Indeed mankind, to his Lord, is ungrateful.

07. And indeed, he is to that a witness.

08. And indeed he is, in love of wealth, intense.

09. But does he not know that when the contents of the graves are scattered

10. And that within the breasts is obtained,

11. Indeed, their Lord with them, that Day, is [fully] Acquainted.

| Verses: 11 | **Surah 101 Al-Qaari'ah** | Makki |

In the name of Allah, the Entirely Merciful, the Especially Merciful.

01. The Striking Calamity -

02. What is the Striking Calamity?

03. And what can make you know what is the Striking Calamity?

04. It is the Day when people will be like moths, dispersed,

05. And the mountains will be like wool, fluffed up.

06. Then as for one whose scales are heavy [with good deeds],

07. He will be in a pleasant life.

08. But as for one whose scales are light,

09. His refuge will be an abyss.

10. And what can make you know what that is?

11. It is a Fire, intensely hot.

Surah 102 At-Takaathur — Makki — Verses: 08

In the name of Allah, the Entirely Merciful, the Especially Merciful.

01. Competition in [worldly] increase diverts you
02. Until you visit the graveyards.
03. No! You are going to know.
04. Then no! You are going to know.
05. No! If you only knew with knowledge of certainty...
06. You will surely see the Hellfire.
07. Then you will surely see it with the eye of certainty.
08. Then you will surely be asked that Day about pleasure.

Surah 103 Al-Asr — Makki — Verses: 03

In the name of Allah, the Entirely Merciful, the Especially Merciful.

01. By time,
02. Indeed, mankind is in loss,
03. Except for those who have believed and done righteous deeds and advised each other to truth and advised each other to patience.

Surah 104 Al-Humazah — Makki — Verses: 09

In the name of Allah, the Entirely Merciful, the Especially Merciful.

01. Woe to every scorner and mocker
02. Who collects wealth and [continuously] counts it.
03. He thinks that his wealth will make him immortal.
04. No! He will surely be thrown into the Crusher.
05. And what can make you know what is the Crusher?
06. It is the fire of Allah, [eternally] fueled,
07. Which mounts directed at the hearts.
08. Indeed, Hellfire will be closed down upon them
09. In extended columns.

Surah 105 Al-Fil

Verses: 05 — Makki

In the name of Allah, the Entirely Merciful, the Especially Merciful.

01. Have you not considered, [O Muhammad], how your Lord dealt with the companions of the elephant?
02. Did He not make their plan into misguidance?
03. And He sent against them birds in flocks,
04. Striking them with stones of hard clay,
05. And He made them like eaten straw.

Surah 106 Al-Quraish

Verses: 04 — Makki

In the name of Allah, the Entirely Merciful, the Especially Merciful.

01. For the accustomed security of the Quraysh -
02. Their accustomed security [in] the caravan of winter and summer -
03. Let them worship the Lord of this House,
04. Who has fed them, [saving them] from hunger and made them safe, [saving them] from fear.

Surah 107 Al-Maa'un

Verses: 07 — Makki

In the name of Allah, the Entirely Merciful, the Especially Merciful.

01. Have you seen the one who denies the Recompense?
02. For that is the one who drives away the orphan
03. And does not encourage the feeding of the poor.
04. So woe to those who pray
05. [But] who are heedless of their prayer -
06. Those who make show [of their deeds]
07. And withhold [simple] assistance.

Surah 108 Al-Kawthar

Verses: 03 — Makki

In the name of Allah, the Entirely Merciful, the Especially Merciful.

01. Indeed, We have granted you, [O Muhammad], al-Kawthar.
02. So pray to your Lord and sacrifice [to Him alone].
03. Indeed, your enemy is the one cut off.

| Verses: 06 | **Surah 109 Al-Kafiroon** | Makki |

In the name of Allah, the Entirely Merciful, the Especially Merciful.

01. Say, "O disbelievers,
02. I do not worship what you worship.
03. Nor are you worshippers of what I worship.
04. Nor will I be a worshipper of what you worship.
05. Nor will you be worshippers of what I worship.
06. For you is your religion, and for me is my religion."

| Verses: 03 | **Surah 110 An-Nasr** | Madani |

In the name of Allah, the Entirely Merciful, the Especially Merciful.

01. When the victory of Allah has come and the conquest,
02. And you see the people entering into the religion of Allah in multitudes,
03. Then exalt [Him] with praise of your Lord and ask forgiveness of Him. Indeed, He is ever Accepting of repentance.

| Verses: 05 | **Surah 111 Al-Masad/Lahab** | Makki |

In the name of Allah, the Entirely Merciful, the Especially Merciful.

01. May the hands of Abu Lahab be ruined, and ruined is he.
02. His wealth will not avail him or that which he gained.
03. He will [enter to] burn in a Fire of [blazing] flame
04. And his wife [as well] - the carrier of firewood.
05. Around her neck is a rope of [twisted] fiber.

| Verses: 04 | **Surah 112 Al-Ikhlas** | Makki |

In the name of Allah, the Entirely Merciful, the Especially Merciful.

01. Say, "He is Allah, [who is] One,
02. Allah, the Eternal Refuge.
03. He neither begets nor is born,
04. Nor is there to Him any equivalent."

| Verses: 05 | **Surah 113 Al-Falaq** | Makki |

In the name of Allah, the Entirely Merciful, the Especially Merciful.

01. Say, "I seek refuge in the Lord of daybreak
02. From the evil of that which He created
03. And from the evil of darkness when it settles
04. And from the evil of the blowers in knots
05. And from the evil of an envier when he envies."

| Verses: 06 | **Surah 114 An-Naas** | Makki |

In the name of Allah, the Entirely Merciful, the Especially Merciful.

01. Say, "I seek refuge in the Lord of mankind,
02. The Sovereign of mankind.
03. The God of mankind,
04. From the evil of the retreating whisperer -
05. Who whispers [evil] into the breasts of mankind -
06. From among the jinn and mankind."

The End